THE LAST CAVALIER

THE LAST CAVALIER

RICHARD TALBOT
(1631–91)

PÁDRAIG LENIHAN

UNIVERSITY COLLEGE DUBLIN PRESS
PREAS CHOLÁISTE OLLSCOILE BHAILE ÁTHA CLIATH

2014

First published 2014 by
UNIVERSITY COLLEGE DUBLIN PRESS
UCD Humanities Institute, Room H103, Belfield, Dublin 4
www.ucdpress.ie

ISBN 978-1-906359-83-6 hb

CIP data available from the British Library

*The right of Pádraig Lenihan to be identified as the author
of this work has been asserted by him*

Text design and typesetting
by Lyn Davies
in Adobe Caslon and Bodoni Old Style
Printed in England on acid-free paper by
Anthony Rowe, Chippenham, Wilts.

Contents

List of Illustrations

Acknowledgements

I have been working on this biography for more years than I care to remember, snatching time between surges in teaching and administrative duties. I would not have finished but for the encouragement and practical assistance of many people. Bríd McGrath and Professor Aidan Clarke read and gave invaluable criticism on my opening chapter as did John Cronin and Manus Lenihan with later chapters. Manus also helped me greatly with my research; James Greaney and Megan Howell brought an eye for detail to presenting the bibliography and critical apparatus. Colleagues past and present in Limerick, Galway, Derry and elsewhere listened and encouraged: among them Professors Daibhí Ó Cróinín, Nicholas Canny, Keith Sidwell and Anthony McElligott. Also, John Logan, Ciara Breathnach, David Fleming, John Cunningham, Alison Forrestal, Mark Stansbury, Éamon Ó Ciardha, Billy Kelly and Alistair Malcolm. My thanks also to Donncha, Cora, Conor and Síle Lenihan. The staff of libraries and cultural institutions were generous with their time and expertise: my thanks must include, Noreen Ellerker, St Mary's Cathedral Limerick, James Harte, Manuscripts Department, National Library of Ireland, Patrick Walsh, Gérald Andres, Bibliothèque municipale de Lyon, Tricia Buckingham and Helen Gilio, Bodleian Libraries Imaging Services, Oxford, Joanna Parker, Librarian, Worcester College, Oxford, Máire Kennedy, Dublin City Libraries, Ken Bergin and Jean Turner, Glucksman Library, Marie Boran, Margaret Hughes, Bríd Walsh and Geraldine Curtin of the Hardiman Library, NUIG. The Executive Editor of UCD Press, Noelle Moran, and the two readers she commissioned and the editor Barbara Mennell gave me encouragement and valuable guidance. Last, but not least, my wife Caitriona Clear: I could not have done it without you. *Go raibh maith agaibh go léir.*

PÁDRAIG LENIHAN
Galway
April 2014

Abbreviations

In the notes, manuscripts, books and articles are cited for the first time by their full titles and thereafter by an abbreviated version. The most frequently cited manuscripts and books are listed below and referred to throughout by the appropriate abbreviation.

Anal. Hib. – *Analecta Hibernica.*

Bagwell, *Stuarts* – Richard Bagwell, *Ireland under the Stuarts* ... (3 vols, London, – 1909–16; reprint, 1963).

BL – British Library (Manuscripts Department).

BNF – Bibliothèque nationale de France

Bodl. – Bodleian Library.

Coll. Hib. – *Collectanea Hibernica.*

Civil Survey – *The Civil Survey, A. D. 1654–56,* ed. R. C. Simington, (I. M. C., 10 vols, Dublin, 1931–61).

Clarendon S. P. – Calendar of the *Clarendon State Papers* Preserved in the Bodleian Library: 1649–1657, ed. W. Dunn Macray (6 vols, Oxford, 1869–76), iii, 1655–7.

Comment. Rinucc. – Richard O'Ferrall and Robert O'Connell, *Commentarius Rinuccinianus, de sedis apostolicae legatione ad foederatos Hiberniae catholicos per annos 1645-49,* ed. Rev. Stanislaus Kavanagh (IMC, 6 vols, Dublin, 1932–49).

CSPD – *Calendar of State Papers, Domestic Series, preserved in the State Paper Department of Her Majesty's Public Record Office.*

CSPI – *Calendar of State Papers, Ireland.*

DIB – James McGuire and James Quinn (eds), *Dictionary of Irish Biography* (Cambridge, 2009) (dib.cambridge.org).

Dick Talbot – P. W. Sergeant, *Little Jennings and Fighting Dick Talbot* (2 vols, London, 1913).

Duc de Tirconnell – Anon. 'Le Duc de Tirconnell' (NLI, MS 118).

EHR – *English Historical Review.*

Gilbert, *Contemp Hist.* – J. T. Gilbert (ed.), *A Contemporary History of Affairs in*

ix

Ireland, from 1641 to 1652... (Irish Archaeological Society, 3 vols, Dublin, 1879).

Gilbert, *Ir. Confed.* – J. T. Gilbert (ed.), *History of the Irish Confederation and the War in Ireland, 1641-3 ...* (7 vols, Dublin, 1882–91).

Gilbert, *Jacobite Narr.* – J. T. Gilbert (ed.), *A Jacobite Narrative of the War in Ireland, 1688-91* (Dublin, 1892; reprint, with introduction by J. G. Simms, Shannon, 1971).

HMC – Historical Manuscripts Commission.

IHS – *Irish Historical Studies.*

IMC – Irish Manuscripts Commission.

Kildare Arch. Soc. Jn. – *Journal of the County Kildare Archaeological and Historical Society* (Dublin 1891–).

Kilkenny Arch. Soc. Jn. – *Journal of the Kilkenny and South-East of Ireland Archaeological Society* (Kilkenny 1856–71).

Life – *Life of James II*, ed. J. S. Clarke (2 vols, London, 1816).

'Irish Narrative' – 'Irish Narrative Ormond' (Gilbert MS 227), Dublin City Library, Pearse Street, Dublin.

L'homme fidele – A. Anselme, 'L'homme fidele où Discours Panegerique en faveur De Monsieur Le Comte de Tirconnel Viceroi d'Irlande', in Recueil de copies de pièces françaises et latines, en prose et en vers, sur les affaires d'Angleterre, d'Irlande et de France, sous Jacques II, Jacques III et Louis XIV, etc.' (BNF MS Français 12160), fos 169–94.

Macariae Excidium – Charles O'Kelly, *Macariae Excidium or The Destruction of Cyprus*, ed. J. C. O'Callaghan (Dublin, 1850).

'Mountjoy's History' – (Gilbert MS 109), Dublin City Public Library, Pearse Street, Dublin.

NA – National Archives.

New History of Ireland – T. W. Moody, F. X. Martin and F. J. Byrne (eds), *A New History of Ireland III: Early Modern Ireland 1534-1691* (Oxford, 1976).

NLI – National Library of Ireland

ODNB – *Oxford Dictionary of National Biography* (Oxford, 2004–5)

Oraison funebre – 'Oraison funebre de Milord Richrad Talbot Duc de Tyrconnel, Vive-Roy d'Irlande' in *Recueil de Diverses Oraisons Funebres* (Lille, 1727), pp. 289–337.

'Ormond' – John Gibney (ed.), 'Some remarks on those who were friends and enemyes to the Duke of Ormond and to the Acts of Settlement of Ireland', *Anal. Hib.* no. 42 (2011).

'Poema' – 'Poema de Hibernia', *c.*1695 (Dublin City Public Library, Gilbert MS 141).

PRONI – Public Record Office of Northern Ireland.

SP – State Papers, National Archives U. K.

TCD – Trinity College Dublin.

Thurloe SP – *A collection of the State Papers of John Thurloe, Secretary of State 1652-8*, ed. Thomas Birch (7 vols, London, 1742).

Tyrconnel – Charles Petrie, *The Great Tyrconnel: A Chapter in Anglo-Irish Relations* (Cork, 1972).

'Tyrconnel Papers' – 'Tyrconnel Papers some and presumably all of which were captured at the Battle of the Boyne' (NLI, MS 37, np).

unk. – unknown.

Vindication – *A Vindication of the present government of Ireland, under His Excellency Richard Earl of Tirconnel* (London, 1688).

Introduction

Richard Talbot was significant, he has been neglected, and the time is ripe to re-evaluate him. He was the leading Irish Catholic political figure for the latter half of his life. The pattern for his neglect was set by many nineteenth-century historians given to romantic mythologising. They chose not to elevate Talbot to the Irish nationalist pantheon, shoulder to shoulder with Patrick Sarsfield or Eoghan Rua O'Neill, figures of less stature by objective standards. Perhaps, too, he was neglected because his character and actions did not always lend themselves to heroic mythologising. A disgruntled secretary and fellow countryman, for instance, thought him 'most insolent in prosperity and most abject in adversity, a cunning dissembling courtier, of mean judgement and small understanding'.[1]

Yet biographers have neglected a fascinating life. A novelist would hesitate to throw the hero into as many memorable events as Talbot underwent, for fear of straining credibility. As a callow youth, he survived the annihilation of an Irish army at Dungan's Hill (1647) and Cromwell's sack of Drogheda (1649). He tried and failed to assassinate the Protector, was captured and interrogated by Cromwell himself, and escaped in circumstances which aroused Royalist suspicions of double-dealing. He would live to fight on land and sea at the battles of Valenciennes (1656), the Dunes (1658) Solebay (1672) and the Boyne (1690). Yet he was more courtier than colonel. A gallant, gambler and duellist, Talbot embodied the Restoration's courtly vices. These three attributes yield partial clues as to his character. Nicknamed 'Goliath', he was exceptionally tall and considered handsome, before he ran to fat in his mid-forties, 'laden with folly, flesh and ill-got land'.[2] His coarse language belonged more to the camp than the Stone Gallery, and he could be violent in deed as well as word, being a notorious duellist even for the time and place. 'Fighting Dick' was one of the three most common epithets (the others being 'Lying Dick' and 'Mad Dick') heaped on Talbot that signpost his key character traits: combativeness and resilience, most evident in that *resource dans les disgraces* or capacity to claw his way back after falls from grace, that were extolled in his funeral oration.

Talbot is especially worth studying because he was by no means a natural courtier. He could be plain-spoken to the point of rudeness with his betters, forgetful, careless and wildly indiscreet. As an Irish papist, he was an outsider, often despised and feared in equal measure, even in the family of James, Duke of York. It would be more than a decade after Talbot insinuated his way into York's household before that prince began to turn to Rome. Talbot would not have been able to establish himself in peacetime, but his war record as a die-hard royalist cavalryman, and the reflected prestige of his Jesuit brother's connections with the ministers of His Catholic Majesty Philip IV gave him access to the penurious royalist court in exile.

History has not been kind to Richard Talbot. He left few papers, and the most voluminous and accessible archives of all were bequeathed by his enemies, especially by Ormond.[3] Bias is accentuated by the fact that his master, James II, was driven from the throne, and the winners, Whig opponents like Gilbert Burnet, spun backstairs intrigue and foreign invasion into a 'Glorious Revolution'. Drawing uncritically on Whig historiography and adding his own spiteful touches, Macaulay's Victorian-era *History of England* endows Talbot with contradictory vices: he was at once a foul-mouthed thug, brazen liar, childish braggart, shameless pimp and 'a coldhearted, farsighted, scheming sycophant'.[4] In their asides on Talbot, historians followed the path beaten by Macaulay until about the 1950s, abusing the Irishman as a swaggering thug, lying upstart, or 'purblind bogtrotter'. Kenyon, from whom one would have expected better, opined that Tyrconnell was a suitable representative of the 'rapacious, ignorant, anarchic forces of Irish Catholicism, at the lowest stage of civilisation in western Europe'.[5] Modern historians, while generally disapproving of Talbot, at least acknowledge his charm, forcefulness, political astuteness and disinterestedness.[6]

Not all abuse of Talbot can be blamed on lazy and prejudiced historians or discounted as mendacious Whiggery, because some Irish Jacobites were almost as unflattering. Colonel Charles O'Kelly of Screen, Co. Roscommon, claimed to be one of the hardliners who wanted to fight on into the winter of 1691–2 and beyond. The following year, he penned his allegorical *Macariae Excidium*, which depicts 'Coridon' or Talbot as 'blown up with arrogance', sly, self-interested, defeatist and prejudiced against Irishmen of Gaelic descent (the 'O's and the 'Mac's).[7] But the force of O'Kelly's criticism is dissipated because it is so indiscriminate – he dismissed Tyrconnell's master as a 'weak prince' and also accused the dashing Patrick Sarsfield, Tyrconnell's bitter factional rival, of treachery.[8]

In contrast, only two long texts in praise of Talbot have appeared in print. His funeral oration, published in 1692 and 1712, is turgid, vague and often inaccurate. The other text was edited by the indefatigable nineteenth-century antiquarian and historian, J. T. Gilbert, as *The Jacobite Narrative* and forms part of a much bigger manuscript, 'A Light to the Blind'. The anonymous author was probably a Palesman named Nicholas Plunkett, and his narrative is often seen as the Old English counterpoint to O'Kelly's *Macariae Excidium*. Plunkett looked back over a quarter century after the guns fell silent at a 'great man'.[9]

To these I can add four untapped pro-Talbot primary sources. The first is a collection of notes written at the dictation of 'The Coll' (Colonel Talbot). These notes cover from the late 1650s to 1673. Richard self-importantly presents himself and his brother Peter, the Jesuit, as clever, behind-the-scenes manipulators enjoying great 'creditt' (the word is used several times) at the Restoration court.[10] 'Interest' or influence was the lubricant of politics, and 'credit', the belief held by others, rightly or wrongly, that one enjoyed such influence. The scribblings were probably among papers captured during the Williamite War (1689–91) and handed over to Sir Robert Southwell, wartime secretary of state for Ireland. J. T. Gilbert assembled and bound these notes together with unrelated writings, in quite distinct hands, mainly pertaining to James Butler, 1st Duke of Ormond, and political intrigue in the 1660s and 1670s. Southwell was an Ormond client, charged with writing a vindication of his patron's life and career. He penned a manuscript history of Ormond, which also ended up in Gilbert's possession and has been recently edited and published by John Gibney.[11] So it is likely that Gilbert associated the Colonel's closet-boasting with notes and materials for Southwell's 'memorial'. A second untapped source is an anonymous biography in French penned in or about 1700, the tone of which is set by the opening motto, '*vivit nunc gloria immortali*' [his glory now lives for all time].[12] The work is untitled but will be referred to by the first four words of the biography, '*Le Duc de Tirconnell*'. It is especially revealing about the critical months after the Glorious Revolution, when Tyrconnell was faced with the agonising choice of striking a deal with William or remaining loyal to James. A third significant new source is an epic poem in Latin that is mainly about the Jacobite regime in Ireland, 1685–91. This epic of 5,500 lines organised into seven books is modelled on Lucan's *De Bello Civili* and was composed by a member of Tyrconnell's wartime inner cabinet.[13] The poet presents Talbot in a very favourable light, as a selfless patriot and a sane, moderating and unifying influence: '*Arbiter omnes*'. Finally, a funeral oration published in 1722 and a manuscript panegyric, both in French, are prolix and repetitive but help fill in some biographical blanks.[14]

Talbot has attracted three biographers. Philip Sergeant's *Little Jennings and Fighting Dick Talbot* (1913) is a parallel biography of Talbot and of his second wife, the widowed court beauty and sister of Sarah Churchill, Frances Jennings. Sergeant delves fullys into such primary sources as were available at that time, though he reacts against Whiggish history so strongly that he paints a somewhat rose-tinted picture of the Talbots.

Sir Charles Petrie's *The Great Tyrconnel: A Chapter in Anglo-Irish Relations* (1973) leaves too many biographical gaps and neglects important sources that should have been accessible to him, such as Tyrconnell's correspondence with Mary of Modena between 1689 and 1691. Talbot's bid for Catholic dominance in 1685–91 was also the subject of an article in a compilation on noted losers in Irish history by James McGuire, who also wrote Talbot's entry in the *Dictionary of Irish Biography*.[15] McGuire refreshingly presented that bid, not as some ludicrously ambitious attempt to dam the Whig and Protestant tide, but as a scheme that was carefully thought-out, boldly implemented and by no means foredoomed to failure.

Since the last full biography by Petrie, a half-century's worth of secondary literature has enriched and nuanced our understanding of subjects as diverse as court cultures and Irish political and religious aspirations in the 1640s. Historiography has moved on, but apart from entries in the *Dictionary of Irish Biography* and the *Oxford New Dictionary of National Biography*, there have been no biographies to reappraise Talbot in the light of even relatively dated historiography, like John Miller's reconstruction in the *Historical Journal* (1977) of how Tyrconnell discredited rivals by argument and insinuation, over-rode his royal master's fears, and wrested the army and government in Ireland from Protestant control.[16] Miller depicts Tyrconnell as commonsensical and realistic, even his brazenness and verbal abusiveness often proving useful in cowing rivals in the cut-throat world of court politics.[17]

Using fresh or under-used primary sources, this study will try to paint a rounded portrait of the man. Talbot's warts are not painted over, but some virtues become clearer: adaptability, courage, resilience, and above all a purpose bigger than greed or personal ambition.

Talbot was seldom as influential as he claimed to be, yet episodes where he played an important part in three-kingdom or archipelagic history stand out: especially the two years before and the six months after the Glorious Revolution. I believe separate national histories within the archipelago are worth pursuing for their own sakes, and this will be mostly an 'internalist' exercise in Irish biography though appropriately enriched by awareness of three-kingdom interconnectedness.[18] An 'egocentric network analysis' of how Talbot the courtier wove, patched, renewed and used a web of personal contacts should uncover much about the inner workings of court and council.[19] 'Credit', 'interest', 'friends', clients, agents, brokers, factions, allies and enemies: the many manifestations of patronage form the strongest unifying thread of this study.

The first chapter, 'Peter's Brother 1646–56', explains the Talbot tradition and legacy of political leadership and activism which illuminates our subject's political career. It traces the political and military activities of Richard Talbot's brothers in the formative decade of the 1640s, especially those of Robert, the eldest of his brothers, who sided with Charles I's governor in Ireland against the overwhelming majority of his countrymen. Their story tells us much about the aspirations of the Irish Catholic community which Richard would lead one day, and explains their shock and lasting bitterness at unrequited wartime sacrifice. Talbot's wartime experience coarsened him but bestowed a swaggering self-confidence that would be useful to a down-at-heel outsider in carving out a niche at the Stuart court in exile.

Chapter two, 'York's man, 1657–62', explains how the nature of the Restoration devalued claims on Stuart goodwill from Richard Talbot and his brother Peter, in particular, and Irish Catholics, in general. Consequently, the Irish Protestant community contrived an Act of Settlement which maintained the wholesale confiscations of Irish Catholic land carried out the previous decade. The chapter describes the physical and moral setting in which Dick Talbot operated as a client courtier, specifically the household of James, Duke of York and the lattice of clientship and faction he created and nurtured. It explains how the role of leadership was thrust upon him to oppose the Act and defy Ormond, his erstwhile patron.

Chapter three, 'Arlington's Friend, 1662–72', picks up as Talbot embarked for Dublin in July 1662 to enrich himself and his patrons and to reverse, subvert or evade the Act. Ormond resented his insolence in presuming to speak for the whole Irish Catholic community and manoeuvred to have him thrown in the Tower. This temporary disgrace and the loss of Charles Berkeley, an influential patron, helps explain why the Act stood, albeit tweaked in favour of Catholics. The chapter sets Talbot's subsequent bid to restore the political status and regain the lost estates of Irish Catholics within the diplomatic and political context of Charles's 'grand design' of toleration for papists, French subsidies and rule without Parliament.

The fourth chapter, 'Ormond's Enemy: 1673–87', describes a trough of disgrace, exile, and imprisonment falling between the two crests of his political life. This low point happened because English political life polarised over the question: should Talbot's patron, the avowedly popish York, be excluded from the succession? Shortly after Ormond returned to Dublin Castle, Talbot was caught up in the tendrils of Oates's fabrications and imprisoned. The chapter speculates about the strings Talbot pulled to secure his release and his life, because the Popish Plot frenzy would have demanded his trial and execution. Charles weathered the plot and his last two years, as it concerned Ireland, flowed seamlessly into his successor's reign.[20] Talbot, ennobled as Earl of Tyrconnell, returned in triumph to Ireland as lieutenant general of the Irish army. He was buoyed by the favour of the newly crowned James II and an alliance –

albeit a short-term, instrumental and mutually distrustful one – with Robert Spencer, Secretary of State.

Chapter five, 'Lord Deputy, 1685–9' evaluates Tyrconnell's achievement in boldly Catholicising key institutions of a Protestant state and chivvying an initially hesitant King James to back him, even to the extent of reopening the land question. The chapter considers the wide parameters of his policies, which ranged from the extremes of breaking with England in the event of James dying without a Catholic heir, to quietly accepting William III after the Glorious Revolution. It also challenges the assumption that Talbot was biased against the Gaelic Irish and favoured New Irish or Old English. Tyrconnell was at one with James in seeing Ireland in archipelagic terms as a 'stepping-stone' whence to win back Britain and this perspective put him potentially at odds with most of his countrymen and with the advisers sent by Louis XIV. The chapter concludes with Jacobite Ireland within a hair's breadth of collapse in the summer of 1689, as the Jacobite siege of Derry was broken, an Irish army annihilated near Newtownbutler, Co. Fermanagh, and a large Williamite army trundled south from Ulster towards Dublin.

The title of Chapter six, 'Lord Lieutenant, 1690–1', reflects Tyrconnell's titular promotion, which contrasted with a sudden loss of grip after the Boyne. The chapter plumbs the psychological basis of Tyrconnell's demoralisation when, despairing of help from France, he called a council-of-war at Limerick and concluded that 'all was lost'.[21] He was shouted down, and never fully recovered the army's confidence.[22] The chapter assesses the prevalence and persistence of internal Jacobite divisions until briefly after Aughrim when the lord lieutenant kept his head and implored the squabbling Irish to stand together, thereby maintaining a strong bargaining position. His re-emergence was brief and he died in the city of Limerick, about to be beleaguered for the second and final time, on 14 August 1691.

The lord lieutenant's death 'pulled down a mighty edifice, videlicet, a considerable Catholic nation'.[23] The epilogue considers if his death really made a difference and asks: could the Irish have repulsed the siege under his leadership or at least capitulated for better terms?

ONE

PETER'S BROTHER
1646–56

PROLOGUE: IN BRUGES

As history had passed by this backwater in Spanish Flanders, so it would seem to be slipping by the exiles lodged in the 'Seven Towers'. In the young duke's upstairs chamber a large fireplace wrought of gilded vine leaves framed an empty grate, even as ice froze on the canal below. The prince perched stiffly on the edge of his chair as if to catch every word of excitable chatter from the man in a black habit standing before him. The Jesuit spoke to the duke in the brogue of his boyhood mutated by the lisps and inflexions of one who has spoken Spanish for most of his adult life. A spy set around the Stuart court described the priest as 'a well-sett man, of a middling stature, full-faced, brownish hayre, a fair complexion'.[1] He had a companion. His brother stood much taller, six foot and more, his bulk emphasised by the full periwig, the gaudy orange of his old-fashioned wide breeches, and the Tyrean purple of his short-sleeved jacket. Bunches of bright new ribbons were sewn on the seams of his breeches and more ribbons looped around his waist, but stopped short of his sword-hilt. He spoke when spoken to, which was seldom.

The encounter in Bruges imagined here between James Duke of York and Richard Talbot the gaudy cavalier represents a defining encounter of Talbot's life. During the winter of 1656–7 Talbot insinuated his way into the household of a man who was but a younger brother of an exiled king, his later importance as an heir apparent and monarch unimaginable. Chapter One will fill in the background of Richard Talbot's life before that encounter but only insofar as it is necessary towards revealing how he came to be there at that time.

*   *   *

Richard Talbot was a Palesman. The late medieval inner Pale, the core of English lordship in Ireland, encompassed Co. Dublin, an adjacent north-east corner of Co. Kildare, and most of counties Meath and Louth. Use of the term 'Pale' and 'Palesmen' lingered as late as 1631, the year of Talbot's birth, to describe the most English of the so-called 'Old English' as distinct from the Native Gaels who once lived, literally, beyond the Pale.[2]

The Old English boasted descent from medieval settlers who chose Counter-Reformation Catholicism rather than conform to the established church and by this refusal set themselves apart from a new wave of settlers from the island of Britain, the 'New English'. Sir William, the Talbot patriarch, was a sharp lawyer (spurious claims of shared ancestry with the earls of Shrewsbury reflect Talbot sensitivity about their undistinguished pedigree) and official of the sort who elsewhere closely identified with the centralising early modern state and thereby rose to *noblesse de robe* status. But he was papist and the state Protestant. He served only briefly (1602–5) as recorder of Dublin, the corporation's most senior legal officer, before refusing to take the oath of supremacy on account of his religion.[3] He belonged to that generation of the Old English which moved from nostalgic affection for the old faith to recusancy, an outright refusal to attend services of the state church. One sign of that zeal was that three of his sons, Richard Talbot's brothers, took holy orders as regular clergy.[4]

As well as being a sort of transitional identity or way station from Englishness to Irishness, Old Englishness was also a term of exclusion that embraced only those who were English by descent, Catholic and wealthy.[5] And Sir William was wealthy, for all the sneers that he was but a 'petty attorney'.[6] His wealth grew from his position as legal adviser, agent and trustee to the Fitzgeralds, Earls of Kildare. Sir William got the 'use and behoof' of Carton Castle, Co. Kildare, and an estate of 1,592 acres adjoining it rent-free from the earl in 1603. He set up his eldest son Sir Robert in an estate of 1,700 acres at Castlesallagh in Glen Imall hard by the spine of the Wicklow Mountains. The crown had seized these lands from Turlough Mac Shane O'Toole who had fought the queen in the Nine Years War (1594–1603) and awarded them to a 'servitor' or English official named Francis Annesley in 1607. Talbot bought it off him twenty years later. Moreover, Sir William and (probably) his son Sir Robert bought over 1,000 acres in a half-dozen distinct parcels scattered across Co. Meath and south Kildare.[7] Such piecemeal acquisition was typical of the way cash-rich Old English merchants, physicians and attorneys obtained land by purchase or by advancing mortgages to landowners mired in debt. To accumulate so much ready cash Sir William must have looted Kildare's 'encumbered and decayed estate' over a period marked by untimely deaths and minorities following the demise in 1612 of Garret 14th Earl of Kildare, the last Catholic to hold the title.[8] Or perhaps it was it all down to 'prudence and management'.[9] The beginning of the end of Talbot's stewardship came when Richard Boyle the parvenu 1st Earl of Cork married his daughter Joan into Ireland's oldest noble dynasty. Cork insisted that he alone should manage his son-in-law's estate and that the young man proclaim his acculturation to New English ways by denying 'ear or entertainment' to his 'Irish kinsmen and followers'.[10]

Sir William led a walkout by the Catholic opposition from the 1613 parliament, disgusted at the packing of the Commons by Protestant members returned by newly created boroughs. He acted as spokesman for the deputation sent to complain to James I. At the audience the learned monarch demanded that Talbot give his opinion on the recently published teaching of the Spanish Jesuit Suarez that it was lawful to kill or depose a heretical monarch.[11] Talbot prevaricated and was duly imprisoned in the Tower of London: he would not be the last Talbot to suffer that fate. Petitioning for his release, he offered many 'different declarations of his duty and allegiance', but would not answer James's question, replying that this was a matter of faith on which only the pope could pronounce. After languishing in the Tower for more than a year and paying a massive fine he was released, unrepentant.

Sir William's dilemma epitomised the persistent Old English belief that one could be loyal to monarch and pope at the same time, a dubious proposition at a time when political and religious loyalty was seen as inextricable. He served as a member of the delegation that extracted the 'Graces' from a financially strapped Charles I in 1628. These concessions would have re-opened office to Catholics and called a halt to plantations by confirming existing land titles. Sir William's death in March 1634 provoked rhapsodies from his son's hagiographer:

> When this great man died it hardly seemed to count because he had the good fortune to leave behind an image of himself [*un autre lui-même*] The son [Richard Talbot] faithfully followed the footsteps of his father & those of his ancestors.[12]

It would be surprising if the three year old did not eventually come to feel the weight of family tradition and expectation, and so it is necessary to outline that collective experience. No one of Sir William's stature emerged to lead the Catholic community when Lord Deputy Thomas Wentworth brusquely reneged on most of the Graces. Worse, Wentworth dusted off old plantation projects in which it would be clear that the Old English would be treated just like the Gaelic Irish, as 'so many papists'.[13] Before that could happen Stuart authority began to collapse in the face of Scottish refusal to adopt a state-sanctioned prayer book. At first, Irish Catholics saw opportunities, as usual, in royal weakness but by three years on, in the summer of 1641, it looked as if the Scots and their allies in the English parliament would prevail over Charles I and be in a position to 'raze the name of Catholic and Irish out of the whole Kingdom'.[14]

A plot to surprise Dublin Castle miscarried, but insurgents overran a swathe of south and mid-Ulster on the night of 23 October.[15] After probing north-east and north-west over the following weeks, Phelim O'Neill, leader of the Ulster insurgents, reoriented his forces south to take Drogheda and, ultimately,

Dublin. As the Ulstermen drew a noose around Drogheda, a relief column from Dublin blundered into them on 29 November at Julianstown and was quickly routed. Four days after the rout, a hosting called by the chief lords of the Pale, Gormanstown, Fingal, Slane, Dunsany, Trimlestown, Louth and Netterville joined the Ulstermen near the Hill of Tara. Old English apologists would later disavow the Ulster rising as 'delirious madness' begun by 'a rabble' and blame the authorities for driving them into the arms of the Ulstermen by disarming them, proroguing the parliament where they hoped for redress, and attacking them. In fact, widespread popular violence erupted spontaneously before Julianstown across much of Leinster.[16] The insurgency in the Pale was home-grown. It began among the lower classes, and crept up to include younger sons of the gentry, the perennial reservoir of blighted ambition in a society based on primogeniture, who led many of the earliest manifestations.[17] Later it sucked in their older brothers and fathers and, ultimately, as at Julianstown, many Catholic peers. One attack on 24 November saw Gilbert Talbot of Carton, one of Richard's brothers, leading a band claiming to be 'the Queen's Soldiers'. The claim to have the implicit or explicit sanction of Charles's Catholic consort, Henrietta Maria, was commonplace. They plundered cattle, household goods and money from a settler near Naas.[18] On 23 December a gang of 'rebells' led by Garrett Talbot, another brother of Richard's, robbed a Protestant neighbour as he was fleeing with goods and stock to Dublin, burnt the pulpit and pews of the Protestant church, and disinterred the remains of clergymen's wives from the chancel.[19] Such disrespect to the dead reflected an atavistic notion that foreign heretics polluted the land: the living and the dead had to be expelled. On St Stephen's Day Garrett's band overran Maynooth Castle, and one Edward Mac Thomas Fitzgerald subsequently installed himself there claiming that he was the 'real' earl of Kildare of that line that Henry VIII had cut short in the 1530s.[20] Here, as in Ulster, the rising envisaged turning the clock back: as the poet Gofraidh Óg Mac an Bhaird, penning his excitable lines in the heady early months of 1642, put it; 'biaidh gach duine 'na dhileas' or 'everybody will be in his own'.[21]

Insurgent hopes of victory depended on seizing control of Dublin, and other beleaguered settler enclaves before parliament and king in England had time to recruit and send reinforcements. The Irish posted strong garrisons near the main axial roads out of Dublin, including Kilsallaghan on the north but a relief fleet broke through to Drogheda on 20 February and on the same day almost 2,000 English soldiers disembarked at Dublin, the advance party of a second wave.[22] Three days after the reinforcements landed, the lieutenant general of the government forces, James Butler, Earl of Ormond, marched on Kilsallaghan Castle. Garret and Gilbert Talbot had brought companies to reinforce the castle where, outnumbered and outgunned, the insurgents were swept out of their entrenchments at the gate.[23]

Over the following weeks the Irish were beaten back from around Dublin and there followed a grim few months when Ormond, to dispel suspicions of sneaking sympathy for the insurgents, let loose his troops to kill soldiers and civilians alike: 'We have banished, hanged and killed all the Irish, and Papist in the Town of Naas', boasted one pamphleteer.[24] One victim was the eighty-year-old Mrs Eustace of Cradackstown near Naas, an aunt of the by now ten-year-old Richard Talbot. She played hostess to a group of passing English officers but 'after dinner, her selfe and another old Gentlewoman, and a girl of eight yeares of age, were murdered'.[25]

As he took his followers south-west, Garrett Talbot set fire to Maynooth Castle and neighbouring Protestant-owned houses.[26] By March Talbot was one of the captains guarding the bog-island of Allen.[27] In April, Ormond's troops plunged deep into Irish held regions but found their way back to Dublin blocked by three tercios drawn up atop Bull Hill, in south Co. Kildare. Standing in one of the tercios with 'banners displayed' was 'Colonel' Garrett Talbot.[28] Ormond's musketeers 'shot at them so thick and sure' that they broke the Irish formations whereupon his cavalry pursued, cutting down a hundred or so.[29] This defeat 'entirely dispersed' the Irish army but there could be no question of the Talbot brothers submitting to mercy. They were marked men.[30] Nor would any mercy be shown to the Irish collectively. In the months before he went to war with the English parliament, Charles had bowed to the demands of that body and decreed that the cost of reconquering Ireland would be paid by confiscated Irish land. This seemed to close off any possibility of a negotiated settlement and in this crisis the Irish belatedly set about creating a government, the Confederate Catholics.[31]

As the English Civil War dragged on into its second year Charles grew increasingly keen to strike some deal with the Irish in order to persuade them to send an army to save him. For their part, the Confederate Catholics asked, early in 1643, to be 'left free in the profession of their faith and given security for their estates'.[32] But what might such religious freedom actually mean? For Rome, freedom meant Catholicism 'established in its former splendour'.[33] Clergy and pious laity who shared this aspiration – a group dubbed clericalists – tended to regard the outcome of the war in Britain with equanimity, while publicly professing loyalty to the king. They argued privately that the Irish should consolidate their hold over Ireland by mopping up the isolated pockets of Scottish, English parliamentary and English royalist control. From this position of strength the Confederate Catholics might fight or treat with whoever won the war in Britain and insist on something more attractive than the grudging promise offered by Charles to apply existing anti-Catholic laws leniently.[34]

Many wealthy lay Catholics would settle for this nod and wink connivance. Robert Talbot, oldest of the Talbot brethren, professed himself equally happy 'to have mass with solemnity in Christ or St Patrick's Church [the two largest churches in Dublin] or privately at his bedside'. [35] Robert was 'a brave instrument of faction and treason' to his clericalist enemies and his overriding priority was to sign a treaty with Ormond, by now the king's lord deputy in Ireland, send troops to Britain, and win the war for Charles. Proponents of this policy constituted a numerically small but influential clique who dominated the supreme council until summer 1646. Critics dubbed them the 'Ormondist' faction because so many of them had close ties to the lord deputy.[36] These men gambled on the unlikeliest outcome of all to the Civil War in Britain, namely complete victory for Charles. A parliamentary victory or a compromise peace was a more likely outcome and in either case it was entirely predictable that Charles would break his promises to his Catholic supporters. This subterranean fissure has been usually presented as a case of Old English versus Gael but to see a Donough O'Callaghan, Daniel O'Brien or Donough MacCarthy Viscount Muskerry aligning with the Ormondists cautions against simplifying the split as an ethnic or cultural one. [37] Provincial rivalries and class tensions were more significant. The 'ignorant and misled multitude', in the words of one Ormondist, might be clericalist but most of the 'best men', in the words of the same speaker, were not.

In September 1643 the Confederate Catholics had agreed a ceasefire with Ormond which froze that territorial status quo. Over the next three years they fought only the king's – and their own – enemies, attacking the Scottish Covenanter enclave in east Ulster in 1644 and the parliamentary enclave in Munster in 1645.[38] All the while they tried to conclude a definitive treaty with Ormond whereby they could embark an army to Britain but Ormond proved obstructive because he personally would have far preferred to strike a deal with the English parliament and the Covenanters.[39]

The Ormondist clique steering the supreme council kept control of the talks with Ormond by nominating like-minded negotiators like Sir Robert.[40] However, the council fatally overreached itself by promulgating a treaty, the Ormond peace, on 3 August 1646. The Jesuit Peter Talbot, brother of Richard, later insisted the treaty was 'seasonable' and 'very advantageous'.[41] It was neither. The Catholics were at the peak of their military power while the king was a prisoner of the Scots, the allies of the parliamentarians. Yet the Peace was skewed towards Ormond and Charles. Repeal of the penal laws was left 'to his Majestie's gracious favour', a naïve act of faith in Stuart promises, and the supreme council agreed to dissolve the entire Confederate Catholic regime before the final ratification of the Peace. [42]

At this juncture, Richard Talbot strides, or rides, on to the stage. Dick was the second youngest of sixteen children and his sister Mary, who married into the neighbouring Dungan family of Castletown, the second eldest. Her son Walter Dungan had fought in England but as the royalist position there crumbled he returned to Ireland and offered his services to Ormond who sent him to join the Leinster army of the Confederate Catholics under General Thomas Preston. When Dungan raised a cavalry troop for the Confederate Catholics for the campaigning season of 1646 his fourteen-year-old uncle put aside his schoolbooks to serve as a cornet.[43]

A cavalier like Talbot wore a feathered hat, doublet, thigh-length buff coat and heavy jackboots.[44] He carried a short-barrelled carbine or a brace of pistols, hanging in holsters on each side of the saddle, but firearms played a subordinate role in fighting and he usually hacked and slashed with the short and curved blade of his sword.[45] Irish infantry battalions massed unwieldy sixteen-foot long pikes and slow-firing matchlock muskets in a ponderous battle square that derived from the tercio of the Spanish armies where the ageing Irish generals had learnt their trade. Cavalrymen gave the Catholic armies the shock and mobility that they otherwise sorely lacked. The best of the cavalrymen were refugees from the Pale where tillage farming bred bigger horses and nurtured traditions of horsemanship and cavalry fighting. Talbot's comrades were élite troops, and they knew it.

The Leinster army split in two. One part, which included Cornet Talbot, was sent to capture the massive medieval keep of Roscommon which anchored the southern edge of an enemy salient that thrust from west Ulster deep into Connacht.[46] Towards the end of the siege Talbot was blooded when enemy horsemen fell on the Irish lines by night. At first light the Leinster cavalry caught up with the enemy rearguard and 'pursued for fully nine miles, cutting down stragglers wherever they came up on them'.[47]

After taking Roscommon, Preston's offensive stalled while the priests and politicians bickered over the Ormond Peace. Kilkenny had thrown open its gates to Ormond but townspeople in other urban centres like Limerick and Clonmel rioted when the Peace was proclaimed. Reflecting the popular mood, Papal Nuncio Rinuccini and the clergy spurned the Peace. The nuncio could count on Eoghan Rua O'Neill's Ulster army but that had scattered after crushing a Scots Covenanter army at Benburb.[48] If Preston had hastened to reinforce Ormond, together they probably could have overcome Clericalist opposition. On 3 September Sir Robert Talbot penned an urgent letter to Preston appealing to what he claimed was their common 'Old English of Ireland' heritage and insisting that his opponents were disloyal: 'though they claim to be for religion I fear they want to destroy English rule'.[49] Preston wavered but ultimately

backed the Clericalists when he realised that his soldiers were not 'excommu-
nication-proof'. The clergy locked up the Ormondists, Sir Robert among
them. Later a General Assembly voted down the Peace: Sir Robert was the
sole dissenting voice.

When Preston rejected the Peace, Walter Dungan had sought instructions
from Ormond who told him to remain at his post with the Confederate Catholics
'in hopes he might be useful on a favourable opportunity to reduce them to their
due obedience': in other words, bide his time until the chance came to suborn his
comrades.[50] Soon Dungan got his chance. When Rinuccini sent a combined
Ulster and Leinster army to take the capital, provisions ran short and the
November weather was predictably wet. Dungan was foremost among Ormond's
supporters who worked on Preston to turn against the clericalists. Unsettled by
reports of these intrigues, O'Neill broke camp and the expedition – the largest
single operation ever mounted by the Confederate Catholics – was abandoned.
Robert Talbot's snobbery, disdain towards his fellow-countrymen and cravenness
to a lord can be seen from the fact that as late as March 1647, knowing that
Ormond would very shortly surrender Dublin to the Roundheads, he was still
bemoaning his 'country's ingratitude towards your lordship'. [51] Untroubled by
self-doubt, he regretted only that he and those 'best affected to the king, religion
and country' have been 'overborn with vote and not weight or strength of reason'.

Having evidently given up hope of seizing a reinforced Dublin outright,
the Supreme Council ordered Preston to mop up outlying garrisons and ravage
the countryside around the capital. [52] On 8 August 1647 Michael Jones, the
parliamentary commander of Dublin, caught up with Preston who hastily
deployed on Dungan's Hill, near modern day Summerhill, Co. Meath. [53]
Preston posted his cavalry in a narrow boreen, hemmed in by ditches so that
when the English charged the Irish were 'not able to stir forward, backward,
or to either side for want of ground'.[54] Pioneers knocked a gap in a ditch and
the horsemen fled the battlefield as did the cavalry reserve behind them.[55] The
cavaliers rode so hard that they lost only fourteen men of their number taken
prisoner, Cornet Talbot among them. The main body of Irish infantry stood
their ground 'for a long time' but eventually clambered over a ditch and scattered towards the illusory safety of a nearby bog.[56] Here some 3,000 soldiers
'did capitulate for quarter, as the Irish say, and the English deny it' and threw
down their weapons.[57] Jones spared officers and some 200 common soldiers,
but 'without mercy put the rest unto the sword'.

Despite the catastrophe at Dungan's Hill the Confederate Catholics
limped along until the following summer when the political context abruptly
changed. Victory for the Parliamentarians and the capture of King Charles
opened up fissures between those in Britain who favoured constitutional

monarchy and peace talks with Charles and those who pressed for more radical change. The royalist court in exile sent Ormond back to Ireland to juxtapose loosening components of the Scots-Parliamentary alliance into new alignments in Munster, Murrough O'Brien Lord Inchiquin declared for Charles in April 1648 and agreed a ceasefire with the supreme council the following month. Rinuccini's partisans were appalled by an alliance with 'Murrough the firebrand' [Murchú na dtóiteáin].

A desultory conflict followed in which O'Neill and his Clericalist allies seldom came to blows with their Ormondist opponents. [58] The most significant engagement of this little civil war involved Dungan and, presumably, Talbot: the last of the Dungan's Hill prisoners had been exchanged in July 1648. Angus Mac Donald of Glengarry's 'Redshanks' (Scots Gaelic mercenaries) had escaped the Battle of Dungan's Hill and joined Charles Kavanagh, an ally of O'Neill's. They fled north from close-by Wexford town on hearing of an Ormondist advance but Dungan's cavalry caught them in open countryside while making for the safety of Davidstown Wood and 'barbarously slaughtered both man, woman and child': Gaelic armies were usually trailed by as many camp followers as fighters. [59]

Meanwhile talks between the general assembly and Ormond for a definitive settlement ground on until Ormond offered major new concessions, after Queen Henrietta Maria ordered him to soften his stance. Catholics were promised free exercise of religion and assured that an overwhelmingly Catholic standing army would be kept in being until the agreement was finally ratified. Reports that Charles would be tried as 'a tyrant, traitor, murderer and implacable enemy' finally helped break the deadlock in January 1649, and his execution prompted mass defections by Protestants to the royalist cause. [60]

In Ormond's reconstituted army Sir Robert Talbot nominally commanded a troop in the horse regiment of Thomas 4th Viscount Dillon (who had led the Irish cavalry so feebly at Dungan's Hill) but almost certainly Walter Dungan acted as Sir Robert's place-holder and Richard Talbot, in turn, served under Dungan. [61] Ormond had to prise back the capital from Jones (he had handed it over to him only two years before) with a field army that was not much bigger than Jones's and vulnerable to a sally by the besieged. Nonetheless, Ormond split his forces, leaving Dillon at Finglas while he pitched the main camp at Rathmines, two miles south of Dublin. At daybreak on 2 August Jones swooped on the camp and quickly scattered the royalists. Oliver Cromwell landed less than a fortnight later. [62]

Defeat at Rathmines had not 'grievously weakened' the royalist resistance: Ormond guessed he lost only about 600 men. [63] If Drogheda remained in royalist hands, Cromwell would have to turn his back on the Covenanters (now supporting the Stuarts) in east Ulster while turning towards south Leinster and Munster. Indeed, Dublin would be under threat because O'Neill now threw in his lot with the royalists, belaboured by emissaries who included yet another of Richard Talbot's brothers, the Franciscan Fr Thomas, one of Henrietta Maria's chaplains.[64] Hamstrung by logistical constraints, Ormond did not have the manpower to challenge Cromwell in open battle and, he reasoned, Drogheda should delay Cromwell for a few precious weeks until the end of the campaigning season when autumnal rains and impassable roads usually made it very difficult for large field armies to march and manoeuvre.

While skirmishing near Castleknock, Co. Dublin, Dungan had ridden 'too far forward' and was taken prisoner.[65] Talbot now commanded the troop which, as ill luck would have it, was sent to Drogheda to form part of its 3,000-strong garrison.[66] Cromwell had not the temperament, training or time for a methodical siege in the form of fortified lines and approach trenches. His advance guard reached Drogheda on 2 September and he summoned Governor Aston on the 10th soon after his cannonade began: 'If this be refused, you will have no cause to blame me'. The royalist cavalrymen kept busy in the days before the summons, guarding the northern bank of the river and pressing the English back across Oldbridge Ford (the site of the Battle of the Boyne forty-one years later), three miles upstream.

The Boyne divided Drogheda into two parts with the smaller part lying on the south bank nestling within curtain walls twenty feet high and nine feet wide at their base. Solid as medieval defences went, the walls could not stand up to the pounding of heavy siege guns. By the morning after the summons Cromwell's heavy guns had knocked a 'very great breach' at St Mary's church-yard near the south-eastern corner of the town walls. In response, Aston had his foot soldiers throw up breastworks inside the breaches and seems to have massed horsemen in gaps between these earthworks. When the roundheads clambered over the main breach on the afternoon of 11 September the royalist horsemen dashed into the open space between wall and works and drove them out, inflicting heavy losses.[67] A second breach gave Cromwell's guns a clear shot and they peppered the royalist horsemen with shot forcing them to recoil. Meanwhile, Cromwell led a second attack through the main breach. This time the attackers captured the breastworks and so were secure from counter-attack by the royalist cavalrymen. The handful of cavaliers still in their saddles (eleven out of fifteen horse officers had fallen by now) rode across the bridge, whereupon the foot soldiers began to scurry after them, the English at their heels.[68] The collapse must have been sudden because by the time the surviving cavaliers reached the north-west of the town they had to cut their way through English foot soldiers milling outside Sunday's Gate.

Cromwell admitted in a letter intended for publication that he 'forbade' his troops 'to spare any that were in arms in the town'. Measured by the customary 'laws of war or arms' and the grim usages of siege warfare, Cromwell's order was unexceptionable. Everyone knew that a commander-in-chief would be hard put to restrain troops enraged by heavy losses from running amok once they swarmed into the streets. Aston, 200 officers and men, sheltering behind palisades on the Millmount, a motte dominating the south part of the town, laid down their arms, were locked in the eponymous windmill, and later slain. Cromwell may have broken a promise of quarter in this instance. This was, or would have been, dishonourable behaviour according to the 'laws of war'. It is unsurprising, therefore, that the English clubbed, hacked, stabbed or incinerated, as Cromwell himself admitted, thousands of soldiers and 'many inhabitants'.[69]

A parallel code to the 'laws of war' was based on Christian principles and forbade killing prisoners and civilians in almost any circumstances. A Scottish veteran of the Irish wars could opine that, however justified by the laws of war, it was 'horrible cruelty' to kill a prisoner in cold blood.[70] This was not a fanciful or utopian aspiration. Ormond's soldiers stormed Rathfarnham Castle some days before the Battle of Rathmines and 'all that were there were made prisoners', Ormond was proud to recall.[71]

Lieutenant Talbot was one of the handful of Royalists to survive the Drogheda massacre. A pamphlet extolling his governorship of Ireland almost forty years later insisted that Talbot showed himself 'brave to the last extremity' at Drogheda and retreated when just a dozen men were left alive around him. This sounds plausible and of a piece with his apparent valour at Dungan's Hill. Taken prisoner, his life was spared and this was read as 'a providence that marked him out for greater things'.[72] Such providentialism might be no more than a pious platitude or an intellectually empty retrospective justification through success (we won so God must have been on our side) of the kind often used by Cromwell himself.[73] But when unlikely and unexpected boons such as Talbot's survival were granted it was hard to avoid seeing miraculous confirmation of God's will and providential interpretations could then be convincing and fortifying.

He sustained so many wounds that if he was not dead he was as good as dead & lay for almost three days amongst those who were certainly so. In the normal course of events he could not have survived. But the patron saint of Ireland who is especially honoured in the county of Tyrconnell [Donegal] interceded for he who would bear that name [Tyrconnell] so gloriously & begged the same God who kept Jonah alive for three days in the belly of a whale to repeat this miracle for the young warrior.

His prayer was answered. Providence led a soldier to a place where the dying lay, he detected a spark of life in him [Talbot] and resolved to save him. But he was not strong enough to carry out this act of piety unaided and asked another soldier for help. The latter, too obedient to the barbarous order of his general against the beaten Catholics, would not help anyone but a Protestant & no sooner had he asked this when the wounded man, weakened by loss of blood, revived at this question and answered boldly 'I am a Catholic'... Hardly had these words been spoken when the soldier interrogating him made to finish him off. But the guardian angel of the island working through the agency of the first soldier overcame and disarmed the second.[74]

The first soldier brought the wounded man 'within the town' (this detail indicates that Talbot fell near the breach) and put him under medical care. Talbot eventually recovered and slipped out of Drogheda. The claim by one contemporary source that Talbot escaped dressed in woman's clothing has to be a legend: a hulking youth could not have carried off the imposture.[75] Stripping away the pious fiction, some of this account tallies with another French-language biographical source which recounts how Talbot was 'pierced' by many thrusts or cuts and fell to the ground where he lay for almost twenty-four hours (rather than the three days of the 'Oraison funebre') amidst the dead.[76] In addition we can identify his saviour. A survivor remarked that some prisoners were 'privately saved' in defiance of Cromwell's orders and we know from yet another source that Dick Talbot owed his life to John Reynolds, a colonel leading the cavalry that drove back their royalist counter-parts.

Cromwell piously opined that the massacre was a 'righteous judgement of God upon these barbarous wretches who have imbrued their hands in so much innocent blood' and, more convincingly, used the 'lesser evil' plea that 'this bitterness will save much effusion of blood'. [77] Certainly, smaller wards surrendered rather than risk 'Drogheda quarter' but it was an unseasonably mild winter that really derailed Ormond's Fabian strategy and let Cromwell campaign unrelentingly late into the winter and resume unexpectedly early in 1650. [78] He was on the march before the end of January, denying the Royalists a chance to draw breath, and by March two pincers were closing on Kilkenny, one from the south-west and another from the north-east. Dungan, by now Commissary General of the Leinster Horse, engaged the latter column with five troops of horse (Talbot probably among them) near Bolton Hill in Co. Kildare but was worsted.[79]

By the time he left Ireland Cromwell had taken Kilkenny and Clonmel so that his forces controlled the coast from Derry to Bandon inland to a depth of about thirty miles. Yet the tempo of war would slow after Ireton, Cromwell's son-in-law, took over. This was partly because of Ireton's caution but also because the Irish fought more doggedly, even desperately, as Cromwell clarified his unremitting hostility to Catholicism; 'if by liberty of conscience you mean liberty to exercise the mass' he had told the defenders of Ross in October 1649, 'that will not be allowed of'.[80] Charles's public repudiation of his 1648 alliance with Irish Catholics, Ormond's departure for France and the defection of most Protestant Royalists to Parliament, all clarified what was at stake: the very survival of an Irish Catholic community.

At the outset of the 1651 campaigning season the earl of Clanricard, Ormond's successor, held the Shannon line but since Connacht and Clare could not sustain all his forces he left thousands of soldiers behind the somewhat notional front lines to wage guerrilla war.[81] These guerrillas were often decried by their enemies as 'tories': tóraí denotes a robber or cattle rustler. Dungan's 'tories' were assigned five counties (Dublin, Kildare, Wicklow, Wexford and Carlow) while Talbot now commanded Dungan's troop. Clanricard had not enough men to hold the Shannon line and in late May 1651 Charles Coote marched from west Ulster and squeezed through the gap between Sligo and the Shannon. He next veered away from the most direct route south over the Curlew Mountains (where Clanricard had fortified the passes against him) and swung around by 'an unexpected way' on a wide arc through Mayo, then south towards Athenry. Irish cavalrymen, 'Captain-lieutenant' Richard Talbot among them, had been hastily recalled from Leinster.[82] The Irish fell on 300 of Coote's outriders, and killed them all or took them prisoner, together with a company of foot soldiers nearby. This reverse did not stop Coote and he pressed on to Loughrea. In a skirmish near the town, Richard Talbot was taken prisoner for the third time in four years. Talbot's survival as a prisoner could not be taken for granted: Coote was brutal, even by the standards of English warfare in Ireland. To take one example, Coote had a prisoner named Henry rua O'Neill, son of Eoghan rua, bludgeoned to death with a tent pole after the battle of Scariffhollis.[83]

Meanwhile, Ireton crossed the Shannon just above Limerick and sent a detachment to link up with Coote. Clanricard pulled back closer to Galway, leaving Athlone isolated. Viscount Dillon, Sir James Dillon and Sir Robert Talbot surrendered Athlone on 18 June without facing a siege or even an assault, even though they had ample gunpowder and enough supplies for three months. A Clericalist author accused Talbot of 'treason, faction and perjury' and even Ormondists muttered darkly about 'treacherous' and 'ignominious' surrender.[84]

Coote blocked up the eastern approaches to Galway while Clanricard's army lurked on the west bank of the Corrib. In July Clanricard circled behind Coote to a rendezvous near Kilconnell in east Co. Galway, thereby forcing Coote to temporarily lift the siege of Galway city. Soon, however, most of Clanricard's army scattered, 'not able to subsist'.[85] Among those forced to disperse were Dungan's horsemen who crossed the upper reaches of the Shannon, rode south to the bogs of Offaly, and dashed across open countryside to reach his fastness at Glenmalure, a deep cleft in the Wicklow Mountains.

Much of the English army was thinly scattered in garrisons while a large field army sat and waited before Limerick from May to October 1651. Meanwhile, skulking fragments of the royalist armies emerged from hideouts like Glenmalure to raid, and sometimes overrun, garrisons, intercept supplies and ambush patrols. In early September Irish horsemen had taken prey and prisoners in a raid on Baggotrath (modern-day Baggot Street) almost within a stone's throw of Dublin Castle. These prisoners were released on parole and in return the parliamentary commissioners directed Coote to release Richard Talbot. He may have been let go in time for Dungan's raid on New Ross in the small hours of Saturday 29 September, where he seized much booty before marching north along the River Barrow.[86] His band brushed aside a force trying to hold a ford near Monasterevan against them and had swelled to about 3,000 men in and around Naas by 28 October.

But by now Limerick had capitulated, as would Galway in April 1652. In spring and early summer of 1652 the English were at last able to deploy powerful and mobile forces for counter-insurgency sweeps to harry and starve out the guerrillas, having first congregated civilians into villages of at least thirty households within 'lines of protection' and destroyed or taken up foodstuffs and crops 'without the line'.[87] One such no-man's land, comprising the whole of Co. Wicklow and the northern half of Co. Wexford, took up much of Dungan's assigned zone.[88]

Straitened for provisions, Dungan and Talbot took a raiding party of 250 cavalry and 500 infantry to forage within the line, right up to the walls of Wexford town, during the first week of May 1652. Such raiding parties were always encumbered and most vulnerable on the return leg and an equally strong English detachment cut between Dungan's men and their line of retreat. Running skirmishes followed and at length the Irish faced about, shuffled into battalion formation, and bore down, 'push-a-pike', on their pursuers.[89] But after a 'very sharp dispute' the Irish broke, losing some 200 men in a five-mile pursuit. It must have been a shattering blow because just days later Dungan headed the list of signatories on 'articles of agreement' on behalf of the Leinster forces. Robert Talbot, always to the fore when it came to capitulating, was another of the seven subscribers who were assured of 'pardon for life and protection for themselves and their personal estates'. The Parliamentary commissioners promised, for what it was worth, 'our utmost endeavours' to let the families of the exiles keep as much of their landed estates as would suffice for their 'comfortable maintenance' and reassured those capitulating that it was not the Commonwealth's intention 'to compel any of the Recusants in this nation to their worship or divine service contrary to their conscience'.[90] The officers were free to ship themselves and their soldiers to any foreign state 'in amity with the Commonwealth of England'. Over a year later, in August 1653, seven vessels left Waterford carrying troops to north-western Galicia.[91] Richard Talbot was among them.

The Bourbons and Habsburgs were grimly fighting in a mutually destructive conflict that was outlasting the Thirty Years War. The Commonwealth was happy enough to feed their insatiable demands for cannon fodder by facilitating troop transports. Over 18,000 men left for Spain or Spanish territories between 1651 and 1655 and anything from 10,000 to 18,000 also took service with the French.

Plague, famine and the flight of the fighting men left Ireland, in Cromwell's words a 'clean paper' ready for a fresh chapter to be written.[92] The native leaders were to be written out of this chapter. While the Act of Settlement, passed in August 1652, disclaimed any intention to uproot 'the whole nation', anyone owning property worth more than £10 a year would be judged according to their 'respective demerits'. Memories of the 'barbarous, cruell massacres' perpetrated by Catholics during the first months of insurgency were selectively recalled and rhetorically exaggerated to justify collective and punitive land confiscations. [93] All Catholic landowners would forfeit their estates to English grantees of various stripes such as 'adventurers' who had loaned money in 1642 to finance the reconquest and army men owed arrears of pay. Dispossessed Catholics would be awarded a portion of land in the 'natural prison' of Connacht and Clare, bound by river and sea. On paper what they were to get was calculated according to their forfeited estates and their individual 'delinquency': all were presumed delinquent in some degree. Sir Robert Talbot lost almost 2,800 acres in Counties Wicklow and Meath but despite being awarded thousands of acres on paper in Burrishole, Co. Mayo, he did not apparently secure this property.[94] All of Co. Sligo and one third of Co. Mayo was clawed back from lands set aside for dispossessed Irish like Talbot, leaving insufficient land to satisfy them. The available land was further cut back when commissioners helped themselves to estates and Irish were transplanted who were supposedly exempted for pardon for life or estate. However, special consideration was taken of English-born papists and lands were set aside for 'widows of English extraction'. Robert was married to Grace, a sister of Cecil Calvert who had resigned his office as secretary of state in 1625 after he publicly avowed Catholicism. The king had awarded Calvert an

Irish peerage lest it be thought he was in disgrace and the newly created baron of Baltimore would later found colonies in Newfoundland and Maryland.[95] On the strength of her English parentage, Grace Talbot secured 500 acres in and around Castle Sampson, Co. Roscommon.

The Protector's agents displayed consummate administrative skill in survey-ing confiscated land but the actual assignment was a free-for-all in which guilt or innocence counted for less than wealth or influence. When the dust settled, natives owned as little as nine per cent of land compared to an estimated sixty per cent before the war: half the land in the country had changed hands. It was a massive loss of wealth, status and power.[96] The towns and cities were mostly captured by mercantile and artisan immigrants but in the countryside the Protectorate created not a whole new population but a Protestant upper crust decried by a Catholic author as 'robbers and rebels', 'Cromwellian mechanics', 'Protestant canaille', and 'trash'. [97] It would be Richard Talbot's lifelong work to uproot them.

By the time Talbot disembarked a handful of followers in Cantabria he had begun to style himself 'Colonel Talbot'.[98] The self-appointed colonel parted from Dungan who remained in Iberia and was one of those officers who subscribed to a collective condemnation of the thousands of Irishmen who deserted to the French in 1653.[99] Dungan later commanded an Irish regiment, fought against the Portuguese rebels and their French backers, and was eventually promoted maestre de campo in the Armada del Mar Océano.[100] Various Talbot brothers took the French or Spanish sides: Thomas and 'Colonel' (he had about as much claim to assume that style as Richard) Gilbert Talbot usually worked for French interests but Peter the Jesuit continued to identify strongly with Spain.[101] Richard began his rise as a cour-tier by dogging Peter's footsteps and so knowing the pathfinder's career helps explain that rise.

A lecturer in philosophy at the University of Coimbra and later an envoy of John IV of Portugal, Peter Talbot switched allegiance to Spain. In the first of many chimerical schemes to advance the causes of 'king, faith, fatherland and family' he arrived in London in April 1653 with royal letters to Spanish ambassador Alonso de Cárdenas.[102] The ambassador was instructed to help Talbot win some degree of toleration for priests, albeit in an unobtrusive man-ner that did not prejudice Anglo-Spanish friendship.[103] From England Peter crossed to Ireland where he reported on the transplantations to Connacht and transportations to the English West Indies.[104] Hopes of toleration were quickly dashed on this occasion but Peter's backstairs diplomacy flourished in the interstices opened up by Charles II's realignment from France to Spain.

This realignment began when both sides, locked in debilitating war, courted Oliver Cromwell as an ally who could give them the winning edge. Cromwell finally chose to ally with Mazarin out of old-fashioned antipathy to Spain.[105] The first tentative steps towards alliance with France were taken in July 1654 and Mazarin accordingly expelled Charles II and his household from French territory, in complete disregard of Bourbon dynastic loyalties: Charles was first cousin to the young Louis XIV. In December the Protectorate launched a 'Western Design' to descend on Santo Domingo, the largest city in the Spanish West Indies.[106] The Spanish monarchy was so weakened that it turned a blind eye to such provocations so as to avoid open hostilities in Europe and war was not formally declared until 1656. During this interlude of phoney war (1654–6) the Spanish cast about for someone to distract Cromwell from foreign adventures.

That someone would be Charles Stuart, once he had left his mother and her pro-French policies behind and moved his little court to Spa, Aachen and eventually Cologne. The idleness, poverty and homesickness of exile often sparked bitter personal rivalries and sterile intrigues, but the 'Louvrian' and 'Old Royalist' factions in the Stuart courts also formed over fundamental questions of policy as the relative merits of allying with Irish Papists or Scottish Covenanters. Henrietta Maria, principal of the Louvrians, had always tried to persuade Irish Catholics to side with her husband, saw Catholic powers as offering the best hope of her son's restoration, and argued for more concessions to Catholics and English Presbyterians.[107] The Old Royalist faction was typified by Edward Hyde, Charles's chancellor who would re-establish an Anglican religious monopoly and was more sceptical than the Louvrians about foreign aid. The influence of Henrietta Maria and Henry Jermyn Earl of St Albans over Charles was strongest in Paris and widening the physical distance from Henrietta Maria consolidated the influence of Hyde and his ally Ormond.

The Old Royalists embraced a disproportionate number of Protestant exiles from Ireland who were mostly deeply suspicious of Catholicism. Bramhall, bishop of Derry and religious ideologue of the Old Royalists blamed Jesuit conspirators for the killing of the martyred Charles I. Peter Talbot would be, on the face of it, unwelcome to the Old Royalists yet one cannot generalise completely. The faction included three Catholic exiles from Ireland, Ormond's brother-in-law George Hamilton, Richard Bellings and Theobald Taaffe. [108] Ormond was a friend of the Talbots who had, after all, helped wreck the Confederate Catholic regime at his behest. Conscious of the need for aid from Catholic powers, Ormond personally invited Peter to attend on the king at Cologne in July 1654. [109] Later that year Charles authorised Peter to petition the general of the Society of Jesus and the pope for money to raise an army to fight for his kingdom. In return, Charles promised to repeal laws against Catholics in the three kingdoms. [110] In Hyde's view the most the king should do was to dispense with, but certainly not repeal, anti-Catholic laws. Neither Charles nor Hyde could satisfy the religious aspirations of Talbot whose contempt for Anglicanism is amply proclaimed by the title of his *Reflexion upon the Nullitie of the English Protestant Church and Clergy* (Rouen, 1657). Talbot repeatedly suggested that if Charles should (secretly) become a Roman Catholic then the pope and the king of Spain would 'engage themselves to get him all his own again'.[111] It is doubtful if the Spanish seriously expected Charles to convert to Catholicism and the latter's real feelings are probably captured by his stern warning to his younger brother York not to convert to Catholicism or else 'you must never think to see England or me again'.[112]

In January 1656 Peter Talbot urged Charles to come to Antwerp in person to meet Juan-José of Austria, the new governor of the Spanish Netherlands, along with Cárdenas the former ambassador to London. Muttering about Talbot's 'overmeddling', Hyde rebuked Talbot and reminded him that Henry de Vic the long-time English resident agent in Flanders had negotiations in hand and that the king would stay at Cologne until the negotiations were concluded. Talbot replied tartly that Charles would, in that case, remain 'long enough at Cologne'. He smeared de Vic by claiming that Cárdenas and others suspected him of being a French spy and warned Charles not to entrust these delicate negotiations to Ormond or Hyde. Ormond, for his part, cited the 'unhappy experience I have had of the Irish clergy' to contend that negotiations were too important to be left to a scheming Jesuit. [113] Hyde kept Talbot on as interlocutor only on condition that Charles II's conversion was not up for negotiation.[114] To sum up, Peter Talbot's bid to monopolise Stuart negotiations with Spain failed and set him at odds with the Old Royalists.

The Spanish were also drawn to another mischief maker, besides Charles Stuart. The one-time parliamentary Colonel Edward Sexby, a radical 'Leveller', now execrated the Protector. Peter, the multilingual connector so apt at flitting between different circles, enjoyed great credit with Philip IV's chief minister Don Luis Méndez de Haro. Consequently, Peter served as Sexby's main intermediary with the Junta de Estado and as interpreter in talks with the Count of Fuensaldaña gobernador de las armas in the Spanish Netherlands about how to fund Leveller revolt in England.[115]

True to form, Peter overstepped his role by lobbying de Haro to demand that Sexby's Leveller revolt should happen only in tandem with Stuart plans, an 'ill office' that Sexby resented.[116] Talbot failed to bring about any real cooperation because of the mutual suspicions that divided Old Royalists and Levellers. The 'chief end' of the Levellers, noted a royalist agent at Antwerp, 'is to pull down Cromwell, and to set up a parliament by which they will rule' and maintain Charles only as an 'administrator' rather than a 'master' of the constitution. For his part, the 'swearing, drinking, whoring, and little secrecy' of the Royalist exiles repelled Sexby. [117]

The Louvrians, too, had their Talbot schemers. In 1655 Thomas shuttled between Henrietta Maria in Paris, Charles in Cologne, other royalists at Brussels, the Irish in Flanders and, finally, Rome with the apparent objective of securing papal help in return for a Stuart concordat on the Catholic question. Thomas professed dislike of Hyde and Ormond in order to ingratiate himself with the recently exiled vicar general of Dublin Edmund O'Reilly, one of those clericalists so embittered by Ormond that he collaborated with the Cromwellian authorities. Together they set about the 'designing of great things' for Irish Catholics. [118] Their scheme later came unstuck when Thomas learned that O'Reilly, by now archbishop of Armagh, would not support his bid to become archbishop of Dublin. Peter conceded of Thomas that 'sometimes he may speak truth', but wrote him off as a giddy fantasist. A cousin condemned Thomas as 'a disgrace to his function, name and nation' and a confrere listed his vices: wearing civilian attire, smoking heavily, spending freely, and 'wilful indiscipline'. [119]

The importance of Irish clergymen like Thomas and Peter Talbot to the various Stuart factions can be readily explained. Whatever help Charles could reasonably hope for would come from Catholic states and Irish royalist clerics were at home in a Catholic cultural ambience of Spain, France, the Spanish Netherlands or Cologne. One can see how a Jesuit intellectual and controversialist conversant in three continental languages (Spanish, French and Italian) could impress a statesman like De Haro. Contrast Talbot's accomplishments to Hyde's little Englander distrust of popery and his poor language skills: he could not speak French and could barely understand it, even when spoken slowly and carefully. [120] George Digby Earl of Bristol briefly took over dealings with the Spanish from Peter. Bristol spoke French and Spanish, possessed charm and dignity and was 'exceeding dextrous in all the arts of insinuation, and gaining the favour of great men, tho' not of keeping them'. [121] Because of Bristol's shortcomings, Peter Talbot would occasionally prove indispensable, however much Hyde might loathe him.

Hence Peter and by extension Richard still had an entrée, however grudging, to Old Royalist circles. Richard hoped to perform a daring and conspicuous service and so win a more secure foothold as a courtier at the exiled court. After Penruddock's rising flopped, Daniel O'Neill broke out of gaol and made his way back to Cologne about May 1655. [122] O'Neill's origins were wholly Gaelic and Catholic. His mother was a niece of Hugh O'Neill, the Great Earl of Tyrone who led the resistance of the Ulster lords in the Nine Years War

(1596–1603). Daniel's father Con O'Neill was the last lord of Upper Clandeboy. He lost all his country (the northern third of Co. Down) and died leaving his heir Daniel a minor. When a Catholic landowner died in such circumstances the Court of Wards usually removed him from his family and subjected him to English and Protestant education, influence and guardianship. If the minor was a malleable pre-teen, the acculturation usually took root. So it had proved with Ormond and so it would with O'Neill. Charles valued O'Neill as an intrepid undercover agent, able to scrounge food and lodgings, bribe gaolers, encourage the faint-hearted, rein in the foolhardy and win friends: he kept on good terms with successive ministers and even the irascible Hyde's trust and affection for the 'Infallible subtle' leaps out from his correspondence.[123]

O'Neill and Colonel John Stephens, an Ormond client, set in train the latest of many assassination plots.[124] Given that the Protectorate rested on one man, killing that man could be expected to throw the regime into confusion. Dick Talbot volunteered for the hazardous assignment of killing Oliver Cromwell. Most royalist exiles saw nothing discreditable in killing the Protector as revenge for the judicial murder of Charles I and so Hyde and Ormond, though perhaps not the king himself, were privy to this plot.[125] Unfortunately, they were not the only ones in the know. On 13 July 1655 Henry Manning, Secretary Thurloe's spy at Cologne, warned that Talbot, 'a tall young man', and Robin Dungan, Ormond's page and Talbot's nephew, would pass through Dover on their way to help Stephens and Colonel James Halsall assassinate the Protector. Stephens, Talbot and Dungan were duly arrested sometime before July was out but even though they were unmasked, they were eventually set free. Once released they badgered Halsall to go forward with the plot. Halsall temporised and a thoroughly disillusioned Stephens crossed back over the channel. There is a sense of playacting about this business. For instance, no murder weapon was chosen: the 'musketoon', a cut-down flintlock that fired several balls, was usually the assassin's weapon of choice. On 16 November Halsall was seized in his lodgings and his cipher and papers were pulled from the lining of his hat. Talbot and Dungan were also rounded up. Nine days later, Thurloe interrogated Halsall who admitted to collecting large sums of money for 'Charles Stuart, whom he calls the king' and to helping organise Penruddock's rising. He presented himself as hapless, ineffectual and unable to recall incriminating information. Above all, he made no mention of the assassination plot or of his co-conspirators.[126]

Thurloe also questioned Talbot at Whitehall, with Cromwell apparently present in person. Whereas Halsall's examination was recorded in the state papers our only source here is a hearsay retelling of Talbot's own account. The Protector opened proceedings by offering 'great preferments' and flatteringly claimed kinship through the Talbot earls of Shrewsbury. Next he abruptly demanded why Talbot would kill a man who had 'never prejudiced him in his life'. Peter Talbot recounted what his brother told him of the interrogation and snorted that 'nothing made me laugh more'.[127] Talbot found it no laughing matter at the time. Cromwell insinuated that Halsall had cracked under interrogation and had sold Talbot out but the young cavalier kept his nerve and flatly denied a connection with any plot. As luck would have it, his name was not in Halsall's captured cipher. Cromwell also questioned Talbot about Sexby. Frustrated, Cromwell gave up but paused at the door to threaten that he would get the truth even if he had to 'spin it out of his bones'. Talbot defiantly retorted that even if he were to 'spin him to a thread' he had no wrongdoing to confess and would only invent lies. Thurloe again visited the prisoner, making 'large promises' and 'great offers of money'. [128] That night Talbot 'bestowed much wine' on Cromwell's servants and slipped down by a rope cast from a window down to the Thames where a getaway boat waited. After ten cramped days hidden between decks he disembarked at Calais.

Later on, Talbot's escape looked retrospectively suspicious when he happened to be accompanying his brother Gilbert as the latter was caught red-handed with incriminating correspondence at the Antwerp post-house. Gilbert pleaded unconvincingly that his correspondence with parliamentary spymaster Thurloe was really 'for the king's advantage'.[129] Quick to seize on the incident, Hyde wrote off Richard, Peter and Gilbert Talbot as a 'pack of knaves' and hinted broadly that they had betrayed the assassination plot to Thurloe.[130] Explaining himself to Ormond on 1 February 1656, Talbot was in a bind. He suspected (wrongly, as it happened) that Halsall was his accuser and insinuated that the latter may have resented Talbot for egging him on and even hinted at 'cowardice or some private end'. He could not disprove Hyde's accusations other than by protesting that 'I am a gentleman' and pointing out there was no hard evidence, only the 'bare surmises' of those let down by the failure of the assassination plot. Talbot laid a claim to the protection due to a client 'since you have always been a patron of us all, I humbly crave your assistance'.[131] Ormond responded by publicly demonstrating his confidence in Gilbert and Richard by having them accompany him to meet the Princess Mary Stuart, Charles's older sister and wife of the stadhouder of the United Provinces, at Breda. Were Hyde's suspicions justified?

The context of such suspicions was the experience of poverty, perceived neglect by the King, 'the inglorious inaction and the hopes deferred', and imprisonment which could embitter and wear down trusted agents and courtiers.[132] The most shocking case of a good man gone bad was that of Sir Richard Willys, unmasked by the fall of the Protectorate. [133] Gilbert Talbot's mean little betrayal was, in comparison, hardly a shock. He was generally regarded as a 'half-witted fellow' whose spending on fine clothes and gambling left him desperately short of money.

There were, however, other plausible suspects besides the wretched Gilbert. Henry Manning, Thurloe's most prolific and imaginative correspondent at Cologne, fell under suspicion 'of Halseys, Dick Talbots and Robin Dunghens taking' after he was arrested for spying, interrogated and shot. [134] Another suspect was Halsall's servant William Marston who 'knows all his business', including where he had hidden his papers. Indeed, Halsall himself concluded that Marston 'is a rogue' and passed on a scribbled warning to Ormond through a fellow prisoner in January 1656. There could easily have been other informants besides Manning or Marston with so much loose talk among the royalists and levellers at Brussels that 'Cromwell shall not live long'. Robin Dungan, in particular, had blabbed about his mission.[135]

Talbot's twice escaping from custody might smack of connivance by the authorities. On the first occasion, Thurloe evidently underestimated Talbot's importance until a spy warned him to 'Take a care of releasing the Irish Talbot'. The warning came too late and Thurloe had already released him along with Dungan and Stephens, probably as unwitting bait to net bigger fish.[136] The second escape seems implausibly theatrical until one remembers that time and again royalists escaped from imprisonment by scrambling out windows, tying sheets together to make ropes or dressing up in women's clothes. [137] The fact is that the Protectorate's security was poor and turnkeys often took bribes to look the other way. Perhaps Sexby's Leveller underground contacts offered a bribe or hired the getaway boat. [138] Dungan was later released and Halsall escaped from the Tower so they must have turned traitor too, if one applies Hyde's beady-eyed logic.[139]

Richard Talbot narrowly escaped disgrace but his bid to gain credit with the Old Royalists had backfired. He made at least one more bid to impress Ormond. The Spanish commissioned Richard, or so he said, to find out how much the Protector knew about Sexby's plot to 'hazard something considerable'. Richard wrote to Ormond, betraying his instructions and offering to give whatever reply the king deemed politic.[140]

Foregoing court politics for the campaigning season of 1656, Richard joined a group of English gentlemen serving with Louis, Prince de Condé as volunteers. Condé's great rival the Vicomte de Turenne had slowly pushed the Frondeurs and their Spanish allies back from the gates of Paris towards Flanders and that summer Turenne encircled and besieged Valenciennes for eight weeks. On seeing a Spanish relief army arriving those within the town opened all the sluices and the flood broke a bridge of boats across the river, effectively cutting part of the besieging army under Marshal La Ferté off from the main body under Turenne. Before dawn next morning the Spanish vanguard smashed through La Ferté's lines and took a redoubt. Condé's corps, Talbot riding with them, quickly followed. La Ferté led a counter-attack to regain a redoubt but had advanced only 50 yards when his cavaliers fled in panic: most of them were drowned or killed in the slaughter that followed. Valenciennes was Turenne's worst defeat. He lost about a third of his army and the Spanish happily speculated that the strategic consequences are 'like to be very great'.[141] In fact Valenciennes proved strategically inchoate because Mazarin's English allies outweighed any Spanish advantage.

The Anglo-French alliance provoked a reciprocal, if loveless, match between Philip IV and Charles Stuart. The Spanish promised Charles a subsidy and let him move his court to their territory, albeit to sleepy Bruges-la Morte, as its detractors dubbed it, rather than Brussels. In the event that an English port town declared for him, the Spanish authorities promised to furnish an invasion army. In return, Charles's immediate task was to detach Irish troops from the French service. He promised after his restoration to suspend anti-Catholic laws in England and implement Ormond's 1649 treaty with the Irish.[142] Charles's definitive alignment with Spain widened the gap between mother and son and between their respective Louvrian and Old Royalist factions. This family quarrel would open up fresh fields for Peter Talbot's meddling and bring Richard Talbot into the household of the duke of York. Henry Jermyn, who ruled Henrietta Maria's household at the Louvre, had managed to place his nephew Harry and his cousin Sir John Berkeley within York's household. Berkeley grew to be a special favourite of York's and so he managed, in turn, to insinuate his nephew Charles Berkeley into the charmed circle. The Jermyns and Berkeleys identified James with his mother's faction and tried to draw him into Louvrian schemes to woo Presbyterians and Catholics.[143] York had not wanted to leave Paris but did so in August 1656 at his brother's insistent command. As Charles saw it, his younger brother's household was a nest of Francophile Louvrians who could damage his rapprochement with Juan-José.[144]

Three months after James came to Bruges, Charles struck. With the help of moles within the duke's household, Henry Bennet and Harry Killigrew, Charles set a client of Ormond's to purging York's household of Louvrians. Bristol pitched in with a claim that Don Juan José detested Berkeley for 'being so much a Frenchman', or in other words being anti-Spanish. York refused to give up Berkeley, fled from Bruges across the border to the United Provinces, and even threatened to return to Paris. Thoroughly alarmed lest this undo his arrangements with the Spanish, Charles backed off, reinstated Berkeley and promised to treat York's household 'with all kindness'. York came back to Bruges and dismissed

Killigrew and Bennett so he 'had none left in his family, but such as were absolutely his own'.[145] By fleeing Bruges, York had shown that dutiful as he was, his
obedience could not be taken for granted. Charles treated him more tactfully ever
after and allowed him a position of power and some autonomy as commander
of the fledgling Royalist army and master of, in a sense, a rival court.[146] James
irritated his older brother by acting autonomously as, for instance, when he
later sent Peter Talbot to Spain (in October 1658) to demand a bigger pension
and more authority in military affairs.[147] York had also shown that unquestion-
ing loyalty to his servants which made him an exceptionally worthwhile patron:
'Those the king loved', said one, 'had no faults.'[148] This was a household worth
striving to join and Peter Talbot was in a strong position to push his younger
brother into a newly vacated place. Peter Talbot attached himself particularly
closely to York ('He is with the Duke where he is', noted one correspondent)
and the younger man took the Jesuit at his own estimation as someone whose
word carried great weight with the Spanish.[149] The duke was especially grateful
to Talbot for confirming his own suspicions that Juan-José had never criticised
Berkeley and that the tale had been concocted by Bristol. Peter Talbot duly
supplanted his discredited rival in York's dealings with the Spanish and
manoeuvred to have Richard commissioned lieutenant colonel in a regiment of
foot being assembled from Irishmen who deserted the French service in obedience to Stuart summons.[150] This regiment would form part of the projected
Stuart brigade within the Spanish army.

Richard Talbot was a poor choice for lieutenant colonel. A colonel's 'merit'
(to use the contemporary term) was not based primarily on his experience or
competence but on his wealth and status which, in an era of seigneurial
recruitment, attracted and kept soldiers. Ideally, then, a lieutenant colonel
made up for any deficiencies in his colonel's martial skills; it was he who
instilled drill and discipline and drew up the battle formations. Talbot was of
course a veteran of more fighting than most of his fellow exiles but he had little
grasp of infantry battle tactics and formations. Thirty years later Hyde's son,
the second earl of Clarendon, observed that Talbot could not even draw up a
regiment in formation.[151] More telling than Talbot's inexperience was his lack
of connection. York was the titular colonel but the effective commander was
Cormac or Charles MacCarthy, Viscount Muskerry's son (he took the
Muskerry title when his father was created 1st earl of Clancarty in 1658), and
Ormond's nephew. The troops were mostly Munster men and many were tenants and dependants of Muskerry who had followed him into Spanish service,
into French, and now back to Spanish service. MacCarthy naturally expected
to nominate a lieutenant colonel of his own choosing and resisted Talbot's
pretensions. The dispute escalated into a duel, the details of which remain
unknown. What is known is that Peter Talbot successfully lobbied the Spanish
who then interceded with York to override MacCarthy's objections and give

Richard the lieutenant colonel's place. York had, yet again, asserted his influence by this 'impolitic contrivance', as Hyde decried it.[152]

So bitter was the rancour between Talbot and MacCarthy it is hard to
imagine how the pair could have worked together at the sieges of Ardres and
Mardike in 1657. York's *Life* describes MacCarthy digging a lodgement in the
ditch around a bastion salient at Ardres and goes into some detail about the
duke's proximity to the action. Talbot is not mentioned in this detailed and
vainglorious narrative.[153] Talbot's lieutenant colonelcy probably served as a
contrivance to enhance his standing in his patron's household and he may have
spent little, if any, time with his regiment. He rode in York's entourage at the

Siege of Mardike. James's *Life* notes Talbot and Lord Newburgh as 'servants' of his who, while exercising their horses on the sands near Mardike, were approached by John Reynolds, commander of the English contingent. Reynolds reminded Talbot that he had once saved his life and now asked Talbot to fix a face-to-face meeting with York. The meeting on the sands went ahead, compliments were exchanged but nothing definite was settled. Accused of treason, Reynolds was recalled. His boat ran aground during the homeward crossing and he was drowned.

In May 1658 Turenne laid siege to Dunkirk and Juan-José led some 14,000 men to relieve it.[154] Early on the morning of 14 June Turenne's army lined up outside Dunkirk, his right wing stretching towards the Bruges-Furnes Canal and his left wing anchored on the sand dunes at the seashore. His attack began the Battle of the Dunes. Spanish tercios stood on a high sand hill close to the shore, inland and to their left three Royalist battalions of foot (one of them MacCarthy's) waited. Further inland stood German and Walloon regiments.

English pikemen from Lockhart's regiment clambered up the steep-sided dune and pushed the Spaniards off the hill. They were quickly followed by other English regiments while York led a lone squadron of forty men in desperate efforts to break them: 'being come up almost within reach of their pikes, I found the ground to be such, as rendered it almost impossible for me to break into them'. Talbot was probably with his duke rather than with his regiment, luckily for him. The receding tide left room for Turenne's cavalry to pass along the beach and Juan-José's right flank, York's horsemen among them, began to disintegrate. The front-line infantrymen were unsettled by the fear of being outflanked and they too began to flee. The Royalist battalions stood 'a little longer' than the rest until 'a voice coming behind them, that the foot should save themselves'. MacCarthy's battalion broke but his fleeing soldiers were run down by enemy cavalry. A mere twenty common soldiers got off and, apart from Mac Carthy himself, 'not an officer escaped taking'. Eleven days after the battle, Dunkirk surrendered but Oliver Cromwell had little over two months left to savour his triumph.[155]

'When time your wondrous story shall unfold, /Your glorious deeds in arms, when yet but young, /Your strange escapes, and danger shall be told': the encomium related to James Duke of York but might just as well have applied to his Irish client.[156]

TWO

YORK'S MAN
1657–62

Richard Talbot's career began in Peter's shadow and for the first few years of that career his activities and alignments may be inferred from those of his older brother. This close relationship between the two was by no means inevitable. Peter was fourteen years older than Richard and when they met in Spain in 1653 he would hardly have seen him since he had been a babe in arms.[1] He would not have taken Richard under his wing out of mere fraternal loyalty because, as should be apparent, there was no cohesive Talbot brotherhood presenting a united front to the world. They shared a strongly hierarchical and élitist view of the world in which the natural form of government was an overlapping and mutually sustaining triad of monarchy, church, and nobility/gentry. To this they added an unusually well-developed self-importance and disdain for the credulity of (to use Peter's words) the 'simple people of Ireland'.[2] Yet the brothers often acted at cross purposes and even betrayed one other. The alliance between Richard and Peter, which lasted until the latter's agonising death in a prison cell over a quarter of a century later, must have been based on something more than their sibling bond, perhaps on mutual usefulness or even affection.

Peter had, as discussed in the last chapter, plotted with the Leveller Sexby. This intrigue was later subsumed in a scheme orchestrated by the talented but wayward George Villiers 2nd Duke of Buckingham, Charles's boyhood companion, to return to England and foment an uprising against Cromwell.[2] Hyde accused Buckingham of wanting to return to pursue his own private interests and warned the king that he should not trust a man who attracted so many presbyterian, dissenter and papist misfits. Peter turned down a bribe from Hyde to spy on the duke but Sexby's betrayal and capture in 1657 marked the end of this latest design, though Peter still stoutly maintained to anyone who would listen that 'all is not lost'.[3] The end of royalist co-ordination with the Levellers, the inability of the Spanish to pay pensions to Charles and his court, and the 'little thankes' Peter got from Hyde and the Old Royalists pushed Peter and Richard Talbot to burrow more deeply into York's court. In summer 1658 Peter went to Madrid to petition Philip IV to increase York's pension and put him in command of a cavalry regiment in return for which the young prince, Peter assured him, would convert to Catholicism. No doubt this was wishful thinking on Peter's part but in any event King Philip did increase the pension, thereby consolidating the Talbot position in York's household.[4]

Cromwell's death in September 1658 suggested that would-be assassins had the correct instincts after all: without the Protector there would be no Protectorate. The Council of State nominated Cromwell's eldest son as his successor and in March 1659 Marshal Caracena, commander-in-chief in the Spanish Netherlands, sent Peter Talbot secretly to London to sound out Richard Cromwell about ending the war.[5] By way of further illustrating the want of cohesiveness among the Talbot brethren, Gilbert would betray the secret of his brother's talks to Cardinal Mazarin. Peter's mission was overtaken by rapidly changing events as Richard Cromwell floundered and in May 1659 was forced out of power by army grandees who set up the Commonwealth again and recalled the 'rump' parliament: those members left after Oliver Cromwell had successively purged the Commons of presbyterians and others who favoured compromise with Charles I.[6] In the end the rump parliament was unwilling to disgorge Dunkirk and so a peace deal with Spain proved elusive.

Peace with republican England would necessarily have meant Spain repudiating her English royalist protégés: for all his noisy professions of loyalty, Peter was working against the interests of his king. Hyde suspected this 'greatest villain alive' not just of ingratiating himself with the republicans but of all sorts of double-dealing. Talbot had, Hyde heard, publicly mourned the passing of Oliver Cromwell with whom he had been 'very intimate' and had actively opposed General Monck, the man who would eventually restore Charles. Moreover, Talbot was supposedly trying to block France and Spain from uniting to restore Charles, working to have Charles expelled from the Spanish Netherlands, and scheming to put York on the English throne.[7] In support of the latter surmise, Hyde seized on a report from one Colonel Bampfield, an irrepressible double-dealer, who claimed that Talbot boasted to him on board a ship to France that he followed York and 'would have nothing to do' with Charles. The ship was blown back to England, Bampfield rode post haste to London and reported what Talbot had told him to the authorities who elected not to arrest Talbot. Bampfield embarked again with Talbot, and laid the whole business open to Hyde.[8] The story is riddled with internal contradictions (why would Bamfield denounce Peter Talbot to the republican authorities for remarks against a Stuart?) and inconsistencies, yet for once Hyde's suspicions may have been on the mark.

Peter Talbot renewed his contacts with Buckingham after the latter's release from imprisonment in February 1659. Buckingham had fallen out of favour when he married the daughter of Thomas Fairfax, one-time parliamentary commander in the North of England.[9] Hyde detested Buckingham's rhetoric of religious liberty and rapprochement between royalists and

Presbyterians while Talbot was captivated by these very ideas. Talbot may have intrigued, along with Buckingham, to have Catholics and Presbyterians support James (without the latter's authorisation) rather than Charles as a restored monarch and may have had tacit Spanish backing. Whispers that he had wanted to secure the crown for James by marrying him to Oliver Cromwell's daughter could still be heard at court a decade later.[10]

Looked at from Charles's or Hyde's point of view, Peter Talbot was the treacherous and duplicitous schemer of anti-Jesuit myth, preferring politicking to preaching. Looked at from the point of view of someone who wanted to improve conditions for Irish Catholics, Talbot's schemes are understandable. The English Commonwealth seemed firmly bedded-in as the de facto government for the foreseeable future, so securing toleration for Catholics involved dealing with that regime. Charles could do nothing for them. Other Irish clergymen like Edmond O'Reilly had reached that more or less disagreeable conclusion much earlier. Charles had complained of Talbot to the Father Provincial of the Jesuits in Flanders and in June 1659 the restless Jesuit was ordered to leave England. Peter disobeyed, claiming his mission to England had sanction from the Vatican. [11] In response, the General dispensed Peter from his vows.[12] Rumour had it that he was dismissed:

> due to the fact that when he was sent to the mission in Ireland Talbot had spent a much longer time in England, at court, than his obedience permitted, so that he seemed more interested in courtly affairs than in saving souls[13]

Gloating at Charles's court about Talbot's dismissal was so public as to discomfit the Spanish ministers in the Netherlands. Talbot always insisted that this did not amount to dismissal from the Society for which he continued to profess admiration. Rather, the Society and he had parted company by mutual agreement for a greater good, namely to allow him greater latitude to lobby at court.

Waiting at Calais in early August 1659 to take ship for England, Charles heard that Booth's rising in Lancashire had been a flop and so he changed his plans and made for Fuentarabia on the frontier between France and Spain. Nearby, de Haro and Cardinal Mazarin met for over three months in closed sessions to conclude decades-long Bourbon–Habsburg conflict. Sir William Lockhart, plenipotentiary for the English Commonwealth, fretfully waited to be presented with the final outcome. So too did Charles, who hoped to solicit assistance from de Haro, re-establish cordial relations with France and even persuade both powers to co-operate against his enemies in England.[14]

Peter Talbot went there too, ostensibly to 'do what services he could for his king' and secure 'favour for Irish Catholics'.[15] The two objectives were not always compatible. Lodged in the Tower awaiting execution after the Restoration, Thomas Scot, an 'intelligencer' for the Commonwealth, confessed that he had arranged

> to send & furnish Peter Talbot to the interview at the Frontiers to observe the transactions of the two Crownes in relation to us, and to keepe them as well as hee could from uniting to any dangerous Engagement against us, or to acquaint us timely there with, but he did us no other service than to help us of with fifty pounds.[16]

While taking the Commonwealth's money, Peter talked his way back into favour with the royalists, by telling Charles what he so desperately wanted to hear, namely that Mazarin and De Haro had agreed in writing to restore him: they hadn't. He won back Ormond's support by persuading the Spanish to pay the ever necessitous great man £3,800. Relying on Peter Talbot's agency, Henry Bennet, Charles's minister at the Spanish court, had already bypassed Hyde and Ormond in negotiating support for Charles II's restoration. Peter finally convinced Bennet that he was a loyal royalist by brandishing papers that he claimed to have presented to de Haro. These papers made a case to continue supporting Charles as the embodiment of the only party enjoying widespread support in England. Bennet now stood by Talbot in the face of Hyde's denunciations of the Jesuit's 'wickedness and malice': if Talbot was a rogue, insisted Bennet, he was a useful one.[17]

By now Hyde had completely lost hope in royalist insurrection or 'powerful friends' abroad: only 'God Almighty' could bring Charles home.[18] Indeed, the Restoration seemed providential. The political and military authority of the generals collapsed and one of their number, Monck, marched his army south from Scotland to London in January 1660, dissolved the rump and in March 1660 secretly established contact with Charles and committed himself to his restoration.[19] A strongly pro-royalist convention parliament assembled in April 1660 and invited Charles home. Hyde drafted the Declaration of Breda which gave assurances of a general pardon, 'liberty to tender consciences', arrears of army pay and forfeited estates. In Ireland, Lord Deputy Henry Cromwell, Richard's younger and more able brother looked to the 'Old Protestant' or pre-war English interest for support. Parliamentary commissioners displaced Henry in 1659 but Old Protestant officers led by Charles Coote the younger mounted a coup d'état against them. By appearing to align the Protestants of Ireland with the winning party before anyone else, the coup put them in a strong bargaining position.[20]

The form the Restoration took disadvantaged Irish Catholics in general but was doubly disadvantageous to Peter and Richard since Charles need not feel beholden to the Spanish or, by extension, to them. Even more worrying was the alliance with Portugal which brought a royal bride-Catherine of Braganza – and a huge dowry. Mazarin agreed to pay the dowry, mindful that the marriage alliance would create a permanent rift between England and Spain because, among other reasons, Charles committed himself to helping to the Portuguese in their twenty-year-long revolt against Spanish domination. [21] Whether Hyde could claim full credit or hidden Louvrian machinations played a part, Charles showed himself to be an ingrate by turning on Philip IV who had sheltered and supported Charles' entourage for four years.[22] Peter and, to a lesser extent, Richard were associated with a pro-Spanish alignment and so one would expect this diplomatic about face to leave them stranded high and dry. On the contrary, they were catapulted to greater prominence.

By the Restoration, Richard Talbot had secured his place in James Duke of York's 'family' which he succeeded in using as a springboard for further advances, despite the initially unpropitious anti-Spanish court alignment. To understand how he did so one must consider the physical setting he occupied, examine the factions he followed, understand the codes of behaviour he observed, trace the client–patron relationships he cultivated and, above all, grasp the character of his most abiding patron. He accompanied York back to London and eight months later, Richard sailed for Portugal on the *Royal Charles* to present a letter from York to the Infanta. With him was Edward Montagu the bearer of an official letter from Charles to his soon-to-be bride. The English fleet arrived in Lisbon road on 26 January 1661, 'saluted by all the guns, for three miles round'. Richard may have been chosen for his linguistic accomplishments, but his mission really amounted to a public mark of trust and an equally public sign that he had turned his back on Spain. Insofar as the mission involved work of substantive importance he fumbled it, being 'so forgetful and absent-minded' as to leave the formal letter behind in London and only remembering it when going in to his public audience with the Infanta.[23]

Until the fire of 1666, London was a wooden city crowding for six miles along the north bank of the Thames. The Palace of Whitehall took up nearly half a mile of river to the west. King Street, the main road from the city to Westminster was thick with carts, carriages, livestock, courtiers and soldiers and cut through the middle of this sprawling series of connected buildings that had accumulated organically over time. North of the road lay the tennis court and various apartments, the whole taking its name from the octagonal Cock Pit where those who were most intimate with, or necessary to, the king lived. Hyde (now Earl of Clarendon), Buckingham, and, not least, Charles's mistress Barbara Palmer all lodged there at various times. At the height of his influence, in 1688, Talbot would have chambers in St James's Palace, further to the north.[24] To the south of the road lay the Privy Garden, Bowling Green and the enormous banqueting hall outside of which Charles I had been beheaded. Between these comparatively open spaces and the river was the long Stone Gallery while behind guarded doors lay a warren of closely compacted apartments housing king, queen, duke of York and their retinues.[25]

The privy council at the Restoration consisted of an unwieldy thirty members, a dozen of them servants of the previous regime. Clarendon headed the council as lord chancellor and Charles, bored by routine business, delegated much authority to him. Next came Ormond as high steward and lord lieutenant of Ireland, York as lord high admiral and Sir Edward Nicholas as secretary of state. A smaller committee or cabinet sometimes made decisions without the knowledge of the privy council. There was no unity of action among these ministers who often opposed one another in parliament. All of them answered to king, not parliament, and could be instantly dismissed by him. The monarch could also be influenced by a word in his ear from hangers-on and mistresses who had no official standing in cabinet or council. Buckingham for instance did not become a privy councillor until 1662 but his position, while undefined, was influential. In contrast to the institutional power of the office holder, the influence of the favourite was based on the monarch's personal affection and he could become the focus of petitions from swarms of suitors.[26] Patronage, 'the exercise of influence and the doing of favours', was the glutinous lubricant of Stuart politics and the court was the point of contact for petitioners since the privy council was small and easily bypassed and parliament was an occasional event rather than a permanent institution.[27]

It was neither practical nor desirable that everyone have close access to the monarch, and so palace rooms, great chamber or guard, presence chamber or privy chamber, antechamber or withdrawing room, filtered out some of the throng. But Whitehall, a French visitor sniffed, was 'nothing but a heap of houses' and was so sprawling that it was not possible to eliminate chance meetings.[28] Privy counsellors were allowed go as far as a lobby near Charles' bedchamber, while, in theory, only ministers, secretaries of state and York could penetrate further. The Bedchamber was a complex of apartments containing bedrooms, libraries, closets and so on and was the most intimate and private of the Stuart court's components. The groom of the stole—first gentleman of the bedchamber controlled access and supervised the assorted gentlemen and grooms who slept at the foot of the royal bed and dressed, fed, and attended the king by day. These courtiers had the best chance to catch the king's ear. One of them recalls importuning the harassed monarch in what should have been his most private moment: 'he [Charles] went to ease himself ... nobody having entrance but the lord and groom of the bedchamber in waiting and I desired of him there to bestow a colours in the guards to a relation of mine'.[29]

The courtier waited within the lattice of vertical links of patronage/clientship and the horizontal ties of faction. Ideally the patron 'recommended' his client to higher-ups and 'defended' him against 'emulators' and 'enviers', while the client publicly and loudly acted out the role of devoted follower and 'friend'. All the better if the client was a poor relation, was witty or handsome, had a gift for flattery or a head for business. The patron's magnanimity and the deference of his client nurtured mutual trust and solidarity.[30] In practice the relationship usually fell short of this ideal. The client-courtier feared social eclipse, political collapse, loss of honour or dismissal from office. He was envious and sensitive to slights and mockery since he spent so much time in a hothouse of gossip. The courtier's life had been especially tense and unstable at the exiled court, what with cramped lodgings and the fluctuating size of the court, swelling and shrinking as it moved and courtiers came and went. If, after the Restoration, cavalier courtiers were given to duelling and debauchery the reason may lie in the legacy of exile. The Irish Catholic courtier Theobald Taaffe personified the duellist and debauchee. He acted as Charles's chamberlain, valet, clerk of the kitchen, cup bearer, master of entertainments, and more: Charles left his first mistress Lucy Walter under Taaffe's protection but on his return to Paris found that Taaffe had fathered a baby on her.[31] In August 1658 Taaffe, and two seconds, one of them Richard Talbot, fought Sir William Keith of Ludquhairn, a Scotsman, and his seconds over an unpaid wager of seven sovereigns laid on a game of tennis. This was deadly business. The sword was far more lethal (an estimated fifth of duellists were killed) than the pistol which supplanted it in the latter part of the eighteenth century and, moreover, the seconds threw themselves into the fight, rather than standing aside to regulate and restrain participants.[32] Typically, two groups of three lined up opposite each other and at a signal rushed at each other with thrusting and slashing blades. Taaffe slew Keith, while Talbot restrained himself and disarmed rather than killed his opponent. Charles's reaction typified social ambivalence about duelling: he banished Taaffe from court for only a short while and always retained 'great affection' for him.[33]

Even in more settled conditions at Whitehall the client-courtier was on tenterhooks; his loyalty was not usually exclusive or unconditional and he would be foolish to follow a failing patron. Consequently the pyramid of patronage blurred at its base into other pyramids making 'faction' too static a term to capture the scramble for favour. Moreover, brokerage further blurred the boundaries of faction. The broker was a middleman putting people in touch with each other through direct introductions or acting on a customer's behalf. Their arrangement did not have the durability of a client–patron relationship or the warm rhetoric of friendship, but was based on kickbacks commensurate to the value of the favour, land, office, farm or monopoly.[34]

James was less striking than his older brother: he was of average height, wore a grey wig, was fair-skinned and, to cite the inimitable pen picture of Lorenzo Magalotti, a Tuscan visitor, 'all the outlines of his face are prominent: a square forehead, the eyes large, swollen, and deep blue, the nose curved and rather large, the lips pale and thick, and the chin rather pointed'. Lacking good looks or an easy manner, York tried to project an aura of 'severe majesty' but Buckingham deftly distinguished the languid but wryly perceptive Charles from his earnest brother: 'The king could see things if he would, and the duke would see things if he could'.[35] York had:

> not much penetration into political affairs, because his rough and impatient spirit does not let him stop for long to examine things, but makes him follow his first impulses blindly. Nevertheless he is very often influenced by people, and once he has chosen them it is not so easy for him to free himself from their sway; his mind is always like wax, ready to receive and retain indelibly every slight impression of their ideas without considering whether these proceed from reason, or from self-interest, or malignity or ambition. [36]

The criticism that York was too malleable comes not from a vindictive scribbler exulting after his dethronement, but from an observant outsider. That malleability and stubborn loyalty made the duke a dependable patron to the fortunate few who contrived to be among his favourites. York controlled a household of 110 persons in 1662 which supported no fewer than fourteen top courtiers most of whom had followed him in exile. They resembled Charles's servants in 'their rapacity, their incapacity for business and their love of intrigue'.[37] Sir Charles Berkeley, York's groom of the stool, was the top courtier. York's memoirs depict a selfless, modest and loyal courtier whom both Stuart brothers 'much esteemed and entirely trusted'.[38] Not especially witty or handsome, he was affable and became a valued confidant to king and duke alike. He was well on the way to growing into a 'truly influential' favourite when he was killed by a cannon shot in 1665.[39] Below Berkeley was a second rank of five courtiers who included the purser Giles Rawlings, a Catholic, along with Master of the Horse Henry Jermyn the younger (another Catholic) and Comptroller Sir Henry De Vic, Peter Talbot's old rival. The third tier included York's secretary William Coventry, a one-time Louvrian, who sometimes had the temerity to jostle with Berkeley over which of them 'should have most interest' with James.[40] Also in the third rank were a half dozen grooms of the bedchamber, Talbot among them. [41]

York continued to publicly receive the sacraments of the Church of England until 1672 and quite when he privately converted to Catholicism is not clear. Though York's household included rather a lot of papists, he had not picked members of his household for their religious affiliation but for their usefulness, congeniality and (probably in Talbot's case) soldierly qualities.[42] High, or strategically useful, office fell into the laps of many courtiers in York's household and Talbot thereby made contacts that he could nurture into useful, if often equivocal and short-term, friendships. Let us take just two examples. When York became lord high admiral of England, his secretary imperceptibly took on the wide and ill-defined range of business associated with that office and became one of four navy commissioners. Coventry proved an efficient if corruptible administrator: 'The constant magnet to the pole does hold, /Steel to the magnet, Coventry to Gold'.[43] Buckingham contrived to discredit him for issuing an ill-advised challenge to a duel and in 1669 Charles sent Coventry to the Tower and stripped him of his offices. A second example is that of a humbler but still significant courtier, the Scotsman Sir Ellis Leighton. He would convert to Catholicism, try to have his master 'engage' with Buckingham in 1670, and serve as secretary to a lord lieutenant of Ireland, John Baron of Stratton, a kinsman of Charles Berkeley where he would prove a useful friend for Talbot. Leighton was committed to Newgate in November 1678 during the 'Popish Plot' but by then he had been tainted by corruption charges.[44]

The returned exiles shared some important values. In the 1679–81 years of crisis, for instance, they opposed bills to exclude York from the succession but they did not form a 'faction', 'party' or any grouping that suggests a long-term association of men who were of like mind on some key issue or principle.[45] It is more illuminating to see them, and courtiers and officials in general, as divided between those who were 'in' and those who were 'out'.

Political prudence dictated that government include those like Monck (now duke of Albemarle and captain-general for the army) who had brought Charles home and could yet send him back on his travels. Disappointed cavaliers were disgusted that Charles, and his chief minister, on whom they displaced much of their anger, were more forward in appeasing former enemies than rewarding old followers. Chief amongst those complaining was Bristol who disdained such appeasement and despised Hyde for his cautious pursuit of a negotiated settlement with parliament. The flamboyant Bristol advocated French alliance, a pro-Catholic policy (he had converted while in exile) and untrammelled monarchy. In summer 1663 Bristol tried to impeach Clarendon for treason, accusing him of accepting French bribes in exchange for the sale of Dunkirk. The impeachment failed, Clarendon survived and Bristol was discredited.

Clarendon forged some new alliances with men whom the cavaliers dismissed as time-servers, like Roger Boyle Earl of Orrery who had wanted to crown Oliver Cromwell. A marriage between Orrery's niece and Clarendon's son followed but Orrery's 'boundless ambition' and his dislike of Ormond made him an inconstant Clarendonian.[46] For the most part Clarendon tended to neglect his patronage network and was too apt to dismiss suitors disparagingly, thereby alienating potentially useful clients like Bennet and Coventry.[47] He forbade his wife to call on Barbara Palmer, the king's chief-mistress for most of the 1660s, when perfunctory civility might have won over the lady. Worse, while Charles wanted to ennoble Mr. Palmer so as to honour his mistress, Clarendon refused to pass a patent granting Palmer an English peerage, and so Barbara had to make do with an Irish title as Countess of Castlemaine. Clarendon's chief ally was Ormond whose absence as lord lieutenant of Ireland necessarily curtailed his usefulness at court.[48]

Clarendon's slow displacement had begun when Bennet was recalled from Madrid to be keeper of the privy purse. Bennet stood out in the throng, being tall, pale, grave in demeanour and affecting a thin black patch on the bridge of his nose where a sword had scratched him during a fleeting military action in the Civil War. Peter Talbot boasted that he had 'importuned' Charles to recall Bennet and had then smoothed over factional rivalry between Bennet and Charles Berkeley so that the pair now 'fell into an entire friendship'.[49] Bennet next eased out Clarendon's old friend and colleague Sir Edward Nicholas to become de facto principal secretary of state in October 1662 (Irish matters lay within his broad remit) and with that came his 'open rupture' with the lord chancellor.[50] Berkeley replaced Bennet as keeper of the privy purse and so was responsible for payments and other dealings with Castlemaine. Berkeley soon grew to be Charles's prime favourite and would be appointed (absentee) Lord President of Connaught and ennobled (to another Irish peerage) as Viscount Fitzhardinge of Berehaven. When Castlemaine was installed at Whitehall in April 1663 her apartment became a rival court where Bennet, Berkeley and Buckingham could plot and inveigh against Clarendon. Buckingham's party piece was to thrust out his belly and mimic the gouty chancellor's limp and his disapproving frown. Nor was Buckingham alone: with pursed lips the diarist Pepys records how Peter Talbot 'made sport' of the lord chancellor.[51]

Such sport was deadly serious. If the butt of the joke let such mockery go unpunished, he or she lost face and publicly admitted their waning influence. Coventry knew this when told that an actor was rehearsing a skit which would expose him to the 'mirth of the world'. Discredited and lodged in the tower, Coventry nonetheless threatened to hire toughs to beat up the actor and 'cause his nose to be cut'.[52] An anecdote from the fag end of Bennet's career (he was earl of Arlington by then) further illustrates the potency of public mockery. Talbot had been long absent from court (this dates the anecdote to the late 1670s) and:

> Upon his return [Talbot] found the earl of Arlington's credit extremely low, and seeing him one day acted by a person with a patch and a staff, he took occasion to expostulate this matter with the king, with whom he was very familiar, remonstrating how very hard it was that poor Harry Bennet should be thus used, after he had so long and faithfully served his majesty, and followed him everywhere in his exile.

Sensitivity to mockery was of a piece with the preoccupation with honour and shame in the eyes of one's peers that was such a constant in small exclusive societies like royal courts where face-to-face relations were paramount and where the personality of the courtier was as significant as his office. Duelling was the preferred way for a courtier to assert his honour amongst his peers. This ritualised violence was formally prohibited by the king but sanctioned, even demanded, by the courtier's peers. Magalotti deplored Buckingham's notorious sodomy but was far more shocked at the 'unnecessary tolerance' he showed when Prince Rupert dragged him off his horse, mounted, and rode off. The modern reader finds it hard to imagine how Buckingham could be faulted for cowardice given that he had already fought three duels (in one of which he fatally wounded an opponent) his right arm was strained by the fall and Charles was on hand to insist on restraint.[53]

Stung by mockery and with Bennet nipping at his heels, Clarendon would grimly cling to office for another five years because he retained his son-in-law's support and Charles, who did not want to be dominated by any one minister, was content to let the rivalry play out.[54] Until 1667, then, the Clarendon/Ormond interest looked imposing enough but could be undercut whenever enough of their many and diverse enemies could coalesce long enough to do so.

Despite the promptings and insinuations of courtiers and favourites like Buckingham, James never allowed his household to be used as a rallying point for his brother's political opponents.[55] Supporters and opponents of Castlemaine's bedroom cabal could be found in Charles's and James's households. Out of family loyalty James kept up fairly close relations with his father-in-law (see below), as evidenced by a definable Hyde–Yorkist party in parliament and by the reach of Clarendon's patronage into the York household. Edward Colman, victim of the Popish Plot and secretary to Mary of Modena between 1673 and 1676, first entered York's household because he was a remote family connection of Clarendon's.[56]

A client like Talbot could not, so to speak, lay all his bets on one horse especially at a juncture of bewilderingly fluid and unstable alliances and rivalries.

Talbot claimed Ormond along with York as a patron for as long as he possibly could. He also hitched his star to that of Berkeley as suggested by the allegation that, at Berkeley's bidding, he, Thomas Killigrew (a fellow-groom) and Harry Jermyn immersed themselves in a sordid intrigue. Shortly after returning to England in 1660, a pregnant Anne Hyde claimed that York was father of the child and her husband by a clandestine marriage.[57] His mother, his sister Mary Princess of Orange, and the lord chancellor (the girl's father) were all set against the match. Clarendon rightly feared that his enemies would blame him for throwing the couple together in order to set up his daughter as the mother of a king.[58] Other conspiracy theorists even saw proof of his manipulations in his encouragement of Charles's marriage to the Portuguese princess Catherine of Braganza, knowing somehow that she would be barren. The duke was torn. His infatuation had cooled and he recognised that as a commoner and daughter of his brother's servant she was 'particularly ill-suited' to be his bride. On the other hand, he felt pity for the girl's predicament and remorse at his own caddishness. He 'opened his heart' to Berkeley who first tried to persuade him that the match was unsuitable and a purported marriage without the king's consent invalid. It may have been Berkeley who sent James to consult Peter Talbot for moral guidance, early evidence of the duke's bent towards Rome. After some equivocation Peter reassured the unhappy duke that to break off the purported marriage would not breach the decrees of the Council of Trent. Berkeley also blackened Anne Hyde's name to give James an excuse to cast her off. He gathered as witnesses Richard Butler Earl of Arran (Ormond's wastrel second son), Talbot, Jermyn and Killigrew. Closeted with York they feigned reluctance but then confessed to know from personal experience that the girl was a slut:

> Talbot said that she had made an appointment with him in the chancellor's cabinet, while he was in council; and, that, not paying so much attention to what was on the table as to what they were doing, they had spilled a bottle full of ink on a dispatch of four pages, and the king's monkey, blamed for this accident, had been in disgrace for a long time.[59]

Not to be outdone, Killigrew boasted not only of groping and fondling Anne but that 'he had the honour of being intimate with her' in a privy and so, he affirmed, had 'many others'. In the end, Charles drew a line under the business by flatly insisting the child was York's (though court gossip that York was 'not the first to have knowledge of her' would persist) and the marriage contract accordingly binding: they married in September 1660, six weeks before she gave birth.[60] The duchess affected not to blame her traducers, telling them 'nothing was a greater proof of an honest man's devotion than his being more solicitous for the interests of his friend or master than for his own reputation'.

Like most of the intriguers, Richard Talbot chafed at Clarendon's 'insolent authority' and so he had a motive to wreck the marriage plans. Yet Clarendon does not identify Talbot as one of the culprits when he surely would not have hesitated to blame someone whose very name he detested. Only the Memoirs of Gramont names Talbot as deeply involved in the charade, and Anthony Hamilton, author of the Memoirs, may have tainted him with this intrigue in order to settle a score or pay back for some injury, real or imagined. Talbot would later (see chapter five below) promote and patronise the Hamilton brothers, and his support was probably crucial when Anthony faced accusations of cowardice under fire at a skirmish preceding the Battle of Newtownbutler in 1689. Another officer was blamed but, perhaps, Anthony Hamilton felt that Talbot did not intervene strongly enough on his behalf. For whatever reason, Hamilton certainly made up or at least exaggerated other sordid anecdotes that show Talbot in an equally unflattering light. According to Hamilton, the duke of York usually brought a friend with him for appearance's sake when calling on his current mistress Anne, wife of Robert Carnegie, son and heir to James 2nd Earl of Southesk. One day he chose Talbot as his companion. Talbot had recently returned from a Portugal (this would date the supposed incident to between May and July 1662) and knew York's paramour only as Lady Southesk.[61] Carnegie, the lady's husband, came home during the tryst and found Richard lolling in the ante-room. Talbot, who knew Carnegie only by that name, demanded what he was doing there. If he had come to see Lady Southesk, warned Talbot, 'you may go away again; for I must inform you the Duke of York is in love with her, and for your private ear is at this very moment in her chamber'. Talbot then advised Carnegie/Southesk to seek a mistress elsewhere and escorted him to his coach. Hamilton further relates that Southesk deliberately contracted a venereal disease in a brothel so that he might get revenge by passing on the disease, via his wife, to the duke. The fantastic tale hinges on Talbot's supposed slow-wittedness in not catching on that Robert Carnegie and the 3rd earl of Southesk were one and the same. He could not have caught on because Carnegie did not become earl until 1669, seven years after the supposed incident.[62] No doubt Talbot did act as York's pimp and pander if one chooses to see his role through the lens of Macaulay's Victorian censoriousness. By his own boast Richard also acted as a go-between for Charles and his chief-mistress Barbara Palmer, as did Charles Berkeley.[63] But this was but an aspect of his business as broker, 'fixer' and messenger scurrying between the ankles of the great.

We must judge Talbot by the standards of his time, place and status. 'Rank' or 'quality' rose or fell by how one dressed, who one associated with, what office one held or work one did and other worldly yardsticks. 'Virtue', 'honesty' and 'character' referred to moral standing while several terms like 'honour', 'reputation' or 'credit' conflated worldly and moral considerations. Sexual incontinence was ostensibly sinful and dishonourable among all social classes and both sexes but by a contrary code of libertinism, sexual rapacity actually enhanced male reputation. This code was most influential in fashionable circles of metropolitan society during the latter decades of the seventeenth century and was a primary means of setting oneself apart from the lower orders. [64]

Talbot was a libertine. He had fathered a child with 'a Lady that he had promis'd marriage to, tho' he never perform'd his Promise'. [65] That the injured lady may have been a connection of the O'Neills of Shane's Castle or Edenduffcarrick in Killileagh, Co. Antrim, may be inferred from two facts. First, the child, Mark Talbot, would maintain connections with Co. Antrim and with the O'Neill family. Second, the O'Neills and Talbots were connected. Sir Henry O'Neill had, like the Dungans, fought for Charles I in England before coming back to Ireland in the later 1640s to enlist in Ormond's forces. He married Eleanor, youngest of the Talbot girls, sometime before the early 1650s and she continued to live with her mother at Carton. [66] Perhaps a sister or cousin of Henry O'Neill also lived at Carton. The injured lady, whoever she was, may have been cut off from the usual protective pack of older family members by the upheavals of war and flight and liable to be smitten by a dashing cavalier. Such things happened in times of civil war. [67]

The young Irishman was 'very handsome', wore 'good clothes', stood well 'above the ordinary size' and played the 'gallant' at Whitehall. [68] A lampoon penned in 1673 by 'Colin' (here the satirist has taken the persona of a shepherd, a naïve outsider, shocked by the depravity of court) claimed that Anna Maria Talbot, née Brudenell, Countess of Shrewsbury 'had the mishap/to give the King Dick Talbot's clap'. [69] Satirical references to the 'pox' and the 'clap' can often be read, not as literal truth, but as condemnation of the popish corruption and sickness at the heart of Whitehall and there is no other evidence that Talbot was afflicted by venereal disease. However, he may very well have been Anna Maria's lover for a time in the early 1660s, though he insisted any sexual relationship was 'imagined' by gossips. He would have been one of many: Hamilton acidly observed that no courtier 'could complain of ill treatment at her hands' and among her other lovers were Talbot's cronies Jermyn and Killigrew and one Colonel Thomas Howard. [70] Sir Peter Lely's portrait depicts mousy-coloured ringlets framing a face with, a longish nose, full lips, slightly heavy chin and Lely's trademark heavy-lidded eyes. Brudenell's bodice is pulled down to bare one breast thereby conveying the sitter's womanly allure and her availability, using symbolism particularly associated with mistresses and suggestive of notoriety.[71] Lely's portraits of court beauties lack individuality and so it is hard to see why Anna Maria sparked 'duels, quarrelling and scandal'. In August 1662 Howard and his second accosted Jermyn and Giles Rawlins coming from the tennis court. They had come prepared, wearing buff coats and carrying swords while the others 'had only the usual bodkins'. Rawlins was killed in the one-sided sword fight.[72] By late 1666 Anna Maria had settled down with one paramour, Buckingham, for the next eight years and was installed in his home alongside his wife. The long-suffering Lord Shrewsbury challenged Buckingham to a duel in January of the following year. He was pierced through the chest by Buckingham's sword and died two months later. Killigrew persisted in publicly abusing his former mistress: Buckingham first snatched his sword from him at the King's Theatre and beat him till he begged for his life and two years later, in 1669, he hired a gang of thugs who stopped Killigrew's hackney coach, beat him severely and killed his servant.

Dick Talbot was no more of a libertine and duellist than most of his set, young blades who had shared the experience of defeat, exile and seemingly miraculous restoration. After the restoration there was only a single report of his fighting a duel (with 'Lord Anieer' or Aungier) and this proved false.[73] Gaming, rather than sexual conquest or brawling, was his distinctive vice and he played cards for very high stakes. The fashionable card games, Piquet, Gleek and L'Ombre were not purely games of chance but demanded skill and judgement in bidding, together with nerve and bluff in betting: useful traits for a political career. Hamilton tells of Talbot losing 300–400 guineas one evening in December 1664. This was a big stake: Talbot's income as a gentleman of the Duke of York's bedchamber was just £300 a year and by the mid-1660s he was drawing some £3,000 a year from newly acquired Irish estates.[74]

To sum up, once he had established himself in York's satellite court Richard Talbot's prospects were reasonably good. He was strikingly handsome, a conspicuously gallant cavalier, displayed 'honour' – as that quality was understood at the Restoration court – and was above all 'obliging'.[75] But he was also hot-tempered and liable to blurt out indiscreet truths.

Talbot's main work as a lobbyist and broker in connection with forfeited Irish estates (the subject matter of the next chapter) drew him from Whitehall in July 1662 to spend the next year in Dublin. He was still very much within Ormond's orbit and when he left for Ireland he had, in his own words, a 'privity' or understanding with Elizabeth Hamilton, Ormond's niece. The Hamiltons illustrate the truism that religion trumped all other indices of identity. Sir George Hamilton was a younger son of Sir James Hamilton, a favourite of

James I. During the Plantation of Ulster he had, notwithstanding his
Catholicism, been awarded estates in west Ulster and in Co. Tipperary. The
latter estates were settled on the younger sons, including George who married
Mary Butler a sister of the future Duke of Ormond, and a Catholic like nearly
all her family.[76] Their daughter Elizabeth was not attached to either of the
royal households and was not a wealthy heiress but her beauty, accomplishments and 'lively wit' nonetheless made her a mark for high-born suitors at
court. No sooner had Talbot left than Arran, Ormond's younger son (one of
the false witnesses against Anne Hyde) began paying court to his cousin. The
family packed Arran off to Ireland 'for fear of marrying': a connection with a
client and poor relation was not what Ormond had in mind for his sons. Soon
after this a visiting Frenchman, the count of Gramont, 'cast his eyes' on the
beauty. His intentions may very well have been dishonourable but her two
brothers, James and George, harried Gramont into a public avowal. This
happened in the winter and spring of 1663 and when Dick Talbot heard of the
business he was enraged; 'coming over [he] broke all off, and advised her to
marry Gramont. He would fain fall back but James her brother misused him
and so it went on'. Talbot's recollections are confusingly terse but apparently
in summer 1663 James Hamilton attacked Dick Talbot and what 'went on'
afterwards was a quarrel with the Hamiltons and their patron Ormond. The
Memoirs of Gramont were, as noted, penned by Anthony Hamilton, a younger
brother of Elizabeth and Sergeant has great difficulty in constructing a linear
and credible narrative from the *Memoirs*. Anthony Hamilton has Talbot quarrelling with Ormond, being thrown into the Tower as a punishment, securing
his release and then, improbably, paying court to Ormond's niece. The *Memoirs*
transpose a quarrel and imprisonment that happened two years later and that
arose, as Talbot's own story makes clear, for entirely different reasons. Sergeant
attempts to resolve the confusion by supposing that Talbot was twice thrown
in the Tower and by so doing compounds the muddle.

   While in Dublin in 1662 and 1663 Talbot still showed Ormond the outward
forms of deference but had begun to doubt his goodwill to Irish Catholics.
Even some of Ormond's 'fastest friends' and dependents like the Franciscan
Peter Walsh expressed similar concerns.[77] Talbot cultivated other patrons in
Bennet and Berkeley whose usefulness, respectively, lay in the authority of
office and the influence of daily and congenial contact with Charles II. Joseph
Williamson, the head of Bennet's secretariat, sent Talbot all the news and
reminded Bennet of Talbot's clients.[78] Ensconced at court as one of the four
almoners to Charles's new queen (she also had no fewer than a dozen chaplains
and a confessor) Peter could watch out for brother Dick's enemies.

   Peter's proficiency in Spanish was probably the reason for this appointment, as it probably was for Richard being chosen as Catherine's escort from Portugal.[79] Foreign Catholic princesses like Henrietta Maria could expect sullen suspicion in England but the position of Catherine of Braganza (Charles's queen from 1661) was even more fraught. Her husband was notoriously unfaithful and insisted on installing Castlemaine as a lady of the bedchamber. Catherine objected that this would expose her to the 'contempt' of the court but she was forced into humiliating acquiescence by November 1662 after months of protesting and threatening.[80] Peter Talbot was caught in the crossfire of this quarrel. There are two versions of what happened. One is that Peter was outraged on Catherine's behalf at the king's blatant philandering and, while encouraging her to stand firm, blurted out in Spanish that Castlemaine was an enchantress. She took the remark literally as an accusation of witchcraft and cautioned Charles against her rival's sorcery.[81] This 'lost in translation' story is unconvincing. Talbot was friendly with Castlemaine and was, or had been, pro-Spanish. Catherine, for her part, must have been suspicious of Talbot on both counts. Consequently, Talbot's remarks about Castlemaine may have been a deliberate gambit to break up the marriage rather than artless prattling. The Talbots were convinced that Catherine had complained of Peter and that she had been put up to it by Ormond and by the Portuguese ambassador.[82] Richard tried to mobilise Berkeley to save Peter. He protested to his patron that he could not 'imagine' why his brother had 'fallen into the king's displeasure' and flatly denied that he himself had acted improperly:

> Though I have as much confidence in your friendship as in any man alive, yet you may believe me I would not make use of it if I were not as innocent of this as the child new born last night, for I call God to witness I never discoursed with the Queen of this subject …

Berkeley declined to help and objected to Talbot's 'pert' tone. Talbot next reproached Berkeley for not defending him to Charles and to Castlemaine and implored him, 'pray do not delay it longer'.[83] Evidently, Berkeley ignored Talbot's pleas. Peter was stripped of his post and banished from England in November 1662, the same month that Charles finally managed to install Castlemaine in his wife's household.[84] Dismissing Peter Talbot may have been Charles's consolation prize to his wife for foisting his mistress on her. Evidently the rift lasted some months until the latter lady interceded with Berkeley on Peter's behalf. Castlemaine's intimacy with Charles endowed her with significant influence but yet she was, in a sense, a protégé of Berkeley, keeper of the privy purse. In gratitude, Peter responded with unctuous professions of gratitude to Berkeley:

my brother Dick is very sensible of your favours and resolved to obey your commands in todo [Talbot sprinkles his letters to Berkeley with the occasional Spanish phrase, perhaps as a way of reminding the latter of their shared exile in the Spanish Netherlands]. Now I shall desire you to assure yourself that I am as grateful a servant as any, and none know better what I owe to you than myself, nor pray more for your health and prosperity. My most humble respects to my noble Lady Castlemaine, to whose goodnesse I am much obliged, and shall acknowledge it in all occasions and fortunes.[85]

The rift had been healed not a moment too soon, because Talbot would need all the friends he could muster.

The 'Old Protestants' or pre-1641 'New English', most of whom had favoured Oliver Cromwell as the saviour of Protestant Ireland, had entrenched themselves in government under Henry Cromwell. As noted above, when Cromwell was dismissed they mounted a coup d'état which they could later represent as an early blow for the royalist cause. The convention they held in spring 1660 urged Charles II to freeze the landed status quo and this formed the basis for the royal declaration of 30 November which formally disavowed the Treaty of 1649 that Ormond had negotiated on his behalf with Irish Catholics. The declaration also confirmed that the general promise Charles had made at Breda before sailing home would apply to those who now owned confiscated estates in Ireland: except for the 'regicides' (those who had signed his father's death warrant) they would keep their estates. Special provision was made for the kingmakers who had secured Ireland for the king: these included Charles Coote, now elevated to the earldom of Mountrath, and the slippery Roger Boyle Lord Broghill (who had orchestrated the defection of the royalist garrisons in Co. Cork in 1649), now styled earl of Orrery. However, Charles's Declaration named 38 Irish Catholics who should be 'restored to their former estates', no questions asked. The list was top-heavy with aristocrats and included four earls, eight viscounts, and five barons besides a disproportionate number of people with Ormond connections like George Hamilton, his brother-in-law, Richard Lane, a kinsman of his secretary, and Sir Robert Talbot.[86]

This was an empty expression of goodwill because Charles left the enactment of a land settlement to an Irish parliament convened in May 1661. This was an all-Protestant body and the single Catholic returned was promptly expelled. The 'Old Protestants' who dominated parliament (of 254 members all but 66 were pre-1641 settlers) struck up an alliance with the less radical elements of the Cromwellian newcomers and maintained 'united and effective action', all the while insisting on confirming all the confiscations rather than throwing the newcomers to the wolves.[87] The preamble to their draft bill for an Act of Settlement conjured up a mythic past where the 'Old Protestants', if 'seemingly rebels', were driven to it by the Irish massacres while the 'Adventurers' and 'Soldiers' had risked their money and lives to put down these barbarous rebels. The massacre legend was such a useful stick with which to beat the Irish because it had a grim basis in fact, however selectively recalled, numerically overblown and spiced up with ghastly atrocity stories. During the winter of 1641–2 Irish insurgents had killed thousands of British settlers in Ulster (about 600 were killed in Armagh, the worst hit county) and on a smaller scale elsewhere, usually when they were being conveyed as prisoners to a safe haven. There had been probably as many Protestant killings of Catholics, like the killing of Talbot's aunt Mrs Eustace, perpetrated weeks and months later but these were elided from the narrative of victimhood.[88]

Despite furious lobbying by Irish Catholic delegates, the Act passed and confirmed virtually all the confiscations. The Act was so drafted that nearly any category of Irish person to be restored could get his estate back only if the existing soldier or adventurer occupier were compensated or 'reprised' by an estate of equivalent value elsewhere. This qualification weighed the whole process heavily towards the occupier. Always anxious to avoid unpleasantness, Charles had let himself be convinced by smooth talkers like Irish vice-treasurer Arthur Annesley (elevated to the peerage as earl of Anglesey in 1661) that somehow there was enough land to leave the new owners in possession or reprise them, compensate Protestant royalist officers (the '1649 officers') for arrears of pay, reinstate the 38 nominees and even reward the 'ensignmen', well over 200 Irish Catholic officers who served in his regiments in exile, and others to whom he promised redress. 'There must be new discoveries made of a New Ireland', Ormond commented.[89] Charles, despite his relatively benign feelings towards Irish Catholics in general (at least compared to Scottish Presbyterians), and some in particular, seemingly left them at the mercy of their enemies. The king 'can hate without harming and like without helping', French ambassador Cominges perceptively noted. Charles was, he admitted, 'good and very fair', but as regards this 'unhappy nation', the Irish, 'the dispossessed [les chassés] are weak and the possessors strong'.[90]

They were indeed strong and faced no comparable counterweight. It has been claimed that Charles, Clarendon, and Ormond all wanted 'substantial catholic restoration'.[91] Perhaps: but how badly did they want a restoration and how 'substantial' would it need to be? Charles, for the moment, took the line of least resistance. Clarendon was not unhappy to see the Irish punished by mass confiscations since he wholeheartedly endorsed the black legend that the Irish had (to quote from his *History of the Rebellion*) 'with most barbarous Circumstances of Cruelty, within a space of less than ten Days, murthered an Incredible Number of Protestants, Men Women and Children promiscuously without distinction of Age or Sex.' Moreover, his account of Cromwell's conquest in Clarendon's *History* unrelentingly hammers home the message that the Peace of 1649 was annulled by the disobedience, treason, disorganisation, and cowardice of the Irish. Consequently, the king owed them nothing.[92]

As for Ormond, he had accepted a £30,000 gift from the Dublin parliament when he was nominated in November 1661 as lord lieutenant. Even his Protestant 'old friends' regretted that he accepted the payment, while the Irish and their sympathisers at court called it a 'downe right bribe against them' and prompted accusations that he 'sells his country for an estate'.[93] Moreover, Ormond would also amass far more land than he had before the war: his rental of about £25,000 a year was equalled only by that of the head of the Boyle interest, the second earl of Cork and first earl of Burlington. Ormond liked to pose as a neutral reluctantly forced by a Protestant parliament to pursue a land settlement that did not, he freely admitted, have 'reasonable regard' for Irish landowners: 'If it be [so], it will not pass'.[94] Claims of benevolent neutrality are incompatible with the fact that Ormond would not stir himself on behalf of the Irish in general, since he was embittered by what he would ever see as their disloyalty and treachery in 1646. The treaty three years later did not temper his hostility. Catholics expected that Ormond would actively support and lobby for the fulfilment of the 1649 treaty which formed the 'central argument' for the recovery of their estates.[95] He may or may not have assured Orrery that 'it must be laid as a ground that noe adventurer or soldier shall be removed from his lot', but he acted in that spirit.[96] Putting the most favourable construction on his attitude to his Irish Catholic followers, Ormond was predisposed to accept that the transfer of power and wealth was more or less irreversible because the new owners were too powerful to be trifled with. There were real grounds for nervousness: the wave of popularity that greeted Charles II ebbed rapidly in Britain and within two years disaffection was widespread, even before the Medway disaster, the Plague and the Great Fire of London led many to believe the Stuarts had forfeited God's favour. The army in Ireland, that ultimate arbiter of power, was still controlled by the 'Cromwellians of Ireland' and so Protestant disaffection there was potentially even more threatening.[97]

At this pivotal moment the clergy, the natural leaders of Irish society, plunged into a needless and distracting wrangle. There was potential enough for splits among the Catholic clergy already as secular clergy jostled with regular clergy (that is, clergy bound by a regulum or 'rule' belonging to orders such as Franciscans, Dominicans and so on) at the drastically reduced font of lay patronage. The 'Remonstrance' controversy was even more divisive and cut across secular versus regular rivalries. It began with a sham plot, a perennially useful anti-Catholic ploy. In December 1661 a forged letter duly surfaced, purportedly sent by two priests, which prophesied an imminent Catholic rebellion. The letter sparked parliamentary outcry and a round-up of priests, army mobilisation and some transplantation to Connacht.[98] The squall of persecution drove Catholics to seek royal protection and it was in this fearful climate that Richard Bellings, a client of Ormond, drafted an abject statement of Catholic temporal loyalty to 'assure his Majesty of their allegiance, vindicate their religion from the scandal of unwarrantable tenets, and move in the king's breast that pity which is implored by the Roman Catholics of Ireland.'[99] The main 'unwarrantable tenet' at issue was the vague and anachronistic power that popes claimed to depose monarchs. Unfortunately, Rome took a different view of the deposing power and, inevitably, the issue split Irish clergy and laity precisely at a time when the latter needed to keep their eyes fixed on the main chance: getting their estates back. Thomas, Gilbert and Sir Robert Talbot subscribed to the Remonstrance. Robert is probably Roibiord an réaghghúna, the gowned sharpster of Ó Bruadair's A Dia na n-Uile: the gown was associated with lawyers or 'gownmen'. Richard ignored the Remonstrance and Peter opposed it furiously.[100]

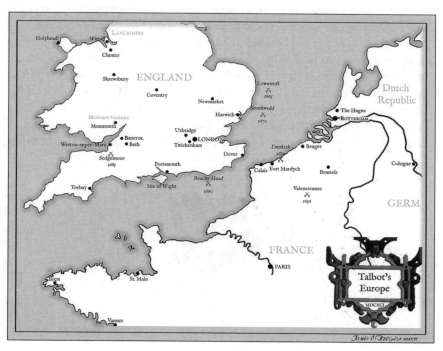

Ormond had not instigated the Remonstrance (he would not arrive in Ireland until July 1662) and initially he saw it merely as a useful test to identify some 'better and more sober' priests and so punish the rest.[101] In 1666 Ormond facilitated a national convention of clergy where they showed eagerness to mollify their critics, short of adopting the precise words of formulary devised by the Franciscan Peter Walsh which Rome had condemned. But Ormond insisted on the formulary or nothing. Walsh was Ormond's creature and recipient of a £200 annuity from the duke and by now it is clear that he was Ormond's instrument in deliberately perpetuating a knotty problem of church-state relations.[102] Louis XIV tried for most of his long reign to assert and define his authority over a Gallican church: 'The more Pope and king tried to define and establish their respective authority, the more insoluble questions they raised, and the more they rendered convenient old compromises unserviceable.'[103] Ormond's minion spun out the controversy in order to set the Catholic clergy against each other and thereby weaken the only remaining institution around which the Irish could unite at a pivotal moment when the shape of the Restoration land settlement had not yet been set: 'My aim was the work a division among the Romish clergy', boasted Ormond a decade later.[104]

So far, so bad. Yet Charles had begun to claw back some control over the land settlement. 'Innocents', those free of any taint of involvement in the Irish rebellion of 1641–2, could be restored right away, without the occupiers being compensated or 'reprised'. Anglesey had framed the qualifications of innocence so narrowly 'as made it almost impossible for an Irishman to escape'.[105] Or so he thought. The same month that Talbot set out for Dublin (and the timing is not coincidental) Charles appointed a seven-man court of claims to implement the act. They were supposedly impartial 'Englishmen and Protestants', 'learned in the law' and reputed to be 'of good reputation' and 'integrity'.[106] Fortunately for Talbot, most of them were nothing of the sort.

THREE

ARLINGTON'S FRIEND
1662–72

This chapter examines how Talbot acted as a go-between for a minister and for a powerful courtier both enriching themselves from confiscated Irish estates and as a lobbyist and agent for dispossessed Irish Catholics. By demanding a cut of any restored property, he built up an enviable property portfolio. He later took on, or had thrust on him, the role of spokesman and tribune of the entire Catholic community, when he would lobby for restoration of Catholic estates and the rightful place in law, politics and administration that went with property ownership. His struggles pitted him against Ormond, the deadliest enemy of collective Irish Catholic organisation and political activity. Talbot's backstairs activism would be intimately bound up with political intrigues and upheavals in England, and with international diplomacy.

It was whispered that some of the commissioners first nominated to the court of claims had 'secret instructions' to award decrees of innocence at the behest of powerful royal ministers, especially Henry Bennet.[1] The rumours were probably true and three of the commissioners would consistently find most applicants innocent. These were Sir Richard Rainsford, Sir Thomas Beverley and Sir Winston Churchill: the latter was Bennet's client and father of John Churchill, the future duke of Marlborough. On the other hand, three members with Anglo-Irish connections proved, in contrast, niggardly in voting for innocence. These were Sir Edward Dering, Edward Cooke, a former colonel in Cromwell's army and now MP for Clogher, and Sir Edward Smith MP for Lisburn. Ormond preferred the naysayers: he reckoned Smith 'a very honest, well-natured man' while Dering was connected by marriage to his Southwell clients.[2]

Talbot hoped that the seventh member, Sir Henry Coventry (brother of Sir William Coventry of York's household), would swing the balance against the naysayers but Coventry was recalled before the court actually began its hearings in mid-January 1663. He was replaced by Sir Alan Broderick, a cousin and client of Clarendon's.[3] Broderick criticised Rainsford's inopportune 'zeal' and assured Ormond that 'the least intimation you could let fall' would be taken by him as 'an absolute command'. Evidently, then, Talbot had reason to worry that

Broderick's appointment 'destroys us all', but his fears proved unfounded.[4] 'O'Broderick' (as disgusted Anglo-Irish Protestants dubbed him) tended to vote with 'McRainsford', 'O'Beverley', and 'McChurchill'. Yet the chairman had no casting vote, and after eleven weeks of proceedings Churchill informed Bennet how the court was often tied '3 to 3' and if it happened that he, Beverley, or Broderick were absent 'almost every case is dismissed', though the party be 'ever so innocent'.[5]

Using Talbot as a go-between, Rainsford, Beverley and Churchill all drew Bennet's attention to profitable legal loopholes and fed him insider information.[6] To take just one example of a murky speculation: Rainsford and another commissioner made a 'discovery' of an estate worth £100,000. Such 'discoveries' were a well-tried precursor to plantations during the reigns of Charles's father and grandfather, whereby the defective title would cause the estate to be vested in the king. Rainsford and the other commissioner suggested to Talbot that he ask Bennet to get a grant of the estate from the king. They promised a helpful adjudication on the property though, Talbot reminded Bennet, 'no man living must know that any of them are interested in it'.[7] Talbot promised the commissioners that Bennet would then kick back one half of the estate's value to them. Whenever he was challenged publicly, Talbot kept a straight face, denied having 'any influence' over the commissioners and protested indignantly that this allegation was 'dishonouring to them'.[8]

Maybe it was simply good fortune that two of Talbot's brothers-in-law (Henry Talbot and Sir John Dungan) were heard on the second day the court of claims sat and that both were adjudged innocent.[9] William Dungan, the second son of Sir John Dungan would benefit from this finding because the eldest son Sir Walter (Richard Talbot's captain during the war) had evidently renounced his inheritance. Perhaps he had to. The latter's claim to innocence would founder because he had signed a collective renunciation of the 1646 Ormond Peace though he was acting, in effect, as Ormond's double agent at the time.[10]

Three other disputes further illustrate the part Talbot played as a double-dealing agent for Bennet and for Berkeley. Hugh Montgomery Earl of Mount Alexander had got a grant of the estate of James Allen of St Wolstans, near Leixlip, Co. Kildare. To disprove James Allen's innocence and thereby secure Allen's estate, Montgomery procured witnesses to swear that Allen took charge of throwing a boom across the Boyne estuary during the 1641–2 blockade of Drogheda. Talbot involved himself closely in upholding Allen's innocence in expectation that he would be 'well rewarded', as would Berkeley who bought out Allen's interest in the estate. Berkeley claimed to have been moved by pity in cases such as these, lest 'the poor Irish would be destroyed by the number and malice of those that sought their ruin'.[11] A 'supposed friend' of Montgomery's, tore an incriminating page out of the record in return for £2,000. This timely bribe, the 'knavery' of Allen's witnesses, and 'some private directions' from Charles, moved the court of claims to find Allen innocent in February 1663. Montgomery was flabbergasted and even Talbot was pleasantly surprised since he had given up hope for Allen's innocence. To spoil Montgomery's expected win Talbot had asked Bennet to use St Wolstan's to reprise adventurers and soldiers displaced from the Clanmalier estate (a joint project of Bennet's and Talbot's discussed below) and 'say nothing about it to Lord Berkley'.[12]

The second case study is that of Sir Philip Hore of Kilsallaghan, Co. Dublin, who was decreed an innocent by the court of claims. His father's house had been an insurgent headquarters, as noted in chapter one, but Philip relied on a claim that a feoffment preceded his father's attainder and so secured the estate, which comprised some 11,000 acres. To complicate matters, Ormond's secretary Sir George Lane, who had obtained a grant of the estate, disputed the legality of the feoffment. Hore proved a stubborn adversary, prepared to use every legal device open to him. Ultimately Talbot intervened and brokered an agreement between the rivals in 1665. As a reward, Hore granted Talbot a satellite estate of 285 acres in Castleknock, Co. Dublin.[13]

Talbot brokered other deals for Berkeley, besides St Wolstans, and promised to 'doe all I can for you hear ['here': Talbot often lapsed into Hiberno-English phonetic spelling] and you shall give me a snip out of it'.[14] Talbot acquired rather more than snips. In January 1663 he reported that William Steele, former lord chancellor in Ireland and commissioner for the affairs of Ireland, had been implicated in plotting against Charles in the dying days of the interregnum and so his property was liable for sequestration once he was attainted. One item of property was a debt of £6,000 registered by statute staple against Sir John King, Baron Kingston. This was 'good mony' Talbot reminded Fitzhardinge (Berkeley as was) and pressed him to 'gett the grante of it'. Talbot, acting on his own or on Fitzhardinge's behalf, agreed to accept annual payments of £600 from King. Three years passed and the annuities went unpaid until, at Ormond's mediation, Talbot settled for an annuity of £300 so that he and King 'may not meet each other uneasily as we do now'.[15] Kingston disgorged lands he bought from an adventurer in 1659 to William Dungan (created Viscount Clane in 1662), heir to the original owner, without the usual fuss and protests. Perhaps it proved all so easy because Richard Talbot was able to use the assignment of the debt as leverage against King.[16]

The court of claims sat for eight months, from January to August 1663, during which time the Court heard only a fraction of the 4,800 or so claims. Those who got a hearing were mostly Palesmen and while this is usually attributed to

Talbot's machinations it is more probable that the commissioners called the most likely-looking category of innocents first, namely those who lived in what had been the English quarters during the 1640s. The commissioners were unexpectedly lenient, or fair, towards Papists and this enraged the House of Commons which demanded that land claims be reserved to local, and reliably Protestant, juries.[17]

While Ormond privately shrugged off the more hysterical Protestant accusations, he affected to share the fears expressed in the House of Commons of a revolt by 'fanatics' (Protestant dissenters) and, indeed, rumours of rebellion in Ireland were the talk of London town in March and April 1663.[18] Ormond claimed he could not trust an army that was underpaid, billeted in small detachments across the country and purged of only the most diehard Cromwellians. Clarendon proved an unsympathetic confidant and accused his old friend of feebleness: 'You do not enough make yourself obeyed'.[19] For his part, the king was 'horribly angry' at the House's recalcitrance and its affronts to the members of the court of claims and threatened armed action. A showdown was averted with an abortive plot by 'fanatic spirits' to seize Dublin Castle in May 1663, kidnap Ormond, and reinstate the Solemn League and Covenant. The ringleaders were known to be Cromwellian officers like Colonel Thomas Jephson MP for Trim but there were 'so many' implicated in the plot (including eight MPs) that Ormond 'was glad to look no further'. The members of the House, now falling over themselves to show their loyalty, shied away from further antagonising the king over the court of claims.[20]

The case of Randal MacDonnell Earl of Antrim finally stretched the concept of innocence beyond breaking point and discredited the court of claims. Ormond fumed that seven hours of hostile testimony showed that Antrim fell foul of no fewer than eight debarring 'qualifications' in the Act of Settlement, not least in opposing the second Ormond Peace of 1649 and (probably) collaborating with Cromwell to bring about the fall of Wexford. Badgered by Antrim's wife, Daniel O'Neill's niece, Charles II unilaterally declared Antrim innocent in July 1663 and ordered Ormond to make his views known to the commissioners of the court of claims. Ormond ignored the order but Lady Antrim made the order known anyway. The commissioners duly decreed by a four to three majority that Antrim be restored and adjourned shortly afterwards, shaken by the outrage of local Protestants. The statutory time limit of twelve months on their sessions expired in August and they never reconvened.[21]

Within weeks Ormond was at work on a draft bill which purported simply to 'explain the king's meaning' but was, in effect, 'an alteration'.[22] Ormond sent his draft bill to Whitehall in September 1663 but the English council thought it too generous to the Cromwellian interest and debated several amendments over the next six months. Charles had three of the biddable commissioners, Rainsford, Broderick and Beverley, come to London to advise him.[23] The most contentious question was Ormond's insistence that his bill be 'so transmitted that it may pass' the Irish House of Commons. By accepting that as his touch-stone, Irish Catholics must lose out: indeed, Ormond especially valued a clause that the court of claims could never be resumed and urged Whitehall to turn a deaf ear to Irish complaints. On the question of innocents, Ormond suggested that he and six Irish privy counsellors choose those worthy of innocence but the English privy council rejected this idea, anticipating that Ormond and the privy counsellors would take a very narrow view of innocence.[24] By now Talbot had shuttled back to London where, to Ormond's chagrin, he claimed credit for delaying the bill.[25] The delay was 'not because Colonel Talbot desir'd it', Bennet (or the Earl of Arlington as he was by now) reassured Ormond but because of a last minute draft bill prepared by Rainsford.[26]

After rising to become secretary of state over Clarendon's objections, Arlington subsequently took some pains to try to re-establish working relations with the chancellor. Arlington was never one for either implacable enmity or unreserved friendship. However, the chancellor snubbed him and Ormond proved disobliging. Twice Arlington asked Ormond to give a vacant cavalry troop command to his brother who had spent a decade in exile following the Stuart court and twice Ormond passed him over for other candidates. Neither 'time or alliance could ever entirely remove' Arlington's irritation at this slight and his sometimes strained relations with Clarendon and Ormond opened up opportunities to Talbot.[27]

Talbot was Arlington's 'solicitor' or agent in acquiring the forfeited estate of Viscount Clanmalier, Laoiseach O'Dempsey, which was worth about £4,000 a year.[28] The long-running Clanmalier estate saga was the *Jarndyce v Jarndyce* of the Restoration land settlement. There were competing interests to be bought off, outmanoeuvred or, in the case of the original proprietor, ignored. 'Poor Lord Clanmalier hee is lost', mused Talbot, but he made a token effort to salvage a third of the estate for him by way of a special proviso in the Act of Explanation.[29] More significant opposition was mounted by a number of brokers like Anglesey and Francis Lord Aungier (Talbot's supposed duelling opponent) who surfaced on behalf of the soldiers and adventurers on the Clanmalier estate.[30] Men like these wielded considerable influence in the Irish parliament where, after all, it was necessary to pass the Act of Explanation and have Bennet's claim secured by a proviso or clause.[31] In October 1662 Ormond offered to act as an honest broker between Aungier and Bennet and hinted that Talbot should be paid off and dropped as an intermediary: 'I never expected Dick Talbott's martyrdom in that cause, he is up to his ears in provisos, reprisalls & the language of the Act of Settlement and has an honorable pretence of retreat'.[32]

Two months later, Talbot grumbled to Arlington that it took a gruellingly long argument to persuade Ormond to take even the smallest steps towards helping the secretary acquire his Irish estate.

> I took the opportunity of finding him alone in his closet, and truly I told him that most people here of his own friends did very much admire [wonder] that his Grace was not warmer in serving you in your pretention to the estate the King had given you here, especially since it was obvious to all mankind that the proprietor was altogether irredeemable. I added likewise that no man had more reason than myself to know how much you desired his friendship and how you would endeavour to deserve it, and much more upon that subject. Long discourses there were upon it, but after a long hour's dispute I concluded with him that I would bring Mr Brien and Mr Churchill to him with a bill to present him, interesting you in that estate with provisoes also for the old proprietor; and likewise orders that the new provisors of it shall be forthwith reprised.

It quickly emerged that Ormond had no interest in the fate of the original Irish proprietor and his sole concern was that reprising the present occupiers elsewhere might be too big a drain on the reserves of available land. Talbot breezily tried to reassure him it was but a 'small matter' of draining 'one drop of water out of a hogsett [hogshead].' Talbot next bypassed Ormond and persuaded Anglesey (who was anxious to curry favour with Arlington) to intimidate the present occupiers into believing that their position was in 'great uncertainty'.[33] By April 1663 Ormond was more pliable. Talbot had regained Fitzhardinge's favour, lost when Peter Talbot meddled in the affairs of Barbara Palmer, and Daniel O'Neill had let Ormond know that the king was displeased that the duke was 'not kind' to Arlington. The Clanmalier estate wrangles dragged on until March 1664 when Talbot argued Arlington's case for two hours before the privy council and won his point, though only on condition that he let the largest of the Cromwellian grantees, a Lieut-Col. John Nelson, stay on as tenant on an estate of 1,387 acres at a rent that other brokers, Cork, Anglesey and Orrery would think fit. Two years later, Nelson's widow was still importuning for a lease and compensation for improvements.[34] Displacing the Cromwellian grantees was fairly easy if they, as one of their spokesmen put it, had not enough 'interest' (political connections in modern language) to block the scheme.[35] Arlington had got his Irish estate and the town of Portarlington in Co. Offaly is a tangible reminder of his fleeting involvement.

In dealings with Arlington, Talbot's key contact was Joseph Williamson, head of Arlington's secretariat. Arlington had inherited Williamson when he displaced Nicholas and, 'loving his ease more than business', he delegated much of his correspondence to Williamson who by 'subtlety, dexterity and insinuation' got to be Arlington's main workhorse. Williamson drew Arlington's attention to Talbot's clients and kept Talbot posted about doings at court. In return, after many promises and false starts, Talbot secured an Irish estate for Williamson.[36]

The Act of Explanation would not be passed for another two years and as it was being prepared at Whitehall in 1664–5, Talbot lobbied indefatigably to block it or ensure that it would not damage his interests or the interests of those he represented. Another draft bill was sent to London in September 1663, by which time Talbot was back at Whitehall, and was delayed while Charles picked out Catholics who would benefit from special clauses or 'provisos'. By April 1664, Ormond had drawn up a detailed list of those Irish who had tried most often to bring the Confederate Catholics 'to the obedience and service of the crown'. The Act of Explanation ultimately confirmed that no further decrees of innocence should be given. Charles, who was surprisingly well-briefed about the Explanatory Bill, assented to this only after insisting he should name in the act 54 dispossessed Irish individuals or 'nominees' to be restored to their chief mansions, and 2,000 adjacent acres.

The act having declared that the adventurers and soldiers were to be first provided for by a reprise of equal worth, four (Smith, Deering, Churchill and Broderick) of the seven commissioners heard representatives of the Irish, the Adventurers and the Soldiers until by May 1665 agreement was reached that most adventurers and soldiers (Orrery and some other prominent Cromwellian grantees were exempted to secure a passage of the act) would surrender one third of their lands to create a land bank for reprisals.[37] The process ground on slowly and the adventurers' and soldiers' deficiencies seemed more than enough to exhaust the whole of the land available for reprisals: two years later, not a single one of the nominees had 'got so much as a cottage'.[38] In 1667 Edward Nugent of Carlanstown, Co. Meath, petitioned in vain to be restored as his father was one of the 36 persons named in the 1660 Declaration to be restored without further proof, and was likewise one of the 54 persons named in the 1665 Act of Explanation of 1665. Barnaby Fitzpatrick Lord Upper Ossory was also named twice but got no relief by 1666.[39]

During the two crucial years of 1663–5 a swarm of agents and brokers emerged to peddle their influence to regain estates. The older Henry Jermyn (now earl of St Albans) reportedly took bonds of £1,000 up front from Patrick Sarsfield of Lucan, Co. Dublin, and Philip Hore, for acting as their agent. Sir

Maurice Berkeley, Fitzhardinge's brother, procured Thomas Luttrell's proviso in the Act of Settlement. William Domville, the Irish attorney-general, concluded an agreement with Robert Preston and Marcus Fitzsimons (the latter had also enjoyed the backing of Queen Catherine) to regain their estates.[40]

But Talbot outshone them all. Arriving from Ireland in summer 1663, he brought £18,000 in bonds and securities from 'hundreds' of dispossessed hopefuls who 'had no friends of their own to solicit for them' and who believed him to have a 'mighty interest' at Whitehall.[41] He attracted clients mostly from Leinster, including Gerald Lynch and Hugh Hussey (Co. Meath), Sir Thomas Nugent (Co. Westmeath), Philip Hore (Co. Dublin), John Magennis (Co. Down), George Chivers (Co. Wexford) and Sir Robert Nugent (Co. Roscommon).[42] He might secure a bond in return for successful restoration or gain an income from it for an agreed time: in 1671 he got the fee simple of quit-rents payable out of part of James Allen's former estate.[43] Most often the client promised a hefty portion (a half to two thirds according to one hostile account) of the estate to secure the rest.[44] Talbot had the effrontery to enforce such under-the-counter agreements in the courts when he sued Thomas Nugent's heirs because they balked at paying-up the agreed sum. The heirs complained that they did not owe the recovery of the estate to Talbot's efforts because, after an initial flurry of activity, he had 'taken no further trouble in the matter'.[45]

Table 3.1 Richard Talbot's lands c.1690

COUNTY	ACRES	COUNTY	ACRES	
Kildare	3,781	Kildare	843	† R. Loeber, H. Murtagh, J. Cronin,
Meath	3,605	Meath	2636	'Prelude to confiscation: a Survey
Dublin	1,992	Dublin	633	of Catholic Estates in Leinster in
Louth	339	Wicklow	9,650	1690' in *Journal of the Royal Society*
TOTAL	9,717*	TOTAL	13,762†	*of Antiquaries of Ireland*, 131, (2001),
				pp. 63–5, 67, 69, 73, 74, 75, 77, 92–5.

* J. G. Simms, *The Williamite Confiscation in Ireland 1690–1703* (London, 1956), p. 182; 'Proceedings upon the petition of Frances, Countess-Dowager of Tyrconnel' 13 Aug. 1692, W. J. Hardy (ed.), *CSPD, William and Mary, 1691–1692* (London, 1898), p. 406; HMC Appendix to 8th Report, (London, 1881), p. 499; W. Fitzgerald, 'Carton' in *Kildare Arch. Soc. Jn.*, iv (1903–5), p. 11.

Ormond, in November 1663, wryly remarked: 'In their endeavors for their countrymen, Colonel Talbot & his brother have not omitted to consider themselves'.[46] There is no doubt that Talbot did well. There is some confusion between various sources with a survey completed shortly after the Williamite War (1689–91), crediting Tyrconnell with over 9,000 acres in Co. Wicklow around Castlesallagh, Talbotstown, and Donard while the returns of the

Forfeiture Trustees a decade later include the Carton estate, but not the Castlesallagh–Talbotstown one. Another source would put his estate around Carton at almost 1,600 acres which would adjust the larger figure upwards. So, by 1690 he owned (see table 3.1) anything from in excess of 9,000 to almost 14,000 acres. His estate was built up from lands granted by York in Counties Dublin and Meath: York had been awarded over 87,000 Irish acres belonging to regicides, those men who put their hand to his father's death warrant. The rest of his estate was made up of various little 'snips' he took in the 1660s.

Ormond could ill afford to cast stones at Talbot since he himself had augmented his pre-war estate by 35,000 acres or about three times Talbot's pickings. Ormond's cynical remark reflected his growing dislike of the family.[47] In August 1662 he had given a lukewarm promise to assist Talbot and had mediated in the claim of Sir Henry O'Neill, Talbot's brother-in-law. O'Neill had not been able to establish his innocence because he had fled to the Irish quarters in 1642 before embarking for England to fight for Charles I.[48] O'Neill's neighbour Sir John Skeffington 2nd Viscount Masserene had been granted O'Neill's lands and was not minded to give them back. At Ormond's request, Massereene met with O'Neill, Richard Talbot and others of O'Neill's 'friends' in October 1662 but Massereene complained that the more concessions he made 'the more proposals were multiplied' and agreement proved elusive.[49] In autumn 1663 Ormond's brother-in-law George Hamilton warned Talbot that the duke was irritated by what he construed as Talbot's disrespect. While professing to understand his 'zeal for his countrymen and friends' Ormond stood on his official dignity and would not discuss the draft Act of Explanation with him.[50] For his part, Talbot strove to avoid an open rift and repeatedly apologised to Ormond, pleading that he had not meant to give offence.[51]

As Ormond cooled towards them, the Talbots forged an incongruous alliance with the ultra-Protestant Boyle interest. This alliance was cemented in 1664 when Gilbert Talbot married the widowed Dorothy Loftus, sister of Orrery and of Richard Boyle 1st Earl of Burlington. The earl was unimpressed by his sister's new husband, describing Gilbert as a 'half-witted fellow' interested only in clothes and gambling. Burlington had earlier absolutely vetoed Richard Talbot as a bridegroom for his daughter.[52] Burlington's brother Orrery, on the other hand, was keen on the match and for a few years Richard was a welcome guest in Orrery's new palatial mansion at Charleville (so named as a compliment to the king), Co. Cork.[53] Orrery shared a dislike of Ormond with Talbot but little else and he warned that their 'friendship' would not avail where the 'English & Protestant Interest was concerned'. Orrery proved a useful tactical ally, in the short-term. He assisted the earl of Antrim in getting his estates back on condition that he leased a portion worth £300 a year to his Talbot brother-in-law. Orrery took care to keep such transactions at arm's length and, for example, he assured George Chivers (one of Talbot's clients) circuitously, via his secretary and Gilbert Talbot successively, that he would lobby for his restoration to his estate only on condition that Chivers then convey 400 acres to him.[54]

Sir Robert Talbot was legal counsel to the duke of York and one of four agents for Irish Catholics enjoying a quasi-official standing: this status was reflected in a 1666 order that they be paid a fee levied on lands restored to Catholics. Even though Robert was named as one of 36 and, later, 54, especially favoured Irish Catholics singled out by name, he never regained his estates. Robert Talbot had twice petitioned the English parliament in the 1650s for confirmation of his estate assigned in Connacht and this implicit acceptance of Cromwell's regime had been seized on (by, for instance, Orrery in his 1660 *Answer to a Scandalous Letter*) as a powerful argument against his restoration.[55] In April 1664, Richard begged Ormond's 'protection' for Robert and four other kinsmen who had served the royalist cause in the 1640s.[56] Two years later Orrery's nephew Richard Jones (later earl of Ranelagh) and Orrery importuned Arlington to have Sir Robert Talbot's lands given back to him. Orrery now insisted that Robert 'has a better title than any man of his religion in the kingdom.'[57] Ormond's failure to help Robert Talbot really rankled: here was a man who had raised a lone voice in his favour before the Confederate Catholic general assembly and suffered prison on his account. Even Clarendon grudgingly admitted that of all the Talbot brothers, Robert 'had less malice than most of the rest' and noted that Talbot's disenchantment with Ormond arose when he did not show them the 'friendship' they expected.[58]

The Talbots belatedly realised that Ormond looked out only for 'his own friends and relations' and 'the rest are to be left'. Sir Robert, professing a hitherto unsuspected zeal for Irish Catholics collectively, protested that through Ormond's contrivance 'an English interest is to be first settled in Ireland, and what is left is to be for us'.[59] Such disenchantment was to be found even among Ormond's MacCarthy in-laws and their followers. It was a MacCarthy protégé who pithily summed up the injustice of the acts as '*neart gan ceart*': brute power unconstrained by justice.[60] Ormond rebuked his nephew Cormac Mac Carthy for using 'opprobrious language against the English in this Kingdom' but the young Viscount Muskerry was unfazed and demanded of his uncle why the 'scum of Cromwell's Army' together with 'Adventurers that advanced their money against the king' should keep ill-gotten Irish lands. Muskerry's mother, Ormond's sister, also complained bitterly about the injustice of the land settlement.[61] *A Narrative of the Earl of Clarendon's Settlement and Sale of Ireland* (Louvain, 1668) reminded an ungrateful monarch and his lord chancellor of Irish dutifulness, though criticism of Ormond was as yet muted. Just eight years later, however, *The Unkinde Deserter* lambasted Ormond for his 'cunning artifices' in winning over individual Confederate Catholics, 'craft' in breaking their union, disobedience and treachery in handing over Dublin to the English parliament in 1647, and 'malice' to the Irish. Both pamphlets were penned by the exiled Bishop Nicholas French, though Ormond blamed Peter Talbot for writing them.[62]

Charles's 'wavering temper and open ear' demanded that his top officials attend him closely and quickly scotch the insinuations and projects of rival courtiers. Absent from court and uneasy about the Talbot-led 'Irish caball' undermining him at Whitehall, Ormond send over his brother-in-law Donagh MacCarthy (Robert Talbot's ally in the mid-1640s and now earl of Clancarty) in December 1663 to act on his behalf. That was not enough to ward off his detractors and Ormond had to come in person at the end of May 1664. His presence and authority together with Clarendon's support outweighed Arlington and Berkeley (earl of Falmouth since March 1664) who quickly realised that Ormond would now get his way on the Act of Explanation. They then advised Richard to desist from lobbying for the Irish: 'he had better look after his own interest than break his head in the contending for others'. Talbot ignored their advice.[63]

Back in Dublin, Lord Mount-Alexander had got his hands on letters revealing the fraud that Richard Talbot had perpetrated in the case of Allen of St Wolstan's. He laid this evidence before Lord Ossory (Ormond's eldest son and his deputy) and the privy council, demanding a reversal of the decree of the court of claims. At around this time Ormond suggested to the privy council that a clause be inserted in the Bill of Explanation to annul decrees of restitution obtained by bribery. Richard Talbot took this 'obnoxious clause' to be aimed at him in particular.[64] By late December 1664 he was, according to Clarendon's version of events, publicly threatening to kill the lord lieutenant. The threat was reported by Sir Robert Talbot to Clancarty who, in turn, passed it on to the king rather than to Ormond. Charles, 'with a very visible trouble in his countenance', next consulted Clarendon. The latter was sure Talbot 'had courage and wickedness enough' to carry through his threat. Charles was angered and York, who might be expected to stick up for his client, expressed equal indignation. Charles punished Talbot for his 'insolent presumption' by sending him to the Tower of London on 22 December. Apartments in the tower accommodated state prisoners of consequence in some comfort and the tower also did duty as menagerie, arsenal, mint and record office. The punishment was not as grave and irretrievable as might appear: courtiers like Buckingham and John Churchill would all be sent there only to make triumphant comebacks.[65]

Reading between the lines of Clarendon's account, it seems that Richard Talbot announced his intention to challenge Ormond to a duel and passed this on via Sir Robert and Clancarty who, in turn, notified his brother-in-law. On Christmas Eve Ormond confided to his son Ossory in Dublin that Talbot was publicly threatening his life to frighten him lest he frame a clause against Talbot in the Bill of Explanation. Clancarty then, likely on Ormond's advice, informed the king of the challenge while letting on that Ormond knew nothing of it. As a royal office holder it was beneath Ormond's dignity and a reflection on the king that he should be held to account by every aggrieved petitioner for decisions he had made in his master's name. As a nobleman, on the other hand, avoiding a challenge stained his honour. Having Clancarty pass on the threat directly to Charles sidestepped the dilemma because, however ambivalent the king was about duelling, he could be expected to forbid this particular duel and to sharply reprimand Talbot.

An account that probably originates with Talbot makes no mention of this or any challenge to a duel but claims a face-to-face quarrel precipitated Talbot's imprisonment. Ormond admitted Talbot at his house in Chelsea where both men stepped out on to a balcony. Talbot began bemoaning the land settlement. Ormond replied that Talbot merely 'affected popularity, and how came it about that he of all others should become so publick an Advocate?' Stung by this insult, Talbot hotly answered 'that it was not popularity he affected but the doing of Justice'. Ormond 'should have done that' and those he wronged must now 'right themselves'. 'He [Talbot] says he does not know well if he said more than this'. Ormond reddened with rage at Talbot's rebuke and broke off the exchange. Talbot cooled down quickly enough to anticipate that Ormond's next move would be to complain to the king. Talbot dashed to Somerset House where he confessed to Falmouth that he had 'some warm words' with Ormond. Shortly afterwards, Ormond entered the same room and begged the king to withdraw with him to an adjoining chamber where he breathlessly gave his version of what Talbot had said on the balcony and reiterated the threats to his life. He rhetorically asked if an official of a quarter-century's standing should have to 'pull off his doublet' to fight a duel with Dick Talbot. Charles was duly 'incensed'.[66]

Each of the competing accounts contains evasion and vagueness but few outright contradictions. Both events happened: the challenge to a duel/death threats and the heated interview. But which came first and which was the proximate offence that enraged Charles? The account of the argument and its aftermath mentions 'loose discourses and menaces' directed against Ormond and so this face-to-face meeting at Chelsea was probably the precipitating event. To sum up: Talbot's challenge to a duel, or words that could be so construed, was passed on to the king who did not, one must assume, respond sharply enough for Ormond's liking. Ormond then invited or admitted Talbot to his home with the apparent intention of discussing and composing their differences. A second possibility is that Ormond set up the interview to goad Talbot into angry expostulations and thus give grounds for a renewed complaint to the king. The outcome may have been less than Ormond hoped for but it hushed Talbot at a delicate juncture when the Act of Explanation was to be passed. Next day at a meeting of the Committee of Foreign Affairs Clarendon called for Talbot's banishment. However, York, Buckingham and John Maitland Duke of Lauderdale (the long-term supremo in Scotland) opposed this 'so hotly' that Charles postponed a decision and in the meantime sent Richard to the Tower while Sir Robert and Friar Thomas were incarcerated in the Fleet. Falmouth began interceding for Talbot right away. He pleaded that York's reputation and prestige was dented by allowing a 'servant of so near relation' to be locked up for what were just 'hasty and unadvised words'. Tempers cooled after a few weeks. After 'owning the words', or admitting to uttering the threats against Ormond, Friar Thomas became the designated scapegoat and was duly banished from all Charles's dominions.[67] Talbot was released late in January 1665, whereupon he was rusticated for a short time.

Anglo-Dutch trade and maritime rivalry erupted into three full-scale wars, the first waged by the Commonwealth in the 1650s and the second in 1665–7. This latter war gradually escalated, on both sides, from privateering under flags of convenience to open raids on merchant shipping. In April 1665 York as lord high admiral was directed by his brother to 'assert our right and dominion in the narrow seas'.[68] At the end of May York led an English war fleet of over 100 set sail, 'the bravest fleet of Christendom', against an equally huge Dutch fleet prowling near the Dogger Bank. After two days of tacking and manoeuvring the two fleets passed each other in line of battle on opposite tacks at around four o'clock on the morning of 3 June off Lowestoft. The line of battle was a new tactic, hardly more than two decades old, designed to let broadside cannon pound enemy ships. Both sides, especially the Dutch, handled the line clumsily and after a second ragged pass Lowestoft disintegrated into individual dogfights, the most notable being fought between the opposing flagships York's *Charles*, and Admiral Von Obdam's *Eendracht*: 'The tall Batavian in a vast ship rides,/bearing an army in her hollow sides,/Yet not inclin'd the English ship to board,/More on his guns relies than on his sword/…'.[69] York stood on the quarterdeck, surrounded by his entourage and by gentlemen volunteers. They were there to beat off boarding parties and otherwise to stand fast and serve as an example of coolness under fire. In the absence of evidence to the contrary one must assume that Richard Talbot was there alongside

Falmouth.[70] Cavalry combat was quick and mobile: dash, cut, thrust, shoot, flee or follow, and a man's own ferocity and prowess counted for much. Standing on the butcher's floor of the quarterdeck within a stone's throw of the *Eendracht* as she swept the decks with shot called for a different species of courage, a stoic and calm impassivity. Sometime between noon and two in the afternoon a single 'great shot' knocked down three gentlemen standing 'close by' York like ninepins. The ball took off the head of Richard Boyle (Orrery's nephew and son of the Earl of Burlington) before killing Cormac MacCarthy and Falmouth, whose blood and brains spattered and jellied over York: 'His shatter'd Head the fearless Duke distains/ And gave the last-first proof that he had brains'.[71] Talbot lost a patron on the *Charles* but one whose usefulness was expiring because Falmouth was about to defect from the Arlington–William Coventry axis and realign with Clarendon.[72] At around three o'clock a chance shot touched the *Eendracht*'s powder magazine and she blew up in an instant. The leaderless Dutch faltered and fled westward that night. They had lost eight ships sunk and another eight destroyed beyond repair, whereas York lost just one vessel. Lowestoft was one of the biggest naval battles of all time and yet it proved strategically indecisive because the duke did not seize the chance to destroy Dutch fleet while it was beaten, scattered and vulnerable.

York was back in London as bubonic plague began to break out. We know that Talbot accompanied the duke and duchess at the beginning of August 1665 as they fled to York to outrun the pestilence.[73] Among the party was Frances Jennings, a maid-of-honour to the duchess. The French ambassador appreciatively lauded the striking blonde as 'one of the finest girls in England', 'small but with a fine figure, brilliant keen eyes [and] the whitest and smooth-est skin I ever saw'. The ambassador was watchful because Hugues de Lionne, secretary for foreign affairs, had sent his gauche teenaged son to the English court for three months in 1665 to lose his shyness and make a man of the world [*honnête homme*] of him. The youth soon fancied himself in love with Frances,but she had the good sense 'not to dispose of her heart until she gave her hand'. The youth switched his attentions to Catherine Boynton, another maid-of-honour, when Jennings would not permit him to kiss her hands.[74] Harry Jermyn and Dick Talbot also vied for Frances' affections. Talbot had a clear field when Jermyn was laid low with a fever after he overtaxed himself in a wager that he could ride twenty miles in an hour: we learn nothing of the horse's condition. Talbot was usually the one to take Fanny's hand as she got in and out of the coach and she talked more readily to him than to anyone else in the company. Thus encouraged, Dick screwed up his nerve to the point of renewing his declarations of undying love and fidelity but as luck would have it another member of the company entered the chamber and read out a new poem by Rochester, the notorious debauchee and satirist. Rochester expressed pity for 'Little David' (the diminutive Jermyn) having to contend with 'Goliath' (Talbot). Hearing Fanny sigh for 'Poor little David', Talbot turned on his heels and swore to forget all about this 'giddy girl'.[75] The younger George Hamilton, brother of Elizabeth Hamilton, swooped and snatched the prize from both Jermyn and Talbot.

Talbot returned to Dublin where there was still much work to be done. Five commissioners were appointed to apply the provisions of the Act of Explanation 'to particular cases' and they had to be either nobbled or neutralised.[76] The Act was a crushing disappointment for Irish landowners, who clawed back no more than a third of the land they had lost. The Talbots did rather better than most.[77] Richard secured a lease on Carton and – as we saw – gained much land besides. Garrett got lands at Haggardstown, Co. Louth. Robert, the senior member of the family, had not recovered Castlesallagh, Co. Wicklow by the time of his death in 1670, but the Act of Explanation of 1665 contained a proviso that his son and heir William be restored to possession 'fully and beneficially'.[78] William was serving as secretary to his cousin Charles Calvert, governor of Maryland at the time of Sir Robert's death in October 1670, but was recalled by 'uncle Dick' who now assumed a paternal role. Eventually, Richard acquired the Co. Wicklow estates for himself and installed William in Carton. He also fixed William up with a plum appointment as manager of York's Irish estates from which he drew a generous salary of £500 per annum and levied 'extravagant' charges.[79] Robert's widow was, however, left in a 'bad condition' and the Talbots (or so the Calverts believed) neglected her.[80]

Richard Talbot's name is closely associated with Carton: for example, nearly all of the recurrences of his name in the outlawry lists denote him as being 'of Cartown'.[81] Yet, while in Ireland, he mostly lived elsewhere. He would rent Luttrellstown Castle, and, during the glory days of his viceroyalty, abide in Dublin Castle or in the viceregal summer residence at Chapelizod. There are occasional references to his family retiring to a country house at 'Talbotstown', which Sergeant and Petrie assume to have been a synonym for Carton.[82] But by far his biggest contiguous estate was the 9,650 acres he acquired around Hollywood and Donard in the barony of Talbotstown, Co. Wicklow. From this landholding derived his titles, Baron of *Talbotstown* and Viscount Baltinglass. It is far more likely that the house in question was in or near the townland of that name in Co. Wicklow. William, Robert's son, probably lived full time at Carton and was apparently 'seized in fee' of the property at least until 1683, the year of his marriage, when he made provision from the estate for his new bride. Tyrconnell acquired Carton some time later, subject to a £10 per annum 'chiefry' or rent owing to the earl of Kildare: post-war official documents clearly indicate that he was the owner. Either William or Richard transformed the 'ruined and decayed' stone house noted in the civil survey into 'a very fine house with all manner of convenient offices and gardens'.[83] The mansion, as depicted by William Van der Hagen c.1720 (by which time it was three decades out of Talbot possession) was one of the largest in the Pale, done in classical style, flanked by two separate single-storey blocks of out-offices and surrounded by extensive geometrically formal gardens, paths and plantations.[84]

Meanwhile, Ormond did his best to dissuade dispossessed landowners from dealings with Talbot who flitted, as always, between Dublin and London: we have a glimpse of him as a bystander when the celebrated healer Valentine 'the stroker' Greatrakes attempted a 'dispossession' of a young woman at York house in 1666.[85] Ormond's influence and his capacity to harm Talbot was fading, in part because of Clarendon's fall in 1667. The ageing and cantankerous chancellor had simultaneously neglected and tried to monopolise state business. He was an obvious scapegoat, if not for plague and fire (everyone knew the latter catastrophe was papist work) then for a ruinously expensive and inglorious Dutch war. Spitefully, Charles encouraged Clarendon's enemies to impeach him on treason charges. The not-so-merry monarch threatened that Buckingham, Clarendon's deadliest enemy, would preside over a packed jury and this threat frightened the chancellor into fleeing abroad for his life.[86] The reasons for King Charles's cold anger remain unclear but the last straw seems to have been when Clarendon thwarted his lustful designs on Frances Stuart because (or so Charles half believed) a fertile bride and legitimate royal children would have displaced the chancellor's grandchildren, York's heirs, from the succession.

The heave against Clarendon must have put Richard Talbot in an awkward position because his patron York stood by his father-in-law as long as he possibly could and even dismissed prominent members of his household, William Coventry and Henry Brouncker, who took sides against the lord chancellor. After all, Richard was also a client of Arlington, one of those rising young men orchestrating the heave from behind the scenes. Meanwhile, Peter Talbot had kept up his contacts with Buckingham and never lost hope that he would be a key ally in securing 'liberty of conscience'. Peter would dedicate his 1670 *Treatise of Religion and Government* to Buckingham and in it he affirmed that Roman Catholicism was 'more favourable to kings' than Protestantism which was a 'monstrous shee-conspiracy' to foist Anne Boleyn's daughter on the English people.[87]

Much as the chancellor had before him, the serious and hard-working Arlington dominated English politics over the next five years, certainly more than any other member of the so-called 'cabal' (Arlington, Thomas Lord Clifford, Buckingham, Lord Ashley (Anthony Cooper), and Lauderdale), which was in reality an incoherent and unco-ordinated grouping of men holding strong and usually opposed opinions and prejudices. All they shared was a distaste for Anglican intolerance of Catholics or dissenters, as their personal feelings lay. Buckingham, a 'debauched maverick', basked in the apparent favour of his king but Charles knew full well that he was as useless in power as he was dangerous in opposition, and so any offices he gave 'that vile man' (Ormond's characterisation) were ornamental rather than ministerial. Buckingham was so erratic, violent and dissolute that one must conclude Charles kept him on only as a check on Arlington's ambitions.[88] Of the cabal only Clifford and Arlington, one a papist and the other a deathbed convert, would be privy to the innermost purpose of Charles's 'grand design'.

In January 1669 Charles, with tears in his eyes, confessed to his brother James (a secret convert to Catholicism since the previous year), Clifford, Arlington and Lord Arundell of Wardour that he was convinced of the truth of Roman Catholicism. Then, James recalled, those at the meeting decided to offer Louis XIV an offensive and defensive alliance. For the next one and a half centuries enmity to France would so be ingrained in English foreign policy and national identity that for Charles to think that he and his cousin Louis XIV were natural allies now seems bizarre. The Treaty of Dover of 1670 committed England to allying with France and declaring war on the United Provinces. By a secret codicil to the treaty unknown to most of the cabal, Charles promised to declare his conversion openly, 'as soon as the welfare of his kingdom will permit'.[89] The king laboured under no illusion that a Third Dutch War would be popular but he gambled that generous French subsidies would fund a speedy military conquest and so mute criticism at home.

Clarendon's fall was not necessarily fatal to Ormond who had already been distancing himself from a fading star, as he had from his patron the earl of Strafford in 1640–1. Proof of this distancing can be seen in the fact that Ossory, a close personal and political friend of Arlington, voted against the beleaguered chancellor. The king soothingly reassured Ormond that the chancellor's fall has not 'in the least diminished the value and kindness I ever had for you'.[90] But all the while, Ormond's enemies were blackening his name. Typical of these smears is the report passed on by Magliotti that Ormond had shown little skill as a governor or bravery as a soldier but was guilty of 'infinite venality'. Ossory begged his father to hasten over to Whitehall, 'look the court in the face' and ask Charles outright 'to tell him of his faults'.[91] When Ormond came to court in May 1668 he met a frosty reception and failed to find what specific complaints Charles had to lay against him.

What were Ormond's 'faults'? James McGuire rejected the traditional view that Ormond fell because his main ally had fallen and the pack of enemies snapping at his heels had grown too noisy to be ignored. Charles, McGuire insisted, was not a passive nullity who bent his ears to those who shouted loudest. He chose to have Ormond removed, knowing he would not be a pliable enough tool of his new pro-papist and pro-French policy. Williamson, for one, suspected that Charles dismissed Ormond 'for reasons arising out of his own affairs', yet the strength of the factional alignment against Ormond may, at the very least, have suggested to Charles that his dismissal was now feasible. [92] Political and factional rivals were, then, important as a proximate cause of Ormond's fall and Talbot had a key role to play in co-ordinating their attack on his 'professed mortal enemy'. [93]

Talbot was a 'connector' who was on hand to facilitate a diverse coalition of Ormond's rivals in common action. Buckingham was one such rival. Why this was so need not detain us: perhaps, as Ormond's follower Robert Southwell claims, he would pull down any man 'that did but look great'. [94] During debates in the Commons on Clarendon's dismissal, an MP client of Buckingham's demanded an enquiry into allegations that Ormond had accepted hefty bribes in connection with the Irish land settlement. [95] This smear had Talbot's fingerprints all over it as we know that he was at this very time gathering or fabricating evidence of Ormond's bribe-taking. Peter Talbot's long-standing connections with Buckingham and Barbara Palmer gave Richard access to this circle. Talbot later boasted of his closeness to Buckingham at this time, as Robert Southwell recounted:

> Yett here lett me observe what I was once told by the Earl of Tyrconnell who still spoke freely of all men and things, and more loudly and openly than I think ever courtier did. He was one who ever stood at defiance with Ormond. But he told me, that when Buckingham and he would often sport together in their success, and to see how they had beaten him downe, Buckingham would yet wonder at Ormond's patience and conduct under it.

The other two who beat Ormond down, Orrery and Ranelagh, were also allies of Talbot's. Orrery may simply have been jealous of Ormond's pre-eminence: 'a boundless ambition has nothing, if not all'. For whatever reason, from the mid 1660s Orrery began carping about the lord lieutenant's financial incompetence and malfeasance: one of his letters of complaint ran to eight sheets. [96] Dick Talbot's co-operation with Orrery was always equivocal and was strained by now, but his friendship with Orrery's nephew, Richard Jones 3rd Viscount Ranelagh was just warming up. Writing in 1671 two years after Ormond's dismissal, Ranelagh professed that Talbot 'is one to whom I am as much obliged as I can be to any man'. [97] This smooth-talking, clever and crooked young libertine was chancellor of the Irish exchequer from 1668 to 1674. He and Talbot had probably formed their 'strict friendship' by now: Talbot would lobby for Ranelagh to, for instance, secure the farm of the Irish revenue in return for which Ranelagh allegedly paid Talbot a £4,000 bribe and bestowed pensions on Talbot's friends.[98]

The £4,000 payment was not actually a bribe but the king's bounty or dowry for Talbot's bride which Charles ordered to be paid out of Irish revenues. Disappointed in Elizabeth Hamilton and Frances Jennings, Talbot would be third time lucky in love or, at any rate, matrimony. Anthony Hamilton, that pitiless chronicler of female form and foibles, describes Catherine Boynton maid-in-waiting to Queen Catherine, thus:

> Her [Boynton's] figure was slender and delicate, to which a good complexion and large impassive eyes gave at a distance an appearance of beauty. This vanished on closer inspection: she affected to lisp, languish and have two or three fainting-fits a day. The first time Talbot cast his eyes on her she was seized with one of these fits. He was told she swooned on his account. He believed it.

As well as being a decorative adornment to the court, the maid of honour (Queen Catherine and the Duchess of York had about a dozen such satellites between them) waited in the presence and privy chambers or withdrawing rooms to help entertain ladies calling on her mistress or kept her company as required. Often the maid of honour was a pretty teenage daughter of a down-at-heel royalist who hoped to attract a husband in a year or two. The aristocratic Whitehall rake might amuse himself with a maid of honour but would be unlikely to marry one, though a poorer man might if the deal was sweetened by the customary parting royal bounty which was, however, normally far smaller than Boynton's. The maid of honour could then free up her place for a replacement, sometimes a younger sister.

Frances Jennings and Catherine Boynton both fit this description, though Catherine took longer than was considered seemly to land a husband. Her father, Matthew Boynton of Barmston in Yorkshire's East Riding, sided with parliament in the English Civil War but defected to the royalists in 1648 while governor of Scarborough Castle. Colonel Boynton was slain three years later during the Worcester campaign, leaving six daughters.[99] The daughter of a baronet's deceased younger son, Boynton was no wealthy heiress. One court satire, a coarse lampoon dripping with hatred and disgust for female physicality, linked her and the notorious Jane Middleton, to the Archbishop of Canterbury Gilbert Sheldon, abusing him 'as very a wencher as can be'.[100] Some maids of honour fell victim to the sexual double standard of the day. One such

unfortunate was Hellene Warmestry on whom William Lord Taaffe fathered
a child: pressed by Queen Catherine, he denied his offspring and scathingly
enquired why 'he should be given the honour more than anyone else'.[101]
Others, like Winifred Wells or Arabella Churchill (daughter of the Winston
Churchill who served as one of the members of the court of claims in Dublin)
were preyed on by one or other of the Stuart brothers. Most kept their reputa-
tions, though another satirist twisted such virtue into hypocritical vice:
'Boynton, Price and all the rest./Take heed of leap-frog, though in jest,/Obey
your reverend Mother,/Who warns you all/To none to fall/But Caesar
[Charles] and his brother'. Satirists routinely blasted the other women at
court as sluts and harlots and their fulminations, whether against maids of
honour or archbishops, need to be treated sceptically in the absence of
corroboration. Most of the satirists were themselves hangers-on at court in
some capacity or other and wrote from sexual and social envy rather than from
any wish to improve manners and morals.

Richard and Catherine married in 1669 and the marriage lasted until her
death a decade later, during which time she bore him two daughters, Catherine
and Charlotte. John Michael Wright portrayed the girls in the year their mother
died. Catherine, who cannot have been more than nine years of age, is depicted
in adult hairstyle and clothing: a plain grey-blue dress with a split bodice, a
showy red underskirt, and a black shawl hanging on one shoulder as a token
gesture to mourning dress for her mother. She plucks a petal from an apron held
by her infant sister whose reddish-blond curls are set off by a black silk veil.
Catherine never reached the adulthood anticipated by her portrait.[102] Dick
Talbot was unfaithful to his wife, if one accepts the admittedly questionable
evidence of a scurrilous satire that claims 'Goliath' was one of the many 'roaring
roist'rers of Whitehall' who slept with Lucy Brydges, wife of Adam Loftus of
Rathfarnham, Co. Dublin, pilloried by Rochester as 'Cornus', the cuckold.[103]

The timing of the provision of Peter Talbot as archbishop of Dublin
(January 1669), Oliver Plunkett as archbishop of Armagh (July 1669) and
other bishops together with the fact that they were allowed reside in Ireland
suggest that this was the first instalment of Charles's pro-Catholic pro-
gramme. Charles had let it be known in Rome that he would let no one other
than Peter Talbot reside in Dublin as archbishop.[104] Ormond's replacement,
John, Baron Robartes, was linked with Clifford and Arlington. All in all, the
context for Catholic political interests in Ireland was unusually favourable.
Robartes did not arrive in Dublin until September 1669 and then lasted only
seven months during which time he tried to tighten up the government
finances and stamp his authority on the army but raised such a storm of
protest that he asked to be recalled.

Peter was consecrated in Antwerp in May 1669 and announced he would hasten to London to lobby Charles's ministers against Peter Walsh and his 'iniquities' and proceed from there to his archdiocese.[105] Soon after his arrival in Dublin, Peter Talbot drafted a master plan to undo the land settlement, start to Catholicise the army, and infiltrate Catholics into the corporations, the magistracy and onto the judicial bench. This would serve as a blueprint for Richard's plans fifteen years later.[106] The confident planning reflected Peter's insider knowledge about the secret Treaty of Dover: twenty years later, the Church of Ireland cleric William King claimed to have seen a paper dated 1 July 1670 among Richard Talbot's papers that revealed a 'design' between Charles and Louis to 'Establish Popery in England by a Toleration, to suppress the Insolency of the Dutch, and to maintain a strict Alliance between the French King and the King of England'.[107] One can speak of both Talbots collectively since they worked to the same plan and Peter lived at his brother's home at Luttrellstown within three miles of Dublin. Even with a tail wind from Whitehall at their backs, Richard and Peter needed to move warily, disarm existing opponents, avoid making too many new ones, and keep close watch on their friends. Completely ignoring the need for stealth, Peter proved gratuitously irascible in his dealings with the new lord lieutenant and with his fellow-archbishop. On the face of it, John Berkeley of Stratton, who disembarked in Dublin in April 1670, seemed to be everything the Talbots might have hoped for in a governor. A kinsman of the late Falmouth, he disliked Ormond, was married to a Catholic and his secretary, Ellis Leighton, was a Catholic convert who hoped his fellow papists would win toleration if only 'they will be prudent'.[108] However, Peter had expected his ally Buckingham to be named for Dublin Castle and made no attempt to hide how disgusted he was at Berkeley's appointment. For his part, Berkeley tried as much as he could to have 'nothing to do' with Talbot, 'neither for nor against him'. Peter Talbot quickly set about punishing those Catholic clergymen who had not retracted their subscription to the remonstrance and he abused Peter Walsh the 'wrangling friar' and instigator of the remonstrance in print. Berkeley gave Peter free rein against the remonstrant clergy, despite Ormond's protests and Arlington's warnings. Even so, Berkeley's support was not wholehearted enough for Peter who threatened to have Buckingham supplant him, complained of the lord lieutenant to his contacts at Whitehall and even insulted him to his face: having secured Barbara Palmer's backing for his 'projects' he rounded on Berkeley 'in a great huff' asking if he 'was the King's or the Duke of *Ormond's* Lieutenant'?[109]

Peter's falling-out with Archbishop Oliver Plunkett of Armagh was just as gratuitous and imprudent. In 1670 Plunkett convened a national synod (surely a grandiloquent title for a handful of bishops meeting in a private house near

Bridge Street) to agree on a prayerful protestation of allegiance to the king and so finally bring the remonstrance controversy to an end. The synod generated fresh wrangles as Plunkett and Talbot disputed which of them was entitled to preside as primate of Ireland. The bishops let Archbishop Plunkett preside, agreed to refer the thorny question of primacy to the Holy See, and picked Sir Nicholas Plunkett as bearer of their address to the king. Plunkett was a suitable spokesman, being a veteran Confederate Catholic parliamentarian and negotiator who had also argued against the Act of Settlement before the king in the early 1660s. Talbot, however, demanded that he himself should be the one deputed because Whitehall had authorised him to oversee the Irish Catholic clergy in civil matters of this kind. Arlington had, claimed Peter, passed on such a request by a third party but did not supply authorisation in writing. The archbishop of Armagh now coolly demanded written proof. His bluff called, Talbot backed down.[110]

A humiliated Talbot pursued a vendetta against Plunkett. Brenan of Waterford, a neutral observer, recognised that they were, 'both one and the other, touchy and of a hot disposition', but cast most of the blame on Talbot. One would have to agree with Brenan. Peter may have spread slanderous reports that Plunkett kept a mistress, though he solemnly assured the archbishop that he was not behind the rumours. He patronisingly attributed what he saw as Plunkett's mistakes to 'imprudence' (itself a highly damaging accusation to send to Brussels or Rome) rather than 'bad intention.' To Rome he loudly denounced calumnies that Plunkett 'greatly inclines to Protestantism' while still passing them on: thus he could at once pose as Plunkett's defender while slyly casting doubt on his orthodoxy.[111] In November 1672 Bishop O'Molony of Killaloe, Richard Talbot and Colonel John Fitzpatrick (a one-time follower of Ormond and a rival Catholic lobbyist) brokered a reconciliation that culminated when Peter, together with his brothers and nephews, came to dine with the archbishop of Armagh. Uneasy peace lasted for the few months more until Peter had to flee Ireland in June 1673. But that is to get ahead of the story.

Not only were the Talbots distracted by feuds but the 'Orrereyan' party comprising Orrery himself, Ranelagh, and the earl of Carlingford (none other than Theobald Taafe the duellist seconded by Talbot in 1658) began to fall apart, mainly because of the president of Munster's renewed hostility to Catholics. [112] Orrery pulled down new convents in Limerick and Waterford during the summer of 1670 and discovered evidence of a papist plot by an anonymously delivered and suitably seditious letter.[113] Orrery had not grasped the seismic reorientation of the Cabal ministry and two years later he was shocked when Arlington passed on the king's warning to desist from persecuting Catholics in his presidency. Orrery and Richard Talbot, in particular, were pulled apart by the contestants in the political struggle. Clifford and Arlington showed Talbot bundles of intercepted letters from Orrery to Lord Lieutenant Berkeley in which Orrery heaped abuse on Talbot and on the Papists. In April 1672, Ormond claimed to Burlington (the senior member of the Boyle family) that he had picked up the charred remains of a letter from Peter Talbot to Buckingham while poking in the fireplace of the king's bedchamber: what business had he poking about? The supposed letter cast doubt on Orrery's loyalty to the king.[114] Talbot and Carlingford also grew estranged after the latter described Barbara Palmer as a 'whore' and Talbot ungallantly passed on the remark to the lady herself.

Catholics could now practise law and sit as justices of the peace, a service which, though unpaid and burdensome, conferred and confirmed local status. Significant numbers of Catholics (enough to perturb most Protestants in Ireland at any rate) could now live, trade and vote in corporate towns. Boroughs returned just under four-fifths of all members of the Commons and so an ongoing trickle of potential Catholic voters might ultimately threaten the Protestant stranglehold of parliament. Yet a more fundamental improvement demanded that the land settlement be overturned. The Cromwellian confiscations had slashed the proportion of profitable land owned by Catholics from 69 per cent to perhaps less than 10 per cent and by the late 1660s Catholics had clawed back to only 30 per cent of all profitable land. Ownership was concentrated in fewer hands, and so whereas there had been 6,758 Catholic landowners in 1641, there were only 1,353 by the late 1660s.[115]

In January 1671 Talbot was in London as 'general agent of the Roman Catholics of Ireland' endowed 'with full power' to prevail on the king that they might 'return into their lands and possessions'.[116] In February Peter convened a meeting of prominent Catholics to arrange financial backing for his brother's mission.

While Richard was in London, six 'bold and wicked' horsemen tried to assassinate Ormond while he was walking to Clarendon House but inflicted only a slight sword cut. Ormond blamed the notorious fanatic Colonel Thomas Blood, but believed that Buckingham had put Blood up to it. It would have suited Talbot every bit as much as Buckingham to have Ormond put out of the way because the latter was nominated as one of the thirteen privy counsellors to hear Talbot's petition and report to the king. Ormond later boasted that when the 'whole settlement was brought into danger' by Talbot he stood alone on the English privy council in defending 'the English interest.'[117] Ormond cast doubt on Talbot's standing and authority to speak for such a 'vast number' of Irish Catholics. He had a point. Scrutiny of the list of fifty petitioners does show that they were not nationally representative: nearly all of them hailed from north Leinster and the adjacent part of Connacht and belonged mostly to Old English (there were exceptions like James Ferral, Thomas Naghton, William Fallon, and Conly Geoghegan) and Talbot-connected families.[118] With the single exception of Edmund Butler Earl of Mountgarret, Talbot had not tapped other Catholic regional interests like those of the Butlers in Co. Kilkenny and south Co. Tipperary, the MacCarthys in Co. Cork or of the Clanricard Burkes in Co. Galway.

The privy counsellors present overrode Ormond's quibbles (like Bucking-ham, most of them were more interested in discrediting Ormond than helping Talbot) but the English attorney-general, Sir Heneage Finch, landed a more telling blow. He pointed out that some of the subscribers had already been restored in whole or in part: William Viscount Dungan, Matthew Plunkett, Richard Nugent Earl of Westmeath, Theobald Dillon and Sir Nicholas Plunkett, while others on the list, like Gilbert Talbot, never owned estates in Ireland.[119] Finch pleaded it was in the public interest to keep even an imperfect settlement intact or risk Ireland forever being 'always settling and never settled'.[120]

> Here Colonel Talbot began to interrupt the Attorney, and said his memory was short, and therefore desired to answer by parts. The King and Council seemed not to be pleased with the interruption but the Attorney desired he might be inter-rupted; for (he said) he came not as an advocate to plead a cause but as a servant to his Majesty to give his observations and opinion upon the whole. Whereas if he should fall into any mistake, he would take it as a favour from Colonel Talbot to rectify him in it. [121]

In looking at specific cases, Finch confirmed that Ormond's secretary Sir George Lane had been granted part of Philip Hore's estate but had acquired this with Talbot's connivance. Richard Talbot was standing behind the king's chair and burst out: 'I deny that!' Finch calmly replied: 'have a little patience Mr Talbot, you yourself shall prove it' and flourished an agreement written in Talbot's hand and signed by the colonel and Sir Robert as counsel to the duke of York: 'At this all laughed indeed, and so did the colonel for company, swearing out that he had never minded such impertinent [irrelevant] things.'

Despite being publicly caught out in an artless lie, Richard was unabashed and even ebullient when he wrote to Peter: 'I have forgot the part of a courtier as to fear offending any man in power in speaking the truth' and trumpeted that he would risk 'the frowns of the powerful' to remedy the 'ruin of my country, relations and friends' and make the king and his ministers 'very sensible' of the land settlement's iniquities. Talbot won this round. Charles chose to appoint another smaller committee to report if the Irish land settlement really was in accordance with his declaration of 1660. The membership of this committee was sympathetic to Talbot and included Buckingham, Anglesey, Ashley (who had spoken out in Talbot's defence against Ormond) Denzil Baron Holles, Lauderdale and Thomas Trevor. Anglesey's report of June 1671 confirmed, to Ormond's dismay, that 'the ends which your majesty proposed to yourself by your declaration have not been accomplished'.[122] The following month Richard disembarked in Dublin where he soon opened another small crack in the paper wall against Papists by obtaining command of a cavalry troop on the Irish list. He was the first, and last for quite a few years.[123]

Talbot was frantically shuttling between London and Dublin (in the twenty-eight months from December 1670 to March 1673 he made four round trips) trying to hold his design together, rein in Peter, and lobby to have Berkeley dismissed. Not content with haunting the Stone Gallery, Talbot had to be on hand in Ireland often enough to encourage his supporters in facing down the hostility of Protestants amongst whom Talbot's petition had made 'no small noise' in Ireland. Colonel Henry Ingoldsby, a diehard republican even in the last months of the Commonwealth, quarrelled about the petition with Thomas Cusack, one of Dick Talbot's many nephews. The pair fought a duel in which Cusack broke his sword in closing with the colonel but still managed to overpower him. He spared Ingoldsby, showing what would turn out to be impolitic mercifulness.[124]

Berkeley was dismissed in January 1672. This was yet another confirmation that the viceroyalty, however honourable and lucrative, was a 'hazardous' posting as it entailed absence from the political arena in London.[125] Talbot had less success lobbying for a biddable successor. 'How he came to be raised to this post', Arthur Capel Earl of Essex professed he 'could never understand'. Charles may have chosen a man known to dislike papists as a way to deflect criticism from his pro-French and pro-toleration policies. On the other hand Talbot may have been speaking the truth when he claimed that York blocked the first choice, George Savile Viscount Halifax, as being too 'stiff against Popery'.[126]

In September 1672 Peter Talbot, relentlessly harrying the Remonstrants, excommunicated John Byrne, parish priest of Kilcock, and even sent five neighbouring parish priests to 'excommunicate all the parish' for daring to back their pastor. Peter prevailed upon his nephew William Dungan, a recently appointed justice of the peace, to frighten Byrne by committing him in February 1673 to Naas gaol and clapping him in irons. Too late, the blundering pair realised that they had presented Ingoldsby with a tailor-made cause célèbre. A public trial at the next assizes would serve to expose how common law process had been scandalously abused to enforce the illegal claims of a popish cleric purporting to exercise papal jurisdiction.[127]

Yet did it really matter if Peter was quarrelsome or Richard careless? Their design was a small cog in the wheel of Charles's grand design which faltered for weightier reasons altogether. Charles issued a Declaration of Indulgence in March 1672 as part of his preparations for war with the Dutch: he did so reluctantly, urged by all his chief advisers. They each pressed him for different reasons. Arlington and Lauderdale saw it as a security measure in advance of war, Buckingham and Ashley saw in it toleration for dissenters while Clifford and York hoped it would be a first step towards removing penalties against Catholics.[128]

> The coll [Richard Talbot] was in Ireland when the Declaration came forth, but coming [to London] a fortnight afterwards Clifford told him with all the joy imaginable that now a fair step was made & c, but he frankly told him he was so far from rejoicing thereat that he feared it would turn to the ruine of them all.[129]

Talbot was not alone in judging the Declaration as 'too furious': a French diplomat likewise deplored York's 'obstinate and over-hasty enthusiasm'.[130] The Declaration would, as Talbot presciently feared, set back the Catholic cause.

All might have been well for the design if Charles and Louis had won a quick victory over the Dutch. War began with what seemed irresistibly strong French armies pushing down the Maas and the Rhine in May while an Anglo-French fleet was expected to disembark an expeditionary force on the coast of Holland. Master of three of the seven provinces, Louis peremptorily rejected Dutch offers of peace and territorial concessions. He wanted to dismember that upstart little republic. With their backs to the sea, the Dutch led by William of Orange flooded the polders and by August 1672 the French advance had bogged down. A year later, Louis would have to give up his territorial gains in the United Provinces and confront a growing number of enemies on other fronts.[131]

Of course the Dutch could not have stood with their backs to the sea if an Anglo-French fleet had, as planned, decanted an expeditionary force on their shores. Talbot himself fought in the naval battle that doomed this plan. De Ruiter failed to press home a successful attack before the components of the Anglo-French fleet led by York successfully massed. The Dutch admiral now pulled back from the Dover road to home waters. The English ships, carrying

5,000 troops for the descent, drew more water than their Dutch counterparts and so could not pursue them on to the sandbanks near the coast. Thereupon, York's fleet turned back and dropped anchor at Southwold or Solebay on the Suffolk coast, about ninety miles north-east of the Thames, where the fleet took on water and stores and many volunteers went ashore 'to refresh themselves'. Sailing through the night De Ruiter almost achieved total surprise in the pre-dawn hours of Tuesday 28 May; but the wind slackened before he had quite reached the Anglo-French fleet. Startled, the French cut anchor cables and moved in one direction, the English in another and De Ruiter was able to concentrate his attack on the latter. York had time to improvise a line of battle, though with 'difficulty enough', by seven o'clock in the morning.[132] What followed until ten that night was, admitted De Ruiter, 'the hardest battle' he ever fought.[133] York's flagship *Prince* stood windward of her own division and faced heavy gunfire unaided. With the captain killed and mainmast shot down, York shifted to the *St Michael* and raised his standard there.[134] The *Royal Katherine*, a second-rate warship 'newly come' from the shipyard with a novice crew, served as one of the 'seconds' screening the stricken *Prince*. Talbot served on board *Royal Katherine* as a volunteer, having scrambled on board just in time for the battle: an eyewitness had seen him dashing on a borrowed mount from nearby Harwich towards the anchorage early the morning before.[135] Such volunteering was the height of fashion and 'it was looked upon, among nobility and gentry, as a blemish not to attend the Duke of York aboard the fleet'.[136]

Two Dutch fire-ships were 'clapped' onto the *Royal Katherine*: fire-ships were so vital because, while cannon could do terrible damage to human beings, it was rare for even a heavy 32-pound ball to hole a properly braced and reinforced wooden hull and rarer still to do so under the water line.[137] The crewmen of the *Royal Katherine* promptly struck their ensign. The Dutch boarded, took the captain, lieutenant and 'several others' (including Talbot and Sir John Chichely Master of the Ordnance) off the ship, put the rest of the crew 'under hatches', and left a skeleton crew to set the *Royal Katherine* and its crew ablaze.[138] In a dramatic turnabout, a French ship cut the cables of the fire ship whereupon the captured crew broke out of the *Royal Katherine*'s hatches, overpowered the skeleton crew and regained control of their ship. Next morning she sailed into Sheerness 'in a very shattered condition'.[139] The captain of the *Royal Katherine* was imprisoned at Rotterdam and released in a prisoner exchange over a month later: so, one assumes, were the other prisoners taken on the ship, though the Dutch sources are silent on this. The silence reminds us that Talbot was not considered a very significant personage, yet.[140]

Sporadic fighting continued throughout Wednesday and Thursday as York tried to collect his ships. Counting vessels and casualties, the Anglo-French fleet had the best of it, losing just the *Royal James*, which blew up when two fire-ships were placed on her. Yet dispassionate observers could conclude that the Dutch 'have gained some advantage' in thwarting an Anglo-French descent.[141] It would be three weeks before the English navy repaired its ships and was able to put to sea again in strength. Strategically, De Ruiter won at Solebay.

The war would now drag on and Charles would have to recall parliament to vote him subsidies. As he feared all along, the Commons would give voice to widespread public disquiet about the French alliance and the Declaration of Indulgence. Charles's 'grand design' of an Anglo-French Catholic alliance was threatened, and with it the Talbots'-little design.

FOUR

ORMOND'S ENEMY
1673–87

Richard Talbot's little design began to unravel, even before the grand design. With the English parliament due to reconvene in February 1673, Arlington was increasingly worried that recent concessions to Irish Catholics would give ammunition to the opposition. He quickly rowed back, warning Lord Deputy Essex not to admit any more Catholics to corporations and had Ormond nominated to the committee on the Acts of Settlement and Explanation. When the Commons came to sit, Arlington's fears proved well founded. Instead of a floating population of 'country' outsiders and 'courtier' insiders, something like two ideologically distinct groups began to congeal. A grouping of York's 'friends', Old Cavaliers, and Clarendonians was pitted against 'Buckingham's party' which comprised the hardcore of the country opposition and the residual Presbyterian interest.[1]

Members from both groups seized on the activities of the Talbots in Ireland to show that the toleration for dissenters and Catholics that Charles asked for was a popish stalking horse. Sir Trevor Williams MP for Monmouthshire side-tracked the Commons debate on the 'Bill for Ease of Dissenters' in March 1673 by pointing out the 'great danger' of allowing papists to enter Irish corporations or serve as justices of the peace. Williams was probably inflamed by the fact that the shire he represented was the last redoubt of popery in Wales, but the pair who rose to support him showed that the attack on the Talbots was not just a solo run by a backwoods bigot.[2]

These next two speakers were Sir Maurice Berkeley, an Ormond client, and Ormond's son Arran, both members for Wells. Both expressed trepidation about 'so many Papists in command and trust there [Ireland]' and they singled out Talbot by name. Next on his feet was the Presbyterian Sir Edward Massey, a one-time parliamentarian who switched sides after Charles I's execution.[3] Henry Powell, usually a court supporter, delivered the most bruising and personalised attack of all, insisting that Talbot had been given a captain's command of a troop of cavalry in Ireland 'but to break the ice, for many others to follow' and complained of Peter Talbot the 'pretended' archbishop of Dublin excommunicating 'several' Catholics for their allegiance. Powell's anger was personal: his brother had been displaced from a troop on the Irish list.[4] The Talbots, then, had stirred up a diverse parliamentary alliance that would prove unbeatable.

Office holders like Secretary of State Henry Coventry and John Duncombe, chancellor of the exchequer, together with Arlington's brother-in-law Sir Robert Carr, talked up Talbot's services for the Royalist cause: Duncombe lauded him as a 'gallant' man.[5] Coventry also drew attention to the absurdity of baying for strict enforcement when by the letter of the law 'every [Papist] man would be hanged'. Two backbenchers claimed in Talbot's defence that he was but a 'qausi Papist' and one of them cited Catherine Boynton's as evidence: 'he has a Protestant in his bed'.[6]

A Commons address to the king demanded that Talbot be stripped of his command and barred from coming within five miles of the court, and that all Irish Catholics be stripped of commissions of the peace and debarred from all corporations.[7] The Commons again condemned Talbot for presuming to act as an 'Agent for the Catholics of Ireland' and castigated him as one of three 'chief promoters' of popery alongside Fr Patrick Maginn and Henry Baron Arundell of Wardour. Arundell was one the three most prominent Roman Catholic peers in England and a go-between in concluding the secret treaty between Louis and Charles in which the latter expressed his intention of announcing his reconciliation with Rome. Maginn was Catherine of Braganza's almoner, a close friend of 'Madame', Charles's late sister, and also Clifford's spiritual adviser. While keeping up a brave front, Talbot was frightened that the commons had named him in such dangerous company as the 'chief ringleader' of a French and papist conspiracy.[8]

Before agreeing to vote desperately needed supplies the commons forced Charles to withdraw his Declaration of Indulgence (March 1673) and impose a test, obliging all office-holders to swear the oaths of supremacy and allegiance, make a declaration rejecting transubstantiation, and produce a certificate proving they had recently taken communion in an Anglican ceremony.[9] The main target of the Test Act was James Duke of York, who had probably converted secretly in 1668 and publicly revealed his conversion in Easter 1673 by failing to receive communion at an Anglican service.[10]

A lone voice in the Lords, Lord Treasurer Clifford railed against what he saw as the impertinence of the Commons in pronouncing on purely ecclesiastical matters. Arlington deplored Clifford's excessive zeal and asked York and Talbot to persuade Clifford to tone down his opposition. Charles would probably have dissolved parliament without withdrawing the declaration had not the French ambassador intimated that he could expect no more French subsidies. Charles's Grand Design had collapsed and the public was as sullen and truculent 'as ever it was in his father's days'.[11] The Test Act, passed in March 1673, duly forced James to resign as high admiral and Clifford to resign as lord treasurer, a post he had held since November 1672.[12]

By openly avowing Catholicism, York had raised the spectre of a Catholic succession. Queen Catherine suffered one miscarriage after another, in contrast to Barbara Palmer's exuberant fecundity. By the time of Catherine's final miscarriage in 1669, it was clear that she would not produce an heir and that she was a block to the direct line of succession through Charles. So long as Charles could not sire a legitimate heir (he had fifteen surviving children born out of wedlock to seven mothers), an avowed papist stood next in line of succession.

Ashley, by now first Earl of Shaftesbury, suggested that Charles do one of three things: divorce Catherine and remarry, declare Monmouth his oldest bastard son to be legitimate, or exclude York from succession. Hitherto Charles had sometimes given the impression that he was considering divorce. Smitten with lust for Frances Stuart he had, in 1667, consulted with Gilbert Sheldon, Archbishop of Canterbury about divorcing Queen Catherine.[13] Sheldon temporised and asked for time to ponder the problem. Later, Charles supported a bill allowing divorce on the grounds that the wife proved to be barren.[14] Renewed whispering during the summer of 1673 suggests the king may have been again considering divorce. According to Talbot's account, Arlington, Shaftesbury and Clifford, out of enmity to York, wrote to Archbishop Peter to come to court because the king wanted to consult him about divorcing Catherine and indicate if Rome was likely to acquiesce in such a divorce. Clifford is referred to as 'Mr Treasurer' thus fixing a date for the business sometime after November 1672. The trio must have expected Peter to be eager to revenge himself on Catherine but he proved uncharacteristically coy about intriguing and wrote to Richard asking him to try and have him excused. Richard warned York about the request for divorce advice: perhaps that had been Charles's intention all along and he was just toying with the dynastic succession question to put James in his place and remind him that he needed his older brother's goodwill. Richard also requested the king to excuse Peter from coming to court. Charles gave the impression of being 'indifferent' about the business but Clifford again pressed for the archbishop to come to Whitehall secretly. In June 1673 Peter left Dublin in apparent compliance with Essex's proclamation against 'the Popish clergie', and stayed in England for a month before embarking for France.[15]

Sometime during this month the archbishop met Charles and gravely warned him that divorce proceedings would meet insurmountable obstacles at Rome. Peter admitted afterwards to Dick that he had magnified the procedural obstacles because he was genuinely convinced that the marriage was a valid one and a wife could not be set aside just because she was barren, unless it could be medically proven that this condition was 'an original impotency in the blood' that pre-dated the marriage. It is conceivable that Peter Talbot was afflicted by genuine scruples about divorce proceedings, but the greater likelihood is that he was pursuing some Yorkist and pro-French agenda, while leaving a medical get-out clause for the king to pursue if he wished. To round off the business, he detached Clifford from his co-conspirators, convinced York that Clifford had called him over to head off the divorce threat, not the reverse, and so attached Clifford to York's interest.

For his part, York was anxious to remarry before parliament, due to reconvene in October, could meddle in his plans. Anne Hyde had died in 1671 leaving two daughters, but no sons. York's remarriage and the birth of a male heir was a matter of state, too important to be left to James's fancies. Charles's first preference was for a Habsburg princess, the archduchess of Innsbruck, as a counter-balance to his increasing dependence on France.[16] James had wrested some control over the negotiations from his brother by insisting that a member of his own household, Henry Mordaunt, Earl of Peterborough, act as his agent. Talbot boasted that he had first introduced Peterborough into York's circle and had been the one to advise York to choose Peterborough. The Habsburg negotiations shuddered to an abrupt halt in March 1673 when the newly widowed emperor announced that he would marry the archduchess himself. At this point Talbot reinserted himself into the negotiations by steering his patron towards seeking either a French bride or one from a state within France's diplomatic orbit. This was a crucial reorientation because 'a marriage of French contrivance' would be far more unpopular with parliament and people than a Habsburg match.[17]

Peterborough accordingly set out in March on a series of journeys to Paris, Dusseldorf and Modena to choose a bride for the heir-presumptive from a list of a half-dozen eligible ladies. Peterborough's account of the marriage negotiations is incomplete and too much should not be read into the omission of Richard Talbot from his account.[18] Talbot claimed that the father of one jilted girl, dejected that Peterborough (or possibly Joseph Williamson, yet another agent) thought his daughter dumpy and plain, wrote to Talbot urging him to visit for a 'more equall survey'. York then sent Talbot to Paris to 'join eyes' with Peterborough in the agreeable task of assessing the charms of some of these girls. And girls many of them were: the youngest, promoted by Charles' current mistress Louise de Kéroualle, Duchess of Portsmouth, was under thirteen and childish for her age. Talbot was offered a hefty bribe to make a match for one of Louis XIV's three preferred candidates: she was probably a daughter of the 'rich and potent' duke d'Elbeuf. Because the lady was lame, Talbot would not accept the bribe to foist her on James: 'the king of France was heard to say that Monsieur Talbot's eyes were hard to be satisfied'.[19]

Mary Anne, niece of the reigning duke of Württemberg-Neunenbürg, was an early front runner. Peering through the parlour grate of the Paris convent where she lodged, Peterborough noted approvingly that she 'had the appearance of a maid in the bloom of youth, and of a healthful constitution likely to bear strong children'. However, Charles disliked the maiden's mother and claimed to recall that Richard had been the mother's 'gallant' and 'consequently that the daughter was his and so his master [York] to become his son-in-law'. Talbot expostulated that he was 'innocent in this matter'.[20] In late July Mary Anne was pipped at the post by Maria Beatrice D'Este of Modena, once it became clear that the latter's plan to enter a nunnery was not as fixed as Peterborough had been led to believe. Louis was perfectly happy with the alliance and promised a hefty dowry. Peterborough was sent post haste to Modena to stand in as York's proxy in a marriage ceremony. Mary of Modena then set out on the long overland journey to England in October 1673, escorted by Peterborough and a sixty-strong retinue.

The Talbots were rewarded for their help in royal matchmaking. Peter was appointed Mary Beatrice's chief almoner and Richard her chief equerry.[21] While we are told that both Talbots set out from Paris to meet the bridal retinue on route, it is likely that Talbot was actually accompanied by Patrick Maginn, rather than by his brother who was stricken by a long and ultimately fatal illness.[22] He suffered agonies from a stone which irritated and ulcerated the wall of his bladder. Surgery before anaesthesia was largely a matter of lopping off limbs, but in a singular example of an internal procedure surgeons could 'cut for the stone'. Peter's stone was presumably inoperable. By the time Mary arrived in England on 20 November the public mood was sullen and the Commons had even passed an address to Charles demanding that the marriage should not be consummated. Charles responded to this effrontery by proroguing parliament until 4 January 1674.[23]

The cabal began to disintegrate shortly after the prorogation. Clifford hanged himself. Buckingham defected to the country opposition. So did Shaftesbury who proceeded to launch an increasingly strident campaign to have York excluded from the succession. Lauderdale still mainly concerned himself with Scotland and Arlington proved a spent force, though he lingered on as secretary until September 1674. When parliament refused to vote supply, Charles was forced out of the Dutch War in February 1674 and he quickly gave up on the core objectives of the Grand Design: religious toleration and a French alliance. Where the ministers of the cabal had represented every shade of religious opinion except Anglicanism, the rise of Thomas Osborne, earl of

Danby, established a Protestant domestic and foreign policy. Danby was Anglican in outlook and insisted that parliament 'must be gratified by executing the laws against popery and nonconformity and rejecting a French alliance.[24] His Protestant foreign policy was crowned by the fateful marriage of James's daughter Mary to William of Orange in 1677.[25]

On his return to England in 1674, Talbot kept house in Twickenham where he lived on-and-off for the next few years and dabbled on the fringes of negotiations that York and his secretary Edward Coleman were conducting with French ministers.[26] Lord Lieutenant Essex rightly suspected that Talbot and Maginn were his 'inveterate' enemies and was careful to 'walk warily' lest they have him toppled and replaced by a governor more sympathetic to the papist cause.[27] At Talbot's behest the duke of York tried, but failed, to 'shake' Essex. The latter's resilience left Talbot no choice, by April 1675, but to obsequiously 'propose a friendship' with Essex.[28] This he did, and acted as an agent in town on behalf of Essex on a matter as sensitive as buying off a blackmailer who was threatening to publicise love letters he claimed had been sent him by the lord lieutenant's wife. The blackmailer owed Talbot money and this presumably gave Talbot leverage to force his debtor to withdraw the threat, or maybe even to make the threat in the first place. [29]

But Essex's days as governor were numbered once he opened Ranelagh's account books. In May 1676 Talbot warned Essex of the threat, reassured him that his 'friends' in London would be on their guard and promised whatever help he could give, 'in the small station I am in'.[30] Essex's investigation threatened a system in which Ranelagh lodged advance payments by revenue farmers in London rather than Dublin and irritated Charles and Danby who were scrabbling to keep the English treasury afloat.[31] Danby and Ranelagh hoped to see Monmouth appointed titular lord lieutenant to replace Essex, with Edward Conway 3rd Viscount Killultagh doing the actual work as his deputy. Monmouth suspected 'some trick' lay behind the offer and confided his suspicions to Talbot, who in turn tipped off his patron. York had no love for Essex but was reluctant to see his dashing nephew get Essex's office and so he persuaded Charles to play it safe and appoint Ormond. For a brief period during this skulduggery Talbot was perceived to be Ormond's 'bosom friend' and even worked on some project with Nicholas Armorer, a follower of Ormond.[32]

Meanwhile, Peter spent over two years abroad, mainly in Paris, where he befriended a prominent English priest named John Sergeant. It was an unlikely friendship because Sergeant dreamed of a Gallican settlement in Britain whereby all Jesuits would be expelled and a bishop appointed who would not take orders from Rome, 'without leave of the state'. The latter aspiration had disturbing echoes of the wretched Remonstrance and Talbot later denounced

Sergeant's writings to the Inquisition: he had, thundered Talbot, 'uttered more errors against faith and morals than Luther or Calvin'.[33] Talbot's *Blacklaonae Haeresis Confutatio* (Sergeant had dabbled in the ideas of Thomas White or 'Blacklo', whence the title 'Blacklo's Heresy Confounded') published at Ghent in 1675 represented a more cerebral response. The archbishop of Paris and Louis XIV himself ordered both parties to leave off squabbling forthwith.

Peter crossed to Britain in March 1676 and spent the next two years living as quietly as his restless spirit would permit under the roof of Sir James Poole of Poole Hall, near Wirral in Lancashire. The Pooles, like Neill O'Neill's in-laws the Molyneuxs, were among the leading recusant families in England's most Catholic shire.[34] Advised by physicians that he had not long to live, Peter 'desired to die in his own country'. Ormond would not give him leave to return but assured him through a go-between that he would ignore his presence, so long as he 'behaved himself peaceably'. Richard and his family had probably been lying low in Yorkshire (presumably with his wife's kinsfolk) for the previous six months or so and it is likely that they accompanied the ailing archbishop. Peter disembarked in Dublin in May 1678 and was borne in a chair to his brother's home at Luttrellstown.[35]

Peter left Poole Hall for other reasons besides terminal sickness. He had continued to excoriate Sergeant, partly because of his natural combativeness, and partly no doubt because he saw himself as the most senior and able Roman Catholic ecclesiastic in the three Stuart kingdoms, duty-bound to defend papal authority against Walshs, Sergeants and their ilk. Sergeant was no less quarrelsome and made it clear he detested 'old-close-crafty-Jesuits' and their patron the duke of York as enemies of 'all honest Catholics'. Sergeant wrote to Poole threatening that if his 'make-hate' guest continued to engage in controversy he would publicise 'letters written in his own [Talbot's] hand to a prime Jesuit in France which contains treason'. The threat was delivered in May 1678, the same month that Peter embarked for Dublin. The coincidence of threat and departure is suggestive.

It may be that Sergeant was already collaborating with Shaftesbury to implicate Peter Talbot in particular and the Jesuits in general in a 'popish plot'.[36] The popular mood was receptive to lurid fantasies because the 1670s had seen sharpening anxieties about a debauched and pro-Catholic court and about Danby monopolising access to the monarch and pulling strings to produce a compliant Commons. The revelations of Ralph Montagu, a former ambassador in Paris, helped Shaftesbury and William, Lord Russell (Shaftesbury's right-hand man in the Commons) to discredit Danby by disclosing that, for all his Protestant and anti-French tub-thumping, he and Charles had continued to take Louis XIV's gold. Danby was impeached in 1678 for intriguing with foreign powers and locked in the tower until 1684. The noise of Danby's fall was smothered by the thunderclap of allegations by Titus Oates.[37]

Oates presented a story that replicated the sequence of events between 1637 and 1641 that had convulsed three kingdoms and sparked over a decade of warfare. He had been an Anabaptist preacher and Leveller activist but prudently conformed after the restoration to the Church of England. He lost two livings, successively accused of drunkenness and sodomy. He next entered two Jesuit colleges in France and was expelled from both.[38] Supposedly armed with insider knowledge of popish intrigue, Oates deposed that in April 1678 he had helped organise a 'grand consult' of fifty Jesuits in London to send priests disguised as Presbyterian ministers to stir up revolt against episcopacy, raise rebellion in Ireland, hire four 'Irish ruffians' to assassinate the king, and put York on the throne. [39]

The plot was a device to strike at York. As early as November 1678, Shaftes-bury moved in the Lords that York should be excluded from public affairs. Coleman, formerly York's secretary, fell victim to the hysteria because he had imprudently kept copies of old correspondence with the Jesuit confessor to Louis XIV, Père de la Chaize, in which he expressed his admiration for 'the mighty work' of 'subduing a pestilent heresy'.[40] In 1679 the House of Commons resolved that York's religion had given the 'greatest Countenance and Encouragement to the present conspiracy' and passed a bill excluding him from succession.[41] A plot aimed at York with, as we shall see, a strong Irish dimension could not but threaten the Talbot brothers.

Public opinion polarised over the question of York's exclusion. Rather than recognisable parties it is more accurate to think of individuals moving forward and back on a spectrum of prejudices and beliefs within loose and vestigial associations in coffeehouses and clubs where they could socialise with fellow-travellers and form groups to draw up petitions and addresses.[42] Already by November 1678, those who would by late 1680 be called 'Whigs' wanted York excluded from the line of succession, removed from the privy council and even banished from England. The controversy was not about a distant contingency: proto-Whigs expected that a Protestant succession would dissuade Charles from 'popery and arbitrary government (the two of course, went together) now'. They were an agglomeration of anti-Catholic groups and individuals held together by a single common aim of exclusion but otherwise divided on questions as fundamental as the identity of an alternate successor.[43] Proto-'Tories'(called after Irish Catholic outlaws) deplored Whig appeals to the people as demagoguery, declaimed that James had a divine and inalienable right to succeed to the throne, and insisted that the Whigs were really 1640s-style republicans and puritans.[44]

The crisis did not unfold as had the crisis of 1639–41. A Presbyterian rebellion in 1679 was quickly put down. Charles was never so short of money that he could not survive without parliament. And, for all the nervous chatter, no rising broke out in Ireland. A popish threat without an Irish dimension would have been a pallid offering to lay before the English public. Oates forged letters from a Irish physician named Fogarty practising in London in which he confessed he was to poison Ormond. He also forged letters from the accused Jesuits in which they referred to a promise from Peter Talbot that Ireland would 'rise in arms' on hearing that Charles had been assassinated.[45] Joseph Williamson's scribbled notes of Oates's allegations confirm that an Irish plot, with Peter Talbot at its centre, was a cornerstone of the whole edifice.

> Ireland – 40,000 black bills provided to arm the Irish. Morgan was sent with Savill into Ireland. Gives an account the people there are resolute. 20,000 foot will arise and 15,000 in the north of Ireland, and, if the French King landed, would let him in. 800,000 crowns promised by the General of the Jesuits, Padre Oliva. Contrived the death of the Duke of Ormonde by letters of Peter Talbot. He saw them. Four Irish Jesuits undertook to kill him. If they could not then Dr. Fogatti was to be sent to Ireland to poison him, and then the Irish should rise...[46]

On cue, the second edition of Temple's gruesome Irish Rebellion (1646) appeared in 1679 to remind readers that they could expect persecution and massacre in the event of a Popish succession.[47]

On 11 October, even before Oates swore his charges, Ormond sent an officer to Richard Talbot's house to take Peter into custody. He put the army on alert and decreed that bishops, Jesuits, and other regular clergy who had allegedly conspired to murder him should 'depart the kingdom'.[48] On 12 November 1678 Ormond received the long expected order from London to apprehend Richard Talbot as well: he stood accused by Oates of being the General designate of an Irish army that would 'bring in Popery by the sword'. As ever, Talbot was well informed and expected that every post would bring his arrest warrant. Ormond immediately picked up Talbot and put him in 'close custody' in Dublin Castle.[49]

Over the next few months an informer, an Irishman named Everard, put flesh on Oates's accusations. Everard claimed that while Richard Talbot was in or about Paris on his journey to England with Mary of Modena (this would have been in the last days of October or first days of November 1673) he had commissioned the informer to secure him an audience with Louis XIV.[50]

> Now in the interval, having before been recommended by Dr. Brien, Dr. Molony Priests, and others, to Colonel Richard Talbot, and to his Brother Peter (the pretended Archbishop of Dublin) for a person that carried on business after the formalities of

the Court of France, and the Colonel himself having made some tryal of me; he on a time desired me to be assistant to his Brother the Bishop, not long since come out of England: The Bishop desired I should go and complement on his behalf, the Marshal Bellefond (Grand Steward to the King of France), and know when he might be introduced by him to the Kings Audience about the business whereof he treated with the Marshal himself while he was in England as Ambassador (in or about the year 1670.) The object was to arm the Irish and they would seize some sea ports. The very same night I did communicate all that past in this Peter Talbot's Negotiation to Sir Robert Welsh ... However Sir Robert most unfaithfully forthwith discovered all to Colonel Talbot ... that I intended speedily to go for England to accuse both him and his brother Peter; the Colonel feigning to keep his bed, desires to speak with me at his own Lodging. The Circumstances of the message with the Premisses weighed, I took one or two along with me to his very Chamber door on another pretext; he presently desired to know when I intended for England, and when I had seen Sir Robert Welsh. But by this much, forthwith perceiving I was betrayed; I pretended another occasion of that voyage; for which besides I seemed not to be very earnest, if either in Paris, or with the now Dutchess of York (then at Paris) he would procure me some fit employment of Secretary, or Usher.[51]

Everard who hailed originally from Co. Tipperary, led a hand-to-mouth existence in Paris, sometimes translating documents from English to French for Walsh, a fellow Munsterman and spy: Walsh claimed that Charles had commissioned him to 'keep intelligence out of France'. Walsh admitted that Everard had mumbled about certain 'designs' against Charles II but that he had not taken any notice of such vague and idle talk. Walsh emphatically denied tipping off Richard Talbot and further denied that he was to blame for Everard's subsequent imprisonment in the Tower: that was due, he said, to suspicions that Everard was plotting to poison the Duke of Monmouth. Walsh's story is not credible and the plot to poison Monmouth seems invented to appease his Whig interrogators. Moreover, Walsh's past was more chequered even than that of Peter or Richard Talbot. He had fought in the English Civil War, embarked an Irish regiment for the French service, deserted to the Fronde, been imprisoned in the Bastille for three years by a vengeful Mazarin, was – he claimed – sent by Ormond as a royalist agent to England and was suspected by Hyde of treachery. Unlike Richard Talbot, he suffered further imprisonment, at Brussels, before clearing his name nearly three years later. On the other hand, Everard's story sounds even more fantastic. [52] A hanger-on, at Versailles it is doubtful if he could open doors to Marshal Bellefonds, still less the Great King. Everard put in credible circumstantial touches (Talbot being bedridden, for instance) into his fantasy, but the timeline does not work. Bellefonds must have seemed a plausible name to drop (he had been a French envoy in England) but it was unlikely that he would have occupied an influential position at court at this particular time because he was under a cloud and in temporary exile.[53] To cap it all, Everard was a spy, informer and agent provocateur for whoever could pay him most: he 'was frequently to change his stories, as well as sides'.[54] His story is even less credible than Walsh's. A Frenchman named Guerard, held prisoner in the Tower of London, also accused the brothers of plotting in Paris.[55] Oates elaborated his allegations against the Talbots at the trial of Edward Coleman, while in spring 1680 Shaftesbury would uncover an Irish plot to the English privy council which involved a massacre of Protestants and a French landing.[56]

It is unclear if Ormond really believed in Richard Talbot's guilt but he certainly was convinced that Peter had dabbled in 'some plot' and regretted that the wily archbishop had time to get rid of supposedly incriminating documents. [57] His long-standing dislike overcame any qualms he might have had about locking up a decrepit old man. So too did his need to protect himself against Whigs who blamed him for keeping up 'familiarity and correspondence' with papists. They grumbled that that he neglected to secure Peter Talbot's correspondence, denuded Dublin of troops, only went through the motions of banishing regular clergy and disarming papists, and even entertained prominent papists like Dungan and Clanricard to cards every night in the Castle until the early hours. They also criticised him for letting Richard Talbot leave prison and spend nights at his own home, where Ossory and Arran frequently visited him.[58] The prisoner was indeed allowed home on recognisances to visit his dying wife, and so some of the other accusations of leniency levelled against Ormond may have been true.[59]

Archbishop Michael Boyle expressed his satisfaction that 'all here was peace and quietness' while England was convulsed by the popish plot.[60] Ormond must take credit for this. He had taken the basic precautions, locking up the Talbots and banishing bishops and regulars. Knowing there were no grounds to fear a rising, he did not delve too deep for evidence of an Irish conspiracy lest he goad the natives and 'rather quicken a Rebellion than prevent it'.[61] Ormond's caution disappointed Whigs who needed an appropriately wicked and dangerous Irish plot with which to terrify the English public. Yet the viceroy was unassailable for the moment, because Oates had unwittingly boosted his prestige when he set him up as an intended victim of the plot.[62]

Catherine Boynton passed away in March 1679 and that very month Richard petitioned Ormond for his release and for permission to go to Paris.

Talbot's nominally Protestant brother-in-law Sir Thomas Newcomen of Sutton, Co. Dublin (a member of the privy council for three years past), had already been lobbying the lord lieutenant. A later lord lieutenant would lambaste Newcomen as 'false and treacherous' and devoted to his brother-in-law's designs. Doctor William O'Meara (the O'Mearas were hereditary physicians to the Butlers of Ormond) supplied medical certification of a 'great and dangerous swelling in an inconvenient and sensible part': one of Talbot's testicles was painful, badly discoloured, and swollen 'near as big as a gooses egg'.[63] The only surgeon who could cut for this frightful tumour happened to be in Paris. 'I think it not hard for a liberal patient to get a favourable certificate from a physician', Ormond snorted sceptically as he passed the decision on to the English privy council. In mid-July 1679 the council sanctioned Talbot's release and embarkation for France. Surprisingly, he did not embark right away but lingered in Dublin to engage in negotiations with Arthur Forbes Viscount Granard, a follower of Ormond and marshal of the army. These talks concerned a dispute between Mary of Modena and someone named Hollywood about an Irish estate.[64] He departed in August and his two daughters Katherine and Charlotte, together with their aunt Mary Boynton, left Dublin in a coach and seven shortly afterwards to follow him into exile.[65]

Talbot was released during a lull in the two-act drama of the popish plot.[66] The first act had reached its bloody crescendo in the summer of 1679 when fourteen Catholics were executed and the intermission lasted until December 1680. We do not know what strings Talbot pulled to win his release. York could not have helped him since he had, in effect, been exiled to Brussels some weeks before Richard Talbot's petition. In April 1679 Charles slimmed down the privy council, co-opted members of the opposition like Essex and Shaftesbury onto that body and made the latter its lord president. It doubtless helped that Talbot had worked with and was known personally to both these leading Whigs. Or perhaps there was no sentimentality involved and Shaftesbury was unwilling to put either Talbot brother on trial because to do so might force him to produce his surprise witness, John Sergeant. What is clear is that Richard Talbot could not have wangled his release any earlier or much later than he did. It is also undeniable that delay would have been fatal to him. Talbot 'slipped out of the hands of his enemies when he could hardly hope to see an end to his imprisonment but by his death'.[67] During the febrile atmosphere of the second act, when ten more victims were executed, Shaftesbury's Whigs resurrected evidence of an Irish plot in which Talbot would surely have been put on stage to act as the leading man.

Encouraged by Orrery, informers languishing in prison embroidered ever richer tapestries. The French landed arms on the coast of Co. Waterford and

Irish officers returning from France, ostensibly to enlist recruits for the French service, were actually organising a 'general massacre by rising in one night'. This massacre would coincide with the French sailing up the Shannon Estuary and, aided by fifth columnists, seizing Limerick. [68] One informer, David Fitzgerald, implicated his landlord Sir Thomas Southwell (a client of Ormond's) and further claimed that the pope sent emissaries to Ireland in 1676 to encourage papists to withdraw their allegiance to Charles II in favour of his brother. Fitzgerald insinuated that Ormond knew of this and did nothing.

Early in 1680 Essex encouraged Shaftesbury to send agents to uncover more information about French invasion plots. Edmund Murphy, a priest who had been suspended and later excommunicated for drunkenness and unbecoming conduct by Oliver Plunkett now came forward to accuse Plunkett of being in league with Tories and plotting against the king: Plunkett had had dealings with Tories some years before, acting as a go-between to persuade them to disband in return for pardons [69] A suitably tailored version of the invasion plot had him recruiting a huge army to welcome the French as they disembarked at Carlingford.

Indeed, informers like Murphy supplied fodder for Whig propaganda, directed at an English rather than Irish audience. The house of commons, duly won over, would ultimately pass a resolution affirming the reality of an Irish plot.[70] By March 1680 Shaftesbury had cobbled together enough evidence to force the privy council to investigate Ormond's handling of the Catholic threat and demand that Plunkett be brought over to England for trial in October 1680. Ormond denounced some witnesses as 'creatures that no schoolboy would trust with the design of robbing an orchard'.[71] The *True Discovery of the Irish Popish Plot* puts words in the mouth of one informer admitting he and his fellow 'cow-stealers, horse-stealers and murderers' were offered bribes for 'Lying and Swearing'.[72] Many of the Irish informers retracted their evidence, turned against each other, or were otherwise proved to be unreliable. At Plunkett's first trial Edmund Murphy fled to England, and in 1681 at the second trial he refused to testify. But by then the hangman's noose was spun for Plunkett. Essex, troubled by his conscience, petitioned Charles to pardon Plunkett on the grounds that the evidence of the witnesses against him had been worthless. Charles refused because he planned to use some of these same witnesses to accuse Shaftesbury.[73]

Peter Talbot's white martyrdom was overshadowed by Plunkett's fate. Whereas Ormond had been prepared to obey a privy council order to release Richard, he was impervious to petitions and to hints from Whitehall that he should release the dying man from confinement in Dublin Castle. Ormond held a personal grudge and he even rejected a petition from Thomas Newcomen that the dying archbishop be allowed a priest to hear his last confession. The edifying story that Plunkett carried out that office before he was taken to England sounds like a wishful fantasy. We are told the two archbishops were confined for a time in nearby cells and that Talbot beseeched Plunkett's pardon for any wrong he did him in the heat of their dispute over the primacy. Plunkett seized an opportunity to break through his guards, embraced Talbot and gave him the last rites.[74] Peter lingered until late October or early November 1680, two years after his arrest. 'I have for two or three posts forgot to acquaint your Lordship', Ormond informed the secretary of state, 'that Peter Talbot, the titular Archbishop of Dublin is dead and that care was taken to have the body looked upon by some that knew him'. Ormond's care lest he be accused of unbolting the prisoner's cell conveys a sense of the popish plot frenzy.

Charles II remained calm, adroitly outmanoeuvred Shaftesbury and coolly ignored mass petitions. He repeatedly prevented parliament from sitting (except from October 1680 to January 1681) for long enough to let Shaftesbury's Whigs embed an institutional basis of opposition. Memories of the 1640s eventually began to cut both ways. Whig demagoguery stirred up fears among 'abhorrers' who pointed out that legitimate monarchy was the guarantor of all property, authority and hierarchy.[75] From 1681 the Whigs were put increasingly on the defensive. A draft 'association' found in Shaftesbury's papers evoked a wave of 'abhorrences'. On 10 May 1682 Oates was committed to prison for calling the duke of York a traitor, and in December two grand juries presented him on separate counts of perjury. He was condemned to be whipped, pilloried, and imprisoned for life.[76] A plot, most likely real rather than sham, was uncovered in June 1683 whereby Whig grandees Essex and Russell apparently hoped to seize the king and force him to change ministers. Russell was beheaded and Essex thrown in the tower, where he contrived to cut his throat to the bone with a razor. A parallel lower-class plot saw a gang of old Cromwellians and Protestant dissenters plan to ambush and shoot dead both Charles and James at Rye House as the brothers returned to London from the horse-racing at Newmarket. A fire at Newmarket sent the court home unexpectedly early and thwarted the assassins.[77] News of the two conspiracies, conflated as the 'Rye House Plot', was publicised by the crown and produced a wave of loyal addresses and demonstrations. The arrests and trials broke the Whigs.

All the while Richard Talbot was safe abroad though his exile 'lacked the consolation of being close to the Duke of York, his master, who had been forced by the same persecution to seek refuge in Flanders and in Scotland'.[78] Why didn't Talbot attach himself to York's household at Brussels? Perhaps there really was an indispensable surgeon at Paris. Talbot had a more tangible 'consolation' than that of following the duke when he renewed his acquaintance with the widowed Frances Hamilton, *née* Jennings, now countess of Bantry. A brigade of Stuart infantry fought alongside the French against the Dutch in 1672–8 and included an Irish regiment under Sir George Hamilton. Newly promoted to *Maréchal de Camp*, Hamilton had been mortally wounded in 1676 during the day-long rearguard action at Altenheim.[79] Henri Gascar painted his widow 'la belle Jennings' in 1677 while she was in England petitioning for an annuity that Charles had promised if she were ever widowed, but instead awarded her an Irish title, countess of Bantry, as a consolation for her impecunious widowhood.[80] Baroness Hamilton lightly grasps a bunch of flowers in her right hand to draw the viewer's attention to her renewed status as an unmarried woman.[81] She is still a blonde beauty, even if her face no longer (to quote Anthony Hamilton's breathless prose) 'reminded one of the dawn'.

Frances remained in England and was living with her sister Sarah in Jermyn Street, London in the winter of 1679–80. Sarah was married to John Churchill, son of the obliging Winston and brother of the even more obliging Arabella, York's former mistress. Churchill remained in York's circle and sojourned with him in Edinburgh. In a letter written in January 1680 he asks his wife: 'pray present my service to the widow and tell her that I am very glad she is not married, and if she stays for my consent, she never will be'.[82] It is usually inferred from this remark that Talbot had already proposed to Frances and that her brother-in-law was attempting to dissuade Frances from a rash marriage.[83] The inference is unwarranted. John Churchill's consent was not required for his sister-in-law's marriage and his remark sounds like throwaway gallantry in which he was reassuring Frances that she was not overstaying her welcome in his household. Frances might not have been contemplating marriage at all, and even if she had been, that person could hardly have been Talbot since he was but a few months released from prison and was at large in Paris, not London. Papist and penurious, Frances could hardly have afforded to discourage Talbot from wooing her, especially since she had three daughters to launch on the world. Evidently she moved back to Paris, he proposed, she accepted and they married in 1681.[84] It was a love match for Talbot but on her side one would have to reserve judgement. Like her sister Sarah, Frances was notoriously grasping and greedy, though Talbot gallantly insisted otherwise, pointing out that she paid off debts incurred by her late husband in outfitting and provisioning his regiment and so earned the praise of the Sun-King as a 'very estimable woman'.[85]

As late as autumn 1682 an informer in Paris was busy re-heating the French invasion conspiracy. A richly detailed story told of descent on Cork, Limerick and Galway, with each landing to be led by, amongst others, Irish officers cashiered from Hamilton's regiment. Justin Mac Carthy would command in Cork and Lieut-Col. Pierce Lacy in Limerick. Over a dozen ships laden with weapons were even now riding at anchor at Nantes and a papal emissary, one Fr Everard, would accompany them. A priest named Gleeson, a former chaplain with Hamilton's troops, worked through Frances to draw Talbot into this plot to the extent that Gleeson and Talbot met Louis on 24 October 1682 and made no fewer than eleven propositions to him. The ambassador who passed on this tattle misread the political mood in Whitehall: Charles had seen quite enough Irish and popish plots discovered to be impressed by this latest one.[86]

In February 1683 Talbot wrote to Ormond deploring the cost of living in Paris for a man with 'so numerous a family', who was obliged to keep up appearances. He thanked Ormond for his release from Dublin Castle four years before, and wheedled to be let come home to live 'under your Grace's happy government'.[87] In fact, Robert Spencer Lord Sunderland, the secretary of state, had already given permission. Was Talbot pointedly showing off his renewed political credit to Ormond or was he putting himself in the position of a supplicant in order to keep Ormond guessing? The anxiety of at least one politically astute and penitent Whig to invoke 'my friend' Richard Talbot when corresponding with the secretary of state suggests that, by the time of his return to Ireland in summer 1683, Talbot had re-emerged as an influential courtier.[88] He secured a royal order exempting him from jury duty or any 'service relating to the public in Ireland' which was probably a precaution against any attempts by Ormond to hobble his movements.[89]

Private tragedy cast a shadow over these hopeful signs of political rehabilitation. Catherine, his by now fourteen or fifteen-year-old daughter with Catherine Boynton, died in June 1684 and was buried in her mother's vault in Dublin's Christchurch Cathedral. Her infant half-sister, born after Richard's marriage to Frances Jennings, followed a month later.[90]

Talbot reappeared in England the following year full of tales of corruption in the army, false musters, run-down stores and sales of commissions to the highest bidder. James and Talbot had Arthur Forbes Earl of Granard marshal of the army summoned to court and told that if he co-operated with them in blackening Ormond, his Whiggish associations would be forgiven. Granard promptly added his voice to those accusing Ormond and Arran of neglecting to root out politically suspect army officers and presented the king with a list of officers who should be cashiered.[91]

James's Irish policy had already been prefigured in the final years of Charles's reign. The king dismissed Ormond from the lord-lieutenancy in October 1684, and told him he planned 'very many and almost general alterations in Ireland, both in the civil and military parts of the government', which would mean removing Ormond appointees. This would be, Charles purred, 'too hard' for Ormond to put into effect.[92] Ormond secured the king's leave to delay relinquishing power until the spring, pleading that he did not want to make the journey to England in winter, 'an unfit time for an old man to travel in'. He was still in Ireland when Charles died in February 1685. The following month Ormond finally handed over to two lords justices, Archbishop Boyle and Granard, and embarked. While on the road to London Ormond read in a news-letter that the colonelcy of his son's cavalry regiment was to be given to Talbot. For his 'prudence and zeal' and 'infinitely great services', James elevated Talbot to the peerage as Viscount Baltinglass and Earl of Tyrconnell in May 1685.[93] He also gave Tyrconnell informal oversight of the army, instructing lords justices Granard and Archbishop Boyle to consult him on military matters.[94] William Stewart Viscount Mountjoy, commander of an infantry regiment, pulls back the curtains to reveal the power play behind-the-scenes:

> my lord Granard being frightened with the story of Argyle, [a Covenanter rebellion broke in Scotland in April and May 1685 led by the Earl of Argyll] might the easier be brought to whatever was desired of him. This contrivance did not miss of success for as soon as he came to London, and that the first he talked to increased his fears, Col T [albot] Got him and with great demonstrations of kindness, enforced to him the injury he had received in not having a regiment of horse in Ireland, how the king was resolved to modell the army in another manner, that he had advised to him as to the fittest man to inform him in what related to that kingdom, with more to that purpose ... and [Granard's] own ambition drawing where his fear drove him, he encouraged the king in the design he had to reform the army of Ireland, and gave him a list of officers not qualified for their Employments, which list was what T[albot]. had first given him, tho he served not to appear in the matter.[95]

Tyrconnell wanted more, as the perceptive Mountjoy noted:

> His great design had been for a long time to raise the Irish since besides the natural bent a man has for his country, he judged as being the most worthy of them, it was a sure way to raise himself ... as soon as his master came to be King, he made no doubt of his having the government of Ireland, but because until matters were a little settled he knew it was too soon for him who was so obnoxious to the English to pretend to a post that that they had so much reason to be jealous of [so] he agreed with Lords Rochester and Sunderland, the only two he could fear, that neither of the three should propose to the King a Lord Lieutenant for Ireland without the consent of the others ...[96]

As it quickly turned out, Tyrconnell's coveted office was a prize to be dangled or withheld in the power struggle between Laurence Hyde Earl of Rochester, old Clarendon's first son, and Sunderland. The latter had an unsurpassable knack of worming his way back into favour and had been retained as secretary of state by James. A turning point in the Rochester–Sunderland power struggle came in August–September 1685 when Rochester manoeuvred to have his rival packed off to Ireland as lord lieutenant. The English Catholic nobles on James's Catholic inner council, Arundel and John, Lord Bellasis, favoured the plan, far preferring to see Sunderland (the reasons for English Catholic suspicion of Tyrconnell will be explored in the next chapter) rather than an Irishman in Dublin Castle. Sunderland turned the tables on Rochester by proposing that his younger brother Henry Hyde Earl of Clarendon go to Ireland. Clarendon jumped at the chance to repair his shaky finances.[97]

Tyrconnell fell sick, 'which I knew was a sign of his being dissatisfied', reported Mountjoy when he visited the great man's chamber. He 'raged at all mankind', and vowed 'to quit the ungrateful court and retire into some corner to meet that sincere faith which he saw was not to be found near princes'. Henry Jermyn Lord Dover, Talbot's old rival for Frances Jennings's affections, placated his friend by writing to assure him that the setback was not irretrievable and that they should work together all the more fervently to ruin the Hyde brothers. This Talbot 'set about doing'.[98] A letter he dashed off to James objecting to an appointment that 'does so terrify your Catholic subjects hear' seems at first reading to be an ill-considered and uncontrolled outburst of anger for which he offered a half-hearted apology, explaining that his bluntness came from 'the abundance of my heart'. Yet the letter was nicely calculated to touch a chord of religious guilt. Clarendon's terrorised subjects are referred to throughout as Catholics rather than Irish to, presumably, emphasise the bond they shared with their king. They 'have little reason to expect any favour' from Clarendon.[99] Talbot was absolutely correct in this surmise. Clarendon shared the commonplace assumption that the Irish were a conquered people who, as a matter of settled policy, should never be entrusted with military or political power. When Catholics were appointed some months later to one position in each of the three law courts, Clarendon expressed unease and specifically criticised the appointment of Denis Daly because he was one of the 'old Irish race' and by that fact alone 'ought not to be a judge'.[100] Ethnicity aside, the new judges were at least as able as the existing ones who were mostly poorly qualified Ormond drones.[101]

By appointing Clarendon, James hoped to allay fears that the English interest in Ireland was under threat especially when the new governor declared that 'his majesty hath no intention of altering the acts of settlement'.[102] Tyrconnell scoffed at fears of alienating the Protestants in Ireland and slyly equated Protestantism and disloyalty:

Could your majesty see with his own eyes the small proportion your ill affected subjects hear hold to the Catholicks whether you consider their number or capacity to serve, you majesty would with indignation resent the suggestions of those whose interests it is to conceal from you your own power in this kingdom and doe therefore so much lessen your Catholick subjects hear in your esteem.

The latter were doomed ever 'to suffer and not to rejoice with your majesty' but would nonetheless stay loyal to the end like the doomed sailors on the foundering *Gloucester* (a deft probe here at a sore spot of royal guilt) who gave up their 'last breath in a huzzá' for the Duke of York as he was rowed to safety. Tyrconnell concluded with a florid invocation of the Almighty of a kind that is to be found only in his correspondence with James: 'God of his mercy preserve your person and direct you to do all things as shall be for his honour and glory'.

While Clarendon was waiting at Holyhead for a favourable wind, a disgruntled Tyrconnell hired a ship at Dublin and pointedly sailed straight for Chester, passing up the chance to pay his respects in order to 'show his neglect' of the new lord lieutenant.[103] By January 1686 he was back at Whitehall where he was as 'kindly received as he could wish'.[104] It was an eventful month in which Sunderland played to Mary of Modena's religious zeal and won her over to him by helping, in concert with Arundell, Tyrconnell and Dover, to displace the king's current mistress Catherine Sedley, who was sponsored by Rochester.[105] In March Tyrconnell threw himself into a formative court intrigue when he sided with Queen Mary in a heave against the king's confessor, with a view to installing the Jesuit Edward Petre in his stead.[106] Though not the black eminence he is often supposed to have been, Petre wielded considerable influence behind the throne: petitioners found that 'if he undertook their business it seldom failed to prosper'. He would prove a valuable, though not uncritical, ally to Tyrconnell.[107] The queen too, proved supportive: 'I never in my life had a truer, nor a more sincere friendship for anybody than I have for you', she gushed.[108] It is probably no coincidence that Tyrconnell was promoted to lieutenant general of the Irish army that very month.

Tyrconnell needed to be personally present at court to play his part in such plotting and exert his 'prodigiously forceful' personal sway over James and so get his orders for whatever measure he was pushing.[109] Having got the go-ahead, he would return to Dublin to make sure these orders were carried out, then hasten back to London to secure more orders. One has only to look at the table listing his journeys to imagine how punishing the week-long journey must have been, cramped, bored and jolted by poorly sprung coach all the rutted miles to Chester followed often by a horseback ride to Holyhead and a tedious wait for favourable winds before finally crossing the storm-tossed Irish Sea. The journeys probably wrecked his health: it is about this time that references to Talbot taking to his bed become more frequent.

Table 4.1 **Tyrconnell's travels to and from Dublin**

May 1685	to Dublin	
January 1686	to London	*Sources* Kenyon, *Sunderland*,
June 1686	to Dublin	pp. 131–2; Barillon to Louis XIV,
August 1686	to London	21 May 1685; C. J. Fox, A *History of*
February 1687	to Dublin	*the early part of the reign of James the*
August 1687	to Chester	*Second* (London, 1808), p. lxxxiii.

The Drummond brothers, James and John, Earls of Perth and Melfort respectively, managed to monopolise power in Scotland by dividing their time between London and Edinburgh.[110] But there were two of them to share the strain of shuttling between two capitals. Tyrconnell may have been on the point of ousting Clarendon and a rumour reported in April 1686 had it that he would go to Ireland as 'something very like a lord lieutenant'. Rumour proved false and at this key juncture Tyrconnell lay ill at Bath.

In May 1686 Clarendon was rebuked for not yet disarming Protestant civilians especially now that Argyll's rising had shown the threat posed by Presbyterian radicals and the danger of their disaffection infecting their many co-religionists in east Ulster just across the narrow sea. Mountjoy recalls being summoned to meet the new lieutenant general:

> I met my Lord T. at my Lord Granard's where he received me with very great marks of kindness, which a more than common civility paid him during his prison gave me some title to, and immediately after he took us both into the garden, where in a retired place, sitting down upon the grass, he began a dark discourse according to his custom when he had a design, first saying that we were the two persons that the King considered to be the most fit and trustworthy then, after many broken speeches, he began to speak of Argyle, of the disaffected, of the number of such in the country, that if the army were called away they would be dangerous [illeg.] before the army went away, it should be employ'd to disarm all the country where the Protestants were so numerous: this, he said, he found my Lord Granard [illeg.] judged requisite, and they had only delay'd it 'till my coming, who, he said, was so entirely devoted to the King's interest, and who was so able to take right methods for it.

Wrapped up in a characteristic mix of flattery and fearmongering, Tyrconnell's plan was to send troops to confiscate weapons in private houses across Ulster. Mountjoy was aghast and protested that muskets would be hidden, soldiers would plunder the houses they searched, and the commotion would draw complaints from Whitehall: 'But whether he really did fear these people, or that he wished a little commotion to arm the natives he would in no way what I said', observed Mountjoy. After much argument, Tyrconnell adopted Mountjoy's less confrontational approach. Since most of the firearms had been issued by the government to arm militiamen, the council could order the militia captains to collect weapons from their part-time soldiers and gather them in their own homes, supposedly to secure them from being stolen and to maintain them properly. Once collected they could be quietly taken back into government stores. That was to be done by July 1685.[111]

As lieutenant general, Tyrconnell commanded the army independently of the viceroy and answered only to Sunderland. Tyrconnell quickly exceeded his rather vague instructions and set about dismissing Protestants en masse, recruiting Catholic troops, and securing commissions for Catholic officers.[112] While the king trusted Clarendon, such was the lord lieutenant's 'zeal against his [James's] religion' that he had to choose 'an other hand' to remodel the Irish army. Argyll's and Monmouth's rebellion had shown the threat of Protestant radicals and, claimed James's *Life*:

> 'tis certain the Protestants in Ireland being much inclined to Presbitery, even of the Cromwellian stamp, were but too susceptible of such impressions, and by consequence the Army stood in need of being purged from that dross. [113]

Tyrconnell played on royal fears and misrepresented the Irish army as a body of disguised republicans and ex-Cromwellians whereas in fact only ten veterans of the Commonwealth and Protectorate remained active officers.[114] James's *Life* stated that the king gave Tyrconnell power 'to place and displace whom he pleas'd' and Granard, for one, was convinced that the lieutenant general was carrying out royal policy.[115] Yet he was not, or at least not entirely. Tyrconnell equated Protestantism and disloyalty and his purges proceeded on that basis, though he was astute enough to proceed more slowly against regiments commanded by Protestants whom he trusted: thus the regiments of Mountjoy and Lord Forbes, Granard's son, retained a significant minority of Protestant rank and file as late as October 1688.[116] James did not fully share Tyrconnell's assumption that Protestants were necessarily of tepid or doubtful loyalty and, for instance, in May 1688 Tyrconnell was forced to justify cashiering two Protestant captains, Brook and Lucas.[117] Faced with accusations of anti-Protestant bigotry Tyrconnell invariably claimed that 'he himself had never put out a man for being a Protestant' and apologists parroted this line: at

Tyrconnell's review of two regiments at Mullingar, Co. Westmeath, expostulated the *Vindication*, many soldiers left the ranks voluntarily when faced with
the prospect of following the colours to a new posting.[118] Even if James had
fully backed Tyrconnell, it would have been impolitic to put such orders in
writing so Tyrconnell necessarily had to put on a bold front, act as if he enjoyed
full royal authority, put nothing in writing and deliver verbal orders which
were vague and capable of double meaning in case he was challenged.

This vagueness and uncertainty gave Clarendon opportunities to impede
Talbot's purges. He disingenuously expostulated with the king that he needed
clear orders as to 'what proportions of natives you will have in your army here'.
If the king wanted no English then he had only to command his obedience.[119]
In effect he was trying to embarrass James by asking for orders which he knew
full well could not be explicitly given.

Sometimes Clarendon demanded evidence in writing of the king's wishes
from Tyrconnell rather than accepting the latter's glib verbal assurances that
it was 'his Majesty's pleasure'.[120] Sometimes Clarendon rebuked Tyrconnell
and his agents for going 'too fast' and cautioned that they should carry out the
monarch's business with 'less noise'. From time to time, he even nerved
himself to confront the lieutenant general. For instance, he administered a
reprimand after a muster at Kilkenny where Tyrconnell publicly stated that
only Catholics were to be recruited. Talbot huffed and demanded who reported
such an untruth, to which Clarendon replied that he had been told by Cary
Dillon 5th Earl of Roscommon. Tyrconnell flatly denied what he had said but,
Clarendon recalled slyly, 'it so happened' that Dillon was in the next room and
was called in to corroborate the report. Tyrconnell, smiling, protested: 'God
damn me, Cary, I could not give such orders'. When Dillon again refused 'to
deny the truth' the lieutenant general floundered, at a loss for words: 'By God',
he mumbled, 'that is strange'.[121] During the purges Tyrconnell habitually
uttered lies, however brazen and refutable, to misdirect and disarm his many
opponents. Broken officers told of how:

> In the Morning he would take an Officer into his Closet, and with all the Oaths, Curses
> and Damnations, that were never wanting to him, he would profess friendship and
> kindness to him, and promise him the continuance of his Commission; and in the
> afternoon cashier him, with all the Contempt he could heap on him ...[122]

He ladled on such plamás to, for instance, Captain Henry Boyle, Orrery's
son, when he summoned him to sit by his bed, had the room emptied and locked
and assured the young man that 'all the friendshipp and service I ever had for
your father, I have for you'. To show his goodwill he assigned him Bandon, a

Boyle bailiwick and Henry's first choice as quarters for his troop.[123] Yet Boyle and the sons of two other Protestant earls, Captain Robert Fitzgerald and Captain Richard Coote, were among the first officers to be cashiered by Talbot.[124]

The purges gathered pace during the last quarter of 1685. In September Tyrconnell singled out the officers of his own regiment who owed their commissions to Ormond, a move that the old duke saw as an act of spite against him. A year later, 5,043 men – or over two-thirds of private soldiers – were Catholics, though less than one third of the officers were as yet.[125] This was truly a revolutionary step. After all, fumed a Church of Ireland cleric some years later, this turned the 'very Design of keeping a standing Army in Ireland' on its head.[126] Of all of James's missteps in Ireland, arming the papists probably offended English public opinion most of all and consequently Williamite propaganda would harp on this affront after 1688.[127] Contrariwise, Ó Bruadair fastens onto the dismissal of Protestant soldiers and officers to illustrate how power and authority has slipped so completely and gratifyingly out of settler hands. Seon or 'John' (other typical English male names used by the poets are Ralph, George, Peter, and Robin) no longer stands sentinel at the gate of forts or towns [port is bailte] calling out 'Who's there?' In his place is Mountainy Tadhg [Tadhg ón sliabh] who calls out the challenge in Irish: 'Cia súd?'[128]

The purges were drastic, they were anti-Protestant, and they were timely. To argue that the purges degraded the military efficiency of the army is to miss the point that a loyal, if ramshackle army, was to be preferred to an efficient but potentially disloyal one. The most effective leaders of the locally raised Protestant forces who would resist Tyrconnell after the Glorious Revolution (Henry Boyle at Castlemartyr, Co. Cork, Robert King 2nd Baron Kingston, Chidley Coote around Sligo, and, most formidable of all, Thomas Lloyd at Enniskillen, Co. Fermanagh) were all cashiered officers who would have been even more dangerous had they remained in command of troops.[129] In many ways the process was comparable to what was happening in England. During his three years on the throne James steadily weeded out gentlemen and aristocrats who were likely to be politically unreliable or unduly scrupulous about 'the laws and liberties of England' and transformed the officer corps into a professional body relying on the monarch for their prospects. The English army quadrupled in size between 1685 and 1686 and three-quarters of the officers of the royal army were appointed between those dates, mostly careerists and professional soldiers. It was a compact, tightly knit and disciplined institution for James to pursue his own personal policies and overawe parliament.[130]

Tyrconnell made slower progress unpicking the Act of Settlement and Explanation than in remodelling the army. Clarendon proposed that Protestants in Ireland should receive royal assurances 'that they are safe in their possessions by laws which cannot be altered but by their own consent': in other words, the acts should never be changed. Clarendon was satisfied the Irish had forfeited any grounds for complaint by the 'barbarous murders committed on us by their fathers'.[131] Dining with Clarendon the day after his arrival in June 1686, Tyrconnell burst out, 'By God, my lord, these Acts of Settlement and this new interest are damned things; we do know all those arts and damned roguish contrivances which procured those acts.' He continued ranting for an hour and a half. Then and later, Clarendon wondered if Tyrconnell was insane.[132] Clarendon did not realize that such madness had its method and that angry tirades often bullied opponents. Sunderland's biographer claims that his greatest asset was not his suppleness or slyness but 'force of personality, over-weening self-confidence and black bad temper'.[133] He could just as well have been describing Tyrconnell.

In another bruising encounter in June 1686, Tyrconnell upbraided Clarendon because he had 'done nothing about the corporations, which the king will have done'. James wanted a start made on calling in corporation charters by quo warranto legal proceedings with a view to changing them to allow Catholics to be admitted. This would create a Catholic electorate in most of the boroughs which returned the majority of members of parliament. Moreover, he chided Clarendon on 'you have approved of the mayor, and sheriffs of Dublin for the next year: and, by god, they are all 3 as ill men as could be chosen; two of them rank fanaticks'.[134] It was highly important to get a reliable and pliable man nominated because sheriffs could exercise great influence in a general election. Clarendon calmly replied that 'very good men, roman catholicks and protes-tants, have given me account' of the character of these nominees and none complained of them. Clarendon recounts Tyrconnell's riposte:

> 'By God, my Lord,' said he, 'you must not wonder if the Catholics do think you a little partial after your making such a set of sheriffs, who are four parts out of five rogues; but, by God, I justified you to the King'. My lord, said he, you must not wonder, many come to me, who will not trouble your excellency. I hope, you are not angry, that men apply themselves to me: I shall always tell you things as soon as I hear them'.

Clarendon's obstinacy must have tried Tyrconnell sorely but the contempt with which he addressed the lord lieutenant is startling. Here we see Tyrconnell reprimanding his nominal superior for appointing 'rank fanaticks' as sheriff, a matter which was really none of his business since it did not concern the army, his special province. He was truculent, freely admitted to plotting behind the lord lieutenant's back and, the final insult, he feigned concern for his wounded feelings.

Clarendon's list for other boroughs included Sir William Evans of Kilkenny who offended Tyrconnell because he was 'Cromwell's baker's son'. Clarendon admitted that Evans had been a humble baker in England, but later made his fortune in Ireland, married well and discharged his duties as justice of the peace 'very honestly'.[135] Long before the year was out, Clarendon had been ordered not to name any sheriffs for 1687. Instead, Tyrconnell handed him a list he had drawn up together with Thomas Nugent, a newly appointed judge of the king's bench. Every county was committed to a Catholic sheriff except for Donegal, where Nugent confused one Hamilton for another.[136] The final list corrected that oversight.

The appointment of sheriffs and the remodelling of corporations was of a piece with a plan to revise the Acts of Settlement and Explanation. The process of transforming the boroughs began in June 1686 when Tyrconnell brought over a letter from the king directing the lord lieutenant to admit freemen without tendering the oath of supremacy.[137] As summer wore on, a Cork-born barrister named Richard Nagle became increasingly prominent as Tyrconnell's legal adviser and political strategist. Nagle told Clarendon that Tyrconnell was 'in great haste' to deal with the iniquities of the land settlement but that it should be done by an Irish parliament passing amending laws. But 'many things were necessary first to be done' before a parliament could be called.[138] These prerequisites included an overwhelmingly Catholic parliament. To head off demands for legislation to amend the acts in a new parliament Clarendon, supported by Sunderland, sought to set up a commission under which Catholics unfairly treated by the acts would be financially recompensed from a fund to which Protestant proprietors would contribute. Crucially, the new proprietors would get to keep their estates. By August, if not before, Tyrconnell seems to have decided that Clarendon's removal was another prerequisite. When Clarendon called a meeting on the land question for 7 August, only the lord chancellor and attorney-general, both Protestants, bothered to show up on time. Tyrconnell arrived three hours late, without Nagle. When taxed with tardiness he replied contemptuously: 'Faith, my lord, it is very late: we cannot talk much now'. When the meeting eventually took place Nagle opined that a commission would confirm estates 'which ought not be confirmed' but otherwise neither he nor Tyrconnell took the trouble to argue their case with Clarendon.

After a busy summer bullying Clarendon and cashiering Protestants, Tyrconnell went back to Whitehall, accompanied by Nagle, towards the end of August 1686 to renew his lobbying for the governorship. Sunderland responded that the king 'will never put the government of Ireland into the hands of a native'. In rebuffing Tyrconnell, Sunderland was probably passing on James's views accurately. In addition to the king, Sunderland had lined up influential courtiers against Tyrconnell's appointment. The king's inner circle of Catholics was split between those 'Papists who have estates' (in George Savile Marquis of Halifax's words) and the 'more talented' (in the opinion of French envoy Barillon) court Catholics like Harry Jermyn, Tyrconnell and the influential Jesuit Father Petre. The former shared Innocent XI's worries about royal absolutism while the court Catholics were more unreservedly Francophile. When Sunderland tried to block Talbot from the governorship he was at one with the three leading English Catholic nobles, William Herbert marquess of Powis, Arundel, and John, Baron Bellasis, who all distrusted Tyrconnell.[139] Bellasis declaimed 'he was madman enough to ruin three kingdoms'. Bellasis ruefully admitted that the 'hott party' of Catholics outmanoeuvred him and convinced the king not to heed his counsel, claiming that he was 'ould and timerous, and that haveing a good estate was in fear to hazard it'. Though the king believed him to have 'a very weak head', Powis was their candidate.[140]

Sunderland worked on Tyrconnell to withdraw his demand for the lord lieutenancy and instead continue as lieutenant general under Powis with a pension of £5,000 a year. He also promised that Powis would be a mere figurehead and in reality Tyrconnell would 'absolutely govern' Ireland. Dissatisfied with vague pledges, Tyrconnell railed against Sunderland's 'falsehood' and counter-attacked by renewing his earlier suggestion that James FitzJames (the king's natural son with Arabella Churchill) the young duke of Berwick could become lord lieutenant and be married off to Tyrconnell's daughter. The marriage alliance is probably an apocryphal appendage to the story: Tyrconnell's sole surviving daughter was not yet of marriageable age. Arlington had married off his daughter to the loutish duke of Grafton, one of Charles's bastards, to consolidate his position as 'first favourite', and this probably inspired the story.[141]

Yet a marriage alliance whereby Berwick would be a puppet governor and Tyrconnell have 'all the power' would have been consistent with his far-reaching plans at that time. Talbot discoursed to Thomas Sheridan, his soon-to-be secretary, of 'the king's declining age, and the improbability of the queen's having any more children'. In that eventuality he blurted out that the Irish would be 'fools or madmen' to accept 'the Prince of Orange or Hyde's daughter'. Rather than suffer as 'slaves to England' they should set up a king of their own and put themselves under the protection of France.[142] The idea is not as outlandish as it sounds. Ireland, relative to Britain, was probably in a stronger position than the Portuguese were when they broke with Spain in 1641. Bypassing the French ambassador and working through an unnamed intermediary, Tyrconnell sent out feelers to Bonrepos, an unofficial French envoy at Whitehall, asking if he could count on French aid to a breakaway Irish kingdom in the event that James died without a Catholic heir. The marquis de Seignelay, minister of the marine, duly promised 'considerable' aid if the Irish could hold out long enough to receive it.[143]

Talbot's sparring with Sunderland dragged out for most of September 1686 and the only point settled was Clarendon's recall, agreed upon in October.[144] Yet James still shrank from appointing Tyrconnell because he was, first and foremost, an English monarch who saw the Irish as a conquered people and feared that to entrust one of them with viceregal office would endanger English domination.[145] Nonetheless, he did want most branches of government in Ireland, privy council, judiciary, corporations, and not least the army, to be thoroughly remodelled to include a majority Catholic presence. He knew it was doubtful if anyone other than Tyrconnell would be tough enough to play the 'rough part' demanded of him and shrug off the likely protests, abuse, threats and plotting. Moreover, Tyrconnell intermittently convinced the king of the iniquities of the Acts of Settlement and Explanation. These acts, both Sunderland and Clarendon agreed, were the bedrock of English control of Ireland and not to be undermined. When the king summoned his Catholic committee to discuss the acts and the 'affairs of Ireland', Tyrconnell spoke with such passion that James was 'visibly moved and adjourned the meeting, directing that he elaborate his arguments in a private audience.[146] Sunderland was strongly of the opinion that a declaration confirming the acts would be necessary before Tyrconnell could be made viceroy. The latter's riposte was to demand that Sunderland be present at an audience with James so the king could hear just how feeble were the arguments for upholding the acts. Nagle ostensibly wrote Tyrconnell a letter of advice from Coventry on 26 October while journeying back to Ireland. Nagle rejected any declaration confirming the acts, reiterating the old argument that a 'Catholick Pious prince' ought not in conscience reward 'those who served the usurpers' at the expense of 'those who spilt their blood in his brother's service'.[147] Instead, a new act should be passed that would restore many of the innocents who had not been heard by the court of claims. On the appointed day Tyrconnell had been well briefed. Sunderland arrived late and apologised for not having sufficient time to prepare his brief and diverted discussion on to the question of Tyrconnell going to Ireland at all.[148]

Court gossips in October still confidently reported that James would never 'make any Irishman deputy' and that either Berwick or Belassis would be appointed.[149] For her part, the increasingly influential Queen Mary was swayed by Henrietta Boyle Countess of Rochester's lobbying for her brother-in-law. Notwithstanding her goodwill towards Tyrconnell, as late as mid-November, she still hoped, against the odds, to keep Clarendon in Dublin.[150]

Another objection to Tyrconnell, albeit less compelling than his Irishness, was that he was of bourgeois rather than aristocratic stock: later, a French princess wondered 'how His Majesty came to promote him [Tyrconnell] so suddenly to such high dignity he being no person of quality having been but a valet de chambre formerly to the Duke of York'.[151]

Tyrconnell finally won the contest with Sunderland by a desperate gambit. He threatened to reveal to the king that Sunderland had agreed to accept a bribe of £5,000 a year from Irish revenues when Tyrconnell was appointed governor.[152] He would also disabuse the queen of any pleasing illusion that Sunderland had schemed to have Catherine Sedley cast off for 'the honour of religion' rather than to discredit Rochester. Finally, he would reveal Sunderland's scurrilous opinion that James could not be managed 'but by a woman, a priest, or both': the queen was one and Petre the other. Sunderland was aghast and thought Tyrconnell 'mad' because while such revelations would damage Sunderland they would also have cost the enraged Irishman much credit at court. Petre brokered a compromise whereby Tyrconnell would be appointed governor, albeit with the diminished title of lord deputy rather than lord lieutenant, for a limited two-year period. Alexander Fitton, an English Catholic, was retained as lord chancellor and Thomas Sheridan was appointed Tyrconnell's secretary and, if he is to be believed, Sunderland's watchdog.[153]

Sheridan is an important character because he wrote an extensive first-hand account of his subsequent quarrels with Tyrconnell and his conviction on trumped up charges of corruption.[154] Even in his own account, Sheridan comes across as prickly, petulant, foolish, and unrelenting in his hatred of Tyrconnell. Allowing for this hatred it is an honest account of the facts as he perceived them, vividly portrays Tyrconnell's character, describes the alternately clumsy and coolly ruthless way he operated, and even gives an insight into his hopes and fears.

Sheridan began as a collector of customs and commended himself to Coleman and to York as an agent in the project to farm out the Irish revenue in the early 1670s.[155] As a follower of York he was imprisoned in December 1680 on suspicion of complicity in the popish plot, and had to defend himself before the English house of commons, eventually gaining release in early 1681.[156] He married a Catholic (one Whig source claims she was a cousin of Petre's) and announced his conversion to Catholicism in 1686.[157] Sheridan was well-connected, thick-skinned and resilient: all in all, a dangerous enemy.

In November 1686 Tyrconnell was back in London preparing for his new posting and putting the best face he could on having Fitton and Sheridan imposed on him by claiming that he had been the moving force behind their appointments all along. As late as mid-December 1686 court gossip had it that

Tyrconnell would not be sent to Ireland, but a stormy cabinet council meeting of 12 December finally sanctioned his appointment.[158] How had Tyrconnell outsmarted Sunderland, the 'subtillest, workingest villain that is on the face of the earth' (in the words of Queen Anne) in the face of royal and ministerial nervousness about the reverberations of his far-reaching plans in England? Talbot was astute enough to see through Sunderland's prevarications; he could beat him in debate before the king, when baulked he exploded into rages that were at least as thunderous as Sunderland's and, finally, he was more desperate, being ready to trigger mutually assured destruction.[159]

The new lord deputy set out from London on 10 January 1687. A week later the viceregal party, which included his wife and Richard Hamilton, his wife's former brother-in-law, reached Chester. Outside the town, the bishop of Chester met them with his coach, lodged them in his palace and, with the governor and officers of the garrison, made merry and banqueted.[160] The following day the party left for Holyhead where they embarked but were driven back to Weston-super-Mare in Somersetshire by contrary winds.[161] In 'Lilliburlero', the best-known Protestant ballad satirising Talbot,[162] 'Muirish' or Maurice tells 'Teague' or Tadgh the good tidings of Talbot's appointment and frets about the 'Protestant wind' that delays him.[163]

> Ho! Brother Teague, dost hear de decree,
> Dat we shall have a new debbitie,
> Ho! By my shoul it is a Talbot,
> And he will cut all the English throat,

The speakers are two Irish Catholics bearing typically Irish names ('Teague' was until recently a slang synonym for Catholic in Northern Ireland). The Hiberno-English brogue in which Teague and Muirish speak is mocked, especially the supposed Irish mangling of 'th' as 'd' and 's' as 'sh'. Lilliburlero's refrain is an accurate rendering of a phrase that must have been lifted from a Gaelic ballad: 'Lilly is clear, the day is ours'. William Lilly (1602–81) was the best known astrologer and prophet in seventeenth-century England.

Tyrconnell's appointment had repercussions beyond Ireland or Britain. No power, or combination of powers, had mobilised to confront Louis XIV's policy of aggression (réunion, or consolidation as the French called it) against Spanish territories on his eastern frontier. His revocation of the Edict of Nantes in 1685 and persecution of French Protestants, which Louis saw as an aspect of réunion, gave a religious dimension to the international opposition to France. William of Orange, stadholder of the Dutch Republic, had emerged as the linchpin of attempts to build up an anti-French alliance after Louis had invaded

and almost destroyed the Dutch Republic in 1672. William's earliest efforts to
cobble together an anti-French coalition were broken by French diplomacy
but he began to build up a powerful anti-French coalition after the mid-1680s.
Some of the German princes joined William in the defensive alliance of
Augsburg in 1686 while a French trade war against the Dutch Republic in 1687
forced the merchants, hitherto opposed to war with France, reluctantly into
the arms of William. England was too important a naval power to be left as an
imponderable or neutral as war alliances hardened and William began to
sound out his uncle's opponents as soon as he heard of Tyrconnell's appointment.[164] According to Count D'Avaux, the special French envoy to the United
Provinces, Tyrconnell's appointment and Rochester's dismissal, also in January
1687, marked a key moment in the ratcheting up of Anglo-Dutch tensions.[165]
Tyrconnell's deputyship started the countdown to invasion, dethronement
and civil war.

FIVE

LORD DEPUTY
1687–9

At last Tyrconnell wielded real authority rather than backstairs influence.[1] He used this hard power to accelerate the greening of Irish government while tolerating a minority Protestant presence in most of its branches.[2] Protestants remained as one of the three judges on each of the courts of justice, and comprised about one third of burgesses and aldermen in remodelled corporations.[3] Only the revenue branch stayed mainly Protestant, in part because Thomas Sheridan, Tyrconnell's secretary and first commissioner of the revenue, would not give places to his 'importunate countrymen'.[4] Sceptics muttered that Tyrconnell left Protestants in office merely as an ostentatious show of impartiality and assumed that if he had a free hand would he have created a Catholic ascendancy, a monopoly of power. Even if one grants the assumption that power sharing was a ploy to reassure English public opinion, the Catholic ascendancy in the making was not the naked, unabashed and total Protestant ascendancy that would replace it.

While he left a significant Protestant presence in many branches of government, Tyrconnell demanded a more thorough catholicisation of key offices and institutions. So the army purges went on. Nagle, the new attorney-general, instigated quo warranto proceedings to recall and amend the charters of parliamentary boroughs in order to pack their electorates with Catholics. An almost entirely Catholic body of sheriffs was put in place to make doubly sure that the new borough and county electorates returned suitable members to the parliament envisaged by Tyrconnell.[5] Where this was not enough, Tyrconnell or his secretary enclosed recommendations with the election writs.[6] After a flurry of writs in spring 1689, only six or seven Protestants out of 230 members would sit in that year's House of Commons.[7]

A viceroy was of necessity an absentee court politician which put him in a position of 'peculiar danger', depending on allies to warn him of threats and present his side of any dispute.[8] Essex, for example, had relied on his brother Sir Henry Capel and from time to time on secretaries. One of these secretaries describes entering the king's bedroom at about eight o'clock in the evening to find that five of the viceroy's enemies, including Ranelagh, 'had gotten [the] king in a corner and were very busy with him' in maligning Essex. The secretary foiled that particular attack. To all appearances, Tyrconnell had no comparably watchful and loyal representative though Lady Tyrconnell must have done her best. It may be for that very reason (what one would give for sight of a letter or two that passed between them!) that the viceregal couple lived apart from January 1687 until August 1688, he in Dublin and she ensconced in St James's Palace.[9] By continuing to purge the army and civil administration Tyrconnell was apparently flouting the king's express command, conveyed on 15 February 1687. Rivals at court eagerly brought a slump in Irish revenue to James's attention as damning evidence of Protestant flight and economic collapse. The figures were supplied by Sheridan's protégés in the revenue and Sheridan may have been a key player in a heave against the lord deputy. He was, around this time, also working with Dominic Maguire, Archbishop of Armagh who shared Sheridan's antipathy to of the lord deputy. There could be a number of reasons for this dislike. Having been chaplain to Spanish ambassador Don Pedro Ronquillo, who would later warmly welcome William of Orange's invasion of England, Maguire probably considered Tyrconnell too Francophile. Or perhaps Maguire's enmity can be traced to the jostling for precedence that was endemic among the higher clergy. Maguire was at 'open war' with Bishop James Cusack of Meath and to the extent that Maguire's estranged episcopal colleagues petitioned Rome to nominate a coadjutor to Armagh who might restrain the assertive Archbishop. Tyrconnell's favourite bishop was Patrick Tyrrell of Clogher, a Franciscan who would serve as his secretary from February 1688 and who shared his goals of a bigger and wholly Catholic army, Catholics in positions of authority and a 'loyal' (that is predominantly Catholic) parliament.[10] Perhaps swayed by Tyrrell, Tyrconnell supported the petition against Maguire.[11] The pro-Spanish Innocent XI rejected the supplication and Petre 'severely reprimanded' Tyrconnell accusing him of fomenting divisions which rendered the Catholic party 'ridiculous and contemptible to the World'.[12]

So, when Tyrconnell was ordered to meet King James at the northern end of his progress in August 1687 he expected to be rebuked or even dismissed and replaced by Roger Palmer Earl of Castlemaine, a Catholic, cousin of Powis and the estranged husband of Charles II's mistress.[13] On landing at Chester a few days early, Tyrconnell hastened to Shrewsbury to meet the king, putting on a brave show by bringing with him a retinue of over sixty nobles and gentlemen.

> I was on horseback by the King, and in waiting, when the Lord Deputy met the King out of Shrewsbury, where he was making his entrance, and the King received him in

the most cold manner I ever saw, and, as I take it, he came not to the Court at Shrewsbury, but ordered to attend at Chester, where the King arrived two days after.[14]

Tyrconnell's political survival hung in the balance, when James summoned Secretary Sheridan early the morning after he reached Chester. Tyrconnell had wanted to leave his increasingly troublesome secretary behind in Dublin, but Sunderland had insisted he come over. Tyrconnell simmered with anger, all too aware of the threat personified by Sheridan. 'God damn you!' Tyrconnell shouted at him before damning himself for accepting him as secretary and bidding him go to the devil. Nagle tried to smooth things over by saying his master had imbibed too much wine. Next day Tyrconnell apologised to Sheridan, 'taking him about the neck and hugging him'.[15] Tyrconnell had, some noted, a 'sly way' of ruining a man while pretending to be reconciled.[16]

Miller depicts what happened next as a defining triumph for the swaggering lord deputy who, once he met his king face-to-face, persuaded him, against his better judgement, that he could favour Catholics without completely alienating Protestants in Ireland.[17] Tyrconnell undoubtedly browbeat a weak and pliable monarch but his task was made easier by the fact that he was by no means completely out of step with his master's wishes. Over the previous eight months James had made a decisive break with his hitherto cautious policies. He had issued his Declaration of Indulgence and dissolved the 1685 parliament in order to have a new one elected to repeal the Test and the penal laws. He was embarked on a high-risk bid for dissenter support as an alternative to the Tory/Anglicans, purging the latter from local government in favour of a ragbag assortment of Whigs, dissenters and obscure Catholics.[18] James was also packing parliament and remodelling the army from top to bottom. Tories, though outraged, remained passive.[19] It is also possible that James even agreed at Chester to Tyrconnell's contingency plan to declare Ireland independent after the king's death.[20] James was a 'radical moderniser', argues Pincus, promoting French-style absolutism as a means to the end of re-Catholicising Britain.[21] The legal, political and psychological obstacles to reversing the Protestant Reformation or even to leaving Catholicism strongly enough embedded to survive a Protestant successor remained enormous. Providence would not have guided him through so many perils, believed the king, unless there was a great underlying purpose. Politics was no longer the art of the possible.[22]

Tyrconnell had been able to report at Chester that quo warranto proceedings had been brought against nearly all corporations. The charters, duly produced, would be brought before Sir Stephen Rice, senior judge of the Exchequer, the only Irish court whence no writ of error lay in England. Rice would exploit every quibble to find technical flaws in letters patent, allowing the deputy, duly empowered in the name of the king, to issue new charters appointing the officers and members by name with powers to return two members to parliament.[23] Tyrconnell's agenda was 'somewhat at odds' with his master's because he wanted to make these new charters unalterable while James did not want to tie his successor's hands. In other words, a Protestant successor (and no other was envisaged in spring 1687) could undo all Tyrconnell's work.[24] It is revealing that, where James and his lord deputy differed, the king was capable of exerting his authority and getting his own way.

On the Acts of Settlement and Explanation, Tyrconnell did not have it all his own way either and he settled for a compromise on those 'damned things'. The acts would stand but Tyrconnell and Nagle would return to Dublin with permission to draft a bill to make 'substantial' amendments. The bill drafted over the winter of 1687–8 allowed 'innocents' who had not been restored to buy back their estates for the equivalent of three years rental. Those in other categories should now get half their old estates, no questions asked or 'reprisals' sought. The grantee or anyone to whom he had sold the estate (so called 'new interest' purchasers) would keep the other half. At least this rough and ready solution would, mused Tyrconnell, mean that the land settlement would not be delayed interminably by the 'frauds and abuses' of the new interest men. A quintessential new interest man himself, Tyrconnell's irritation with the new interest is surprising only if one views all his actions as purely self-interested.[25] He was capable, quite often, of disinterestedly pursuing a greater good. Rice and Thomas Nugent, chief justice of the king's bench, would bring the draft bills to London in March 1688. Later, Sunderland claimed to have turned down a bribe from Tyrconnell and blocked the bills as best he could:

> I diverted the calling of a parliament there, [in Ireland] which was design'd, to alter the acts of settlement. Ch Justice Nugent and Baron Rice were sent over with a draught of an Act for that purpose furnished with all the pressing arguments could be thought on to persuade the King, and I was offer'd forty thousand pounds for my concurrence, which I told to the King, and shew'd him att the same time the injustice of what was proposed to him and the prejudice it would be to the Countrey, with so good successe, that he resolved not to think of it that year, and perhaps never.[26]

But that piece of double-dealing can wait. Returning from Chester, the threat of dismissal no longer hung over the lord deputy and he was last able to openly attack his troublesome secretary. All along, he would have preferred William Ellis as his secretary. 'I know him to be a great knave and a villain', Tyrconnell said of Ellis, 'but yet he is a useful knave and being a Protestant can do me good, but no hurt'.[27] Tyrconnell was often accused of being a 'rigid' or bigoted Catholic but in fact he was quite prepared to employ suitably loyal Protestants. Putting weapons in their hands was another matter. Tyrconnell employed Ellis, claiming that the double-jobbing Sheridan was too busy to attend to his secretarial duties. At his uncle's instigation Neill O'Neill tried to cajole Sheridan into surrendering his secretarial post. Sheridan would have none of it, abused the lord deputy as a 'knave' and called his wife a 'whore'.

Not surprisingly Tyrconnell quickly escalated from coaxing to coercion. He charged Sheridan with taking bribes to appoint officials within and without his remit, collectors, tide-waiters, storekeepers, gaugers, a goaler, a town sovereign, a consul and a lieutenant of foot.[28] The hearing was rigged and the charges trumped up to the extent that most of the payments were perquisites of the sort considered acceptable at the time. Sheridan was duly found guilty in June 1688 and Tyrconnell delayed him long enough in Dublin to let his wife (she had been called over to assist at the birth of the prince of Wales) reach London ahead of him and blacken the secretary's name.[29] Meanwhile, Tyrconnell wrote to Sunderland and prevailed on him to bar Sheridan from court. For his part, Sheridan raised the stakes by insinuating that Tyrconnell had 'entered into a Treaty' with Louis. It availed him nothing and neither Sunderland nor Petre rallied to Sheridan's defence.[30]

Two of Tyrconnell's nephews, O'Neill and William Dungan (soon to be created earl of Limerick) had busied themselves in discrediting poor Sheridan. This was an early indication of the prominent role that Talbot family connections would take in Irish government. Charges of nepotism obviously stung, because the *Vindication* takes the trouble to rebut the accusation:

> If it be a Crime in our *Native Governour*, as is alleged, That he gave little mean Imployments to succour four or five of his *Relations*, who had been Sufferers and Men of Quality, upon so great a Change: What was it in former Governours, who brought over as many Strangers to us, and lick'd up all the Imployments in Church and State?[31]

Rather more than four or five of Tyrconnell's relations were put into official posts. The privy council included representatives of the great Irish houses, Ikerrin and Galmoy for the Butlers, Clanricard for the Burkes, Antrim for the Mac Donnells, and Justin MacCarthy for the MacCarthys. Yet the core of active members was more narrowly based.[32] For example, a privy council proclamation of March 1689 condemning Protestant insurgents in Ulster and north Connacht was subscribed by seven counsellors and of these three (Fitton, Granard and, probably, Newcomen) were Protestants, three were Irish Catholics and one (Plowden) was an English Catholic.[33] More important than religious or ethnic divisions was the fact that the majority were connected to the Talbot family. Newcomen was Tyrconnell's brother-in law, Limerick and William Talbot of Carton nephews and Richard Hamilton he described as a 'brother'. The extent of Talbot infiltration of civil and especially military office is best captured in tabular form (table 5.1).

Table 5.1 **Talbot-connected office holders** [34]

Son

MARK TALBOT, lieutenant colonel in Antrim's regiment, MP for Belfast.

Nephews

WILLIAM OF CARTON, son of Robert Talbot, master of the rolls and secretary of state for Ireland (1689–90).

'WICKED WILL' of Templeogue, Co. Dublin son of Margaret Talbot: lieutenant colonel of infantry, killed at Derry in 1689.

JAMES TALBOT of Templeogue, Co. Dublin son of Margaret Talbot: colonel of infantry, killed at Aughrim in 1691.

WILLIAM TALBOT of Haggardstown Co. Louth MP for Ardee Co. Louth, son of Garrett Talbot.

NICHOLAS CUSACK of Cushenstown, son of Frances Talbot: captain in Tyrconnell's regiment of cavalry.[35]

WILLIAM DUNGAN, 1st earl of Limerick, son of Mary Talbot privy counsellor.[36]

NEIL O'NEILL of Killileagh, colonel of dragoons, son of Eleanor O'Neill killed at the Boyne in 1690.

Other Relation or Connection

THOMAS NEWCOMEN of Sutton, brother-in-law: privy counsellor 1688–90.

WILLIAM NUGENT, married to niece Alice Newcomen, colonel of infantry killed at Cavan in 1690.[38]

MAURICE EUSTACE, married to Margaret, niece, colonel of infantry 1690-1.

SIMON LUTTRELL, married to niece Katherine Newcomen, lieutenant colonel in Newcomen's regiment 1688-9 and governor of Dublin 1689-90.

THEOBALD 7th VISCOUNT DILLON, married to niece Mary Talbot.

JOHN ARTHUR of Hackettstown or Belgard Co. Dublin, MP for Newcastle married to niece Eleanor Cusack.

CHRISTOPHER NUGENT of Dardistown, grand-nephew, major in Tyrconnell's regiment of cavalry.[37]

WALTER DUNGAN, grand-nephew, colonel of dragoons, killed at the Boyne 1690.

RICHARD HAMILTON, wife's former brother-in-law, lieutenant general 1689–90, captured at the Boyne in 1690.

JOHN HAMILTON, wife's former brother-in-law, brigadier, mortally wounded at Aughrim.[39]

ANTHONY HAMILTON, wife's former brother-in-law, major general.

HENRY, 8TH VISCOUNT DILLON, colonel of infantry, married to step-daughter Frances.[40]

THOMAS NUGENT BARON RIVERSTON, chief justice of the king's bench, sister married to Tyrconnell's nephew William Talbot of Carton and his brother William (above) married to Tyrconnell's niece.[41]

Richard Talbot's following in the 1670s had been almost confined to north Leinster and the adjacent part of Connacht. The marriage of a Mount Talbot niece to Theobald Dillon 7th Viscount Costello Gallen deepened Talbot's influence in Co. Roscommon and east Mayo but did not extend really its geographic range. Neither Talbot kin and affinal connections nor Tyrconnell's administration fully represented and incorporated powerful provincial kin groups such as the Butlers of south Leinster and east Munster. For example, back in February 1686, shortly after Clarendon's arrival in Ireland, meetings began among Catholics in various counties for the purpose of selecting agents to send to England to petition on behalf of the old proprietors and to collect contributions to support those agents. Clanricard declined to let his name be associated with this agitation, complaining that the people of Leinster were 'too hot', and too much under Tyrconnell's influence.[42]

Yet Tyrconnell's government was more than a Talbot family extrusion. His greed had been satiated: 'I have nothing more to ask of any kind of honour or riches…', he assured Queen Mary. Consequently he had patronage left over to attract talented outsiders. The half dozen members of what Sheridan sneeringly dubbed Tyrconnell's 'cabinet' included three lawyers, Nagle, Nugent and Rice together with two military men Richard Hamilton and Justin MacCarthy. Hamilton and Nugent were distantly connected but the main reason for their inclusion was their ability not just as judges and legal advisers but also as political strategists.[43] Tyrconnell proved capable of preferring an abler man over a kinsman, as evidenced by a bitter complaint from Limerick to his uncle after a rival elbowed him aside as commander in chief of the forces garrisoned in Munster. He was now but a 'mock-general', Limerick complained, and so it would be 'far more decent to retire to my own old corner'.[44]

The claim that Tyrconnell promoted the Old English and disdained the Gaelic Irish is so often asserted that it must be confronted.[45] Sheridan, conscious of his own Gaelic paternity, grumbled that Tyrconnell was always ready to 'disoblige the O's and Macs'.[46] But Tyrconnell's own words, vividly captured by

Sheridan, do not support this contention. When Tyrconnell expounded why
the Irish should 'set up a King of their own' and blamed their past failures in
conflicts with the English crown on disunity he spoke of the 'Irish', without
distinction. He 'did not like' Sheridan's attempt to draw distinctions between
'old' [Gaelic] and 'new' [Old English] Irish and rounded on Sheridan 'in a
great huff' because he disagreed with the Irish cutting the connection with
England: 'I will no longer dispute this matter with you, who I thought was my
countryman, but now perceive you are an Englishman'.[47] Seemingly, anybody
who shared his frustration with English and Protestant domination, whether
he was old or new Irish, was Tyrconnell's fellow countryman.

The fact that most officers in Tyrconnell's army were Old English (only
slightly over a fifth of the infantry company commanders listed in a 1689
muster bore Gaelic names) does not prove that he was biased against the
Gael.[48] Commanders in more generously resourced armies than Tyrconnell's
ramshackle array often had to feed and maintain their companies out of their
own pockets until paymasters disbursed arrears so that social deference helped
form the basis of military discipline and cohesion.[49] Consequently, it was
usual to commission peers, land-owning gentry, or other men of means as
commanders of companies, battalions or regiments. The relative paucity of
Gaelic captains simply recognised the reality that the Gaelic community had
been more thoroughly stripped of property than the Old English. Wealth was
a less weighty consideration in commissioning the professional career officers
(some fifty out of a total officer corps of 406) sprinkled among the old regiments.
Such 'men of service' were to be preferred to 'some young country schoolboy',
insisted Walter Dungan as he pleaded with his grand-uncle to commission
one 'Toby Birne', a Gael. Of eighty-seven officers who had served in Thomas
Dungan's (formerly George Hamilton's) regiment in France in 1678 before
Charles II recalled them, thirty-six reappeared in James's remodelled Irish
army.[50] Many, perhaps most, of these veteran officers were Gaels, ranging
from Lieut-Col. Lawrence Dempsey (he had also fought in the brigade supplied
by Charles II to the Portuguese between 1662 and 1668) to ensign Terence
O'Brien.[51] Over one third of members of parliament came from Gaelic families
like John Connor, a lawyer and member of Middle Temple who represented
Philipstown, near the ancient O'Connor Faly seat. Given that parliament
represented property rather than people the Gaels were, if anything, over-
represented in the Commons relative to their wealth.

If Gaelic language poetry can be taken to express the mood of the common
people, then Tyrconnell basked in genuine, if fleeting, popularity. Dermot
MacCarthy, who looked to Tyrconnell's old rivals the MacCarthys for patronage,
nonetheless lauded the brave and patient Talbot [an Talbóideach cróga calma]

who has come armed with the king's authority [le cumhachta an rí] to demob the English 'cheese eating churls' [Bodaigh an chaise].[52] His *Céad buidhe re Dia* composed about 1686 is even more enthusiastic. A prophecy current in the seventeenth century and attributed to Saint Patrick or to Colmcille of Derry looked forward to a messianic deliverer who would rout the 'Gall' or foreigner. This hero, Aodh Eangach or Ball Dearg (so called from a red spot or birthmark by which he would be recognised), would, it was supposed, spring from the O'Donnell dynasty. Since, as it happened, Talbot's title was Earl of Tyrconnell, the ancient O'Donnell country, the poet could identify him as the hero who would 'free them from the slavery of their conquerors'. 'Tyrconnell na lann mo bhall dearg sa' [Tyrconnell of the sword is my Ball Dearg] insisted Mac Carthy who acclaimed him a hero like the mythological Fionn Mac Cumhail [laoch mar Fhionn]. Mac Carthy concluded by praying that Tyrconnell would live (evidently his poor health was public knowledge as early as 1686) to drive out the 'Danes' or foreigners [dhanaraibh] like Brian Boru of old.[53] Fault lines such as regional antipathies, rival family alliances and intergenerational distrust undermined Tyrconnell's regime more than racial tensions.

Two events in June 1688 completed the alienation of James's erstwhile Tory supporters. James arrested seven Anglican bishops who had protested against the Declaration of Indulgence. A few days after the arrests, Mary of Modena gave birth to a son and heir, James Edward (later James III or 'the pretender', depending on political preferences). Before his queen's pregnancy, James's hope of establishing a Catholic dynasty depended on his daughter Anne converting. He unavailingly bullied her and Tyrconnell even pleaded with his sister-in-law Sarah, Anne's beloved lady in waiting, to join in the good work. What could have been expected to be a short-lived papist aberration (if James had died at the same age as his older brother he would have expired in 1688) had now become a Catholic dynasty stretching indefinitely into the future. Yet James, buttressed by a strong and effective standing army, could have continued to rule a sullen but inert populace.[54] It took an invasion to topple him.

William of Orange, James's son-in-law and nephew, had tried to weave a web of alliances to oppose Louis XIV's expansionism but without imperial leadership the alliance was too weak. When the Turks sued for peace in June 1688 the emperor could look west. Belatedly realising his weakness, and believing concessions on his part would be seen as a sign of that weakness, Louis decided to build up his already deep defences in Germany by a pre-emptive attack on Phillipsburg in October 1688.[55] As early as May 1688 William had decided to invade England to capture Stuart naval and financial resources for the 'Grand Alliance' he was putting together. His pretext was to defend his wife's right of inheritance and investigate the 'suppositious' birth of James Edward: James's enemies had spread the canard that Mary of Modena's pregnancy had been a pretence and the supposed heir an impostor smuggled into her bed. Lady Tyrconnell was one of the ladies present at the birth to witness it in order to give the lie to any such claims.[56]

By August 1688 it was common knowledge that 'the Dutch are coming'.[57] Tyrconnell among others warned James but such cautions were not taken seriously until mid-September. James then proceeded to fall between two stools, dismissing Sunderland, and disavowing French aid but not winning back Tory support. William of Orange finally disembarked his army at Torbay on 5 November: this was the invasion that Whig historiography retrospectively dressed up as the 'Glorious Revolution'. Jittery because of a trickle of desertions and the speed of William's advance, James suffered a nervous collapse and took the fateful decision to pull his army back from Salisbury Plain towards London on the 23rd. Within days many officers had defected to William including young Lord Cornbury (Clarendon's son), Henry Duke of Grafton, one of Charles's by-blows, and John Churchill, Tyrconnell's brother-in-law.[58]

Though James's military power was collapsing, all was not yet lost. As King Log he could have provided a figurehead around whom Tories could have rallied. Numbed and demoralised, James fled for France, was recaptured, and on Christmas Eve escaped for good, with William's connivance. There is no mistaking the shock felt by potential supporters like Clarendon at this news: 'Good God! What will become of this poor distracted and distempered nation?' James's flight was gratefully seized on by Tories, churchmen and others with scruples about deposing a monarch. A gathering of peers a few days later deemed that 'the government of the kingdom was extinct' and beseeched William 'to take on government'.[59] This ultimately led to the convention parliament and a formal invitation to William and Mary. Ireland, as 'a Kingdom dependent on the Crown of England', William King later argued, 'must follow its Fate'.[60] It very nearly did.

Tyrconnell's grip on Ireland was weak because he had bled the Irish army white to reinforce James in England. As far back as March, overriding Sunderland's objections, he had reassured the monarch that he could call on troops from Ireland 'whither as you shall think fit at any time' and beseeched him to put Chester 'in good hands' as a disembarkation port.[61] In May he had embarked nearly a thousand soldiers, 200 of them trained men, as drafts for the English army. Just weeks before William landed, he embarked another two and a half thousand trained soldiers to prop up James.[62] With news of James's first flight, his regiments at Uxbridge disintegrated.[63] Some of the scattered Irish escaped to Ireland on the Chester packet boat while others were interned on the Isle of Wight whence some 1,200 were sold to the Holy

Roman Emperor for service in Hungary. The four regiments of foot and three regiments of horse remaining in Ireland provided a pitifully small cadre of veteran officers and trained men to serve as a nucleus for the deluge of raw recruits who would need to be enlisted.[64] By stripping his army, Tyrconnell demonstrates how much he conceived of the crisis in three-kingdom terms: as in the 1640s, Ireland was best secured by intervention in England.[65] With hindsight, squandering forty per cent of the regular army's strength in England was an appalling miscalculation that may have doomed Tyrconnell's regime in the long term and gravely weakened its capacity to counter internal and external threats in the short term.

And there was an internal threat. After ninety years of immigration some ten to fifteen per cent of Ireland's population was Presbyterian or Anglican, though nowhere were the newcomers in a majority yet except in the bigger towns and cities and in nuclei of rural settlement like Clandeboye and the Laggan where the towns of Hillsborough and Derry, respectively, would stand as beacons of Protestant resistance. However, Protestant strength lay not in weight of numbers but rather in landed wealth and the deference that went with that in a hierarchical society. Seigneurial influence was the smoothest and swiftest way to recruit and maintain bodies of troops. In no county of Ulster or the adjacent counties of Leitrim and Sligo did the Catholic proportion of landownership amount to over ten per cent, except in Antrim, where the vast Mac Donnell estates stood out. In consequence, would-be Irish captains and colonels were thin on the ground. Without such leaders, the natives could throw up only peasant freebooters and cattle drivers. Protestant apologists invariably claimed that they were forced to take up arms in self-defence against just such robbers and cattle thieves masquerading as soldiers. There may be some veracity in reports like those of one Protestant landowner resident in Ulster: 'all over the north the tenants do insult so much by reason that we have no civil government amongst us. The strongest hand carries all here.'[66] In truth, pleas of self-defence owe more to a self-serving narrative of loyalty tested beyond endurance than to objective truth. As early as 9 December 1688, not a month after William disembarked, amid wild rumours of impending massacre, Ulster Protestants 'began to appear in great Bodies of Horse and Foot, and take possession of Towns and Forts'.[67] Mountjoy's regiment had garrisoned Derry until ordered to embark, leaving Derry temporarily denuded of troops while the earl of Antrim was recruiting a replacement regiment. When his troops came to occupy the city, the gates were shut in their faces. The towns-people of Enniskillen, Co. Fermanagh, also shut out two companies of troops in mid-December.

During the two months of confusion between William's landing and James's successful flight to France in late December, Protestants in Ulster grouped themselves in associations directed by a central council or 'junto': Counties Donegal, Tyrone and Derry comprised one association, Armagh and Monaghan another, Antrim and Down a third. The outlying counties of Sligo, Leitrim and Cavan were also largely out of Tyrconnell's control, as would, from time to time, defiant enclaves widely scattered across the country, like Parsonstown (Birr) in King's County (Offaly), Bandon and Castlemartyr in Co. Cork, Ballinderry in Co. Wicklow, Nedeen (Kenmare) in Co. Kerry and Keenagh in Co. Longford.[68]

One English source gleefully imagines Tyrconnell hearing of Derry's defiance, raging, swearing, and hurling his hat and wig on the fire. Restless Jacobites, on the other hand, reproved Tyrconnell for being 'rather too slow' to move against the northerners. The reproof was unjust. The junto subsided after an initial burst of activity and showed no signs of marching on the capital. With only ten companies of foot and a handful of horse to hold Dublin, an enfeebled Tyrconnell could ill afford to poke at a slumbering bear.[69]

There are two ways to interpret Tyrconnell's actions, or inaction, during those weeks between news of William's landing and of James's flight. One can credit supporters and sympathisers who stoutly assert that right from the beginning the lord deputy was 'altogether for war', won the council round to his point of view, and secured its agreement to begin levying troops right away.[70] If he appeared outwardly to be wavering, they claimed, it was because he was really playing for time.

> While the usurper exhorted him to while he still could and offered rewards proportional to his unjust ambitions: while the insolence of the factious grew so bad that his life was not safe even in Dublin Castle; prudent and brave all at once, he reanimated the faltering courage of some, encouraged the wavering loyalty of others, [and] diverted those he predicted would emerge as leaders of a [hostile] party, cleverly deploying great patience and necessary dissimulation to stop the menacing unrest from growing until he could take appropriate steps to put it down.[71]

The alternative reading is that Tyrconnell was immobilised by shock at the sudden collapse of King James in England and would, if pressed, have capitulated.

Discussion of the capitulation counterfactual is confused by reports of a supposed diplomatic gambit. On 28 December 1688 Rice brought an offer from his master to surrender on terms to the Church of Ireland primate and to Granard, the de facto leaders of the Protestant community in Ireland. The primate and Granard sent a messenger to William bearing news of the overture. Meanwhile, John Keating, a Protestant judge who had escaped Tyrconnell's purges, heard or was told about the overture. Keating wrote the next day to his friend Sir John Temple the former Irish solicitor-general who had fled to England. Keating claimed that the lord deputy, after expiating on the horrors of war, had repeatedly declared that he would disband his army, surrender office and go home if James were so to 'signify his royal will' and if he could be assured that Irish Catholics would be left no worse off than they had been towards the end of Charles II's reign. Sir John was a brother of Sir William Temple, former ambassador to The Hague, whom William trusted and worked on to take office under him. The superannuated diplomat was now more interested in laying out his gardens at Sheene than in politics but he did not discourage his eldest son, another John Temple, from offering his services to William of Orange. One such service was to write to William Ellis, Sheridan's successor as Tyrconnell's secretary, with whom he was surely acquainted: Ellis's brother John had been secretary to Ossory (other brothers in the variegated Ellis family became Catholic and Church of Ireland bishops, respectively) while the Temples had also rotated in the Butler orbit. Ellis may have suggested in his reply that Richard Hamilton be picked as an emissary to convey reassurances to Tyrconnell and so convince him to come to terms. Hamilton had led reinforce-ments from Ireland to prop up James's regime, been stranded by the collapse, and imprisoned in the tower. John Temple the younger was already acquainted with Hamilton, no doubt through the first Duke of Ormond, Hamilton's uncle. Hamilton was also, of course, a connection of Tyrconnell's, indeed a very close one: to judge from the warmth of his expressions of 'love' to Mon cher frère. So Hamilton was a natural choice for go-between to persuade Tyrconnell to go quietly. Temple vouched for his trustworthiness and secured his release from the tower on parole together with a pass for Ireland and licence to gather stray Irish soldiers and take them with him.[72]

However, when Richard Hamilton arrived in Dublin on or about 8 January he promptly disavowed his mission.[73] He boasted that he had hoodwinked William of Orange into believing that he shared his wish for Tyrconnell to lay down arms and denied, even if he had so wished, that he could have influenced his brother-in-law to capitulate.[74] Armchair warriors declaimed that 'all the bloodshed in recovering Ireland would call for vengeance' from the wretched Temple. Three months after the abortive peace mission he would leap into the Thames as his boat was shooting the rapids under an arch of London Bridge where the whirling eddies dragged him under. His suicide note ambiguously apologised for 'folly in undertaking what I was not able to perform': he had been a week in his new post as secretary-at-war and it is more likely that he felt overwhelmed by his responsibilities than that he had been brooding over his earlier naïveté.

A core problem with the smoothed narrative of a Keating/Temple initiative is that the timeline does not work. Keating wrote on 29 December 1688 and a letter posted in Dublin would have taken from four to eight days to reach London, well after Hamilton had left.[75] Clearly the Temple/Hamilton mission preceded Keating's letter.

John Childs believes that Tyrconnell was only playing for time and had no more than a fleeting interest, if that, in a negotiated surrender while J. G. Simms believes that Tyrconnell might very well have capitulated if a timely and attractive initiative had been developed. Which of them is correct?[76]

There can be no doubt that the lord deputy expressed despondency at his master's fall. At a meeting with two Ulster Protestant envoys Tyrconnell admitted he was 'weary of the sword' but asked rhetorically 'what shall I do with it?' With no one claiming the sword of state, 'shall I throw it into the kennel?'[77] To other delegates, both Protestant and Catholic, he wondered aloud if he should cast the sword 'over the Castle walls' or 'in a ditch': the phrase differs but the sentiment rings true. Witnesses testifying in June 1689 to a House of Lords committee 'for enquiring into miscarriages in Ireland' asserted that Tyrconnell had quite lost his nerve on hearing of William's landing in England. He had melted down plate and loaded his moveable property onto a ship. Fretting about a hostile frigate prowling Dublin Bay, he next unloaded his goods and had his 'nephew' (he was in fact married to a niece of the lord deputy) Colonel William Nugent escort a train of sixty wagons, ostensibly laden with ammunition, to Galway. There may be more to this story than black propaganda. Arrangements for Nugent to bring a convoy of wagons supposedly carrying weapons from Dublin to Athlone were made in late December and abruptly cancelled on 6 January, two days before Richard Hamilton would land in Dublin.[78] Some members of the privy council even considered resistance hopeless. In particular, some 'new interest' Catholics feared they had more to lose than gain by upsetting the Act of Settlement. Privy counsellor William Dungan Earl of Limerick was one such. He begged his uncle to come to terms before William arrived: new interest landowners risked forfeiting 'good estates' in any war[79] and it was all very well for 'those who had none' to be bellicose.

Tyrconnell's pessimism was justifiable. Until he heard that James had escaped the hands of his enemies, it must have seemed quite possible that the mercurial monarch would indeed dismiss his lord deputy to smooth the path towards a compromise agreement with William. After all, he instructed his natural son, James Duke of Berwick, to surrender strategically vital Portsmouth and its Irish garrison without firing a shot. A report of 18 December, probably false, claimed that James's council (insofar as it was his any more) had sent an express to Ireland dismissing Tyrconnell and installing

Granard.[80] Too many sharp and suspicious observers were convinced that Tyrconnell was vacillating for his mood to be subtle dissimulation. Tyrconnell was a liar, but not a subtle one. His uncharacteristic wait and see passivity tends to confirm Tyrconnell's apparent depression. Contrary to alarmist reports current in England (one such report in mid-December claimed Tyrconnell had 20,000 men in arms and was 'daily signing commissions for the chiefs of all the tribes') only in January 1689 did he begin to expand the army, backdating commissions to 1 December, before James's 'desertion' from England, according to a hostile observer.[81] As late as February he had only two regiments in all of Ulster, one of them raw recruits (Antrim's) and the other (Newcomen's) still having 150 Protestants enrolled among the 500 private soldiers.[82]

There is a superficially plausible, but specious, logistical explanation for not recruiting troops sooner. As Tyrconnell explained to James, the only way to maintain an army in the field was by something like the French system of vivres whereby food and carriage was bought by ready money, 'but having no money to subsist, all the order and care I can take will not hinder the ruin of your country nor a famine before midsummer'.[83] But later the lord deputy would recruit a massive army of up to 36,000 troops without any assurance of cash and keep it fed hand-to-mouth by levying contributions in produce and by minting gun money.[84]

The 'fatal hour', from a Williamite perspective, came with Hamilton's arrival which heartened Tyrconnell.[85] He now had a competent and seasoned general he trusted whereas mutual dislike simmered between him and Justin MacCarthy Viscount Mountcashel, the next most senior officer. This probably dated back to the late 1650s when Tyrconnell was imposed on the MacCarthys as lieutenant colonel of York's regiment. Hamilton must also have brought confirmation of reports that James had at last fled England. This had to have been the news that really galvanised the hitherto gloomy lord deputy. With the king a free agent, the lord deputy no longer had to fear a royal order to lay down arms. He might suspect that such an order was coerced or know full well that it was the price James paid to rally support in England: regardless, he would have found it hard to ignore.

So, until news of James's flight reached Dublin, William still had a chance to bribe or bully Tyrconnell into capitulating. It is bootless to blame William for not sending troops to Ireland right away: 2,500 would have sufficed, guessed one exiled Anglo-Irish captain. He might as well have pitched on 25,000 as his estimates. William simply did not have troops to spare for Ireland. English troops sent to Ireland 'would probably have joined Tyrconnell': the Whig Bishop Burnet may be exaggerating but, rightly or wrongly, William did not trust his English army officers and still less the navy that would transport

them. Rebuilding and expanding a reliable and professional army would be
slow work and William's priority was to assemble and ship 10,000 troops to
the Spanish Netherlands.[86] William can, however, be blamed for complacently
deeming Ireland 'in a fair way to be settled'.[87] He read too much between the
lines of an intercepted letter from Tyrconnell to James in which Tyrconnell
pressed his king to flee for France or Ireland. William thought Tyrconnell
urged the latter choice 'more faintly'.[88]

In any event, William's trust in a peace deal was surely too fleeting to have
been developed. As part of the Hamilton/Temple mission Sir John Temple
and William Harboard had, at William's orders, drafted a proclamation on 2
January inviting Tyrconnell 'to lay down arms and deliver up the kingdom'.
The terms of the draft are unknown, but one can assume that it contained
assurances to Tyrconnell and to Irish Catholics regarding property and religion.
William had proceeded without reference to the sensibilities of the exiled
'English belonging to Ireland', as Clarendon, their spokesman called them.
They were, as William no doubt suspected, more interested in vengeance than
policy. On 16 December Clarendon had already importuned William to leave
his bed-chamber at Windsor and come out to hear from 'several lords and
persons of quality' from Ireland. Clarendon read out their petition, William
listened, assured them 'I will take care of you' and promptly withdrew. William
continued to snub Clarendon whenever he tried to buttonhole him again on
this or other business.[89]

On Friday 4 January Clarendon finally gained access to William's withdrawing room to emphasise how 'alarmed' the 'gentlemen of Ireland' were at
his proclamation and insisted that any initiative should be mulled over by a
gathering of the Protestant 'nobility and chief gentry' of Ireland who were then
present in town. Rather than continue to snub Clarendon, William suspended
the proclamation that very day and chose to bring in Ormond (the second
duke, old Ormond being dead by now), Burlington, Drogheda and the rest.
Anglo-Irish Protestants were, as the debate over the Treaty of Limerick would
later demonstrate, generally bent on punishment and retribution even if this
meant starting or dragging out war in Ireland. The proposal offered by them a
few days after Hamilton left, as recorded by Narcissus Luttrell, offered to turn
the clock back to 1684, the last full year of Charles II's reign thereby wiping out,
at a stroke, all the gains made by Catholics under James.[90] William had, even as
Hamilton was disembarking in Dublin, thrown away the chances of a timely
and attractive offer to the Irish by surrendering the initiative to the Protestants
of Ireland. On both sides, willingness to conclude a peace deal passed in the
first week of January.

Some days after Hamilton landed, Tyrconnell sent Stephen Rice and

Mountjoy to James's court in exile at St-Germain, supposedly to plead with James to let his Lord Deputy surrender. Tyrconnell briefed Mountjoy, an honourable but fatally credulous man, to be sure to let James know that while Tyrconnell said he could fight and make a 'heap of rubbish' of the country, at heart he believed it 'impossible' to hold out against William.[91] Another correspondent also used the word 'impossibility':

> He can hold the country till he has ruined it, laid it in ashes and made it as bare as it was in the first creation. But he cannot defend it without money and ammunition to maintain it. For though his army is numerous, yet it cannot subsist without the sinews of war and in keeping it on foot he shall ruin the country.

The writer, Francis Aungier 1st Earl of Longford, no friend of the lord deputy, did not doubt his sincerity but doubted that Louis would let James give the go-ahead to surrender.[92]

Tyrconnell also prevailed on Mountjoy to send letters to the Northern Association's leaders telling them of his mission to have the lord deputy 'lay down the Sword' and advising them to desist from attacks in the meantime. It was all a ruse. On arrival Mountjoy was imprisoned in the Bastille (Rice carried secret orders to that effect from Tyrconnell) where he would stay until exchanged in 1692: he was killed that same year at Steinkirk. William, no mean dissembler himself, was not taken in by the mission, dismissing it as but 'an artifice to gain time'.[93] Tyrconnell's trickery did gain time and also swept a potentially very able leader of the Ulster Protestants off the board. Mountjoy was but one of the many Protestants in Ireland, especially those of pre-1640s family origins, whose attitude to Catholics was less hostile and whose reaction to James's regime was more nuanced than apologists like William King would later claim.[94] Because of his associations and personal contacts with leaders of that community over the years, men like Ormond, Orrery, Burlington, Ranelagh, Granard and Mountjoy, to name but some, Tyrconnell was especially well placed to persuade some influential Protestants to co-operate with his government and others not to revolt against it. Men like Rev Alexander Osborn or Sir Robert Colville of Newtown Co, Antrim, a member of the Council of Five governing the Protestant Association in east Ulster, half-believed his assurances, however much they denied this later.[95] The lord deputy played a weak hand with both skill and bluff.[96] It was generally considered his finest hour and it reinforced his sense of destiny: four months later Dominic Sheldon the lieutenant colonel of Tyrconnell's horse regiment wrote to his patron invoking 'God Almighty who has made use of your Grace as an instrument to preserve the King's authority in this Kingdom.'[97]

A week or so after Hamilton, a French emissary arrived. Tyrconnell evidently saw the importance of putting on a brave face to the baron de Pointis. Gone was all talk of capitulation as he briefed de Pointis to report to Minister Seignelay that the Irish would not only hold out but would even carry the war to England if more weapons (Seignelay brought or promised 8,000 muskets), money and officers were supplied. De Pointis was struck by the enthusiasm of recruits he saw training at Waterford but dismayed that only half of them hefted either a musket or pike, with the rest making do with nail-tipped sticks as makeshift half-pikes.[98] By the end of January Tyrconnell had issued commissions for a gigantic army of 35,000–36,000 men in up to 46 regiments though 'without arms to defend them, clothes to clothe them, or money to subsist them'. He wrote to James on 29 January alternating extravagant promises (if he came in person he would be 'entirely master of this kingdom' in a month) with offensively reproachful appeals by asking 'whether you can with honour continue where you are'. If the Irish were to be starved of supplies, Tyrconnell asked James 'to order such course for their preservation as your goodness and mercy will move you for their security in these dismal circumstances'. Decoded, it was an appeal for James to grant permission for Tyrconnell to capitulate.[99] Tyrconnell had not, nor would not, completely forget about this contingency plan.

Tyrconnell's lobbying helped convince the French ministers that James should set sail for Ireland and Louis, in turn, pushed James into going. On the face of it, his yearning to have his king on hand is surprising. He must surely have foreseen the constraints that James's presence in Dublin would impose on him. That Tyrconnell nonetheless wanted the king on hand as the legitimising figurehead shows how strongly he was committed to carrying the fight to Britain. Of course he had a (second) fallback plan: an envoy was sent to Versailles to plead with the sun king to take the Irish under his protection if James would not come to Ireland.[100]

But that was for the future. Meanwhile, his hold on the capital was feeble so long as armed Protestants living in Dublin completely outnumbered the garrison. At last, Tyrconnell nerved himself. On 24 February troops slipped into the city and stood at the gates and at every street junction where they curtailed the movement of civilians. All civilians were ordered to deliver up weapons at the door of each parish church. Though Protestants were not mentioned specifically, the reference to those who might help the 'Rebels' in Ulster was clear enough. The order threatened, in effect, that if arms were found in a subsequent search of a house the soldiers would be unleashed to ransack and pillage it.[101] The order yielded several thousand weapons and soon the scheme to commandeer weapons and serviceable horses was extended countrywide.

By then the chance of a peaceful handover had well and truly passed. The forum for the exiled Anglo-Irish, the 'Committee of Irish Lords and Commons', met on 14 February and left the terms to be offered to Tyrconnell as William 'in his great wisdom shall think fit' while asking that the terms be such as would 'encourage' the Protestants of Ireland. Eight days later William and Mary issued a proclamation threatening the Irish who were resisting their authority 'at the instigation of Romish priests'. The promises offered in exchange for laying down their arms were vague and equivocal. They would enjoy 'all the favour for the private exercise of their religion that the law allows'. What did 'private' mean: that a chaplain could say mass privately in a nobleman's household, that a parish priest could build a recognised mass-house, that a bishop could exercise his functions? Irish Catholics were also assured of 'full and free enjoyment of their respective estates', again, 'according to law'. The insertion of the last qualifying clause cast doubt on guarantees, and was probably intended to do so. Laws can change and the post-war Irish parliament would be a Protestant one. One sees the same phrase crop up in other propaganda and in the terms of the capitulation of Limerick in 1691 which drew a line under the war. [102]

On or about 20 February, too, the Council of the North belatedly and briefly attacked Carrickfergus, one must assume to gain control of Belfast Lough, a prime anchorage for an invasion fleet. [103] Though the Dublin government had lost control of most of Ulster, it still held outposts at Newry, Charlemont and Carrickfergus which could facilitate the reconquest of the eastern part of the province. A fortnight later, Tyrconnell at last sent Richard Hamilton north with a small army of some 2,500 men. [104]

The Protestant Association called a rendezvous at Hillsborough and posted an advance guard at Dromore to delay Hamilton's march on Hillsborough, Belfast and Carrickfergus. Order, counter-order, and disorder followed. Protestant Association troopers waiting at Dromore charged what looked like a scattering of Irish outriders only to stumble on Hamilton's main body. The Ulstermen fled and their panic infected the main army at Hillsborough where other terrified irregulars scattered homeward. The Break of Dromore (14 March 1689) relinquished Ulster east of the Bann to the Jacobites. A repulse to the Irish at Coleraine gave the Protestant Association forces a three-week breathing space before Hamilton was able to gather his men again (they had scattered to forage and pillage) and push them across the Bann at Portglenone. [105] Faced with the danger of being cut off, the garrison of Coleraine evacuated the town and fell back to Derry, the only walled city in Ulster. Meanwhile, Robert Lundy, Mountjoy's lieutenant colonel and governor of Derry, called outlying strongholds like Dungannon, Enniskillen and Sligo back to concentrate in the Laggan, Derry's western hinterland. [106] Lundy ordered up to 10,000 men to hold the crossing points of the river Finn at 'Long Causeway' (probably near Porthall) Lifford, and Clady, to guard the Laggan. Lundy's army was a 'disorganised and unarticulated mob' and, seeing this, Hamilton took a calculated risk to send his cavalry swimming across the river at Clady, foot soldiers clinging to the horses' manes, tails and saddles. Protestant irregulars do not seem to have favoured the pike and so the foot soldiers nervously waiting at Clady, however numerous, could only have hoped to repel cavalry by heavy and concentrated firepower. But they quickly shot off what little ammunition they had and as the Irish formed up on the bank the defenders shouted 'To Derry! to Derry!' and ran. When Lundy heard of the crossing he ordered a general withdrawal, sent away reinforcements from England and advised the council-of-war to surrender, seeing that the city was about to be cut off from its hinterland.[107] To all appearances Hamilton had won the war for Tyrconnell.

James had disembarked at Kinsale on the day before the Break of Dromore, the first English king in three centuries to visit the country. He reached Cork three days later where Tyrconnell conferred with him for two hours:

> The King did him all the honours that sovereigns can do for their subjects, indeed once he saw him he went forward to the door of his chamber, embraced him and lauded the unshakeable firmness he had displayed in his service. He not only did him the honour of bidding him dine at his table but he set him at his right hand side and the Duke of Berwick at his left. In a word, the King conferred on him every mark and proof of his satisfaction due such a subject and made him Duke of Tyrconnell as a token of his esteem.[108]

Departing Cork on Wednesday 20 March, the royal party made a stately four-day progress towards the capital. The king seems to have been testy on the road: 'slobbered with kisses' from countrywomen near Carlow, he irritably bade them 'kept from him'. About a mile from Dublin he called for a fresh horse which broke loose before he could mount, 'so that he said to Tyrconnel, I think you are all boder'd'. Tyrconnell was no doubt bothered and anxious that the upcoming triumphal procession through the capital would go without a hitch. So it did. Even seen through the eyes of a hostile witness, the ceremonial welcome was a splendidly pompous affair. At St James's Gate harpists plucked their strings on a stage covered with tapestry, a 'great number' of friars sang, the Lord Mayor waited, a spokesman for the waiting municipal dignitaries and guildsmen made an eloquent speech of welcome and the Herald and King at Arms presented the sword of state. James promptly handed over the sword to Tyrconnell to carry in the procession. The gesture can be read as something more meaningful than a sop to a old and faithful servant. The person

Anna Maria Talbot *née* **Brudenell, Countess of Shrewsbury, by Sir Peter Lely** *c.*1670

Frances Hamilton *née* **Jennings, by Henri Gascard** *c.*1675.
MOU997163 Photo courtesy of The Bridgeman Art Library, London.

Lady Catherine and Lady Charlotte Talbot, by John Michael Wright *c.*1679.
NGI.4184 Photo courtesy of the National Gallery of Ireland.

imagined. D'Avaux feared that bad blood between Tyrconnell and Mountcashel would cause problems but as it happened the really divisive and bitter personality clash would be between Tyrconnell and Melfort. Both attended, along with James and D'Avaux, an inner council meeting at seven o'clock every evening where the French ambassador noticed 'some little rift' between Tyrconnell and Melfort.[111] A resident secretary of state for Ireland necessarily curtailed the lord deputy's personal and political authority since one of the two English secretaries of state normally handled Irish business. But for James to pick Melfort for this post rather than Henry Jermyn, Viscount Dover, an ally of Tyrconnell's, must be seen as a deliberate curb on the newly minted duke.

Quite apart from political and personal matters, James's three chief counsellors embodied distinct, and sometimes divergent, interests and strategic priorities. First was what one might call a 'British' Jacobite interest which contained within it two policy-based factions. Protestant Jacobites wanted James to 'live a Catholick in devotion, but reign a Protestant in government' and envisaged a peaceful negotiated restoration. James distrusted Protestants and excluded them from positions of real authority and so the Catholic faction won by default. This faction was represented by the insatiably ambitious Melfort who demanded uncompromising restoration by force of arms.[112] This would not be so difficult because, Melfort was sure, James's subjects would welcome him back with open arms.[113] For Melfort, Ireland was a stepping-stone. Just as soon as Derry was taken or even before, an army should embark for Scotland, and thence march south on England.[114]

Irish Jacobitism was not a British ideology and paid relatively little attention to such themes as the sovereign authority of the crown, the divine right of kings and the principle of hereditary succession by primogeniture. It was distinctive in its abhorrence of Protestantism, its support for Ireland's status as a distinct and ancient kingdom and, more immediately, its desire to revoke the Acts of Settlement and Explanation.[115] The admirer of Tyrconnell who penned the 'Light to the Blind' is unusual among Irish writers in favouring an expedition to Scotland, but only if it had been embarked right away: 'there was a great fault committed in not transporting the Irish army into Scotland or England within two or three months of the king's arrival in Dublin'.[116] Implicitly, he conceded that an expeditionary strategy was no longer viable after summer 1689. 'Charity begins at home' insisted Bishop O'Molony, another of Tyrconnell's partisans, when he set out two commonly held and immediately relevant beliefs of Irish Jacobites:

> For never a Catholick or other English will ever think or make a step, nor suffer the King to make a step for your restauration …: and yet by their fine politics, they

would persuade the Irish to come over and save their houses from burning whilst they leave their own on fire.[117]

O'Molony was sceptical about a stepping-stone strategy and hoped the Irish would secure their island from sea to sea before embarking on expeditions. Knowingly or unconsciously, he was repeating the advice of the Catholic clergy in the 1640s in opposition to those like Robert Talbot for whom everything must take second place to shipping an army to Chester.

Where the author of the 'Light to the Blind' had the benefit of more than a decade of reflection, O'Kelly's *Destruction of Cyprus* was written immediately after the war.[118] O'Kelly elaborated a conspiracy theory whereby James II did not want to reconquer Ireland at all having been convinced 'that the only way to recover England was to lose Ireland'. Then 'the English would immediately recall him'.[119] O'Kelly's perception that Tyrconnell, or 'Coridon' as he allegorically names him, treacherously wanted to lose the war all along underpins his entire narrative, explaining every reverse and missed opportunity. Corydon is a stock character representing a shepherd in classical pastoral poetry and quite why O'Kelly chose this allegorical nickname is unclear. Corydon can variously represent homoerotic love, cowardice (in Spenser's Faerie Queene he is afraid to rescue his love from a tiger's claws) rustic simplicity, innocence and constancy, as in Sidney's 'Faire Phillis hath the fairest face, that ever eye did yet behold :/ And Coridon the constants faith, that ever yet kept flocke in fold'. O'Kelly may have intended the latter meanings as an ironic counterpoint to Tyrconnell's real character.[120]

Advocates of an 'Irish' policy like O'Kelly realised that they could not survive unaided and nursed extravagant hopes that Louis XIV would step in as their protector. To take an example of such a fantasist, Daniel O'Brien Viscount Clare heaped scorn on James after the Boyne and hoped that, since he had shown himself an unfit king he would cede Ireland to Louis so that the latter would then adopt her cause 'as his own'.[121]

Irish attitudes to James were ambivalent: 'As bad as James was, it was worse to be without him'.[122] Demand for complete reversal of the Acts of Settlement, in particular, set the Irish at odds with James in the parliament which he called for May 1689. The Commons passed a bill repealing the Acts amidst a clamour of cheers. James opposed repeal, keen as ever to display his attachment to the English interest in Ireland. Tyrconnell's attitude is unfathomable. If the poem of his adviser, Thomas Nugent Baron Riverston, is any guide, he probably opposed complete repeal and supported a compromise bill in the Lords.

it was decreed/That acts be published which would harm the folk/That asked for them. The list of lands is changed,/Estates removed from their new owners judged,/

By alteration of the law, now to belong/To their old masters, though the property/
Had not yet been recovered from the ones/Now in possession of it. So, one time,/A
hunter sold in various lots the skin/From off a bear he had not captured yet:[123]

Anthony Dopping, Church of Ireland bishop of Meath and leader of the
Protestant opposition in the upper house echoed this sentiment, sneering that
the Irish were 'trying to dispose of the skin before the beast had been slain'.[124]
All too aware that frustrated members of the Commons would delay voting
subsidies until the act was passed, Tyrconnell swallowed his pride and had his
nephew and law lord Sir William Talbot of Carton implore the Lords to pass
the bill of the lower house without further delay. The new interest would be
compensated by lands confiscated following an act of attainder outlawing
those who had fled the country or joined the northern associations. This act
brought on a fit of royal anger and a nose bleed.[125] But James had to give way
and complained privately that 'he was fallen into the hands of a people who
rammed many hard things down his throat'.[126] James was also affronted by a
Declaratory Act denying that laws passed by the English parliament applied
to Ireland and he acceded to it only with the greatest reluctance. He would not
agree to repeal Poynings' Law: the latter denied the Irish parliament legislative
initiative and forced it to send drafts or heads of bills to be vetted by the
English privy council. Nor would he agree to disestablish the Church of
Ireland and forbade the seizure of Protestant churches by Catholics.

James, D'Avaux remarked, 'has a heart too English'. He had no special
partiality to Irishmen, whatever his critics might say: for instance, just two of
the seventeen members of his post-war court at St-Germain were Irish.[127]
James held out against Irish nationalist claims even to the extent of forfeiting
their goodwill. To again use Gaelic poetry as an expression of popular feeling,
after initial jubilation and valorising of the réalta ríoghda [royal star] in poems
like Ó Bruadair's Caithréim an dara rígh Séamas, James quickly becomes an
iconic cipher to the common people rather than the object of true feeling:
criticised while in Ireland and only lamented in his absence.[128]

Louis felt sympathy for his kinsman but was not willing to devote the
naval and manpower resources to restore him to all three thrones.[129] 'The Irish
business is admirable', enthused Madame de Sévigné a month before James
embarked for Ireland, 'and occupies the Prince of Orange so completely that
there is nothing to be feared on our coast'.[130] That about summed up French
policy, blinkered, opportunistic and short-term. Louis wanted a war-by-proxy of
limited liability. His primary interest, either to control or deny to the enemy, lay
in territories that abutted France like the Spanish Netherlands, Cologne, the
Palatinate, Savoy and Catalonia and he shied away from heavy commitments

further afield. At the very most Ireland was a diversion and he hoped that a long-drawn-out Irish war might distract and weaken the Anglo-Dutch component of the Grand Alliance. Seignelay, the minister of marine, supported an Irish diversion but war minister Louvois who was by far the most powerful of Louis's ministers impeded Siegnelay, claiming to fear dissipating French resources on far-flung maritime theatres, but really because of the Le Tellier-Colbert feud both ministers had inherited from their fathers.[131] Moreover, such was Seignelay's commitment to guerre d'escarade culminating in the clash of huge fleets in the English Channel that he neglected sending squadrons on the seas around Ireland. As a result of this neglect, Williamite troop transports and provision ships could sail back and forth across the Irish Sea unimpeded at a time when the French were the dominant power at sea. Louis supplied some money, a sprinkling of specialist officers, artillerists and engineers, munitions and poor-quality weapons in 1689.[132] A 6,000-strong expeditionary force would be sent in 1690, but only after a matching number of Irish soldiers was transported to France.[133] Only in the third and last year of the war did the French ship really significant quantities of munitions and provisions.

On paper, Louis backed James's restoration but attached preconditions to any descent on Britain, among them the demand that a large body of armed supporters should be waiting for the French, holding a well-fortified port. Later invasion schemes of England would hang fire on that very point.[134] In the short term, D'Avaux insisted that the Irish had to capture Derry first and only then send a small detachment of 2,000–3,000 to Scotland.[135]

If one had to compartmentalise, Tyrconnell's strategic vision must be seen as mostly 'British', rather than 'Irish' or 'French'. However much he detested Melfort, he shared with him an impatience to invade Britain and a conviction that long-term security for Ireland was contingent on Jacobite revival in Britain. His was not an 'Irish' policy except to the extent that he would have encroached on his master's sovereignty if it embroiled the French more deeply and irretrievably in Ireland by, for instance, proposing that James cede Galway and Waterford, 'or any other ports of this kingdom' to Louis.[136] From time to time he may have toyed with notions of a French protectorate as a fallback plan, as he had before the birth of a Catholic heir, but he was too sceptical about French motives to pursue this chimera. With his back to the wall after the Boyne, Tyrconnell would repeatedly reassure Viscount Clare that he had written to James to ask that he cede Ireland to Louis but he had not and would not.[137] While giving Frenchmen every outward impression of good will he could be surprisingly bitter about them in his correspondence with Queen Mary. He groaned that Louvois was niggardly in supplying arms and munitions. 'We are only destined to serve a present turn' and soon, he sighed, the

Irish will 'be knocked in the head for them'.[138] 'For them': the Irish were fighting for the French.

The British or expeditionary strategy was stillborn. Sending just a single regiment of Irish dragoons to Kintyre had dramatically boosted the cause of the Jacobite fugitive James Graham, Viscount Dundee. He raised eight Highland battalions from some thirty clans by the end of June and while passing through Atholl to the central lowlands on 17 July he cut through a Williamite army that stood in his path. But Killiecrankie was a pyrrhic victory.[139] Dundee was mortally wounded and without his inspirational leadership the Highland host soon lost strategic momentum. It is highly unlikely that Dundee could have overthrown William's regime in Scotland, but with further reinforcements of Irish horsemen he could have campaigned in the Lowlands thereby protracting the counter-revolution in Britain and diverting English attention and resources from Ireland throughout 1689 and into 1690.

But the Jacobites could not simply leave a covering force near Derry and still send a reasonably big expedition to Scotland in the summer of 1689 because this would have left no reserve of armed troops behind in Ireland.[140] Tyrconnell and even Melfort, reluctantly, agreed at the time that a major expedition could not set sail until Derry fell. And that siege went awry from the beginning. Ignoring the pleas of D'Avaux and Tyrconnell, James allowed Melfort bring him north to Armagh where reinforcements for Derry were making a rendez-vous. The royal road show had been a ploy by Melfort to keep the king away from Dublin and apart from Tyrconnell. James made no discernable contribution to operations, indeed he later pushed on to Derry where he cut across and undermined Hamilton's negotiations with the governor and burghers.[141]

Derry's eighteen-foot-thick masonry and earth ramparts could withstand all but close-range fire from big siege pieces, that is culverins and upwards. To take the city would have demanded a 'siege in form', digging sinuous or dog-legged trenches and dragging big guns through them close enough to batter a breach. Encamped at the very end of a long and frangible line of communications, the Irish were not supplied for a proper siege while the defenders had ample troops, more guns and better gunners.[142] An early sortie at Pennyburn, about a mile north of the walls, accounted for Lieut-Gen. Maumont the commander-in-chief and Pusignan his second-in-command. Thereafter, command of the siege fell on Richard Hamilton's shoulders.

Field officers usually lacked the patience and skill to direct a siege in form and typically cut corners with bloody and often futile assaults.[143] Hamilton was no exception. Twice he threw away his men's lives in bungled assaults on a twelve-foot high rampart that ran from the top of Windmill Hill, south of the city walls, down to the Foyle. The attack on 5 May left up to 150 men dead or mortally wounded. Among them was Lieut-Col. 'Wicked Will' Talbot, son of Henry Talbot of Templeogue Co. Dublin and a nephew of Tyrconnell's.[144] Another frontal assault against the Windmill Hill-Foyle rampart on 4 June ground to a halt for want of scaling ladders.[145]

The city was packed with refugees and was held by over 7,000 soldiers. A relief fleet stood off in Lough Foyle deterred by a boom across the river. By 27 July the garrison's numbers had fallen to 4,456 men, the last cows and horses had been slaughtered and morale was low. Next day the fleet broke the flimsy boom and Derry was relieved.[146] The Irish raised the siege three days later and hastened south.

Hamilton's failure reflected especially badly on Tyrconnell, his mentor. The poet Riverston, a loyal member of Tyrconnell's cabinet, declaimed that the defenders could have been starved into submission if Hamilton had not been so ready to give refugees passes to escape the city and go home: 'O noble general! What a chance you lost, By your inertia, to subdue the town/Filled by a starving people and now faint And ready with your orders to comply.' Riverston smelt treachery. Clearly, William had planted a double agent: 'That this man, lately captive, [captivum nuper] to our loss/With evil omen has been by the English sent/To undertake and do the bidding of/The new-made tyrant ...'.[147]

Meanwhile, in a separate operation, a Jacobite army led by Mountcashel began to pull back towards Co. Cavan from the settler enclave around Enniskillen. He was overtaken near Newtownbutler. The Irish horsemen fled, the foot soldiers fired a few volleys and then they too bolted. It was a 'break' or rout just like Dromore or Cladyford except that the runaways did not escape on this occasion. Unfamiliar with the country, they fled west towards the turf-bogs, inlets, ponds and thickets along the shore of Lough Erne where they were trapped and hunted down: at least 2,000 were killed and 300 captured, including Mountcashel. Patrick Sarsfield, leading another advance on Enniskillen, pulled back to Sligo, then hastily fled south out of town. In September the Enniskillen men would use Sligo as a base to capture outposts on the upper Shannon.[148] Twelve days after Newtownbutler a 10,000 strong expedition sailed from near Chester in order to land in east Ulster and from there march on Dublin. The expedition was led by Marshal Schomberg, the 'ablest soldier of his age'.[149]

D'Avaux had counted on Tyrconnell as an ally against Melfort, who he saw as a scheming liar, during that crucial time when the Irish parliament sat and the siege of Derry dragged on. He found Tyrconnell neglectful of business after the latter took to his sickbed in or about late April. The patient was splenetic (here D'Avaux was offering a medical diagnosis as well as a character assessment) and fits of temper slowed his recuperation, suggesting that the problem was partly psychological: as Mountjoy had noted, Tyrconnell tended to sicken when vexed or thwarted. If he should die, fretted D'Avaux, 'it will be a loss for this country [Ireland] and for the King [Louis] to whom he is as devoted as the best Frenchman could be'.[150] The sickness was punctuated by rallies and relapses: in early May a correspondent was already congratulating Tyrconnell on being 'pretty well' now, 'though you had not been so'.[151] The patient was well enough by mid-June to conduct some urgent business from his chamber but from now on he would be permanently weakened by heart palpitations and intermittently bedridden or incapacitated by a weeping wound in his leg.[152] Tyrconnell probably suffered from osteomyelitis, an infection deep in the bone from an old war wound that had ulcerated and turned septic. This was a hazard common to old cavaliers. In his last year Prince Rupert, too, suffered from an ulcerated leg and Henry VIII suffered from a permanently suppurating leg wound, a painful reminder of a jousting accident.[153] Fighting osteomyelitis stresses the body's immune system and often leads to excessive strain on the heart. So, Tyrconnell's palpitations and ulcer were probably linked as an intractable, and ultimately fatal, condition which inflicted chronic pain and no doubt soured his temper.

The rudderless drift of those months is captured by the Munster poet Dáibhidh Ó Bhruadair who bewailed rule by a weak old man 'who could not walk a step' [gan riachtain coiscéime] and a senseless fool [amal gan chiall] and left it to his audience to put names to the pair.[154] Avid for power, if only to deny it to his rival, Melfort showed little intelligence or energy in exercising it and was little more than a cipher and flatterer. The Irish abhorred him, perhaps displacing onto him some of their disillusionment with James. A Commons motion to impeach Melfort was apparently headed off only by Tyrconnell's intervention behind the scenes. Even if the secretary of state had been the most charming of men, he could hardly have endeared himself to the Irish. He was the figure most closely identified with unpopular royal policies and had to handle, or rather put on the long finger, the delicate business of demobilising a bloated, unarmed and unsustainable army and so disappoint the colonels and captains who had maintained them and would now be out of pocket.

Tyrconnell put on the guileless façade of 'a plain man' who bluntly spoke the truth, disdained personal intrigues, and bit back resentments for the public good: 'It's a dissembling age. I must confess I doe not love it, and care not to practice it, but nothing is lost by being civil to all.'[155] However, Melfort had grounds for his suspicions that Tyrconnell hypocritically professed 'friendship and respect' but 'let loose a pack of about fifty nephews against me'.[156] As proof of Melfort's suspicions, Tyrconnell lobbied to have his nephew William Talbot of Carton replace the odious Scotsman.[157]

In August 1689 the Jacobite regime faced a mortal threat. One 'extremely shattered and thin' army retreated slowly from Derry, shedding its sick, wounded, baggage and artillery train, while another had been annihilated at Newtown-butler.[158] The threat energised Tyrconnell whose 'zeal, loyalty and experience', in D'Avaux's words, was never more sorely needed.[159] Tyrconnell finally secured a private audience with James on or about 7 August where he bluntly warned the king to give over any plans to flee: 'to quit the army is to forfeit the crown'.[160] James denied that he had any such plans and countered with an assertion that Melfort had hinted that Tyrconnell wanted to get rid of James and resume undisputed control of Ireland. In frenetic inner council meetings over the next few days Melfort overreached himself. He called D'Avaux a liar to his face, prompting the king to apologise, explaining that Scots were notorious for bad temper and touchiness. Melfort charged Conrad Von Rosen, the ranking French officer in Ireland, with disloyalty and defeatism. It is true that Rosen derided James saying that he 'knows not how to punish or reward'. Army officers as a whole laid the blame on Melfort for all the disaster that had befallen them. Schomberg's disembarkation finally destroyed Melfort's credibility, given that he had pooh-poohed intelligence reports and insisted the siege of Derry drag on hopelessly. When Tyrconnell finally went public and denounced Melfort as 'a Sunderland' he was delivering a grave insult: James's former chief minister was a byword for double-dealing and Jacobites supposed he had treacherously played down reports of the Dutch descent.[161] The comparison was unjust. Melfort, for all his faults, was an utterly sincere Jacobite and had not converted to Catholicism for reasons of political opportunism.

In a last desperate gambit to detach D'Avaux from Tyrconnell, Melfort insisted that he was the victim of petticoat power because Frances Lady Tyrconnell wanted to oust him in order to shield two of the Hamilton brothers, Anthony and Richard, from court martial charges of incompetence and cowardice. Melfort then and later accused Lady Tyrconnell of being a schemer and war profiteer. He also hinted that she had played the whore at Versailles. The first two accusations were justifiable: she was, like her sister Sarah, grasping and greedy. As to the third charge, other hostile commentators like Sheridan and O'Kelly levelled a similar accusation, the latter hinting that as a young widow she had slept with Louvois. A lie does not become truth because enough people retell it but the accusation has circumstantial plausibility. Louvois was notorious for abusing his position to bed officers' wives, Frances was in a very vulnerable position, and she somehow managed to get her hands on back payments owing to her late husband from the court.[162] Maybe she did so through the merits of her case, as her current husband dutifully insisted.

The official version of Melfort's fall is that, worn down by implacable and unjustified hostility, he made a dignified offer to resign the secretaryship and James accepted. To save Melfort's face James bestowed an English peerage on him and arranged that he go to Versailles, to report in person on the Irish situation. Melfort left Dublin on 22 August 1689, the day James marched north, having been tipped off that, given half a chance, Tyrconnell would have him assassinated.[163] His departure clarified the lines of authority and gave an immediate fillip to army morale.[164] Melfort's post was split in two. Civil affairs were assigned to William Talbot while Richard Nagle took up the more onerous duties of secretary of state for war and carried them out with quiet competence. Appointing William Talbot seems to have been a sop to Tyrconnell which the king soon regretted. He dismissed Talbot five months later and replaced him with Ignatius White the Marquis d'Albeville, his former ambassador to the United Provinces.[165]

Schomberg eventually disembarked at Belfast Lough on 13 August but, luckily for the Jacobites, he frittered away the next fortnight besieging the small and hopelessly cut-off outpost of Carrickfergus Castle when he should have left a covering force and marched down the open road to Dublin. The pause let the Jacobites collect men from the debris that washed out of Ulster, and frantically gather recruits. After taking Carrickfergus on terms, Schomberg marched south towards Dublin but made it only as far as Dundalk, about half-way, by 7 September 1689. Here he stopped and waited.[166]

And waited. Nearly half of Schomberg's troops who had marched south perished of epidemic disease by Christmas, or soon after, in camp, hospital ship, base hospital (surely a grandiloquent term for a disused warehouse in Belfast) and winter quarters. For all the recriminations about maladministration and malfeasance, the débâcle at Dundalk was not, in essence, a logistical problem.[167] During his first five weeks at Dundalk Schomberg could have pushed on against an army which was still marginally smaller: he had perhaps 16,000 troops to James's 13,600. He chose to skulk behind earthworks waiting, at first for cavalry reinforcements and later for the Irish to pull back. An epidemic with the characteristic footprint of typhus (sudden onset, sharp deterioration and usually fatal outcome) would sweep through lice-ridden soldiers huddled in squalid bothys for more than a month at a time.

When James reached Drogheda on 26 August, Schomberg was still besieging Carrickfergus. A council of war dominated by D'Avaux and French officers advised the king to mount a delaying action near Newry just long enough for the troops gathering near Dublin to scurry towards Athlone. In other words, the French wanted James to abandon the capital, and all of the country except Connacht and Clare which lay behind the Shannon. Their advice was defeatist and fatuous. The river line was by now an illusory line of defense because Sligo had fallen: the town along with Athlone and Limerick was one of the strategic gateways into Connacht-Clare. James played for time by sending Nagle back to Dublin to consult Tyrconnell, other top Irish officials, and the Hamilton brothers. They declared that if Schomberg came on slowly they would have time to gather and arm enough troops to fight him.

Sure enough, shortly afterwards Tyrconnell joined the king at Drogheda, bringing many reinforcements. Tyrconnell was probably sincere in reassuring D'Avaux that he would not lightly hazard a battle. Having refused to be run out of Ireland as he had been from England, James had grown worryingly bellicose and Tyrconnell feared that he might lead from the front in a battle and be taken prisoner.[168] He might then strike a deal with his enemies and disown his Irish supporters as had his brother Charles in 1650 and 1660.

On 17 September James pitched camp within five miles of Schomberg, along a ridge looking north. Four days later, James led the army to within half a mile of the enemy camp, kept them waiting three hours in line of battle and then marched them back. He had no intention of storming Schomberg's fortifications but perhaps he expected Schomberg to come and really was 'disappointed in his hopes of deciding the war by a battle', as a Jacobite newsletter claimed.[169] At any rate the coat-trailing by raw, poorly armed, underfed, and sickly troops intimidated Schomberg. In the end the Irish had to break off first but then it was too late for Schomberg's army to pursue them.[170]

James had endured the rigours of autumnal encampment and displayed exemplary courage in the face of his enemy. For his part, Tyrconnell had performed prodigies of improvisation. He then overruled D'Avaux (while still maintaining cordial relations with him), arguing cogently that the army's fragile self-confidence would not survive a demoralising retreat to Dublin. It was he, more than anyone, who inflicted the worst military disaster of the war on King William's army without firing a shot.

To sum up, as lord deputy, Tyrconnell had built up a loyalist redoubt but had almost fatally weakened it when he ill-advisedly sent so many troops to England before the Dutch descent. This decision, his abject defeatism in the weeks following the descent, and his acceptance of a compromise on the Acts of Settlement and Explanation all show that he was attuned to the imperatives of British Jacobitism and out of step with the aspirations of the Irish Catholic community. It was for that reason, not for a supposed antipathy towards Gaelic Irishmen, that he would never achieve the sort of widespread or lasting popularity that would survive adversity, though he enjoyed a brief political honeymoon as the 'darling of the nation'.[171] Regardless of popular feeling, he garnered significant support through ramifying familial networks and a handful of able gownmen. Once he learned that King James had escaped from his enemies he quickly recovered from the shock of the revolution, used patience and guile to stay the mortal threat posed by Protestant insurrection and kept a grip on the capital. He energetically raised a strong army from puny resources to, almost, snuff out Protestant insurgency in Ulster. The failure to capture Derry put an end to hopes of exporting counter-revolution to Britain, his preferred strategic choice. Disabling sickness beset him at this crucial moment. The incompetence of cher frère Hamilton at Derry reflected badly on his patron, though others, above all Melfort, shouldered more blame. As before, disaster energised Tyrconnell. He outmanoeuvred Melfort, as he had Clarendon, Sunderland and Sheridan before him and for a second time mobilised an army from scratch. Throughout, he displayed foresight, a sure touch and a cynically realistic appraisal of his enemies and of his friends, especially his vacillating monarch. Above all he understood better than anyone the limitations imposed by half-hearted allies. In September 1689, with Schomberg's army depleted and demoralised, the war was not yet lost. That was largely Tyrconnell's achievement.

SIX

LORD LIEUTENANT
1690–1

After his autumnal surge of energy, James relapsed into gloomy passivity and spent the winter away from the capital, dreaming of a descent on Britain.[1] Back in the real world, the burden of preparing for the next campaigning season fell on Tyrconnell's shoulders. Most contemporary Jacobite accounts found him wanting and condemned what they saw as both his timorous failure to follow up his advantage at Dundalk and his lethargy in preparing for next summer.

As to accusations of timidity, Tyrconnell was all too familiar with the limitations of his scratch army, 'impetuous in advance and headlong in retreat', and it was prudent of him not to dog Schomberg's footsteps north. Winter saw some skirmishing along the southern fringes of Ulster. The Jacobites raided Newry and kept up tenuous contact with Charlemont. For their part, the Williamites burnt Cavan and ultimately took Charlemont. Schomberg had begun the siege in April, unseasonably early, while Tyrconnell was still waiting until May, when the grass would have grown and his cavalry mounts could graze. The guns and munitions left in the fort during the retreat from Derry were now forfeit so losing Charlemont was a defeat, however much Tyrconnell assured Mary of Modena that the outpost had lost its strategic relevance.[2]

More telling is the censure of all contemporary Irish accounts that the winter respite was not used to recruit, arm and train troops or lay in magazines, but that army officers and couriers threw themselves into 'gaming, drinking and whoreing'. A good example of officers behaving badly is provided by Henry Fitzjames, one of the king's natural sons, who broke a wine glass in Walter Dungan's face when he ventured to criticise Melfort. Dungan, colonel of dragoons and Tyrconnell's grand-nephew, did not seek the usual satisfaction but shrugged off the drunkard's attack as the behaviour of a child who could not be held responsible for his actions.[3] Intimations of the approaching Jacobite fin de siècle may have made the revels especially hectic, but any garrison town bursting at the seams with idle officers and bored soldiers was going to be a disorderly place.

It is clear from a run of Tyrconnnell's letters to Mary of Modena that he was acutely aware of what the army needed. He pleaded for enough gunpowder for his recruits to fire practice shots and so 'inure them to fire' (marksmanship was not a practical ambition with matchlock muskets), copper to mint coins to pay troops, cloth to dress them, tents to shelter them, and steel to make 'fusies' (fusils or flintlock muskets rather than the obsolescent matchlock) to arm them. [4]

Tyrconnell also wanted French reinforcements, both as a cadre of trained troops and a tangible mark of Louis XIV's commitment. He would get his way, but at a heavy price. Over 6,000 French regulars would land in March 1690, almost a year to the day after James had disembarked. But they would take away just as many Irishmen on the same ships. On reaching France, the various regiments would be embodied as the regiments of Mountcashel (who had recently escaped from custody in Enniskillen), of Daniel O'Brien, son of Daniel 3rd Viscount Clare and of Arthur Dillon, son of Theobald, 7th Viscount Dillon. [5] Arthur Dillon was yet another nephew of Tyrconnell's by marriage, and the Talbot–Dillon connection had been further strengthened when one of la belle Jennings's Hamilton daughters married Henry Dillon, Arthur's older brother and heir to the title. [6]

Tyrconnell was nonplussed that the French initially demanded up to 10,000 men – not just raw levies but a significant proportion of trained men as well – as was James who rounded on D'Avaux in the council chamber for contriving ways to 'ruin' his army. D'Avaux had also bid for some of the best Irish officers, like Patrick Sarsfield, brigadier of cavalry, and Walter Dungan, who had expressed interest in the French service. Tyrconnell was quite happy to see Mountcashel go and take with him MacCarthy connections like his twenty-two-year-old nephew Ulick Burke Viscount Galway: young Galway did not embark in the end and perished at Aughrim. [7] With the benefit of hindsight, Tyrconnell should have waived his objections to letting Sarsfield go: married to Clanricard's daughter, Sarsfield was aligned to the Clanricard/Clancarthy axis. Evidently, Tyrconnell distrusted Sarsfield, and James, presumably acting on his lord deputy's advice, had tried to block Sarsfield's promotion, patronisingly dismissing him as 'very brave' but stupid [un fort brave homme, mais qui n'avoit point de teste]. In late summer 1689, Tyrconnell may have set up Sarsfield to fail when he sent him to recover Sligo but gave him only a few men. Drawing recruits from his Clanricard connections, Sarsfield had run Thomas Lloyd's Enniskillen men out of Connacht, showing dash and daring worthy of Richard Hamilton at his best. [8]

The bitterest pill of all was that the French troops would be commanded by the comte de Lauzun. He had courted the Grande Mademoiselle, Louis XIV's first cousin, and by doing so made a powerful enemy of Louvois. Allied with Madame de Montespan, Louis XIV's then mistress, Louvois blocked the nuptials and had the bold suitor imprisoned for most of the 1670s as punishment for his presumption. Knight-errant admiration for Mary of Modena brought Lauzun to rush to England soon after William III's invasion. For all that Lauzun was short, scruffy and sharp-tongued he was inexplicably captivating to women, Mary among them. He won the queen's trust and daringly spirited her with her infant son away to France and safety, running the risk of being apprehended by an excitable mob hunting for papists. In gratitude, James conferred him with the Order of the Garter, pinning on the ribbon the medal that his father had given him just before his death on the scaffold.[9] Privately, Tyrconnell was wary of Lauzun because he had encouraged Melfort's cabals and intrigues and he foretold that if Lauzun came, neither Rosen nor D'Avaux would stay. All of this was bad enough, but Tyrconnell put his finger on the main trouble with Lauzun when he implored Queen Mary not to insist that her pet, or any 'creature of his', be sent to command the French expeditionary force to Ireland. Lauzun was detested by Louvois who, moreover, had hoped to bestow the Irish command on his son: 'if that man [Louvois] bee against us, what can we expect except delays and denials?'[10]

Lauzun exerted himself to be agreeable to Tyrconnell, who reciprocated, being determined 'never to have any disputes with him'. Lauzun even flattered himself that his own confidence and good humour had raised the viceroy's spirits. However, Lauzun quickly fell out with Dover and his ally Berwick, much as D'Avaux had with Melfort. Though the quarrels seem personal and petty on the surface, they actually went to the heart of competing strategies. Tyrconnell shared Dover's and Berwick's distrust of French intentions and dismay at niggardly support but he confronted neither d'Avaux nor Lauzun about them.[11] Lauzun blamed Dover for the French force's shambolic disembarkation and tardy march to Dublin. Dover was an unsuitable choice as chief logistician for the march since he had been overwhelmed by the much less complex challenge of unloading French supplies in Bantry Bay and bemoaned his lot to his old friend: 'many a time have we talked of this strange country of yours but never did I think it the thousand part so bad as I find this place'.[12] Dover was engagingly frank about his administrative incompetence: ''tis a great wonder such a head as mine should have thought of so many different things as I have done since my being here', he confessed to Tyrconnell who did his best to protect 'poor Lord Dover'. But Tyrconnell's support would not avail Dover when he took it on himself to demand that James make peace with William and followed up with an ill-judged request for permission to go to the enemy camp in order to get a passport for England. Shortly before the Battle of the Boyne, James gave him leave to depart, 'but I think', Lauzun wrote, 'Lady Tyrconnell will keep him in Dublin while we are away'.[13] The remark may have been innocent, meaning simply that Harry Jermyn was a favourite with the viceroy's family, but given Lauzun's insinuatingly sly character, he was probably alluding to gossip of some affair between Frances Jennings and her former suitor.

Grabbing the throne of England had been a means to an end: forging a coalition powerful enough to face down Louis XIV. So William's interest in England and, *a fortiori* Ireland, was subordinate to this lifelong ambition. When George Savile, Marquess of Halifax, William's lord privy seal, muttered that William 'had a great mind to land in France [as] the best way to save Ireland', he reflected widespread English disquiet. In the final analysis William had no choice but to humour those who held the purse strings especially since he had lost confidence in old Schomberg. He would come to Ireland 'beyond all knowledge of the world', however much he begrudged time spent away from the Netherlands. 'If I can reduce that kingdom quickly', William reassured an allied prince, 'I shall then have my hands free to act with so much more vigour against the common enemy.'[14]

'Quickly' – to that end William built up his forces in Ireland with more English recruits, Dutch veterans, locally recruited Protestants and an off-the-shelf army hired out by Christian V of Denmark. After a flurry of recruiting, refitting and reinforcement, the Franco-Irish field army still did not number more than 25,000 men by the start of the 1690 campaigning season, or about two-thirds the size of William's field army. This margin of numerical superiority meant that William could hope to land a knockout blow, if he could pin the Jacobites down, and finish the war before winter.

But would the Jacobites oblige? A general who adhered to the conventional wisdom of the day would not risk battle unless he had at least as many men, horses and guns as his enemy or, failing that, his battle lines were secured by natural and man-made obstacles. 'Flee or fight?': the answer to Lauzun's rhetorical question was that he hoped to avoid battle at almost all costs.[15] The Moyry Pass north of Dundalk might have blocked the enemy juggernaut, but when the Williamites arrived they were pleasantly surprised to find it unguarded: 'We marched from Newry over the pass at Moyra, where the enemy, if he had any spirit, might easily have stopped us for some time.'[16] In mid-June, the Jacobite army grazed the countryside bare about Dundalk then pulled back, successively, to Ardee and the Boyne. Lauzun's master plan for the Franco-Irish army was to decline battle, abandon the capital, raze the countryside and retreat beyond the Shannon. James must have initially agreed. In a letter penned from Ardee shortly after William had landed, Tyrconnell blithely assured Queen Mary, in contradiction to his earlier evaluation, that losing Dublin would not really matter after all. So long as the army was kept intact: 'whoever has time has life'.[17] At the last moment, when retreating towards the Boyne James changed his mind, for a little while. The king was commendably slow to ravage his own kingdom and starve his subjects. However, other than expressing reluctance to be chased out of Dublin without a fight, James articulated no clear and consistent alternative strategy:

What induced the King to hazard a battle on the inequality [of numbers], was, that if he did it not there, he must lose all without a stroke, and be obliged to quit Dublin and all Munster, and retire behind the Shannon, and so be reduced to the Province of Conough, where having no magazines, he could not subsist very long, it being the worst corn Country in Ireland; besides his men seem'd desirous to fight...[18]

Tyrconnell's strategic vision was even hazier. He griped about French timidity at sea: why wouldn't Seignelay send a squadron into the Irish Sea to interdict English supply ships or, better yet, waft an Irish army across to England?[19] Failing that, he gloomily forecast that William would 'swallow us up' before the end of the year. Why should James bother to keep Ireland, Tyrconnell asked rhetorically, 'if thereby he did not hope to be master of England' within the year? Leave him with but a handful of troops, Tyrconnell promised Queen Mary, and he would keep the usurper busy in Ireland while his other kingdoms slipped from his grasp. Meanwhile, the Irish should not hazard a battle against a much bigger and better-armed enemy unless Dublin was directly threatened: lose the capital, and 'there will be little hopes of keeping the rest long'.[20] After Mary of Modena showed the letter to Louis, he had Louvois firmly reiterate that a descent on Britain would be untimely. After this rebuke, Tyrconnell changed his tune.[21]

The Jacobite army's position south of the Boyne was, on the whole, a weak one. Apart from a small garrison holding Drogheda, the Franco-Irish army stood on a ridge that sloped gently downwards to the Boyne, where the river looped lazily northwards before meandering back to its easterly course. Oldbridge, at the tip of the loop, and other fords were passable at low tide, and shallows upstream could be crossed at any time. The Jacobite position invited an enveloping manoeuvre, whereby William could use part of his army to pin down the Jacobites in the Oldbridge sector while detaching another part to cross upstream and cut in beside or behind James's army.

The Jacobites were also vulnerable to frontal attack. William enjoyed massive superiority in guns and howitzers and he deployed them on a ridge overlooking the fords. Since the Jacobites had no time to dig in properly at the fords their formations would have been pounded had they tried to hold the riverbank. Consequently, the Williamite army could press across the Boyne in an unstoppable mass. If, as was likely, the French and Irish were then pushed back, it was highly unlikely that they could retreat in good order before a strong frontal attack because a stream, the Nanny, cut right across their rear. Retreating columns would take hours to squeeze across the bridge at Duleek during which time the army would be split and those troops waiting to cross could be expected to bunch up ineffectually and then panic and scatter when attacked.

The best hope for the Jacobites was that something might turn up. Something almost did. While William partook of a leisurely breakfast behind a crag overlooking the river bank, five horsemen, Tyrconnell, Berwick, Lauzun, together with the cavalry colonels, Parker and Sarsfield, passed 'softly' on the other side of the river.[22] George Story, the Williamite eye-witness and historian of the war, connects this to a later sighting of a tightly packed horse troop that paced forward slowly and stood still for half and hour, thereby screening the deployment of two field guns behind a hedge. When William remounted to resume his reconnoitre of the fords, the guns fired. One shot flew high, the second low. The latter grazed the river bank, was deflected upwards, struck William on the right shoulder and knocked him to the ground. He was shaken and blurted out, '*dat diende neit nader*' ['that was too close'], but got back on horseback and made sure he was seen by all before having his wound dressed. Story implies that Tyrconnell targeted William but the French artillerist who ordered the shots fired actually thought he had fired on old Schomberg in the midst of a gaudily coloured knot of aides and hangers-on. Had William been killed, a Williamite attack across the Boyne would probably have stalled without his personal drive.[23] The Jacobites almost won the battle, the day before the battle.

That night, the council-of-war plied William with conflicting advice: frontal attack or envelopment. Either would have worked, but William plumped for a compromise.[24] Before dawn, he sent some 5,000 horsemen from his right wing to ford the Boyne upstream at Rosnaree as part of a plan to send cavalry pincers from his right and left to fall on the flanks and rear of the Jacobite army and hold it in place while the remaining two-thirds of his army, nearly all of them foot soldiers, waded over the river and smashed into the immobilised enemy. It was an impossibly complex plan even for a commander with that *coup d'oeil* (a hard-to-define term of the time importing sound judgement of time and space, a feel for the lie of the land and an instinctive recognition of the 'crisis' of battle) that William sorely lacked. The plan did not survive contact with the enemy: Neil O'Neill's dragoon regiment 'did wonders' in delaying the crossing at Rosnaree until a shot struck O'Neill in the thigh and mortally wounded him.[25] Hearing the action at Rosnaree, James was convinced that most of William's army was curling around his western flank and rear and he promptly sent his guns and baggage back and sent his left wing and centre (two thirds of his army) upstream to counter this imagined manoeuvre. This was an egregious error and, insofar as Tyrconnell was one of the top three commanders, he must shoulder much of the blame. He was saved from tasting the full consequences of his mistake because William responded to this move by sending yet more troops upstream. About half of the Williamite army and two-thirds of the Jacobite main body ended up facing each other impotently across a steep and impassable ravine.

The 'Battle' of the Boyne was an 'unequal match', a series of small actions forced on Tyrconnell's rearguard, left behind in the Oldbridge sector and now outnumbered by almost three to one.[26] It is likely that Berwick commanded the 2,000 or so horse, while Richard Hamilton commanded the 4,000 foot soldiers. Tyrconnell left an infantry battalion in and around Oldbridge and another five some 150 yards back, 'behind some little hills'.[27] Whereas foot soldiers could cower from artillery shot behind embankments and hedgerows, horses could not and so Tyrconnell or Berwick posted the cavalry and dragoons out of artillery range and further back up the slope towards a summit at Donore. It is likely that Tyrconnell stayed atop Donore Hill, James's headquarters until shortly before, where he had a panoramic view of the entire river valley from Drogheda to the bend of the Boyne. He may not have possessed, as Berwick observed, 'military genius' but he was no doubt uneasy to see the enemy stirring and hear the beating of drums.[28]

Not long after ten o'clock three battalions of the élite Dutch Guards pressed across the ford near the little village of Oldbridge, closely followed downstream by St John's Londonderry regiment and the vanguard of three Huguenot battalions. After a sharp fight, the Irish battalion in the hamlet was pushed out. But before the third battalion of the Blue Guards had filed across the ford, Hamilton's other battalions sprung up from where they had crouched, probably in the furrows in a field of standing corn. Hamilton took two regiments of the Irish Foot Guards to press the Dutch, North Irish and Huguenots back 'to the very river'.[29] He also sent three other battalions to attach the leading elements of Hanmer's and Nassau's regiments about 200 yards further downriver. They came on as close as 'pike length' or about sixteen feet but did not close. The Allies had better fire drill and were all armed with flintlock muskets, which suffered fewer misfires and was quicker to reload than the matchlock.[30] Moreover, most Irish foot soldiers had no working matchlocks, obsolescent or not, but carried swords, pikes and scythes.[31] Rapid salvos tore into the Irish who began to hang back and trickle to the rear: 'nor could the Duke of Tyrconnel himself rally them, tho' he used his utmost endeavour to do it'. In fact, Tyrconnell was some distance to the south with the cavalry. The infantry officers suffered disproportionate casualties (a dozen captains, a major and a brigadier were killed that we know of), which was a sure sign that they had led from the front.[32] The best chance to hurl the attackers back into the river was now lost.[33]

Berwick now charged at the head of his troop of Horse Guards against the Bluecoats.[34] William watched closely and

> was in a great deal of apprehension for them, there not being any hedge or ditch for them or any of our horse to support them, and I was so near His Majesty as to hear him say softly to himself, 'My poor guards, my poor guards', but when he saw them

stand their ground and fire by platoons so that the horse were forced to run away in great disorder he breathed out as people used to after holding their breath upon a fright or suspense and said he had seen his guards do that which he had never seen foot do in his life.[35]

Some of the Jacobite horsemen charged in on the Dutch who, 'screwing their swords [plug bayonets] into their muskets, received the charge with all imaginable bravery and in a minute dismounted them all'.[36] Allowing for partisan pride and exaggeration, the Bluecoats would surely have been overrun by more horsemen: a troop (about 150 all ranks) was, complained the author of the 'Light to the Blind' bitterly, 'as good as nothing'.[37]

Tyrconnell, too late, now threw in all his cavalry in a desperate charge to dislodge the Dutch, English, Huguenot and Ulster Protestants. One thousand horsemen swept down the slope 'wonderfully bravely as ever men could do'. An Ulster ballad vividly captures what happened next: 'within ten yards of our fore-front/before a shot we fired/but a sudden snuff they got that day/they little it desired/For man and horse fell to the ground/and some hung in their saddles'. Worst hit was Parker's regiment from which only thirty men escaped unscathed out of ten times that number.[38] Though the Dutch and North Irish beside them stood fast, the cavalry successfully rode down English and Huguenot regiments still scrambling up the bank. A Jacobite horseman may have killed Schomberg in this affray, but it is more likely that William's second-in-command fell victim to 'friendly fire', shot down by Huguenots blazing away wildly as they bellowed 'tuer, tuer!' [kill, kill!].[39]

Tyrconnell led his regiment in person into at least one of these attacks. Asserting that Tyrconnell 'led' his regiment's charge does not usually mean that he rode in front right up to the moment of contact, rather, that he veered aside at the last moment and waved on the rest. It would have been unseemly for him to slash and thrust like a trooper in the front rank. Yet, according to Riverston, that is exactly what he did:

> The Satrap Talbot, fierce with drawn sword/And pistol, hastes into th' embattled stream,/And, coruscating fire, beats back and holds/The daring Dutchmen off. Each wound abides,/No wound comes without death. But they cannot/Put up with seeing Talbot's mouth and face,/Fearful in aspect, without breaking ranks/[40]

While trying to rally cavaliers recoiling from the third repulse Tyrconnell was knocked off his horse to be 'dragged along the ground by the mêlee and trampled by the hooves of a whole squadron'.[41] While this desperate struggle was fought, half a mile downstream the 6,000 or so Danish troops struggled struggled across through chest-high water and potholes. Berwick's busy little troop chased the Danish cavalry vanguard back across the Boyne but a squadron of Irish dragoon was unable to repulse the Danish infantry.[42] Deftly, the Danish foot soldiers assembled portable barriers of chevaux-de-frise and huddled behind them.

By now it was midday and at last, further downstream of the Danes, thousands of Williamite cavalrymen began swimming their mounts across the river and whipping them through the mire on the southern bank. An attack that was to have been simultaneous had already lasted two hours and cost William some of the edge conferred by superior numbers. A better commander than Tyrconnell would have exploited the delay and hurled all his cavalry against the Blue Guards before they had a chance to consolidate. A worse commander would not have grasped that William was now unstoppable and that his horsemen would flank the Irish and cut off any retreat.

Tyrconnell evidently decided to draw back the foot soldiers and leave Berwick and Hamilton with a rearguard of horsemen in and around the ruined church and graveyard atop Donore Hill. What with the dust, smoke, variegated uniforms and babble of outlandish tongues, some of the Williamite cavalry who charged up the hill ended up attacking each other, while those who actually reached the objective were thrown back by a vigorous Irish counter-attack.[43] However, Hamilton was captured within a few paces of William, who recognised him and cried out not to kill him. Would, he asked Hamilton, the Jacobite cavalry charge yet again? 'Yes, upon my honour, I believe they will,' responded Hamilton defiantly. 'Your honour?', William snorted more than once: he had not forgotten the abortive peace mission.

By now, the main body of the Jacobite army was filing slowly across the Nanny. All went well until Berwick's stampeding horse rode through the rearmost battalions. Muskets and pikes clattered to the ground as a dozen battalions 'scattered like sheep flying from the wolf'.[44] South of the Nanny, the French and some Irish regiments about-faced to cover the defile, supported by Berwick's horsemen. At this stage, James fled to Dublin. He did so because Lauzun, fearful that the king would be captured, begged him to flee. James should have ignored Lauzun's advice. Not only did he take eight squadrons of desperately needed horsemen with him, but by running off, he conceded publicly not only that his army was beaten – but that it was doomed.

When James made it to Dublin Castle that night, he is said to have complained to Lady Tyrconnell that her countrymen had run off, to which she replied pertly: 'Sire, it seems you have won the race'. The story is apochryphal; for one thing the Irish were not Frances Jennings's countrymen. The reality is more humdrum. James came to Dublin Castle that night, 'very silent and dejected'.

About nine a Clock King James came to Dublin, with about two hundred Horse with him, all in disorder. My Lady Tyrconnel met him at the Castle-gate, and after he was upstairs, her ladyship askt him what he would have for Supper? Who then gave him an Account of what a Breakfast he had got, which made him have but little stomach to his supper.[45]

Withdrawing a beaten and hunted army to safety in good order was the most taxing of all manouevres. Yet Lauzun and Tyrconnell managed this for a time. Tyrconnell would have the rearguard press on to the Naul, a defile on the Delvin River, about seven miles away on the coast road to Dublin. But Williamites nipped at the heels of his cavalry regiment which comprised the rearmost unit of the rearguard until Tyrconnell was forced to turn about in an unnamed hamlet six miles or so south of Duleek, and improvise a battle line with infantry in the middle and horse on the wings. Here Lauzun and Tyrconnell waited until nightfall, when they slipped away to the Naul. The cavalry now led the column and outpaced the foot, opening up a gap between main body and rearguard. Tyrconnell and Lauzun found three infantry brigades of the second line waiting at the Naul, and ordered them to let the French pass through and then take over as rearguard. Undoubtedly, keeping up an organised retreat saved the Franco-Irish army from being destroyed by pursuing horsemen: 'whilst an Enemy continues in a Body, there's no going after them as if Men were a Fox-hunting'.[46]

Until this time, about midnight on the night after the battle, Tyrconnell had done well enough in challenging circumstances. Even French sources which lambaste the Irish as poltroons (often unfairly or ignorantly) exempt Tyrconnell, who is represented as having done 'as best he could'. The severest criticism that they venture is to suggest that he 'is a very gallant man, full of good intentions which he cannot put into effect because he is too tolerant [qui a tant de complaisance] of the natives'.[47] Tyrconnell grasped the essential fact that the enemy had to be thrown back quickly and not given a chance to secure a foothold on the south bank. He predicted where the first blow would fall, and disposed his troops accordingly. The defensive plan at Oldbridge was as sound as it could have been given that he had no guns and the enemy had so many. It would have been wasteful to have left more than a battalion near the ford as what the French called enfants perdus to be cut up by enemy artillery. The battalion did what was expected of it, to absorb the first shock of the attack. The other Irish infantry battalions lay behind cover nearby and promptly counter-attacked, but Dutch musketry stopped them. The Irish foot soldiers put up a poor enough show, but hardly one for which Tyrconnell could be personally criticised. He can, perhaps, be faulted for lacking that hallmark of the great general, the ability to recognise when the crisis of the battle was happening and respond quickly and effectively. He should have hurled more of his cavalry against the Blue Guards once it was obvious that the Irish foot soldiers were faltering, rather than squandering a troop in a tentative and ineffectual cavalry counter-attack. The massed attack, when it came, was too late.[48] On the other hand, Tyrconnell recognised when it was time to pull back or be trapped. A delaying action bought time for the guns and foot soldiers to escape. Up until midnight, then, Tyrconnell had proved a competent and brave commander. But by dawn, the army had broken up. The charge that Tyrconnell showed himself 'brave in danger, [but] pusillanimous in disaster' contains a kernel of truth and his loss of grip contributed to the disaster that followed.[49]

He began to lose his grip once he passed through the Naul, as he apparently did, rather than waiting to be sure the rearguard also passed through and was relieved by the two brigades. 'Throughout this time, My Lord Tyrconnel and I did not leave [the rearguard]', Lauzun protested.[50] Lauzun's account is too full of holes to be credible but it is the only source we have for Tyrconnell's (in)actions that fateful night. The pre-battle strategic dithering meant, not only that no one had designated a rallying point and route in the entirely predictable event of forced retreat, but no contingency plan for the capital had been laid. Late in the day, Tyrconnell chose to skirt around to the north-west of the capital for a rendezvous at Dunboyne, Co. Meath. This would have been a sensible measure if fixed on earlier and if the army had duly retreated from the Nanny south to Rathoath and Dunboyne. But now, belated orders brought disorder. Lauzun's second-in-command and most of the senior French officers slipped away from their troops during the night and reached Dublin an hour before dawn. They had torn their regimental colours from their staffs and stuffed them into their pockets, something done when all was lost and the colours were in imminent peril of being captured by the enemy. The runaways later implausibly insisted that they had been cut off by enemy vedettes and so had no choice but to make for Dublin, where they had tried to persuade James to defend the capital.[51]

A Father Taaffe, Tyrconnell's chaplain, woke James before dawn on Wednesday with the army's new order of march and asked him to send whatever troops were in the capital to rendezvous to the west at Leixlip with the main body of the retreating army. He should himself flee to France without delay, Taaffe advised, since the enemy would reach the city that very day: as it happened, the Williamite vanguard would not reach the city until Thursday night. The sight of the dusty and dishevelled French runaways and their chattering of hot pursuit added to James's terror. He rode from his capital at first light, petulantly complaining about his Irish soldiers to the Lord Mayor and members of the corporation who came to bid him farewell:

Gentlemen, I find all things at present run against me. In England I had an army consisting of men stout and brave enough, which would have fought; but they proved false, and deserted me. Here I had an army that was loyal enough, but that they wanted true courage to stand by me at a critical minute ...[52]

Colonel Zurlauben, the only senior French officer not to desert his men, disregarded or never received Lauzun's orders and shepherded the French contingent through Dublin that Wednesday afternoon, the day after the battle. Hundreds of Zurlauben's soldiers (many were German prisoners, forcibly enlisted) slipped away and hid in back lanes. The rest of the French troops dispersed and drifted in ones and twos towards Limerick, as did the runaways scattered at Duleek who had been gathered and shepherded to the west of the capital waiting for orders that never came.[53]

Accompanied by nervous Frenchmen, James rode hard and reached Waterford Harbour, all of 120 miles away, by dawn of the next morning. James later confessed that he had been wrong to 'seem to abandon a cause which still had so much hopes of life in it'. [54] He blamed Tyrconnell for pressing him to flee the country and speculated that he might have done so out of misplaced 'tenderness' to the queen. Mary repeatedly beseeched the lord deputy to keep her husband out of harm's way, but Tyrconnell had bluntly told her in autumn 1689, and probably would have told her still, that her husband's personal safety could not be guaranteed in the heat of action. It seems unlikely that solicitude for the royal person would now lead the duke to press James to flee the country, having tried so hard to entice him to Ireland in the first place. No doubt Tyrconnell fretted that the king might be taken prisoner, but that danger could be evaded by having James flee Dublin, not Ireland. Might he have wanted James out of the way to have a free hand to negotiate with William? Probably not; the only evidence that Tyrconnell urged James to flee the country comes from James's *Life*. The omissions and inconsistencies surrounding this episode in the *Life* mean that it cannot be wholly trusted. James likely mistook Fr Taaffe's message and this precipitated his blind panic, enlivened by his characteristic stress-induced nosebleeds, as he raced to Waterford Harbour. Moreover, the Life quickly backtracks and contradicts the earlier statement when it claims that James finally chose to embark on a French ship only because he heard news giving him hope that Louis would order a descent on England. The news in question was a report that the French had defeated the Dutch at Fleurus, eleven days before the Boyne. Surely Louis could now move troops to the Channel ports for embarkation, reasoned James, showing a failure to apprehend French perceptions and motives.[55] James's claim that his was a strategic retreat, not a flight, is belied by the generally accepted view that James wrote to Tyrconnell before he sailed away, allowing him to make terms with William or carry on fighting, as he judged best.[56]

Those around him noticed that Tyrconnell aged overnight after the Boyne. Berwick was convinced that he suffered a severe psychological shock, 'growing as dithering in mind as he was heavy of body'.[57] The battle had brought Tyrconnell personal loss; his nephew O'Neill and grand-nephew Dungan, both colonels of dragoons, had been shot down while valiantly trying to hold their respective fords against heavy odds. Being trampled by horses, overseeing a rearguard action against heavy odds and co-ordinating (albeit poorly) a stumbling retreat in darkness would have taxed the strength of a younger and healthier man. His collapse, if that is what it was, manifested itself in gloom rather than panic; his retreat from Dublin was certainly more sedate than that of his master. On Thursday 3 July, Lieutenant Stevens, making for Limerick, was overtaken by Tyrconnell's 'family' south of Kilcullen, Co. Kildare. The lord deputy's entourage confiscated the lugubrious lieutenant's horse, leaving him 'afoot, weary, and without friends or money'. The next day, Stevens witnessed the duke at Kilkenny Castle facing down a mob of looters and beating them back with his cane. No one could doubt the old man's physical courage, though Stevens impugned his motives, hinting that he had taken a bribe to keep the castle's stores of food and drink intact. On Sunday 6 July, Stevens passed through Caherconlish, near Limerick, where he saw an honour guard of peasants armed with 'rapparees' (the term could denote the half-pike itself and the men who hefted them) lined up to greet the duke.[58] On reaching Limerick, Tyrconnell issued a proclamation ordering stragglers and runaways to rendezvous at that city, and later sent a detachment north to relieve Athlone.

Otherwise, for the next eighteen days, he did little or nothing to build up Limerick's fortifications or put the city in a state of defence. He thought that all was lost and sent Frances away before the month was out. Rumour had it that she brought a fortune in cash with her. She arrived at Brest on 14/25 August, reporting that the Irish still held Limerick, 'but not for long'.[59] Together with her retinue, she took up residence in a nearby convent, awaiting her husband's arrival. Chafing at the lord deputy's lethargy, the officers of the army sent a deputation of five of their number to demand that he call a general council-of-war. Tyrconnell gave way in the face of what was, in effect, mutiny. An anonymous French correspondent records what passed at the council, called late in July:

> At once the Duke of Tyrconnel produced a paper signed by him, the count of Lauzun and all the French officers, and by three Irish officers, which insisted that the town

could not be held three days, and the country could not be defended, and recommended they capitulate with the Prince of Orange or accept what terms he offered. Monsieur Boisleau (the only Frenchman of this opinion), Sarsfield, the 2 Luttrells, Mylord Clare, baron Purcell and all the other officers vehemently opposed this [proposal] which greatly annoyed the Duke of Tyrconnel and sent him into a rage. The officers seeing that he would not change his mind nominated the above named, Sarsfield etc. to take over the army and put the town and country in a state of defence.[60]

Lieutenant Stevens corroborates this account of Tyrconnell urging 'surrender before it was too late', and differs only in saying that when shouted down he desperately offered to compromise by hamstringing the horses and gathering all the soldiers into garrisons. Everyone saw this for the hare-brained scheme it was; putting all the foot soldiers behind walls made sense only if the cavalry remained outside to raid enemy supply lines, fall on foraging parties, and otherwise interfere with enemy sieges.[61] Tyrconnell did not give up this foolishness, and Daniel O'Brien, Viscount Clare, gave a first-hand account of what he saw as Tyrconnell's duplicity and defeatism.

Every day he tries to persuade us we cannot hold out [and] no help can be expected from France so we should lay down our arms and treat with the Prince of Orange for the best terms we can get ...

Talbot did not want to incur the odium of opening surrender talks himself, but worked on various people, including O'Brien, to initiate feelers on behalf of 'the whole nation'.[62] Clare scorned the proposal, responding that William would not keep his promises. Talbot eventually found his pliable negotiator in a barrister from Co. Clare named John Grady, who presented himself to William at Goldenbridge camp sometime in the first week of August passing on Tyrconnell's terms that the Irish be let keep half of their pre-war estates.[63] The gambit was poorly judged because William flattered himself that he had won a crushing victory at the Boyne. He coveted Irish land to reward his Dutch favourites and followers, so his declaration of 7 July from Finglas camp promised pardon to 'the meaner sort', but threatened to make the leaders 'sensible of their errors' and pointedly did not promise Catholic landowners that they could keep their estates if they surrendered.[64] William's was a 'foolish edict', and only when the Irish had hung on to Limerick and spun out the war until another campaigning season would he finally listen to those who advised him that all the forfeited property in Ireland would not offset the cost of an extra year's campaigning.[65] Tyrconnell should really have known better than to expect concessions at this point and, predictably,

William ignored Grady's offer, no doubt sharing the optimism of a newsletter of 19 July: 'we believe the war to be at an end'.[66]

After the Boyne, the eastern half of Ireland fell into William's lap. The Shannon Line covered much of what was left and assumed correspondingly great importance. The strategic imperative was to cut this line, so William split his army. Leaving the main body to plod towards Limerick, he sent a detachment under Lieut-Gen. Douglas to seize Athlone, the most important crossing point after Limerick, and so 'break into Connought'.[67] But Richard Grace, a guerrilla diehard in the 1650s, defied Douglas who had to break off and rejoin the main army near Limerick. The breakthrough would come here, or nowhere.[68]

Most officers professed to believe that Tyrconnell was no traitor, but was simply too old and infirm to act the part of a vigorous wartime commander. However, some accused him of outright treachery. The accusers included, or would soon include, the 'darling of the army', Major-General Patrick Sarsfield, Brigadiers Henry Luttrell, Gordon O'Neill, John Wauchope and William Dorrington, Colonels Simon Luttrell, Felix O'Neill and Nicholas Purcell, together with Lieutenant Colonels Thomas Cusack and Maurice O'Connell.[69] This was a formidably broadly based and diverse faction of malcontents that included Gaels, Old Englishmen, an Englishman and a Scot. *Macariae Excidium* probably best summarises their outlook. O'Kelly reads all acts and omissions throughout the war as strands in a seamless pattern of conspiracy by 'Coridon' or Tyrconnell, who could barely dissemble his disappointment at news that Athlone had held out and exaggerated the weakness of Limerick so as to sap the army's fighting spirit. In his dotage, Tyrconnell had fallen under the malign influence of his avaricious lady and of the 'false and cowardly' Hamiltons – all of them, thundered the mutineers, 'declared enemies to the nation'.[70]

Lauzun scorned Limerick's fortifications as absurdly feeble and insisted on retreating to Galway whence he could embark. Some hotheads planned to overpower and disarm the French troops before they left, but Colonel Mark Talbot stumbled on the plot and revealed it to his father. Tyrconnell quietly warned the ringleaders off, while keeping his French allies blissfully unaware of the business. On or about 2 August, the French troops marched to Galway, where the citizens prudently shut the gates and left them outside to huddle in the lee of the walls lest they plunder and rape, as they had done in Limerick.[71]

The scheme yields a sidelight on the wanton irresponsibility of at least some members of Sarsfield's faction. Had the Irish shed French blood, there would surely have been an end to any hope of further assistance from the Sun King. Relations were rancorous enough already.[72] De La Hoguette's hearsay account of the action at Oldbridge typified the contempt that the French had for their cowardly allies: 'the enemy chased the Irish soldiers before them like so many sheep without [the Irish] firing a single shot'.[73] French officers from Lauzun down, with the notable exception of Boisseleau, were quick to give up the Irish war as a lost cause after the Boyne, and their strident defeatism helped blind Louis to the great advantages still to be gained in Ireland. Two days before the Boyne, Admiral Tourville had beaten the Allies at Beachy Head and secured dominance of the seas. When news of the Boyne reached Versailles, there was no thought of salvaging the situation by sending a fleet to the Irish Sea to maroon William in Ireland and cut off his supplies while discontent rose in England and his continental allies fretted.[74] Instead, Louis XIV and Seignelay prematurely decided to cut their losses and withdraw French troops.

Tyrconnell left some 10,000 Irish foot soldiers behind in Limerick, and detached eight infantry regiments, together with about half of his cavalry and dragoons, to cover a ford over a mile upstream. Tyrconnell probably spent a few more days near Limerick, but busied himself for most of the month of August in Galway with arrangements for what he fully expected would be a siege followed by an emergency embarkation of the French and the best of the Irish troops.[75]

Before the lord deputy left for Galway, Berwick requested permission to take the 3,500 horsemen remaining around Limerick across the Shannon at Athlone, raid behind enemy lines, destroy magazines, feint towards Dublin to distract the enemy, and round off the cavalcade by sweeping back into north Connacht. When Talbot refused, a resentful Berwick wondered was it because he had grown 'too old and too fat' for rough riding and was jealous lest someone else make a name for themselves.[76] Tyrconnell had good reason to dismiss a proposal which would have taken all the riders far away beyond recall on a pointless sweep away from Williamite re-supply routes that ran from the south-east, from Waterford to Limerick. As it was, the cavalry failed in an altogether more vital task when they abandoned the ford on 10 August and pulled back from the Shannon west to Sixmilebridge, thereby letting the Williamites cross the strategically vital river without hindrance.

The 'priding cavalry' redeemed their reputation just days later.[77] William had not brought siege guns to Limerick, expecting that the town would surrender on seeing his army, so he had to wait while a siege train lumbered from Cashel hauling cannon, powder, shot and other stores. Sarsfield swam a 500-strong detachment across the Shannon by night, and making a wide circuit he fell the following night on slumbering waggoners and troopers near Ballyneety Co. Limerick. A spy had tipped off William, who duly sent out another cavalry escort to meet the train, but in the early hours of 13 August the troopers 'saw a great light in the air, and heard a strange rumbling noise'. The escort had set out too late. Most of the eighteen-pounders could be repaired and remounted on new carriages, but the loss of horses taken by Sarsfield seriously disrupted Williamite re-supply. Worst of all, burning so much gun-powder limited the width of the single breach that William's guns knocked: a breach was considered 'practicable' breach when about sixteen men abreast could walk upright over it.[78]

Governor Boisseleau threw up a retirade behind the breach in the wall near the south-east corner of the Irishtown, making 'a work resolved to be disputed inch by inch'.[79] Professional soldiers sniffed at such interior retrenchments, and agreed it was unsoldiery conduct to fight 'like Turks' to 'the last extremity'.[80] The author of 'A Light to the Blind' tries to defend Tyrconnell by likewise insisting the 'do or die' defence of Limerick by his critics was bloody minded and irresponsible, even if ultimately successful. There is some merit in this defence. In warfare between Christians it was considered an act of foolish obduracy for besieged troops to fight on once a 'practicable' breach was knocked. Besiegers who suffered heavy losses from the garrison's stubbornness and poured over a breach into a town would likely run amok, murdering, looting, raping and burning.[81] As a young cavalier, Talbot had witnessed these horrors at Drogheda, and it is understandable that he would not have them repeated. His reaction was humane and rational, but he should have known that now was no time for reasonable calculation.

On the afternoon of 27 August, four thousand Allied soldiers clambered over the top and crowded on to the breach, but were quite unable to make it across the fire-swept killing ground to the retirade. Grenadiers shock troops detached from many regiments together with the Danes of the Funen regiment served as shock-troops but were stopped on the breach. The main body of storm troops bunching up behind them outside the walls was ripped apart by musket fire.[82] For the next three to four hours, 'one continued fire' thundered, and smoke 'reached in one continued cloud to the top of a mountain at least six miles off'.[83] Four barrels of gunpowder lying in a corner of the mural tower blew up, 'men, faggots, stones and what not, flying into the air with a most terrible noise'.[84] By the time William called his troops back, he had lost over five hundred killed outright and over another 1,500 wounded.[85] But next day, William's troops repaired their trenches.

Tyrconnell tiptoed back from Galway to the latest horse campsite at Quin, Co. Clare, a prudent fourteen miles from Limerick, to observe the last days and nights of the siege. The lord deputy vowed to lead the horsemen through the stricken city on Friday 29 August, and so fall on the besiegers, 'without which the place is lost'. He was but striking bellicose attitudes so that no one fault his zeal when, as he still expected, the city fell.[86]

But that very Friday William reluctantly raised the siege because 'the whole country was like a puddle' and heavy rain threatened to bog his guns in the mire. [87] The evacuation showed unmistakable signs of jumpiness; fires set to destroy stores spread to the field hospital, and a horrified Jacobite recalls seeing three hundred charred corpses heaped inside. [88] In the circumstances, cavalry pursuit would probably have routed the Williamite rearguard. However, for all Tyrconnell's bluster at Quin, the attack was never launched. Tyrconnell lost his chance to salvage some credit as a military commander. In contrast, Patrick Sarsfield was the hero of the hour: 'Sarsfield – noble Sarsfield/Is not the man to yield/Whether behind a leaguered wall/ Or in the tented field.' [89]

At least Tyrconnell had the political sense to see that victory at Limerick transformed the strategic outlook. [90] Irish troops should not be evacuated yet, because with French help they could at least hold out for the winter. Nonetheless, he chose to go ahead with his original plan to embark from Galway with Lauzun who, for his part, saw no reason to keep his contingent in Ireland. Leaving was a risky decision that left no one in Ireland capable of outmanoeuvring Sarsfield's followers, but it reflected Talbot's long-standing response to adversity: hasten to the seat of power, plea for support with all the charisma and force of his larger-than-life personality, vilify and discredit his enemies, and come back with renewed authority. Moreover, knowing that Sarsfield's supporters intended to discredit him at Saint-Germain and Versailles, he thought it politic to get there first and 'justify his proceedings'. [91] For public consumption, he claimed that James did 'command our attendance upon him' in order 'to consider of the ways to improve the kingdom'. Promising to be back 'in a very short time', Tyrconnell nominated Berwick to take command of the army, on condition that he would be guided by a council of six brigadiers. [92] The members of the council were Sarsfield, Clare, Pierce Butler Viscount Galmoy, John Hamilton, the Englishman Sheldon, and the Scot Maxwell. [93] Tyrconnell's protégés and supporters, Hamilton, Sheldon and Maxwell, just about held the balance on the council. A triumvirate comprising Riverston, d'Albeville and Sir Patrick Trant would see to civil matters, such as they were. [94]

Tyrconnell then sailed for Brest on 12 September, less than a fortnight after William raised the siege of Limerick. [95] The French fleet of over forty sail met two smaller allied convoys, but in keeping with the timidity of French expeditionary ventures to Ireland, the fleet let the convoys pass unmolested. The convoys were carrying troops to descend on Cork. The latter had a biggish garrison, weak fortifications, and scant supplies, while nearby Charles Fort at Kinsale was well fortified, amply supplied and thinly manned. Berwick would have been better occupied evacuating Cork and reinforcing Kinsale, rather than attacking the strategically inconsequential Birr Castle. With no prospect of relief, the governor of Cork had to surrender outright, rather than obtain an honourable capitulation. The bag of 5,000 prisoners represented the single biggest loss of manpower during the war. Kinsale fell soon after, leaving only the Shannon Estuary and Galway Bay as anchorages for a French fleet.

As disaster loomed in Cork, a meeting of nobles, bishops and senior officers (colonels and upward) held at Limerick resolved that Tyrconnell's arrangements were unconstitutional. The assembly members concluded that a legitimate government needed a resident viceroy and they resolved to send envoys to France to explain their position. On 30 September, Sarsfield, Dorrington and Simon Luttrell called on Berwick and offered him a face-saving compromise: he could stay on as commander-in-chief, provided that he take advice from a council of colonels. Two 'able' (anti-Tyrconnell, in other words) persons would help in the administration of each province.[96] Berwick was adamant that he was entitled to command the army by virtue of his former commission as lieutenant general, regardless of Tyrconnell's status, but the deputies rebutted this counter-argument with a Hibernian version of the abdication argument. Since James had fled the country and, they claimed, told his Irish subjects to fend for themselves (a document containing such an order is not to be found), his regime, and all of its organs, constitutionally ceased to exist. After much prevarication and dissembling, Berwick met the assembly, agreed to their proposals and nominated the Bishop of Cork, Maxwell, Simon Luttrell, Henry Luttrell and Purcell as agents. The last two he wanted out of the country; he saw Henry Luttrel in particular as the malevolent mastermind of the factionists, without whom Sarsfield would be more tractable. Maxwell he sent to quietly ask James to detain Luttrell and Purcell, rather as Tyrconnell had disposed of Mountjoy two years before.[97]

On the face of it, Tyrconnell's flying visit (only three months elapsed from his departure until his return) to Versailles and St-Germain was gratifyingly successful. James received him warmly, promoted him to lord lieutenant and conferred on him the Order of the Garter. O'Kelly claims that Tyrconnell boosted his reputation with Louis by double-crossing Lauzun. Tyrconnell and Lauzun had allegedly concocted an agreed version of events which laid blame on Sarsfield for all that had gone wrong. However, while on the road from Brest to Versailles, Tyrconnell received a warning that it would now be impolitic to blacken Sarsfield, whose reputation had been burnished by Ballyneety and Limerick. He feigned illness, allowing Lauzun to go on alone and tell the preconcerted story. Lauzun duly 'ommitted nothing that might be said in commendation of his friend's conduct and courage' but when it came to his turn, Tyrconnell impugned Lauzun for abandoning Limerick and leaving the

Irish to fend for themselves.[98] The story is true in its essentials, though a devious old courtier like Tyrconnell would have known, without needing to be warned, what way the wind was blowing.

Tyrconnell's success can also be attributed to the renewed optimism with which he conjured up a dazzling cascade of triumphs if only Louis sent enough help without delay. William would then need 35,000 to 40,000 men to finish the conquest so he would not be able to send a big army to reinforce his allies in Flanders next summer. The emperor would be forced by recent Ottoman successes to send some of his troops towards the Balkan front. William would then be forced to run down his army in Ireland to reinforce the Spanish Netherlands, letting Tyrconnell win back much of Ireland thereby precipitating Jacobite revolt in England.[99] His charm worked its old magic for a while and he secured promises of more French help than ever before: 'the king is resolved to support Ireland as much as possible', read the first line of the instructions to Commissaire Fumeron, who was sent back to Ireland with Tyrconnell.[100] Eight major convoys arrived in Ireland over the three years of war, but the scale of support only grew to credible dimensions towards the end.[101] It is hard to see any other Irishman with the requisite stature to impress on the French just how useful it would be to continue a diversion in Ireland.

Yet the lord lieutenant was a sick man, unfit for the taxing demands of travel, wartime government and political backstabbing that lay ahead. On his return journey, he passed through Nantes on 1/11 December 1690 but did not reach Brest until seventeen days later, having lain bedridden for three days at Vannes. Thence, he crept painfully onward. On reaching the port, he found the ships loaded and the winds favourable, but took another nine days to actually go aboard.[102] The poet Ó Bruadair, a protégé of Colonel Sir John Fitzgerald of Co. Limerick, would welcome the lord lieutenant back and express relief that he had recovered his health [ina shláinte]. The fact that the poet evidently felt the need to advert to lord lieutenant's health at all tells us that the subject was a contested one.[103]

The time spent waiting at the quayside was not entirely wasted. Tyrconnell was tipped off that the 'mutineers' had landed at St. Malo, sending Purcell and Henry Luttrell on to Paris to complain of him, and that Randall MacDonnell, the most prominent Irishman in James's household, had secured an audience for them with James at St Germain. Angrily, Tyrconnell demanded of Louvois that Purcell and Luttrell be detained in France.[104]

While Tyrconnell was journeying homeward, his supporters there had been hard hit by Sarsfield who claimed that Riverston, acting as secretary of state for war, was the ringleader of a treasonable conspiracy to betray the crossings on the northern reaches of the Shannon, thereby letting a Williamite army pour into

Connacht. Riverston would then have his brother-in-law, Alexander MacDonnell, who was governor of Galway, throw open the gates of his town to the enemy and also, by some means unspecified, sell out Limerick as well.

What lay behind this spate of arrests was the return of Grady, Tyrconnell's negotiator. He reached Limerick early in December 1690, but was not armed with any authority other than to promise security of property to particular individuals who showed themselves especially receptive in behind-the-scenes negotiations. Grady's mission, then, was not a genuine peace feeler, but a baited trap which snared MacDonnell. The latter had incautiously uttered a wish for a peace deal [quelque honneste composition] after Kinsale was lost, and Riverston was probably of the same opinion. It is likely, then, that Riverston also nibbled at the bait proffered by Grady: the fact that 'A Light to the Blind' and Riverston's own epic poem both ignore the episode completely suggests that it was somehow discreditable to Tyrconnell's client. Private negotiations were enough for a factional enemy to sniff out treachery, so Sarsfield insisted that Berwick dismiss and imprison Riverston. Sarsfield misread subsequent Williamite attacks on the Shannon crossings of Jamestown and Lanesborough (both were repulsed) as confirmation that a plot had existed; otherwise would the enemy have been so stupid as to attempt in mid-winter what they could not manage in summer?[105]

But the enemy was that stupid, there was no plot, and poor Riverston was no traitor: indeed, he would remain, long after the war, a diehard Jacobite. Even O'Kelly's condemnation of Riverston is tepid, while he conceded that MacDonnell was 'an honest man'.[106] Berwick believed that the only fault of Riverston, MacDonnell and the third accused, John Hamilton (who would die a hero's death at Aughrim), was that they were Tyrconnell's minions. Yet he was forced to give way and put Sarsfield in charge of Connacht and Galway. As governor of the only province wholly in Irish hands and commander of the biggest corps in the army, Sarsfield was for the moment the most powerful, and most popular, man in Ireland.[107]

Whether he would remain so depended on how persuasive Purcell and Luttrell could be at St Germain. James's first instinct was to punish them, but he was restrained by broad hints that their sympathisers back in Ireland would exact revenge on Berwick for any insult or injury to the deputies.[108] The deputies resiled from accusing the lord lieutenant of outright treachery, but hinted that he was a corrupt and incompetent dotard overwhelmed by the demands of wartime military command, and that:

His age and infirmities made him require more sleep than was consistent with so much business, that his want of experience in military affairs rendered him exceeding slow in his resolves and incapable of laying projects … [109]

Much of this criticism hit the mark. As to 'laying projects' or formulating strategy, in the weeks before the Boyne Tyrconnell dithered between the most fundamental strategic decisions – fight for Dublin or retreat from Dublin – while ineffectually bemoaning Seignelay's fleet-action strategy. In the weeks after the Boyne, he wanted to come to terms at the worst possible time, when the enemy felt invincible and acceptable terms were not on the table. While these criticisms led James to regret his decision to send Tyrconnell back as lord lieutenant with enhanced authority, such misgivings came too late. Seignelay, who had a genuine strategic commitment to Ireland, was dead, and Louvois disgorged as many supplies as he did because he accepted Tyrconnell as a man of substance with whom he could do business. And his business was drawing thousands more recruits from Ireland: 'if he fails me on the recruiting matter', warned Louvois, 'he will find me failing in all matters concerning Ireland'. It helped that Tyrconnell had discredited Lauzun, an old enemy of Louvois. James realised something that evidently eluded Sarsfield and his followers, namely that reports of squabbling would call into question Irish commitment to the war and cause Louvois to stop, as he saw it, throwing good money after bad.[110]

James took the unusually astute step of asking Louis to supply a prestigious and experienced commander, Marshal Bellefonds, to lead the Irish army. This appeased Sarsfield's partisans, who represented themselves (to French officers) as the 'King of France's party' and hoped to embed Louis so deeply as protector of the Irish that he could not withdraw support without suffering loss of face. To that end, they had hoped that Bellefonds would serve as a military and political supremo. While Louis would shy away from committing himself as deeply as all that, Irish appeals for a French commander appealed to his monumental amour propre. James fudged the question of whether this commander should answer to Tyrconnell who was, ex officio, commander-in-chief.[111]

Tyrconnell was a great man diminished, feebly clasping the trappings of power after he had forfeited moral authority to lead a nation-in-arms and, declared Sarsfield, was 'mortally hated by the whole army'. Though the lord lieutenant still had many supporters in the army, even after losing Hamilton, Dungan and O'Neill at the Boyne, most officers distrusted him.[112] He was clear-eyed enough to read the writing on the wall, but would not go quietly. He was who he was and it would be fatuous to deplore his undignified scrabbling. All political careers end in failure, because those who taste high office seldom bow out with dignity. The tensions between Tyrconnell and Sarsfield have nothing to do with the supposedly divergent war aims of Gael and Old English, the latter hoping to turn the clock back to 1641, and the former supposedly yearning to go back a further forty years to before the Ulster Plantation. One of the few to still stress fault lines between 'new and old Irish', as he dubbed them, was Hugo balldearg O'Donnell, Spanish adventurer, self-proclaimed Earl of Tyrconnell and most recent embodiment (for did he not bear the prophesied ball dearg or red birthmark?) of the messianic deliverer. O'Donnell was a dreamer, who turned out to be a turncoat and traitor at the end. [113] The author of 'A Light to the Blind' ignores any Gaelic–Old English distinction among the residual Catholic gentry and aristocracy as irrelevant, given the extent to which they were 'linked in blood' by intermarriage and united by a shared Catholicism. Nor does O'Kelly isolate Gael versus Old English as the defining dichotomy (these often contrasted texts share many features in common) but valorises Sarsfield and his followers as the authentic voice and strong arm of a distinctively Irish national interest sometimes at odds with James, his English and Scottish advisers, and even with D'Avaux and Lauzun. [114] Of course distinctions were not so cut and dried. Some of Sarsfield's adherents were themselves English or Scots, like Dorrington or Wauchope. Moreover, Tyrconnell had, in his time, represented himself as an Irish tribune when undermining rivals like Melfort. Yet distinction there was. Sarsfield put himself at the head of a party that was at once Irish and French: his followers envisioned Ireland as a French protectorate, while owing allegiance to the exiled Stuarts, and so necessarily detached from Britian for ever or until that happy day when the Stuarts came back into their own. Tyrconnell had flirted with the notion of a French protectorate but the birth of an heir to James II and his own suspicions of French motives put an end to this contingency plan. Ireland should remain a component part of the Stuart composite monarchy, though with a Catholic governor and parliament.

Related to these competing visions was the fissure that opens in any losing cause between (to adopt the language of the doomed Boer republics in 1900) 'hensoppers' and 'bittereinders', that is between pragmatists who would avoid pointless suffering and those who flatly refused to contemplate defeat. Such contrasting responses were elicited according to temperament, age and, of course, status; officers with poor prospects in peacetime would more likely swear to 'do or die' [mourir ou vaincre] than the 'gownmen', as O'Kelly dubbed his supporters, who surrounded Tyrconnell and were trained to anticipate disagreeable contingencies. [115]

When Tyrconnell alighted on the quayside in Limerick in mid-January 1691, Sarsfield was away securing the Shannon crossings. He quickly set about reasserting his authority in Limerick and Galway, monopolising the mail packets to and from Brest, reinstating Riverston to the privy council and releasing Judge Denis Daly, who had been thrown in gaol a few days earlier. In so doing he released a traitor who would prove instrumental in surrendering Galway in 1691. [116] Tyrconnell next summoned Sarsfield to Limerick, but Sarsfield ignored the order, all the while waiting for news that James had dismissed his lord lieutenant. Realising after a month that the lord lieutenant would survive, Sarsfield at last came to Limerick where Tyrconnell greeted him with back-slapping and smiles, professed himself Sarsfield's firm friend, and announced that a grateful monarch had created him Earl of Lucan and confirmed his rank of major-general.

Where Tyrconnell was prepared to bite back his resentment, Lucan's faction continued to flout Tyrconnell's authority, especially once it became known (and Lucan did his utmost to publicise the news) that the French general who was to come, the Marquis de Saint Ruhe or St Ruth, would command 'without any dependence' on Tyrconnell. Lucan would not get a Marshal of France but a rough dragoon officer who had made his name brutally putting down Huguenot rebels in the Cévennes. Here he had led some of Mountcashel's troops over high passes and up precipitous peaks and was impressed with their hardiness and fighting spirit. The consolation for Lucan, then, was that his enemy would be stripped of a core function of viceroyalty, especially in wartime, namely military command. Tyrconnell put the best face he could on this humiliation and, to O'Kelly's jaundiced eyes, 'looked big again after his usual manner, for he was naturally proud and arrogant, high and insolent'.[117]

Tyrconnell had now to endure the blame for all that went wrong. If the French did not send enough money and material, it was because he had misrepresented the wants of the army or had embezzled funds. If boats had not been built over the winter to bring grain and meal upriver from Limerick to Athlone, this was due to his 'wilful neglect', because he would starve the soldiers guarding this strategic gateway. If he ordered a cess of coin to buy beeves rather than collecting the beasts themselves, it was to announce to the world that the French fleet had brought no money.[118] These accusations were unfounded. To probe just one smear, the lord lieutenant's enemies spread rumours that he was scheming to sell recruits into French service for cash. The truth was that Tyrconnell had promised Louvois 1,200 troops to top-up Mountcashel's brigade, but he had no sooner disembarked than he claimed he had only promised 200 and 'took no great trouble', grumbled Commissaire Fumeron, to even gather those. Seven months later, Fumeron was still complaining and in the end Tyrconnell sent a paltry nine cadets. Fumeron surmised, incorrectly, that Tyrconnell prevaricated simply to disoblige Mountcashel, whereupon Louvois, himself well able to nurse a grudge, curtly rebuked Tyrconnell for nursing such a 'petty grievance'.[119]

Unrelenting denigration by Lucan and his acolytes undoubtedly eroded Tyrconnell's authority but must also have corroded army discipline. One wonders how officers could demand respect of soldiers when they publicly disdained their commander-in-chief. This must have sapped public confidence in the war effort. A barometer of such confidence was the value of the coinage. After the Boyne, the value of the old brass money plummeted by half. Tyrconnell now recalled the old coin and proclaimed that newly minted brass coins should be accepted at face value. It was, however, a toothless proclamation, since he made no effort to oblige sutlers to accept the money proffered by soldiers to buy foodstuffs, tobacco, beer and spirits. Indeed, merchants and traders soon refused to accept James's wartime coinage, old or new, at virtually any discount – even at a shilling to a penny – while the soldiers muttered darkly that the lord lieutenant was defrauding them of pay, while amassing a hoard of French gold.[120]

'Tyrconnell is chief in name but Sarsfield in power,' commented a well-informed Williamite in May 1691, just before St. Ruth landed.[121] Whichever of the two men was in command, the Irish army was in a sorry state. Connacht and Clare was overburdened by troops and refugees. With food for the troops guarding the crossings of the middle Shannon having run out, most had scattered to forage. St Ruth's flotilla of over thirty warships and over fifty cargo vessels laden with clothing, arms, ammunition, and grain (enough to feed the army until autumn) sailed into the Shannon Estuary on 19 May, not a day too soon. St Ruth gathered the field army and reached the western or Connacht side of Athlone, just as Godard Van Reede Baron de Ginckel, the Dutchman William had left behind to complete the conquest, lumbered into view on the opposite bank of the Shannon.[122]

St Ruth's commission empowered him to command the army, but 'under me', asserted Tyrconnell, though he admitted that James wished him to defer to St Ruth in all matters pertaining to command of the army. When Tyrconnell joined the Irish camp at Athlone, he ostensibly did so as a mere volunteer but St Ruth, while maintaining a façade of respect, wanted no one looking over his shoulder. He encouraged Lucan, Purcell and Luttrell to go from tent to tent asking officers and 'persons of quality' to sign a petition calling on Tyrconnell to decamp.[123] Some of Lucan's followers even threatened to cut the guy ropes of the viceregal tent if Tyrconnell did not pack up and go. Though he still enjoyed support from many officers of horse and most officers of foot, he slunk away, by his own account, rather than provoke further divisive bickering. Such restraint and self-control in the face of insult and provocation sounds quite out of character and, though officers ignored and disparaged him, he does indeed seem to have been still lingering near Athlone on 30 June. That very evening, a storming party surged across a ford near the broken bridge. The two Irish regiments on duty (O'Gara's and MacMahon's) stampeded, and the Williamites seized the ramparts, defying St Ruth's attempts to counter-attack.

Lucan's faction blamed the disaster on Maxwell, the officer on duty, for treacherously leaving his troops without ammunition, assuring them that there would be no action before nightfall. He was quickly taken prisoner during the assault. [124] The Scotsman was no traitor. On 28 June when the Allies laid planks over a broken arch of the bridge it took volunteers from Maxwell's dragoons to unflinchingly run into the firestorm to tip the beams into the water. As the member of a nation that so engrossed royal favour he was a handy scapegoat for Lucan's followers. Tyrconnell's partisans heaped odium on Lucan's mutinous and factious rabble, especially Henry Luttrell, though not on the hero himself:

> But when the Viceroy sees the rooftops brought/Level with ground, the rampart at their backs/He warns must be removed, that cavalry/May enter through the breach and carry death/To Dutchmen swimming o'er the river's stream,/To save their men and drive the foeman back./The sane opinion of the hated man/Advising is rejected. He himself/ Is even reprimanded: 'So, Viceroy,/Will you give orders now for battle, when/Civil affairs have been put in your care,/While Saint Ruth, sent by the French to Ireland's aid,/Sits in command [*armis Praesidet*] of regulating arms?/Let him, without your interference, do/His part, and do you also manage yours./Either be silent, then, or leave the camp./When we are subject to one general,/Dost wish us to obey the word of two,/Who order very diverse things indeed?'/Tyrconnell, by such goads of hate repulsed,/Left, pitying much the fortune [*Athloniae casum*] of Athlone./ A jealous rival, setting up a trap/ Against the man, and favouring the foe/ And treachery, had cooked these insults up,/ That same one who at Aughrim later on/ Was proved a traitor. Him did Lucan aid,/ Credulous, prone to be deceived, but not/ Malicious of his own accord [*nec sponte malignus*] and quite/ Devoid of any covert tricks at all. [125]

Treachery is the facile all-purpose explanation offered by those, like O'Kelly, too dim or too angry to recognise more complex explanations. During the ten-day siege, some 12,000 shots pounded the narrow western or Connacht side of the town, and 600 mortar bombs rained down.[126] Rather then leave his whole army to be pounded in the rubble, St Ruth rotated regiments in and out of that 'hell on earth'. This was a sensible plan if the main body had been left close enough, in the very shadows of the rampart salients, to counter-attack smartly. But the main body was posted too far away and the westward-facing ramparts were left intact, St Ruth having disregarded Tyrconnell's advice to knock a wide breach in them to facilitate quick reinforcement.[127]

St Ruth, stung by the loss of Athlone, fixed on a hill 16 miles to the west where he would 'win the day or lose all'.[128] The hamlet of Aughrim, that gave its name to the battle, anchored St Ruth's left or northern wing. Boggy ground lay between his front and the approaching Williamites.[129] During the afternoon and evening of Sunday 12 July Ginckel successively attacked the Irish right, where his Dutch, Danes and Huguenots were stopped dead, and the centre where his English were overrun and driven back across the morass. To help contain these attacks St Ruth had shuffled infantry battalions from his left, including a battalion near the mouth of a 'togher' or causeway close to Aughrim Castle. This let Willliamite horsemen pick their way two by two across the togher. The Royal Horse Guards crossed on the third attempt, but found themselves hard pressed. Seeing this, St Ruth cried out: 'Boys, the day is ours!' But while he was mounting a cavalry counter-attack, a random cannon ball knocked off his head. Shocked and demoralised, nearby horsemen left the field. Hearing of this, Brigadier Henry Luttrell who was in charge of the first line of horse blocking the causeway also rode off, 'after a small resistance', insists the 'Light to the Blind', as did Major-General Sheldon's second line of the left wing.[130]

Some of the Williamite horsemen now chased their Irish counterparts westward while elsewhere the Williamites rallied and pushed the Jacobite foot soldiers uphill. Sarsfield's cavalry on the right wing kept Williamite horsemen at bay for a half an hour or so before breaking off and leaving their infantry comrades to clamber over ditches and flee. The pursuers broke off when night fell an hour later but by then about 3,000 Irish had been cut down or captured. The toll struck the leaders heaviest: Of the 32 or so colonels of foot present, 17 were killed, mortally wounded or taken prisoner. It was a 'shattering' blow.[131] The war was lost, though not finished.

Writing to Louvois the day after the disaster, Tyrconnell was quick to blame the cavalry on the left wing and a cavalry regiment on the right (he mentioned Purcell's by name) for having fled and exposing the flanks of the infantry. The lord lieutenant did not single out his bugbear Luttrell by name but subsequent historians cast the blame on this 'miserable wretch, bought by filthy lucre' for supposedly ordering his bemused troopers to turn tail on seeing the enemy approach.[132] It is more likely, however, that Luttrell was the scapegoat for a general malaise and war-weariness amongst the cavalrymen, including Sheldon, Tyrconnell's client. There can be no doubt that the cavalry had not fought as well as at the Boyne. Cavalry commanders had been the ones most entangled in the mutually debilitating Lucan–Tyrconnell feud and it may be that this quarrel had sapped their fighting spirit. The cavalry officers were mostly Lucan's supporters, so O'Kelly dwells only briefly on their flight and implicitly excuses their conduct because they had no general officer to lead them. The 'Light to the Blind' scoffs at this excuse: they had been placed where they were to hold the pass and St Ruth's death did not alter that tactical imperative.[133]

Tyrconnell struck an appropriately sombre mood in his report to Louvois informing him that while the horse had come off more or less intact the surviving foot soldiers had yet to straggle to Limerick and so the final death toll was not yet known. He could not resist criticising St Ruth: 'He did not consult me about this last or any other business and I had no idea he wanted to give battle and if he had only heeded me neither Athlone nor the army would be lost'.[134] By that he meant, in the first place, that he should have knocked gaps in the ramparts of Athlone and, in the second, that St Ruth should have declined to give battle and sent the foot soldiers to hold Galway and Limerick and loose the horse to raid behind enemy lines. Yet Tyrconnell was far less despondent after Aughrim than he had been after the Boyne. He wanted to continue the war and sent messengers to France immediately, promising that he could hold out until spring if arms and ammunition were sent quickly. Four days after Aughrim he met the retreating cavalry at Sixmilebridge and sent them to quarters near Limerick and gathered the fragments of the field army into a fortified camp under the guns of the city.

When Ginckel reached Galway a week later he found the town's merchant and landowning 'tribes', the Lynchs, Ffrenchs, Brownes and the rest, ready to surrender. Many of them were new interest men who showed less and less commitment to the common cause as the war went from bad to worse. Lords Clanricard and Dillon (Lady Tyrconnell's son-in-law) and their garrison troops were so demoralised that a town that had held out against Charles Coote for nine months in the 1650s now tamely capitulated in less than nine days.[135] Drearily familiar accusations of treachery followed. O'Kelly pointed the finger at Tyrconnell for countenancing Dillon's defeatism but in fact the garrison did not wait for Tyrconnell's go-ahead before capitulating. The real reason for the apparent collapse in Irish fighting spirit lay in a proclamation by the Williamite lords justices on 7 July, at the psychologically ripe moment following the loss of Athlone. The proclamation offered pardon and, in consequence, retention of their estates to officers who surrendered within three weeks, though it did not promise retrospection to officers who had submitted or been captured or to the heirs of officers who had been killed in action. The proclamation's promise of freedom to practise religion was couched in language of studied vagueness. Nonetheless the proclamation offered a basis for negotiation which the Galway townspeople and garrison eagerly seized upon.[136] The garrison was allowed to march under safe conduct to Limerick.

The fall of Galway cut Jacobite territory into two disconnected blocks. North and west Munster comprised the biggest block, north Connacht the smaller. Yet Tyrconnell had some grounds for cautious optimism. Had Ginckel ignored Galway and marched straight to Limerick he would probably have ended the war at a blow. With Galway taken, he turned about and took a long route back across the Shannon, south through the midlands and south-west to Limerick to approach the Irishtown from the same direction as William had the previous year. But now it would be more difficult to take the city. It was later in the year and the city had provisions enough to sustain 15,000 troops for six months. During the winter hundreds of labourers directed by French engineers had sculpted the ground around the Irishtown into a formidably deep barrier of glacis, covered way, and enormous bastions. Even troops too shaky to put in battle lines could fight from behind such ramparts. Finally, Ginckel had given Tyrconnell a few precious weeks to reassert control and calm shattered nerves.

Tyrconnell was haunted by the fear that, as in the 1650s, some prominent officer would make individual terms [capitulation particulière] whereupon others would follow and any collective bargaining position would be hopelessly undermined. He insisted that every officer subscribe to a covenant promising to stick together to the last. French officers like D'Usson, commander of the garrison in Limerick, recognised that the oath was well-intentioned and indeed he and Tessé, St Ruth's second-in-command, expressed great admiration for the way the harried lord lieutenant 'serves his master with great dignity at a time when he is in a way reduced to trusting no one'. Yet they feared that so much open discussion of the unmentionable would unsettle the other ranks.[137] Tyrconnell probably knew his officers better than d'Usson; if nothing else the oath flushed out those 'caballists' like Purcell and Henry Luttrell who refused to swear it. Luttrell's arrest for treasonable correspondence with the enemy on 6 August tended to further damage Lucan's faction. A later Williamite history recounts how Lucan himself stumbled on the plot:

> But the true Cause of his [Luttrell's] Imprisonment was the Discovery of a Letter, brought by a Trumpeter from a great Officer in the *English* army, when the Garrison of Galway was conveyed to Limerick: For the Trumpeter, having delivered one to Sarsfield, denied his having any other Letters; but being threatened with Death, if, upon search, any were found about him, he produced one to Luttrell…

The letter was phrased in such a way as to suggest earlier correspondence between Ginckell and Luttrell. Tyrconnell promptly convened a court-martial to sit the very next day. He left Lucan off the court, packed it with his supporters and presided in person. Though he pressed for conviction and death penalty, the majority nonetheless voted him down and Luttrell was imprisoned in King John's Castle for the remaining weeks of the war.[138]

If he escaped the judgement of his peers, Luttrell stands condemned by folk memory and nationalist history: Seán Ó Neachtain, a contemporary scribe and historian, slated this faltach bradach [rotten evil-doer].[139] It seems an open and shut case of treachery. While his brother Simon followed Sarsfield to France after the war, Henry brought his entire regiment over to William's service. The authorities awarded him a pension rather than the promised colonelcy and took some pains to secure him in possession of his older brother's confiscated estate at Luttrellstown. When he was shot by an unknown assassin in 1717, the Irish House of Commons concluded that the murder was 'done by Papists, on account of his service to the Protestant interest of the Kingdom'. Quite what this 'service' was remains unsettled.

And yet there is something fishy about the trumpeter's incriminating letter. For one thing, its contents were confirmed by yet another intercepted letter and, if that were not enough, the Williamite general Ruvigny sent a letter to Tessé on a 'feeble pretext' asking him to be sure that Luttrell received the incriminating letter from the trumpeter.[140] It is almost as if this was a psychological ploy by the Williamites to discredit Luttrell, hitherto a known hardliner. But they surely knew that to discredit Luttrell was to bolster Tyrconnell who was, as lord justice Porter conceded, the only man influential enough to keep the French and Irish from falling out.

Two days after Luttrell's court martial, d'Usson hosted a dinner party. Tyrconnell, the guest of honour drank, imbibed ratafia (brandy flavoured by crushed apricot stones) and was altogether 'very merry and jocose'.[141] On retiring to his bedchamber, however, he was struck down by apoplexy: perhaps all that brandy set his heartbeat racing. He lingered four days. On the last day, 14 August, Sir Richard Nagle wrote in a letter that Ginckel was within four miles of Limerick and Tyrconnell 'lies gasping'. He followed up with a second dispatch later that day: 'I am sorry to tell you that my Lord Lieut. Dyed this day about Two of the Clock. It was a fatall stroke to this poor Country in this Nick of Time.'[142] Surprisingly, Riverston does not repeat rumours of poison but otherwise shrouds his hero's death in conspiratorial menace: Tyrconnell 'died of sickness [morbo], a harbinger no doubt/Of that city's sure fall, a mighty loss/To the deliverance of his [Magna laborantis Patriae] struggling country/A grief and dire solicitude to two Kings,/But to those who desired revolt, a boon,/To those who changed allegiance secretly/For gold from Holland and who did construct/An unseen plot, a singular pleasure.'[143]

SEVEN

POST MORTEM

Jacobite Ireland outlived Tyrconnell by six weeks. Would the regime have lasted longer had the lord lieutenant lived? The author of the 'Light to the blind' had no doubts: 'If the duke of Tyrconnell were then alive (I utter it with certainty), he would not hearken to any offer of surrender, because he expected to retrieve the country by spinning out the war'.[1] An English official shared this view, albeit for different reasons. When he heard of Tyrconnell's passing he opined that this death would soon bring an end to the war because it was the Lord Lieutenant's influence alone that had held the Jacobites together for so long.

James had issued a commission to be unsealed in the event of Tyrconnell's death, dividing the civil power between three lords justices, two of them English-men, the Lord Chancellor Alexander Fitton, and Francis Plowden, a revenue commissioner. Nagle made a third. The army was put under the control of D'Usson, not Lucan. James's memorandum of advice for his infant son written the following year specifically advised him to appoint only a disinterested outsider as governor: 'A clearer statement of regret at having appointed Tyrconnell could hardly be imagined.'[2] The appointments probably marked a bid to reassert that British Jacobite pre-eminence that had been lost with Melfort's fall. James's wishes were, in practice, ignored and a council in which Lucan's supporters predominated (Riverston and Sheldon were the only Tyrconnellite members) called the shots in civil and military matters.[3]

After Aughrim, Irish defeat was 'inevitable'.[4] But if a French fleet were to reach Limerick and deliver supplies then the war, hopeless or not, might well drag on for yet another campaigning season. Ginckel's army was little bigger than that of the Irish and he was beginning his siege late in the campaigning season. It was 30 August, a year to the day that William had abandoned his siege, before Ginckel's guns and mortars began to batter and bomb the Irishtown. Reckoning that the Irish were too many and too well dug in, Ginckel did not break ground and sap towards the ramparts, the necessary preliminary to an assault. Rather he 'lay there in expectation of what would happen' in spite of William's warning that the Irish were 'stubborn' and only a full siege in form, with the attackers digging saps and parallel trenches right up to the counterscarp, would bring them to heel.[5] Ginckel next shifted his attack from the Irish town on the south towards the English town even though it was encircled by the Shannon and Abbey Rivers. Ginckel built new batteries to fire across the Abbey River at the walls of the English town where his guns knocked a gaping breach almost 200 yards wide. The Dutch general hoped to bridge the river and send his men trudging through 300 yards of mud to the breach. An Irish raid, however, forced him to give up what would likely have been a costly failure. The shelling of the English town coincided with the circulation of a document purporting to be Tyrconnell's last will and testament which claimed that the French would leave the Irish in the lurch after dragging out the war over the coming winter. Promises of help were a 'mere chimera' and the Irish needed to make the best terms they could now, while they still could. Simms believes that this piece of black propaganda was put about by Tyrconnell's Irish opponents, but that is as unlikely as the rumour that they had poisoned the lord lieutenant. The tone and sentiments of the 'Testament' are redolent of an English hack unable to suppress his dislike of the Irish, not least when the writer began by admonishing his supposed countrymen insultingly, 'if ever you are capable of thought it is now more needed than ever'. Talbot's 'Testament' was, so to speak, a paper version of the cannon shot pounding the walls of the English. [6]

Two of Ginckel's attacks had failed. Yet the morale of the Irish army was steadily deflating, due to an absence of effective and inspirational leadership, rather than to any cool and objective appraisal of the circumstances. Proof of collapsing morale came on the night of 15–16 September when Williamite pioneers laid pontoons across a ford a mile upriver of Limerick. Robert Clifford, a brigadier of dragoons lay nearby in order to support a small detachment of foot soldiers covering the ford. Clifford was warned 'several times' of suspicious noises at the ford by officers on their rounds but he ignored these warnings and at first light was faced with Williamites marching dry shod over the Shannon. His dismounted dragoons (their horses were grazing and could not be retrieved in time) made a show of resistance and retreated. On 22 September, Ginckel led most of his horsemen and somewhat less than half his infantry over a pontoon bridge into Co. Clare, leaving the rest to hold the siege works. [7] Dominick Sheldon with a strong force of 3,500 horsemen and 1,000 infantry nearby tamely retreated, as he had so disastrously at Aughrim, instead of entering the city where there was horse fodder enough for the next three months. Each faction blamed the other. O'Kelly asserted that Clifford, a 'creature of Coridon's [Tyrconnell's]', was guilty at least of 'unpardonable neglect'. The author of the 'Light to the blind' agreed that Clifford was guilty of 'neglect, or ignorance or treachery' but claimed that he had secret orders from Lucan to retreat after a show of resistance and so give a pretext for surrendering. [8] The episode was symptomatic of defeatism among the cavalry officers, especially the minority among them like Sheldon and Clifford who had been supporters of Tyrconnell.

After pushing on to Thomondgate, the Allies drove the Irish back across Thomond Bridge towards the city at which point a French officer raised a drawbridge spanning the central arch and trapped hundreds of Irish outside to be slaughtered, their corpses piled up higher than the parapets of the bridge.[9] Ginckel still remained convinced that an outright attack would be 'impracticable'.[10] Yet that very evening the Jacobites beat the *chamade*, the drum beat whereby the besieged usually announced their willingness to capitulate.

Would they have done so if Tyrconnell were still alive? Or, assuming Tyrconnell were alive and had agreed to negotiate, would he have wrested better terms from Ginckel?

As to the first counterfactual scenario, the Jacobites could have held Limerick even after Ginckel crossed the Shannon. The fact that Ginckel crossed, as William's outriders had the year before, did not alter the fact that winter was nearly on him, that the French were on the sea, and that the Allied squadron in the Shannon Estuary had only seven men-of-war, not enough to block the relief fleet. In a little while longer Ginckel would have had to pull back from Limerick and the French provisions ships would have tied up at the quay.[11] Tyrconnell, still counterfactually alive, would then have spun out the war into the campaigning season of 1692. But to what effect? In May 1692 Admiral Tourville failed to clear the English Channel for a French-Jacobite invasion force waiting in Normandy for embarkation. The Allies followed up their success by burning fifteen French ships off La Hogue. These sea battles marked the end of France's naval superiority and capacity to resupply and reinforce the Jacobites.[12] Without a steady stream of French arms, munitions and provisions the Irish war effort would have collapsed by autumn 1692. Nor would tying down 20,000 Allied soldiers in Ireland for another campaigning season have decisively altered the course of operations in the main theatre of war, the Spanish Netherlands. We know this because, as it happened, most of Ginckel's troops spent that summer after Limerick waiting uselessly in England to embark for a diversionary descent on St Malo. The expedition was called off too late for the troops released from Ireland to be of any use in the Netherlands.[13] To conclude, it is probably as well that the Irish capitulated when they did because they were promised better terms than they would have been promised a year later.

The slaughter on Thomond Bridge discredited d'Usson and de Tessé, the two senior French officers, who would have liked to fight on to the last Irishman. Lucan, who displaced them, was not the fire-eater of yesteryear. The fact that Lucan rather than Tyrconnell dominated negotiations is significant.

Had it been the latter, lamented the writer of the 'Light to the blind', the Irish 'might have gotten much more beneficial conditions' on the lines of those suggested when Ginckel had sounded out members of the Irish peace party eight months ago.[14] These contacts had intimated that the Irish would lay down arms only 'on condition that they retain their estates and the exercise of their religion as in King Charles's time'.[15] Specifically, could Tyrconnell have extracted these terms?

Tyrconnell had been 'a bitter enemy' to those who would submit and, assuming that he agreed to negotiate at all, he would never have agreed to so nebulous a form of words as Article One of the capitulation:

> The Roman-Catholics of this Kingdom, shall enjoy such privileges in the exercise of their Religion, as are consistent with the Laws of Ireland; or as they did enjoy in the Reign of King Charles the II:[16]

The form of words artfully gave the impression that, at worst, the Catholic religion would be connived at as it had been in Charles II's reign. But the laws of Ireland were not consistent with any 'privilege' towards Catholicism, while the other clause of doubtful precedence about Charles II's reign was meaningless given the stark fluctuations in the position of Catholics at different times during his reign from royal favour to murderous persecutions. That the Irish knew of this difficulty is suggested by the fact that they sought initially the same 'freedom of conscience' that they enjoyed in a specific year, the year James II was crowned.[17] While the war lasted, article one stood and no penal laws were passed, other than a ban on foreign education and prohibitions of Catholics carrying arms and owning horses of charger quality. The latter prohibitions were, arguably, matters of military prudence rather than religion. However, once the war was over and William no longer beholden to Catholic allies he did not block the Irish parliament's clamour for penal laws against Irish Catholics. In short, the first article was flannel and the Irish negotiators must have realised that it was not 'warily drawn'.[18]

Guarantees of property protection were offered by article two to 'all persons in the city of Limerick and in the Irish army that is in the counties of Clare, Kerry, Cork and Mayo'. One of the Irish negotiators, Sir Toby Butler, insisted 'there must be an end of the treaty' if this article was not extended to civilians in the Irish quarters in these counties' while Sarsfield bristled that he would 'lay his bones in these old walls rather than not take care of those who stuck by them'.[19] A phrase covering civilians was inserted in the document presented for signature but was left out in the transcribed copy sent to Dublin. The bill eventually confirming the articles as passed by the Irish parliament in

1697 omitted the clause. The problem primarily related to counties Mayo and Clare and in practice landowners in those counties almost never forfeited except where they followed Lucan into exile. In other words, they benefited from the clause, missing or not. Critics blame the Irish delegates for committing a 'grave wrong' by not insisting that the second article's guarantees of property should extend to Jacobite prisoners-of-war and the heirs of those killed in action. Tyrconnell would not have treated these families so shabbily, if only because so many surviving relatives of his own nephews and grand-nephews found themselves in that predicament. 'Wicked Will' Talbot died of wounds inflicted on him during a sally by the defenders of Derry, Neill O'Neill and Walter Dungan had been cut down at the Boyne and Colonel James Talbot of Templeogue and Mount Talbot was slain at Aughrim.[20] Neil O'Neill's widow Frances claimed the benefit of a pre-existing marriage settlement when his estate was confiscated. The gambit failed and the settlement was not recognised: many such settlements and deeds denying ownership by the attainted person at the time of attainder were backdated forgeries. The best she could do was secure a forty-one year lease on the property from the forfeiture commissioners to maintain herself and her four daughters. Walter Dungan's brother Thomas, former governor of New York, had more success than Frances O'Neill when he produced a purported deed showing that Walter had only been entitled to a life interest in the estate.[21]

Lucan had a far different priority than Tyrconnell would have had. The first question Lucan asked, before even discussing articles, was if the Irish officers and men could go 'wherever they had a mind'. George Clarke, Williamite secretary at war, was probably correct to surmise that by this Sarsfield 'reckoned upon making himself considerable'. In other words, Sarsfield would land in France not as a lone refugee but as the leader of a large body of recruits. Ultimately the Williamites even hired vessels to help take the Irish to France. In this respect the Limerick articles do seem, as a French officer noted at the time, to be so 'singular as to be almost without historical precedent'.[22] To be fair to him, Lucan may have had an overriding interest in embarking as many soldiers as possible for strategic as well as selfish motives.[23] Perhaps he did not believe it really mattered what terms were set down for the stay-at-home Irish because the enemy would not observe them. The issue would only be decided by an invasion of Britain and Ireland, spearheaded by Irish troops, with him at their head.

It is bootless to explore counterfactual 'might-have-beens' any further than the signing of the 'Treaty' of Limerick.

The Tyrconnell peerage was an unlucky, or at any rate, short-lived one. The original title had been awarded to the O'Donnells and the title lapsed on Rory

O'Donnell's attainder after the Flight of the Earls in 1607. The title was next conferred on Oliver Fitzwilliam Viscount Merrion in 1661 and became extinct with his death six years later. John Brownlow was created Viscount Tyrconnell in 1718 and the title expired with him in 1746.[24] Richard Talbot's tenure of the title was only slightly longer than Fitzwilliam's and he did not hand this, or much else, on to a successor.

His estates of almost ten thousand acres were confiscated: Tyrconnell had, after all, died an outlaw and so was liable to the same treatment as an officer killed in action. This left his widow among the top half dozen biggest losers from the post-war confiscations.[25] The confiscated estates included James's large portfolio in Ireland whose management had been a source of profit to the Talbots. The twice-widowed Lady Tyrconnell continued to attend the exiled court at Saint-Germain as a lady-in-waiting on Mary of Modena and recipient of 3,000 crowns awarded out of the pension King James received from the Louis Le Grand. The year after her husband's death she gathered many of the Jacobite exiles around Paris for a funeral service in the English convent in the Faubourg St-Antoine. She kept up a correspondence with her sister, Marlborough's wife and Queen Anne's favourite, and fulsomely thanked her for helping in her 'special concerns'.[26] Among these concerns was the recovery of lost income. Sarah Churchill's lobbying helped her sister establish a claim to a jointure on part of the manor of Cabra Co. Dublin forfeited by her late husband: a bill giving effect to that claim was passed by the English Commons, 'both Whigs and Tories striving who could favour it most'.[27] Frances later spent much time at Brussels where she acted as a conduit between Marlborough and the Jacobite court at Saint-Germain during the War of the Spanish Succession so long as the prospect still existed that James III would succeed on the death of his aunt, Queen Anne. Frances returned to Dublin in 1708 and took up residence at Arbour Hill on Dublin's northside.

While reigning in Dublin Castle, Lady Tyrconnell had snagged noble husbands for all three of her daughters with George Hamilton. Elizabeth married a Protestant noble, Richard Parsons, 1st Viscount Rosse (d.1703), Frances married Henry, 8th Viscount Dillon, and Mary married Nicholas, 3rd Viscount Barnewall of Kingsland.[28] She was evidently wealthy, well-connected, and pious, as she demonstrated by her protection and generous endowment of a Poor Clare community that fled in 1715 from the dangerous environs of Dublin Castle to North King Street. Sixteen years later she died, having tumbled out of bed on a freezingly cold night and perishing of exposure: at 82 years of age she was too feeble to rise or call for help. She was buried in the Jones family vault in St Patrick's Cathedral on 9 March 1731.[29]

The Jones connection was through her grandson Richard Parsons 1st Earl of Rosse, a notorious libertine and gambler who was also a grandson of Ranelagh, Tyrconnell's crooked ally. Newspaper reports that she left 'near a Million of Money' may be discounted and probably reflect the rumours of avariciousness that clung to her.[30]

William Talbot, Sir Robert's son, was the nearest Tyrconnell had to a legitimate male heir. He was first in the remainder to his uncle when the latter was made Earl of Tyrconnell in 1685. He became Master of the Rolls on 23 April 1689 and Secretary of State for Ireland in September of that year. He may have incurred disgrace because he was dismissed from his post before the year was out. He died of natural causes at Galway in May 1691, predeceasing his uncle.[31]

Tyrconnell sired two known offspring who survived to adulthood: Charlotte from his first marriage and his bastard son Mark or Marcus. In 1702 Charlotte married her cousin, a son of Tyrconnell's nephew William Talbot of Haggardstown, Co. Louth, who followed the Jacobite cause in exile and claimed the Tyrconnell title.[32] This cousin, Richard Talbot, would become the third Earl of Tyrconnell in his own estimation. He died at sea in 1716 on the return voyage from the French expedition to support Jacobite insurrection in Scotland. [33] Charlotte and Richard's son, Richard Francis, the next 'Earl of Tyrconnell' sailed to Scotland with Jacobite reinforcements after the '45, was captured at sea and eventually exchanged. He subsequently served as French Minister Plenipotentiary to Prussia.

Marcus Talbot was Tyrconnell's son by 'a Lady that he had promis'd marriage to, tho he never perform'd his Promise'.[34] The injured lady may have been a Clandeboy O'Neill to infer from the fact that Mark Talbot described Sir Neil O'Neill as a 'relation' and was on visiting terms with the Lancashire Molyneuxs, Sir Neil's wife's family. From his youth he served in the French army and, after James's accession, in the English army.[35] He returned to Ireland in 1689 where he was appointed lieutenant colonel (wealthy but amateurish colonels usually picked a veteran like him for this key appointment) in the earl of Antrim's regiment and was governor of the strategically vital stronghold of Carrickfergus at the beginning of the Jacobite War.[36] By 1691 he had been promoted to brigadier and was gravely wounded at Aughrim. After his recovery he served under Marshal de Noailles in Catalonia and later under Vendôme in Italy and fought at the Battle of Marsaglia in 1693. Given command of the regiment of Clare in 1694 he was recalled to St. Germain in 1694 to be on standby with his troops for a Jacobite descent on England.[37] His tongue loosened by drink, Talbot blurted out that King James 'was a thousand times fitter for a Convent than for a Throne'.[38] The insult was eventually repeated back to Mary of Modena who demanded that Talbot be punished. This indiscretion may have been the proximate cause of Talbot's disgrace but the deeper cause was a romance that had blossomed between Talbot and the widowed Henrietta FitzJames, daughter of King James and Arabella Churchill. Hearing that the couple were on the point of marrying clandestinely, James packed his daughter off to an English nunnery in Pontoise.[39] Frances, a lady-in-waiting, pleaded with Queen Mary on Mark Talbot's behalf while both Noailles and Vendôme petitioned the Sun King himself. In vain. Louis cashiered Talbot, withdrew his pension, and threw him in the Bastille. James and Mary proved implacably unforgiving and only with the outbreak of the War of the Spanish Succession was Mark Talbot restored to active service as a colonel. He was killed at the Battle of Luzzara (1702) while serving under Vendôme in Italy.[40]

A STUDY IN FAILURE

'Thus heaven preserved him not for small ends', insisted one of Tyrconnell's contemporary hagiographers.[1] But great or small, Jacobitism proved a dead end.

How does the biographer treat a subject like Tyrconnell whose life-project eventually collapsed? The Protectorate fell within a few years of Oliver Cromwell's death and a vengeful Stuart had his body dug up and his skull mounted on a spike. But once reclaimed by later generations (S. R. Gardiner, for instance, thought him the 'noblest and wisest' of English rulers), Cromwell's failure could be reinterpreted as success deferred. In contrast, Jenny Wormald's Mary Queen of Scots, born to power but unequal to its demands, was a failure unredeemed by later admirers. Which kind of failure was Tyrconnell, redeemed or irredeemable?[2]

The answer hangs on whether he was an Irish Jacobite. One might very well argue that Irish Jacobitism enjoyed a post-Culloden afterlife because it articulated a collective sense of calamity and redemption which could outlive its beginnings in Stuart monarchism and so remain relevant to later national aspirations.[3] For those minded to see it, some irreducible continuity persisted from Jacobite monarchists, through Jacobin republicans, O'Connellite repealers, Fenians, Home Rulers, and so on.

But Tyrconnell was more of a British than an Irish Jacobite. At Chester he accepted, perhaps even welcomed, a compromise on the land settlement that would prove unacceptable to his countrymen. When William's invasion loomed, Tyrconnell embarked much of his standing army to support James, even though this ran the danger of losing Ireland. Clearly, he did not envisage Ireland standing alone for very long if Britain fell. His despondency in the weeks after William's landing in England is explicable when events are viewed, as Tyrconnell saw them, through a three-kingdom prism. A captive King James would likely have ordered Tyrconnell to step down and see his Catholic administration dismantled. Where James's flight was an embarrassment for English Tories, to Tyrconnell it was a providential escape that clarified his strategic choices and galvanised him into action. He coaxed his king to visit Ireland even though he must have foreseen that the presence of the monarch and of favourites like Melfort in Dublin Castle would diminish his own authority. His yearning for a legitimising royal presence shows how strongly the lord deputy was committed to carrying the fight to Britain as his preferred strategic plan. However much Melfort might insinuate otherwise, Tyrconnell still clung to this hope (one could hardly call something so formless a 'plan' anymore) as late as spring 1690 in the face of William's personal intervention leading a massively reinforced Allied army. The French navy should interdict the Irish Sea, Tyrconnell pleaded, to leave William stranded in Ireland. He promised to keep William busy while James descended on England. From time to time he toyed with notions of a French protectorate as a fallback plan but he was too sceptical about French motives to pursue this chimera.

In other words, Tyrconnell usually shared the perspectives and preoccupations of British Jacobitism, suffers from its inconsequentiality and so does not fit comfortably into a teleological nationalist narrative.

But there has to be a yardstick of historical significance that does not rest on consequence or resonance to much later generations. To the generations living in the half century between Tyrconnell's death and Culloden a Jacobite restoration seemed a credible possibility. We know better, but to ignore such a weight of fears and hopes would be to perpetuate a narrowly present-centred history. As long as Jacobitism is worth studying, so is Tyrconnell.

To assert that Richard Talbot showed 'constant loyalty' to his monarch was not just hagiographical bombast. [4] Intense, if idiosyncratic, loyalty to the Stuarts forms the golden thread of his entire political career and to fully grasp the complexity and strength of this loyalty it was necessary to reprise his family background and formation.

Richard sprang from a lawyerly family of the sort that elsewhere closely identified with the centralising early modern state and rose to noblesse de robe status. But the Talbots were papists and the state was Protestant. He had imbibed in his youth a peculiarly reflexive and personal loyalty to the Stuarts which did not extend to other institutions and extrusions of the state. The Stuart cult began with the accession of James I/VI, son of a Catholic martyr, and never entirely dissipated. Disdaining the 'rascal multitude', the Talbots were active in the 1640s among those Old English grandees who saw themselves as an enlightened minority siding with Ormond and with their hard-pressed monarch against deluded fellow countrymen and power-hungry priests. [5] Though the Talbots were trenchantly devout products of the counter-reformation, to them Charles came first in the conventional triad of 'God, King and Country', even if this meant wrecking the Confederate Catholic regime. The later Talbot family tradition of political activism would be burdened by the baggage of the 1640s, namely the perception among many Irishmen that the Talbot brothers were Ormondist factionists and wreckers who had betrayed the common good in selfish pursuit of their own interests.

Perhaps a transmitted memory of that betrayal partly underlay the feud with Sarsfield. The latter dreamed of placing Ireland under French protection and so, while owing theoretical allegiance to exiled Stuarts, making her necessarily independent of, and separate from, Britain. Tyrconnell might belatedly and opportunistically represent himself as the champion of Irish separatism but he was the inheritor of the ultra-loyalism of the 'Ormondist' faction of the 1640s which had subverted the Confederate Catholic cause. Sarsfield, grandson of the insurgent leader Rory O'More, was probably more aware of this poisoned legacy than most.

Talbot's career falls into three distinct periods. In the first he was a courtier/ client. In the second he was successively discredited, imprisoned and exiled. In the third triumphant phase he at last attained hard power, not just backstairs influence. Let us evaluate his achievements during these three phases.

When young Dick Talbot elbowed his way into York's circle in 1657 he began the relationship that would structure his personal life and his political career. This was a striking coup, taking into account the cloud of suspicion that hung about him after the futile plot to assassinate Cromwell. Talbot's success in gaining and guarding this station can only be partly explained by the adaptability of Irish exiles to the cultures of the Catholic mainland, as compared to English and Scottish Protestant royalist exiles. Leaving aside an unguarded tongue and lapses of memory, Talbot had most of the qualities of a quintessential client-courtier. Even his vices (gambling, duelling and sexual intrigue) were courtly, both his wives had been ladies-in-waiting, and he survived on the credit accruing to him by his privileged access to the heir-apparent. York was a dependable patron who shielded Talbot more than once from the wrath of jealous rivals. He did so because he was susceptible to the charisma of a follower who was affable, obliging, courageous, handsome and loyal. When Talbot was away from court he took care to befriend those who were still about his patron and close to King Charles himself: Berkeley, Bennet and Castlemaine. He enriched himself by dealing in forfeited Irish estates using insider dealing, perjury and bribery. Seen from his point of view these were not crooked land deals since the land settlement itself was a criminal racket in which 'vast rewards' were bestowed on 'the worst rebels'.[6] Talbot could have lived uneventfully and comfortably in Ormond's shadow and no more merit a biography than, say, Richard Belling or any other of Ormond's Catholic minions. He chose not to because he was driven by a purpose bigger than greed or personal ambition. His eldest brother had disdained wartime Irish Catholic self-government, but Talbot himself began to outgrow such snobbish sectionalism in the 1660s, as he cast about for ways to block, subvert, unravel or evade the interregnum's punitive land confiscations. He was a poor enough tribune, rash and clumsy. One has only to recollect how

Finch demolished his case before the privy council in 1671. But he was the best tribune the Irish had. In retaliation Ormond successfully lobbied to wind up the court of claims and set about drawing a line under the land confiscations for good. Talbot's disenchantment with Ormond marks the moment when he grew into a 'defender of his people', convinced that the 'expectations of many depended on him'.[7] So they did.

In evaluating Richard Talbot's career as a courtier/client one must have regard to the obstacles he faced, especially the chill winds of anti-popery that could gust through the hothouse atmosphere of Whitehall, blasting the corruption, tyranny, and treachery that hostile polemicists associated with popery. Moreover, his brother and closest ally Peter was quarrelsome and incontinently talkative. Above all, Ormond was his enemy. Talbot pitted himself against the viceroy in 1663–5 but was thoroughly outmatched. So thoroughly indeed that Ormond had Talbot thrown into the tower and went on to secure an Act of Explanation which largely confirmed the land confiscations. Only after Clarendon's fall, York's conversion and Ormond's dismissal could the Irish tribune resume his struggle. Talbot was rightly dismissive of grand gestures like the Declaration of Indulgence and instead tried by modest increments to secure practical toleration for a Catholic hierarchy in Ireland and reinsert Catholics into political office, beginning at the bottom as justices of the peace, the unpaid drudges of local government. The opportunity was fleeting and Talbot's plans inevitably collapsed once Charles's 'Grand Design' faltered.

In evaluating his achievements it is sufficient to note of the second phase that he survived, narrowly escaping a show trial and execution during the Popish Plot hysteria. In July 1679 Talbot procured his release and permission to go to France, purportedly for medical treatment. The release is a testament to the range of contacts he maintained beyond York's circle, and it saved his life. Otherwise he would have died in prison like his elder brother or been taken to England for execution like Plunkett.

As to the third and final phase of Talbot's public career, he had always striven to reconcile Old English loyalties to church and state that were ultimately irreconcilable except in the person of a Catholic monarch. His success depended on York getting to the throne, siring a Catholic heir and sitting on the throne long enough to pass it on to that heir. It is simplistic to assume James's regime was a bizarre aberration that was bound to collapse sooner rather than later. Moeover, if James had died before his plans had matured Tyrconnell would probably have had the Irish 'set up a King of their own' and put themselves under the protection of the Great King. Later, William's invasion of Britain could have been reversed, at least until the Boyne finally closed off that chance. Thereafter, a French protectorate owing nominal allegiance to the Stuarts might have secured Irish Catholics. In other words, Tyrconnell's failure was not foredoomed.

Within a remarkably short time he inserted Catholics into what he saw as a natural and proper place among the judges, generals, colonels, and sheriffs and so built a government that would withstand the shock of the Glorious Revolution. A prime reason for Tyrconnell's success must be that 'prudence and zeal', lauded by James II.[8] Berwick juxtaposes by antithesis the lord deputy's strengths and weaknesses:

> He was a man of very good sense, very obliging, but immoderately vain, and full of cunning. Though he had acquired great possessions, it could not be said that he had employed improper means; for he never appeared to have a passion for money. He had not a military genius, but much courage.[9]

Perhaps Tyrconnell had no 'genius' or natural aptitude for war but what he did have was unrivalled first-hand experience and he usually displayed the steadiness that grew from such familiarity: 'he more than any man is accustomed to this [war] with firm resolve even in the midst of dangers'.[10] His normal fortitude deserted him twice, for some weeks after William landed in England and later when William triumphed at the Boyne.

As for his administrative skills and attributes, he possessed 'bon sens', that is, enough judgement tempered by experience to foresee the likely effects of a particular course of action or policy. An 'obliging' disposition was a highly valued trait in a courtier and denoted someone who was willing to exert himself on an ally's or client's behalf, or to project every impression of exertion in order to trade on that favour later on. Tyrconnell was also cunning. He could read other people accurately and adjust his behaviour accordingly so as to chivvy King James, charm Queen Mary, outwit Clarendon and blackmail Sunderland. He dissimulated to, sometimes literally, disarm opponents. He gave out publicly that policies like purging the army were limited in scope and falsely professed particular friendship to potentially dangerous individuals.

He was no greedier or more corrupt than one would expect and, consequently, his inner circle or cabinet of sharp lawyers and seasoned army officers contained able men as well as Talbot drones. Two cabinet insiders, Nugent and Hamilton, were well connected and talented. Hamilton owed his promotion to petticoat power, many said, but he proved himself a capable field commander at Dromore, Cladyford and the Boyne. Two cabinet members, Nagle and Rice, were talented but not connected to the vice-regal family. The myopic Mountcashel, who floundered on the battlefield, was neither talented nor well connected. All, however, represented a broader range of regional interests and familial networks that the

Talbots could draw on from the Pale. All, moreover, shared Tyrconnell's vision. The highest praise Nagle could bestow on the lord deputy who had just passed away was that he was 'always zealous for his country'.[11] His countrymen were not just the Old English of the Pale. Riverston insisted that 'the names of Trojan [Old English] and Rutulian [Gael] were at once alike to him'.[12]

That the Irish were beaten down 'is not so much to be wondered at', admitted a Whig writer some years later, 'as their holding out against the power and wealth of England, and against all nations to admiration as long as they did'.[13] Much of the credit for this must go to Tyrconnell. For a short time in 1689 it even looked as if the Jacobites might roll back the revolution. That summer an Irish army might have embarked for Scotland and reinforced Dundee's hard-pressed loyalists. That fleeting opportunity passed while the Irish army sat before Derry for over three months. Tyrconnell lay at death's door for much of this fateful moment and Melfort, whose ambition outstripped his ability, ran the show. After the relief of Derry the shattered Jacobite field armies retreated south and listlessly waited near Drogheda. Rising from his sickbed, Tyrconnell saved the capital. He manoeuvred to have Melfort sent away and convinced both James and D'Avaux that the army would not survive further retreat and must be prepared to challenge Schomberg's army near Dundalk. By putting up a brave front, Tyrconnell's army inflicted the most severe defeat of the war on the Williamites, with hardly a shot fired.

This was probably Tyrconnell's finest moment, when his cool head and resourcefulness saved Dublin but already his authority was being chipped away. For instance, a Commons handpicked by him had not delivered the compromise land settlement the king and Tyrconnell had wanted. His correspondence grows gloomier as he saw that Louis would not support the war other than by a smallish expeditionary force constrained by restrictive orders and led by an inept and discredited courtier. Tyrconnell grasped just how limited was the French commitment before anyone else and so it is easy to understand why he vacillated so long on the key strategic question, fight for Dublin or flee west? Fighting at the Boyne was an act of do or die desperation for James; ' if he did it not there [the Boyne] he must lose all without a stroke'.[14] Defeat at the Boyne left no apparent strategic alternative to surrender on whatever terms could be gained. Buoyed by an apparently decisive victory, William was in no mood to grant an attractive peace deal and it is a measure of Tyrconnell's psychological collapse that he failed to recognise or anticipate this. He had suffered an almost equally disabling collapse in the weeks after William's landing in England but had quickly recovered his nerve and his authority. This time he lost his grip for good.

An army mutiny denied Tyrconnell effective command of the army, where-upon he tamely withdrew to Galway with the French while Sarsfield attained heroic stature by successfully defending Limerick.[15] That unwonted success caused Tyrconnell to re-evaluate his pessimism. Less than a fortnight after William raised the siege of Limerick, Tyrconnell embarked for France, not to retire, but to blacken the mutineers at Saint-Germain and Versailles, eliminate their ringleaders as he had Mountjoy, secure French backing, and come back with enhanced authority. On the face of it he succeeded. James heaped fresh honours on his now lord lieutenant who, helped by his timely betrayal of Lauzun, secured promises of more provisions and munitions than ever before.

Yet he could neither cajole nor cow the newly-minted Lord Lucan, who had the advantage (as had Tyrconnell in his power struggle with Sunderland) of being so desperate – or irresponsible – as to risk open conflict. Tyrconnell's habitual response was to back down: he even slunk away after being insulted at Athlone rather than call on his many supporters within the army. It may be, as the author of the 'Light to the blind' suggests, that the older and wiser man feared exacerbating a public scandal that would taint both factions. After all, Tyrconnell could remember the Confederate Catholics indulging in fratricidal quarrels that were off-putting to potential backers whether Papacy, France, Spain or the Duke of Lorraine.

Tyrconnell deftly shifted the blame for Aughrim onto Lucan's followers, scapegoating Henry Luttrell while exonerating those of his own partisans like Dominic Sheldon whose performance was just as suspect.[16] He reasserted his authority by demanding that the officers swear a collective oath to stick together and fight on. It was a prudent move: a spokesman for a united army could extract significantly more concessions from a war-weary enemy than despondent individuals. Tyrconnell did not live to conduct those negotiations, but had he lived he might have done better than Lucan. He could hardly have done worse.

Notes

INTRODUCTION: RICHARD TALBOT, EARL AND DUKE OF TYRCONNELL

1 Thomas Sheridan, 'An Historical Account of some remarkable matters concerning King James the Second's succession ...', *HMC Stuart MSS*, vi, p. 46; J. Miller, 'Thomas Sheridan (1646–1712) and his "Narrative"' in *IHS*, vol. 20, no. 78 (Sept. 1976), pp. 105–28.

2 Anthony Hamilton, *Memoirs of the Comte de Gramont*, ed. D. Hughes (London, 1965), p. 192; Henry Savile, 'Advice to a painter to draw the duke by' in G. de F. Lord (ed.), *Poems on Affairs of State: Augustan Satirical Verse, 1660–1714* (3 vols, New Haven, CT, 1963), i, pp. 217–18.

3 R. Hutton, *Charles the Second King of England, Scotland and Ireland* (Oxford, 1989), p. 284; J. G. Simms, 'Review: The Great Tyrconnell' in *IHS*, vol. 18, no. 72, p. 631.

4 T. B. Macaulay, *The History of England from the Accession of James II* (2 vols, London, 1849), ii, pp. 48–50; P. W. Sergeant, *Little Jennings and Fighting Dick Talbot* (2 vols, London, 1913), i, pp. 110–11.

5 B. Duke Henning, *The House of Commons, 1660–1690* (3 vols, London, 1983), i, p. 547; D. Ogg, *England in the Reigns of James II and William III* (Oxford, 1955), p. 165; J. P. Kenyon, *Robert Spencer, Earl of Sunderland 1641–1702* (London, 1958), pp. 141, 162.

6 J. Miller, *James II: A Study in Kingship* (London, 1978), pp. 210, 216–17; D. L. Smith, *A History of the Modern British Isles 1603–1707* (Oxford, 1998), p. 276.

7 Charles O'Kelly, *Macariae Excidium or The Destruction of Cyprus*, ed. J. C. O'Callaghan (Dublin, 1850), pp. 109–13, 145–6.

8 J. G. Simms, *Jacobite Ireland* (London, 1969), p. 38; P. Kelly, 'A light to the blind: the voice of the dispossessed élite after the defeat at Limerick' in *IHS*, xxiv, no. 96 (1985), p. 433.

9 Gilbert, *Jacobite Narr.*, p. 155; Kelly, 'A light to the blind', pp. 431–62.

10 'Irish Narrative', pp. 19–32.

11 'Ormond, p. 45; *The Thirty-Second Annual Report of the Deputy Keeper of the Public Records: appendix one* (London, 1871), pp. 13, 17, 21, 23.

12 'Le Duc de Tirconnell' (NLI, MS 118, p. 1).

13 'Poema', Book 6: 142.

14 'L'homme fidele'; 'Oraison funebre'.

15 James McGuire, 'Richard Talbot earl of Tyrconnell (1630–91) and the Catholic counter-revolution' in C. Brady (ed.), *Worsted in the Game* (Belfast, 1989), pp. 73–83.

16 James McGuire, 'Talbot, Richard duke of Tyrconnell' in *DIB* [www.dib.cambridge.org/view]; Piers Wauchope, 'Talbot, Richard, first earl of Tyrconnell and Jacobite duke of Tyrconnell (1630–1691)', *ODNB* [www.oxforddnb.com/view/article/26940, accessed 23 Apr. 2012].

17 James McGuire, 'Why was Ormond dismissed in 1669?' in *IHS* 71 (1973), pp. 295–8.

18 T. Harris, 'Restoration Ireland – themes and problems' in C. Dennehy (ed.), *Restoration Ireland: Always Settling and Never Settled* (Dublin, 2008), p. 9.

19 P. J. Carrington et al. (eds), *Models and Methods in Social Network Analysis* (Cambridge, 2005), pp. 8–9.

20 Kenyon, *Robert Spencer*, p. 101.

21 Gilbert, *Jacobite Narr.* p. 105; R. H. Murray, *The Journal of John Stevens containing a Brief Account of the War in Ireland, 1689–1691* (Oxford, 1912), p. 144.

22 Rev. John Trench to Bishop William King, 9 May 1691, 'The Lyons Collection of the correspondence of William King' (TCD MS 1995–2008, fo. 126v).

23 Gilbert, *Jacobite Narr.*, p. 155.

ONE: PETER'S BROTHER

1 'A Letter of Intelligence', Spa 17 Aug. 1654, *Thurloe SP*, ii, p. 528.

2 He was eighteen when he fought at the siege of Drogheda in 1649: 'Duc de Tirconnell', pp. 1–2.

3 J. Curry, *An Historical and Critical Review of the Civil Wars in Ireland* (Dublin, 1775), p. 134; C. Petrie, *The Great Tyrconnel: A Chapter in Anglo-Irish Relations* (Cork, 1972), p. 25; E. Hyde, *The Continuation of the Life of Edward Earl of Clarendon* (3 vols, Dublin, 1759), iii, p. 688; 'Oraison funebre', p. 300.

4 See the list of Irish Jesuits in the early seventeenth century in E. Hogan, *Ibernia Ignatiana* (Dublin, 1880), pp. 228–9.

5 A. Clarke, 'Ireland and the general crisis' in *Past and Present*, no. 48 (Aug. 1970), p. 81; A. Clarke, *The Old English in Ireland, 1625–42* (2nd edn, Dublin, 2000), p. 19.

6 'Oraison funebre', p. 300.

7 W. Fitzgerald, 'The County Wicklow barony of Upper Talbotstown, and whence its name' in *Kildare Arch. Soc. Jn.*, v (1906–8), p. 460; *Civil Survey: County of Meath*, v (Dublin, 1940), pp. 9, 137, 138, 155, 223, 231; J. P. Prendergast, *The Cromwellian Settlement of Ireland* (New York, 1868), pp. 209, 235–6; *Calendar of the Patent and Close Rolls of Chancery in Ireland Charles I*, ed. J. Morrin (Dublin, 1863), pp. 251, 346, 438; *CSPI James I 1606–08*, eds C. W. Russell and J. P. Prendergast (London, 1874), pp. 62–3.

8 W. Fitzgerald, 'Miscellanea' in *Kildare Arch. Soc. Jn.*, vi (1909–11) p. 516; 'The Rental Book of Gerald, ninth Earl of Kildare, AD 1518', ed. H. F. Hore in *Kilkenny Arch. Soc. Jn.*, v (Dublin, 1867), p. 529; V. Treadwell, *Buckingham and Ireland 1616–1628* (Dublin, 1998), pp. 114–21; N. Canny, *The Upstart Earl: A Study of the Social and Mental World of Richard Boyle first Earl of Cork 1566–1643* (Cambridge, 1982), p. 49; Sir William Talbot to Kildare, 22 Oct. 1629, p. 30, Charles I to Lords Justices of Ireland ?1630, p. 1, Alice Countess of Kildare to Kildare,

25 Oct. 1632, pp. 73–4, Sir William Talbot to Kildare, 1 Apr. 1633, pp. 106–8 in 'The Earl of Kildare's Letter Book' (PRONI MS D. 3078/3. 1/5). My thanks to Bríd McGrath for generously making her transcript of these documents available to me.

9 T. Carte, *History of the Life and Times of James the first Duke of Ormonde* (3 vols, London, 1735), ii, 233.

10 Canny, *The Upstart Earl*, pp. 49–50; Lady Alison Talbot to Kildare, 2 May 1634, 'The Earl of Kildare's Letter Book' (PRONI MS D. 3078/3. 1/5); J. Ohlmeyer, *Making Ireland English: The Irish Aristocracy in the Seventeenth Century* (New Haven, CT, 2012), p. 161.

11 Clarke, *The Old English in Ireland*, p. 45; *Dick Talbot*, i, 19; English Privy Council to Chichester, 27 Jan 1614, *CSPI James I 1611–1614*, eds, C. W. Russell and J. P. Prendergast (London, 1877), p. 465.

12 'Oraison funebre', p. 301.

13 Clarke, *Old English*, pp. 28–43.

14 'Remonstrance of Catholics of Ireland' in Gilbert, *Contemp Hist.*, 1, p. 360; C. Russell, *The Fall of the British Monarchies* (Oxford, 1991), p. 379.

15 M. Perceval-Maxwell, *The Outbreak of the Irish Rebellion of 1641* (Dublin, 1994), pp. 204–7.

16 J. Lynch, *Cambrensis Eversus*, ed. M. Kelly (3 vols, Dublin 1848–52), i, p. 13; M. Ó Siochrú, *Confederate Ireland 1642–1649 A Constitutional and Political Analysis* (Dublin, 1999), p. 37; Gilbert, *Ir. Confed.*, i, p. 226; Perceval-Maxwell, *The Outbreak of the Irish Rebellion, p.* 258.

17 N. Canny, 'Religion, politics and the Irish rising of 1641' in J. Devlin J. and R. Fanning (eds), *Religion and Rebellion: Historical Studies, XX* (Dublin, 1997), p. 51; N. Canny, *Making Ireland British* (Oxford, 2001), p. 506.

18 Deposition of Patrick Gosson (TCD MS 813, fo. 250r).

19 HMC, *Calendar of Ms of Marquis of Ormond New Series*, ii (London, 1903), p. 3; Deposition of Jane Price (TCD MS 813, fo. 330r); Deposition of William Vowels (TCD MS 813, fo. 331r, 331v).

20 B. MacCuarta, 'Religious violence against settlers in South Ulster, 1641–2' in D. Edwards, P. Lenihan and C. Tait (eds), *Age of Atrocity: Violence and Political Conflict in Early Modern Ireland* (Dublin, 2007), pp. 168–9; Examination of William Whalley (TCD MS 818, fo. 24r); Canny, *Making Ireland British*, pp. 490, 513; Deposition of George Elkin (TCD MS 813, f. 279r); The Examination of Hannagh Ffarrell (TCD MS 813, fol. 148r).

21 Conor O'Mahony, *An Argument Defending the Right of the Kingdom of Ireland (1645)*, ed. J. Minihane (Aubane Historical Society 2010), p. 52.

22 Deposition of George Stockdale (TCD MS 810, fo. 12); Gilbert, *Ir. Confed*, i, 45–50; Carte, *Ormonde*, i, 282–3; P. Lenihan, *Confederate Catholics At War, 1641–49* (Cork, 2001), pp. 46–7.

23 R. C. Simington and J. MacLellan (eds), 'Oireachtas List of Outlaws, 1641–1647' in *Anal. Hib.*, no. 23 (1966), p. 351; Examination of Patrick Dillon (TCD MS 816, fo. 85r); Examination of Charles Connor (TCD MS 813, fos. 39r, 39v); Examination of Walter Hussey (TCD MS 813, fos. 46r, 46v); Examination of Patrick Dillon (TCD MS 816, fos. 83r, 87r); Examination of Teige Kelly' (TCD MS 816, fo. 196r); Examination of Thomas Ash (TCD MS 813, fo. 10v).

24 A. L., *A True Relation of the Late Expedition…* (London, 1642), pp. 3, 6; *Public records 32nd*

Report, p. 115; K. Nicholls, 'The other massacre: English killings of Irish, 1641–2' in D. Edwards, P. Lenihan and C. Tait (eds), *Age of Atrocity: Violence and Political Conflict in Early Modern Ireland* (Dublin, 2007), pp. 184–8.

25 'NN', *The Polititians Cathechisme* (Antwerp, 1658), p. 157.

26 Deposition of Thomas Kilvy' (TCD MS 816, fo. 225r); Deposition of Thomas Bloud (TCD MS 816, fo. 154r).

27 Deposition of William Hollis (TCD MS 810, fos. 235r, 236r).

28 Examination of Daniel Enos (TCD MS 810 fo. 23v).

29 Gilbert, *Ir. Confed.*, i, p. 80; Examination of Edward Walsh (TCD MS 813, fo. 63v).

30 Carte, *Ormond*, i, p. 316; *Calendar of MS of Marquess of Ormonde HMC New Series*, vi (1908), p. 209.

31 J. T Gilbert, *Ir. Confed.*, i, p. 81; Ó Siochrú, *Confederate Ireland*, pp. 47–9.

32 J. T Gilbert, *Ir. Confed.*, ii, pp. 90–1.

33 G. Aiazza, *The Embassy in Ireland of Monsignor G. B. Rinuccini, archbishop of Fermo in the years 1645–49*, ed. Annie Hutton (Dublin, 1873), pp. 414–15.

34 R. Gillespie, *Seventeenth Century Ireland* (Dublin, 2006), pp. 157–8; C. Z. Wiener, 'The beleaguered isle: a study of Elizabethan and Jacobean anti-Catholicism' in *Past and Present*, no. 51 (May 1971), p. 27.

35 G Gilbert, *Contemp Hist.*, i, p. 95; Clarke, *Old English*, pp. 85, 260; D. F. Cregan, 'The Confederate Catholics of Ireland: the personnel of the Confederation, 1642–9' in *IHS*, vol. xxix, no. 116 (1995), p. 504; Anne Creighton, 'The remonstrance of December 1661 and Catholic politics in Restoration Ireland' in *IHS*, vol. xxxiv, no. 133 (May 2004), p. 20; R. Dunlop, *Ireland under the Commonwealth: Being a Selection of Documents relating to the Government of Ireland* (2 vols, Manchester, 1913), i, p. 197; Hyde, *Continuation*, iii, p. 688; Examination of Edmond English (TCD MS 813, fo. 8v); R. C. Simington and J. Mac Lellan (eds), 'Oireachtas List of Outlaws, 1641–1647' in *Anal. Hib.*, no. 23 (1966), p. 366: Deposition of Job Ward (TCD MS 815, fo. 283r); Deposition of John Watson (TCD MS 812, fo. 41v).

36 Ó Siochrú, *Confederate Ireland*, pp. 65–6

37 Ibid., pp. 66, 245–6.

38 Lenihan, *Confederate Catholics*, pp. 64–71, 76–7; P. Lynch (ed.), *The Earl of Castlehaven's Memoirs* (Dublin, 1815), p. 56.

39 Ó Siochrú, *Confederate Ireland*, p. 77: P. Little, 'The marquess of Ormond and the English parliament, 1645–1647' in T. Barnard and J. Fenlon (eds), *The Dukes of Ormonde, 1610–1745* (Woodbridge, 2000), pp. 88–9.

40 Cregan, 'The Confederate Catholics of Ireland', p. 504.

41 'Robert Wilson', *The Friar disciplind, or animadversions on Friar Peter Walsh* (Ghent, 1674), pp. 6, 17; T. Ó hAnnracháin, *Catholic Reformation in Ireland The Mission of Rinuccini 1645–1649* (Oxford, 2002), pp. 128–30.

42 Ó Siochrú, *Confederate Ireland*, pp. 110–11.

43 Gilbert, *Contemp Hist.*, iii (part 1), p. 85; Gilbert, *Ir. Confed.*, vi, pp. 79–80, vii, p. 346; J. T. Gilbert (ed.), *HMC Manuscripts of the Marquis of Ormonde* (London, 1895), i, p. 190;

Memorandum re Barnaby Byrne, 29 Jan 1645 (SP 63/264 p. 58) and 'A Note of what Monies John Carroll esq did outpay to the army at Birr', June 1646 (SP 63/264 p. 79); 'Oraison funebre', p. 302.

44 Cuthbert Mhág Craith, 'Toirdhealbhach Ó Conchubhair' in anon (ed.), *Father Luke Wadding* (Dublin, 1957), p. 432.

45 Gilbert, *Contemp Hist.*, i, pp. 134–5, ii, p. 388, iii, pp. 30, 235; Examinations of Richard Greg and Gyles Curran (TCD MS 810, fo. 388 v); Examination of Captain Marcus Cruise (TCD MS 817, fo. 333r); Deposition of Robert Browne and Examination of James Murphy (TCD MS 819, fos. 287v and 150r); Examination of Teige O Carroll (TCD MS 813, fo. 196r); Confession of John Doelan (TCD MS 814, fo. 152r); Examination of Brian Kelly (TCD MS 830, fo. 75r): Deposition of George Cashell (TCD MS 810, fo. 25r); Examination of James Talbot (TCD MS 813, fol. 26r); Examination of Peter Hooper (TCD MS 819, fo. 40r).

46 *Comment. Rinucc.*, i, pp. 190, 237, ii, p. 263.

47 C. P. Meehan, *The Rise and Fall of the Irish Franciscan Monasteries...* (5th edn, Dublin, 1877), p. 483.

48 *Comment. Rinucc.*, iii, 298; J. T. Casway, *Owen Roe O'Neill and the Struggle for Catholic Ireland* (Philadelphia, 1984), pp. 137–8, 147–8.

49 *Comment. Rinucc.*, ii, pp. 361–2; T. Ó hAnnracháin, *Catholic Reformation in Ireland the Mission of Rinuccini 1645–49* (Oxford, 2001), p. 28.

50 Robert Wilson, *The Friar Disciplined or Animadversions on Friar Peter Walsh* (Ghent, 1674), pp. 79, 93–4: Carte, *Ormond*, ii, p. 285.

51 J. Lowe (ed.), *Letter Book of the Earl of Clanricard 1643–47* (Dublin, 1983), pp. 369–71; George Lord Digby to Ormond, Leixlip, 22 July 1647 in Carte, *Ormond*, i, pp. 560–2.

52 P. Lenihan, 'The Leinster army and the battle of Dungan's Hill' in H. Murtagh (ed), *Irishmen in War: Essays from the Irish Sword* (Dublin, 2006), i, pp. 90–104; Edmund Hogan (ed.), *History of the Warr of Ireland from 1641 to 1653 by a British Officer* (Dublin, 1873), p. 58; Arthur Annesley to unk., July 1647, HMC *Egmont MS*, i, part 2, p. 438.

53 Gilbert, *Ir. Confed.*, vi, p. 32; Gilbert, *Contemp Hist.*, i, pp. 154–5

54 Carte, *Ormond*, iii, p. 319; Gilbert, *Contemp Hist.*, ii, p. 675.

55 Gilbert, *Contemp hist*, i, p. 155; Carte, *Ormond*, iii, p. 319.

56 Gilbert, *Ir. Confed.*, vii, p. 32.

57 Gilbert, *Ir. Confed.*, vii, pp. 32–3; T. Ó Donnchadha (ed.), 'Cín Lae Ó Mealláin', *Anal. Hib.*, no. 3 (Dublin, 1931), p. 37; Lynch, *Cambrensis Eversus*, pp. 279–80.

58 Ó Siochrú, *Confederate Ireland*, pp. 191–20; Casway, *Owen Roe O'Neill*, p. 208.

59 *Comment. Rinucc.*, iii, pp. 501, 505; Gilbert, *Contemp Hist.*, ii, p. 20; Gilbert, *Ir. Confed.*, viii, pp. 114–15.

60 K. J. McKenny, *The Laggan Army in Ireland 1640–1685* (Dublin, 2005), pp. 100–1; J. S. Wheeler, *The Irish and British Wars 1637–1654* (London, 2002), p. 188; Ó Siochrú, *Confederate Ireland*, pp. 198, 200.

61 HMC *Calendar of the Manuscripts of the Marquess of Ormonde* (London, 1911), pp. 204, 209.

62 G. A. Hayes-McCoy, *Irish Battles* (2nd edn, Dublin, 1980), p. 212.

63 James Scott Wheeler, *Cromwell in Ireland* (Dublin, 1999), pp. 79–81.

64 *Comment. Rinucc.*, iv, p. 302; Father Thomas Talbot to Ormond, 27 Aug. 1663 (Bodl. Carte MS 33, fos. 74–5).

65 Gilbert, *Ir. Confed.*, viii, p. 123; G. Hill, *An Historical Account of the MacDonnells of Antrim* (Belfast, 1873), pp. 467–8.

66 J. G. Simms, 'Cromwell at Drogheda, 1649' in H. Murtagh (ed.), *Irishmen at War: Essays from the Irish Sword* (Dublin, 2006), i, p. 109.

67 D. Murphy, *Cromwell in Ireland* (Dublin, 1883), pp. 94–6; Gilbert, *Contemp Hist.*, ii, pp. xxi–xxii; Wheeler, *Cromwell in Ireland*, p. 85.

68 Simms, 'Cromwell at Drogheda, 1649', p. 111; Gilbert, *Contemp Hist.*, ii, xxviii.

69 C. Duffy, *Fire and Stone: The Science of Fortress Warfare* (London, 1975), pp. 57–9; D. Chandler, *The Art of Warfare in the Age of Marlborough* (London, 1997), p. 267; J. Morrill, 'The Drogheda massacre in Cromwellian context' in D. Edwards et al. (eds), *Age of Atrocity Violence and Political Context in Early Modern Ireland* (Dublin, 2007), pp. 254–6; M. Ó Siochrú, *God's Executioner: Oliver Cromwell and the Conquest of Ireland* (London, 2008), pp. 86–7.

70 Sir James Turner, *Pallas Armata Military Essays of the Ancient Grecian, Roman and Modern Art of War* (London, 1683), p. 335: Ronald Dale Kerr, '"Why should you be so furious?": The violence of the Pequot war' in *Journal of American History*, vol. 85, no. 3 (Dec. 1998), p. 880; B. Donagan, 'Codes and conduct in the English civil war', *Past & Present*, no. 118 (Feb. 1988), pp. 74–7.

71 Ormond cited in Murphy, *Cromwell in Ireland*, p. 28.

72 Anon., *A Vindication of the Present Government of Ireland under his excellency Richard, earl of Tirconnel* (London, 1688), p. 3.

73 T. Claydon, *William the Third and the Godly Revolution* (Cambridge, 2004), pp. 31–2.

74 'Oraison funebre', pp. 303–5.

75 A. Lytton Sells (ed.), *The Memoirs of James II His Campaigns as Duke of York* (London, 1962), p. 245; Nicholas Plunkett, 'Account of the war and rebellion in Ireland since the Year 1641', *HMC First report* (London, 1870), p. 228; *Tyrconnel*, p. 48.

76 'Duc de Tirconnell', p. 2.

77 James Burke, 'The new model army and the problems of siege warfare, 1648–51' in *IHS*, no. 105 (1990) pp. 9–13; Patrick J. Corish, 'The Cromwellian conquest, 1649–53' in *New History of Ireland*, p. 340; D. Stevenson, 'Cromwell, Scotland and Ireland' in J. Morrill (ed.), *Oliver Cromwell and the English Revolution* (London, 1990), p. 157: Hill, *God's Englishman*, p. 109.

78 Gilbert, *Contemp Hist.*, ii, p. 466.

79 Anon., 'Diary of the proceedings of the forces in Ireland …' in Gilbert, *Contemp. Hist.*, ii p. 222; J. S. Wheeler, *Cromwell in Ireland* (Dublin, 1999), pp. 133, 156.

80 J. Burke, 'Siege warfare in seventeenth-century Ireland' in P. Lenihan (ed.), *Conquest and Resistance: War in Seventeenth-Century Ireland* (Leiden, 2001), pp. 266–7; Wheeler, *Cromwell in Ireland*, pp. 155–7, 194.

81 Wheeler, *Cromwell in Ireland*, p. 202; Ó Siochrú, *God's Executioner*, pp. 174–7.

82 Gilbert, *Contemp Hist.*, iii, pp. 231, 233, 241.

83 Wheeler, *Cromwell in Ireland*, p. 170; 'A journal of the most memorable transactions of General Owen O'Neill' in *Desiderata Curiosa Hibernica* (Dublin, 1772), p. 521.

84 Gilbert, *Contemp Hist.*, iii, p. 45; *Comment. Rinucc.*, iv, p. 574; Clanricard to Richard Fanshawe, 27 Aug. 1651, *HMC Calendar of the Manuscripts of the Marquess of Ormonde* (London, 1902), i, p. 193; J. H. Ohlmeyer, *Civil War and Restoration in Three Stuart Kingdoms* (Cambridge, 1993), p. 284; Archbishop of Dublin and others to Clanricard, nd. in P. F. Moran (ed.), *Spicilegium Ossoriensie* (3 vols, Dublin 1874–8), i, pp. 354–5.

85 E. P. Duffy, 'The siege and surrender of Galway 1651–1652', *Journal of the Galway Archaeological and Historical Society*, xxxix (1983–4), pp. 115, 117: Examination of Ffarragh O'Kelly (TCD MS 830 fo. 180 r); Gilbert, *Contemp Hist.*, ii, pp. 158, 192–3, iii, p. 392.

86 *The Weekly Intelligencer* no. 25 (10–17 June 1651), p. 198: Patrick Archer to Ormond, 9 Jan 1652, *HMC Calendar of Ormonde Manuscripts*, i, p. 24; Ó Siochrú, *God's Executioner*, p. 192; Dunlop, *Ireland Under the Commonwealth*, i, pp. 33, 38, 49, 56, 61, 68, 75; Anon., *A Great Fight at Sea … Also a bloudy Fight in Ireland* (London, 6 Nov. 1651), p. 6.

87 Dunlop, *Ireland Under the Commonwealth*, ii, p. 425; W. Smyth, *Map-making, Landscapes and Memory: A Geography of Colonial and Early Modern Ireland c.1530–1750* (Cork, 2006), pp. 158–9; P. Lenihan, 'War and population' in *Journal of the Economic and Social History Society of Ireland* (Spring 1998), pp. 1–21.

88 Dunlop, *Ireland under the Commonwealth*, i, pp. 148, 190; Ó Siochrú, *God's Executioner*, pp. 225–6.

89 Gilbert, *Contemp Hist.* iii, pp. xviii, 69, 70.

90 *Comment. Rinucc.*, v, p. 187; Dunlop, *Ireland under the Commonwealth*, i, pp. 187, 197–203; Gilbert *Contemp Hist.*, iii, pp. 38, 66, 85–86: Parliamentary Commissioners to Lenthall, Kilkenny 6 May 1652, in C. McNeill (ed.), *The Tanner Letters* (Dublin, 1943), pp. 357–8; Edmund Ludlow, *Memoirs* (3 vols, London, 1721), i, p. 409.

91 R. A. Stradling, *The Spanish Monarchy and Irish Mercenaries The Wild Geese in Spain 1618–68* (Dublin, 1994), pp. 94, 106, 166.

92 Smyth, *Map-making*, pp. 158–9; Igor Pérez Tostado, *Irish Influence at the Court of Spain in the Seventeenth Century* (Dublin, 2008), p. 35; Stradling, *The Spanish Monarchy and Irish Mercenaries*, pp. 78, 139.

93 Ó Siochrú, *God's Executioner*, p. 226; B. Coward, *Cromwell* (London, 1991), p. 76; P. Corish, 'The Cromwellian regime, 1650–60' in *New History of Ireland*, pp. 357, 362.

94 J. P. Prendergast, *The Cromwellian Settlement of Ireland* (New York, 1868), pp. 35–6, 209; 'Proceedings upon the petition of Thomas Fowle, 24 Mar. 1697', *CSPD, William and Mary, 1689–1702*, viii, p. 71; R. C. Simington, *The Transplantation to Connacht 1654–58* (Dublin, 1970), pp. 185, 236.

95 J. D. Krugler, *English and Catholic The Lords Baltimore in the Seventeenth Century* (Baltimore, MD, 2004), pp. 74–5. 86–7.

96 J. McElligott, *Cromwell our Chief of Enemies* (Dundalk, 1994), p. 53; K. S. Bottigheimer, *English Money and Irish Land* (Oxford, 1971), p. 140; J. G. Simms, *Jacobite Ireland* (London, 1969), p. 4; Dunlop, *Ireland under the Commonwealth*, ii, pp. 524, 570: Corish, 'The Cromwellian regime', pp. 365–6; N. Canny, *From Restoration to Reformation: Ireland 1534–1660*

(Dublin, 1987), pp. 220–1; T. C Barnard, *Cromwellian Ireland: English Government and Reform in Ireland 1649–1660* (Oxford, 1975), p. 34.

97 Gilbert, *Jacobite Narr.*, pp. 20, 22, 24; J. F. Lydon, *The Making of Ireland From Ancient Times to the Present* (London, 1998), p. 201; J. G. Simms, *The Williamite Confiscation in Ireland 1690–1703* (London, 1956), p. 196.

98 Talbot is styled 'Colonel' from his earliest appearance in Royalist correspondence. See George Goring Earl of Norwich to Sir Edward Nicholas, Antwerp, 14 Dec. 1655, G. F. Warner (ed.), *The Nicholas Papers, Correspondence of Sir Edward Nicholas* (4 vols, London, 1897), iii, p. 204.

99 J. J. Cronin, 'The political activities of an exiled royal court and the role played by its Irish courtiers' in Philip Mansel and Torsten Riotte (eds), *Monarchy and Exile: The Politics of Legitimacy from Marie de Médicis to Wilhelm II* (London, 2011), p. 155.

100 Óscar Recio Morales, *Ireland and the Spanish Empire 1600–1825* (Dublin, 2010), pp. 145, 151, 152; Brendan Jennings, *Wild Geese in Spanish Flanders 1582–1700: Documents Relating to Irish Regiments from the Archives Genéral du Royaume and other sources* (Dublin, 1964), p. 453.

101 A letter of intelligence from Paris. 4 Mar, 1654, *A Collection of the State Papers of John Thurloe*, vol. 2; 1654 (1742), pp. 106–27 [www.british-history.ac.uk/report. aspx?compid= 55306& strquery=Talbot, accessed 14 Mar. 2011].

102 T. Clavin, 'Talbot, Peter (1618/1620–1680), Roman Catholic Archbishop of Dublin', *ODNB*; Talbot, Peter [www.oxforddnb. com/view/printable/26937, accessed 16 Jun. 2005].

103 Igor Pérez Tostado, *Irish Influence at the Court of Spain in the Seventeenth Century* (Dublin, 2008), p. 163.

104 *Comment. Rinucc.*, v, pp. 178–9; Peter Talbot to Bishop of Clonmacnoise, 3 July 1654, P. F. Moran (ed.), *Spicilegium Ossoriense Being a Collection of Original Letters and Papers Illustrative of the history of the Irish Church* (3 vols, Dublin, 1874–84), ii, pp. 133–4.

105 N. Greenspan, *Selling Cromwell's Wars* (London, 2012), p. 74; T. Venning, *Cromwellian Foreign Policy* (London, 1995), p. 6; A. Bryant, *King Charles II* (London, 1931), p. 56.

106 G. R. Treasure, *Mazarin: The Crisis of Absolutism in France* (London, 1995), p. 252.

107 G. Smith, *The Cavaliers in Exile 1650–1660* (Basingtoke, 2003), pp. 108, 113, 117, 118; D. L. Scott, 'Counsel and cabal in the king's party, 1642–1646' in J. McElligott and D. L. Smith (eds), *Royalists and Royalism during the English Civil Wars* (Cambridge, 2007), pp. 113, 122–7; J. J. Cronin, 'The Irish royalist elite of Charles II in exile, c.1649–1660' (PhD thesis, European University Institute, Florence, 2007), pp. 234–5; M. A. White, *Henrietta Maria and the English Civil War* (Aldershot, 2008), pp. 157–8; Miller, *James II*, pp. 9, 15.

108 Cronin, 'The Irish royalist elite of Charles II', pp. 240–1.

109 M. R. F. Williams, 'Between king, faith and reason: Father Peter Talbot (SJ) and Catholic royalist thought in exile' in *EHR*, vol. cxxvii, no. 528, p. 1073.

110 Pérez Tostado, *Irish Influence at the Court of Spain*, p. 163; Peter Talbot to Goswin Nickel, General of the Society of Jesus, Cologne 17 Nov. 1654, *HMC 10th Report* (London, 1885), p. 363; Hutton, *Charles II*, p. 87.

111 Dunn Macray, *Clarendon State Papers*, iii, p. 281.

112 Charles II to York, Cologne, 10 Nov. 1654. *A Collection of the State Papers of John Thurloe*, i,

pp. 661–75 [www.british-history.ac.uk/report, accessed 14 Mar. 2011]; N. H. Keeble, *The Restoration: England in the 1660s* (Oxford, 2002), pp. 63–4.

113 Peter Talbot to Charles II, Antwerp 3 Jan. 1656 and 7 Jan. 1656; Peter Talbot to Ormond, Antwerp 7 Jan. 1656; Peter Talbot to Ormond, Brussels 12 Aug. 1656, *Clarendon S. P.*, iii, pp. 80, 83, 84, 158–9; Pérez Tostado, *Irish Influence at the Court of Spain*, pp. 165–6, 169; Scott, *Travels of the King*, pp. 184–5.

114 Williams, 'Between king, faith and reason', p. 1084.

115 Information of Samuel Dyer, 27 Feb 1657, *Thurloe S. P.* vi, pp. 831, 833; Williams, 'Between king, faith and reason p. 1077.

116 Scott, *Travels of the King* pp. 168–9; Sir Marmaduke Langdale to Sir Edward Nicholas, Brussels 16 Nov. 1655, *The Nicholas Paper*, iii, p. 128.

117 Pérez Tostado, *Irish Influence at the Court of Spain*, p. 165; *Clarendon S. P.* p. 315.

118 'A letter of intelligence', Paris 22 May 1655 and Cologne, 2 June 1655, 'A Letter of Intelligence', Cologne, 2 Nov. 1655, *Thurloe S. P.*, iii, pp. 433, 465, 533–4, 659; Kingston to unk., Paris 28 Aug. 1658; *Thurloe S. P.*, vii, pp. 339–52; Mr Kingston to ?Joseph Radcliffe, *Thurloe S. P.*, vi, p. 764; T. Ó Fiach, 'Edmund O'Reilly, Archbishop of Armagh, 1657–1669', Franciscan Fathers (eds), *Father Luke Wadding Commemorative Volume* (Dublin, 1957), p. 180.

119 *Dick Talbot, p.* 78.

120 J. Lynch, *De Praesulibus Hiberniae* (2 vols, Dublin, 1944), i, p. 324; G. Steinman, 'Memorials preserved at Bruges of King Charles the Second's residence in that city' in *Archaeologia or Miscellaneous Tracts relating to Antiquity*, vol. xxxv (London, 1853), pp. 335–6; J. J. Jusserand (ed.), *A French Ambassador at the Court of Charles the Second* (London, 1892), p. 55; R. Hutton, *Charles II King of England, Scotland and Ireland* (Oxford, 1989), pp. 104–5.

121 *Life*, i, p. 293; H. M. Digby, *Sir Kenelm Digby and George Digby, Earl of Bristol* (London, 1912), p. 260; Venning, *Cromwellian Foreign Policy*, p. 116.

122 G. Smith, *Royalist Agents, Conspirators and Spies: Their Role in the British Civil Wars, 1640–1660* (London, 2011), pp. 189–94.

123 D. F. Cregan, 'An Irish cavalier; Daniel O'Neill', *Studia Hibernica*, no. 3 (1963), pp. 63–72, 75.

124 A. Barclay, 'The rise of Edward Colman' in *Historical Journal*, vol. 42, no. 1 (Mar. 1999), pp. 123–6; Steinman, 'Memorials preserved at Bruges', p. 340; G. Aylmer, 'Patronage at the court of Charles II' in E. Cruickshanks (ed.), *The Stuart Courts* (Stroud, 2000), p. 195.

125 A. Marshall, *Intelligence and Espionage in the Reign of Charles II, 1660–1685* (Cambridge, 1994), pp. 283–4.

126 Richard Talbot to Ormond, Brussels 3 Jan. 1656, *Clarendon S. P.*, iii, p. 81; J. T. Peacey, 'Order and disorder in Europe: parliamentary agents and royalist thugs 1649–1650', in *Historical Journal*, vol. 40, no. 4 (Dec. 1997), p. 955; 'A Letter of Intelligence', Cologne, 28 July 1655, *Thurloe S. P.*, iii, p. 659; E. Scott, *The Travels of the King: Charles II. In Germany and Flanders 1654–1660* (London, 1907), pp. 125–6, 129–30; 'State Papers, 1655; Nov. (7 of 8)', A collection of the State Papers of John Thurloe vol. 4; Sept. 1655–May 1656 (1742) pp. 235–50 [www.british-history.ac.uk/report.aspx?compid=55420, accessed 24 May 2011].

127 Scott, *Travels of the King*, p. 134; Richard Talbot to Ormond, Antwerp, 7 Jan. 1656, *Clarendon S. P.*, iii, p. 85.

128 Scott, *Travels of the King*, p. 135.

129 P. Aubrey, *Mr Secretary Thurloe: Cromwell's Secretary of State, 1652–1660* (London, 1990), p. 108; Hyde to Ormond, Cologne, 7 Jan. and 14 Jan. 1656, T. Carte (ed.), *A Collection of Original Letters and Papers concerning the Affairs of England from among the Duke of Ormond's Papers* (2 vols, London, 1739), ii, pp. 64, 68; Gilbert Talbot to Ormond, Antwerp 7 Jan. 1656, George Lane to Ormond, 31 Dec. 1655, *Clarendon S. P.*, iii, pp. 78, 85; George Goring Earl of Norwich to Sir Edward Nicholas, Antwerp 14 Dec. 1655 and 21 Dec. 1655, Warner, *Nicholas Papers*, iii, pp. 204, 217.

130 Hyde to Ormond, Cologne 7 Jan. and 14 Jan. 1656, Carte, *Duke of Ormond's Papers*, ii, pp. 64, 68.

131 Carte, *Duke of Ormond's Papers*, ii, pp. 70–3; George Lane to Sir Edward Nicholas Antwerp, 17 Jan. 1656, Warner, *Nicholas Papers*, iii, pp. 247–8.

132 Smith, *Royalist Agents, Conspirators and Spies*, pp. 204–6; Graham Greene, *Lord Rochester's Monkey* (London, 1974), p. 17; H. W. Chapman, *Great Villiers: A Study of George Villiers Second Duke of Buckingham 1628–1687* (London, 1949), p. 82.

133 Scott, *Travels of the King*, pp. 386–8.

134 Earl of Norwich to Sir Edward Nicholas, Antwerp, 21 Dec. 1655, Warner, *Nicholas Papers*, iii, p. 217; T. Barnard, *Irish Protestant Ascents and Descents 1641–1770* (Dublin, 2004), p. 105.

135 J. Halsall to Ormond, London 6 Jan., *Clarendon S. P*, iii, p. 87; Scott, *Travels of the King*, pp. 130, 132; Sir Marmaduke Langdale to Sir Edward Nicholas, Brussels 16 Nov. 1655, Warner, *Nicholas Papers*, iii, p. 128; 'Examination of the Lady Diana Gennings', Birch *Thurloe S. P.* xxxiv, p. 401; Scott, *Travels of the King*, p. 138.

136 'A Letter of Intelligence', Amsterdam, 2 Nov. 1655, *Thurloe S. P.*, iv, p. 103; Wauchope, 'Richard Talbot', Oxford DNB.

137 Green, *Lord Rochester's Monkey*, p. 23; Scott, *Travels of the King*, pp. 63, 73, 82–3, 126.

138 Peter Talbot to Charles II, 6 Jan. 1656, *Clarendon S. P.*, iii, p. 83.

139 Aubrey, *Mr Secretary Thurloe*, p. 106.

140 Richard Talbot to Ormonde, Antwerp 7 Jan. 1656, *Clarendon S. P.*, iii, p. 85.

141 Charles Sévin marquis de Quincy, *Histoire militaire du regne de Louis le Grand, roy de France* (7 vols, Paris, 1726), i, pp. 209–11; 'A Letter of Intelligence', Paris, 19 July 1656 [N. s.], 'An intercepted letter to G. Rathcliffe' and 'A Letter of Intelligence', Brussels 19 July, 1656 [N. s.], *A Collection of the State Papers of John Thurloe*, vol. 5; May 1656–Jan. 1657 (1742) pp. 187–200 [www.british-history.ac.uk/report/aspx, accessed 11 Aug. 2011]; Ignacio Ruiz Rodriguez, *Don Juan José de Austria en la Monarquiá Hispánica; Entre la Política, el poder y la intriga* (Madrid, 2007), pp. 190–2; C. Ramsay, *The Memoirs of the Viscount de Turenne* (London, 1765), pp. 42–3.

142 *Clarendon S. P.*, iii, pp. 291, 303; Peter Talbot to Ormond, 3 Jan. 1660, *Spicilegium Ossoriensie*, ii, p. 181; Cronin 'The Irish royalist elite of Charles II', pp. 242–3; F. J. Routledge, *England and the Treaty of the Pyrenees* (Liverpool, 1953), pp. 6–7, 40; Aubrey, *Mr Secretary Thurloe*, p. 108.

143 Miller, *James II*, pp. 16–17.

144 Ibid.

145 *Life*, i, pp. 287, 292 293; Cronin, 'Irish royalist elite', p. 239; *Dick Talbot*, i, pp. 82–3; N. A. C. Reynolds, 'The Stuart court and courtiers in exile 1644–54' (PhD, University of Cambridge, 1996), pp. 133, 166; John Callow, *The Making of King James II: The Formative Years of a Fallen King* (Stroud, 2000), pp. 69–73.

146 Miller, *James II*, p. 22.

147 G. Downing, The Hague, 11 Oct. 1658, A collection of the State Papers of John Thurloe, vol. 7; Mar. 1658–May 1660 (1742), pp. 417–429 [www.british-history.ac.uk, accessed 14 Mar. 2011]; Miller, *James II*, p. 23.

148 C. S. C. Brudenell-Bruce Earl of Cardigan, *The Life and Loyalties of Thomas Bruce: A Biography of Thomas, Earl of Earl of Ailesbury and Elgin, Gentleman of the Bedchamber to King Charles II and to King James II, 1656–1741* (London, 1951), p. 112.

149 Richard Overton to Sir M. Langdale, Delft, 30 Oct. 1655, Warner, *Nicholas Papers*, iii, p. 102; Miller, *James II*, pp. 18–19.

150 J. Butler to Thurloe, Flushing, 2 Dec. 1656, *Thurloe S. P.*, v, pp. 645–6.

151 S. W. Singer (ed.), *The Correspondence of Henry Hyde, Earl of Clarendon, and of his brother, Laurence Hyde Earl of Rochester* (2 vols, London, 1828), i, p. 436.

152 Carte, *Ormond*, ii. 234; *Clarendon S. P.*, iii, p. 141; N. Plunkett, 'Account of the war and rebellion in Ireland since the Year 1641', *HMC First Report* (London, 1870), p. 228; A. Creighton, 'The Remonstrance of Dec. 1661 and Catholic politics in Restoration Ireland', *IHS*, vol. xxxiv, no. 133 (May 2004), p. 20; *Dick Talbot*, i, pp. 84–5.

153 *Life*, pp. 312–6, 326.

154 Venning, *Cromwellian Foreign Policy*, pp. 141–2, 147.

155 A. Lytton Sells (ed.), *The Memoirs of James II: His Campaigns as Duke of York* (London, 1962), pp. 260, 269, 271–3; Scott, *Travels of the King*, pp. 358–360; Venning, *Cromwellian Foreign Policy*, pp. 141–7.

156 Aphra Behn, *Oroonoko and Other Writings*, ed. P. Salzman (Oxford, 1994), p. 255.

TWO: YORK'S MAN

1 Peter Talbot was born in 1617: 'Calendar of volume 16 of the Fondo di Vienna in Propaganda Archives: Part 1, ff 1–102', ed. Benignus Millett, OFM, in *Collectanea Hibernica*, no. 38 (1996), p. 73.

2 Williams, 'Between king, faith and reason', p. 1088.

3 Peter Talbot to Hyde, Ghent, 18 Aug. 1657, Dunn Macray, *Clarendon State Papers*, iii, p. 349; H. W. Chapman, *Great Villiers: A Study of George Villiers, Second Duke of Buckingham, 1628–1687* (London, 1949), pp. 81, 85–6.

4 Williams, 'Between king, faith and reason', pp. 1092–3.

5 *The Friar Disciplined*, p. 72; Hyde to W. Howard 6 June 1659, Dunn Macray, *Clarendon State Papers*, iv, pp. 214–215; Extract of a letter from Colonel Talbot to Colonel Preston, Brussels, 12 Apr. 1659 and Bordeaux to Mazarin, London, 7 Mar. 1659 in M. Guizot, *History of Richard Cromwell and the Restoration of Charles II* (2 vols, London, 1856), i, pp. 318, 349.

6 D. L. Smith, *A History of the Modern British Isles 1603–1707: The Double Crown* (Oxford, 1998), pp. 193–4.

7   Hyde to W. Howard 6 June 1659, and Ashton to Hyde 10 June 1659 in Dunn Macray, *Clarendon State Papers*, iv, pp. 215, 232.

8   J. Loftis and P. Hardacre, *Colonel Bampfield's Apology* (London and Toronto, 1984), pp. 186–7; E. Hyde, *The Continuation of the Life of Edward Earl of Clarendon* (2 vols, Oxford, 1761), ii, p. 346; F. J. Routledge, *England and the Treaty of the Pyrenees* (Liverpool, 1953), pp. 38–9; C. H. Firth (ed.), 'Thomas Scot's account of his actions as intelligencer during the Commonwealth' in *EHR*, vol. xii, no. 45 (Jan. 1897), p. 122.

9   Smith, *Cavaliers in Exile*, p. 198; M. Coate (ed.), *The Letter-Book of John Viscount Mordaunt 1658–1660* (London, 1945), p. 11; Routledge, *England and the Treaty of the Pyrenees*, pp. 42–4.

10 Lorenzo Magalotti, *Lorenzo Magalotti at the Court of Charles II: His Relazione d'Inghilterra of 1668*, ed. W. E. Knowles Middleton (Waterloo, Ontario, 1980); F. C. Turner, *James II* (London, 1948), p. 56.

11 Bordeaux to Mazarin London 5 June 1659 in Guizot, *History of Richard Cromwell* i, p. 193; Cronin, 'The Irish royalist elite of Charles II in exile, c.1649–1660', p. 324.

12 Fr Joseph Le Clerque to Hyde, Brussels, 26 July 1659 in Dunn Macray, *Clarendon State Papers*, iv, pp. 278–9; Bordeaux to Mazarin, London 3 Nov. 1659, Guizot, *History of Richard Cromwell*, ii, p. 269; Routledge, *England and the Treaty of the Pyrenees*, pp. 42–4; *The Friar Disciplind*, pp. 72, 76; J. D'Alton, *The Memoirs of the Archbishops of Dublin* (Dublin, 1838), pp. 431–2; Gilbert Talbot to Colonel Preston, Brussels, 12 Apr. 1659, Guizot, *History of Richard Cromwell*, i, p. 348; T. D'Arcy M'Gee, *The Irish Writers of the Seventeenth Century* (Dublin, 1857), pp. 175–6; Anon., *Foxes and Firebrands...* (Dublin, 1682), pp. 96–7; Miller, *James II*, p. 23.

13 B. Millett, O.F.M., 'Calendar of volume 16 of the Fondo di Vienna in Propaganda Arcives: art 1, ff 1–102' in *Coll. Hib.*, no. 38 (1996), p. 73.

14 C. Eden Quainton, 'George Lockhart and the peace of the Pyrenees', in *Pacific Historical Review*, vol. iv, no. 3 (Sept., 1935), pp. 273–7; L. Williams (ed.), *Letters from the Pyrenees: Don Luis Méndez de Haro's Correspondence to Philip IV of Spain, July to Sept. 1659* (Exeter, 2000), ix–xi.

15 Lynch, *De Praesulibus Hiberniae*, i, pp. 324–5; *The Friar Disciplind*, p. 73.

16 C. H. Firth (ed.), Thomas Scot's account of his actions as intelligencer during the commonwealth' in *EHR*, vol. xii (1897), p. 122.

17 Hartgill Baron to Lord Mordaunt, 14 Oct. 1659, *Letter-Book of John Viscount Mordaunt*, pp. 61–2; Carte, *Ormond*, ii, pp. 272–3; Routledge, *England and the Treaty of the Pyrenees*, pp. 40–1, 63; J. Wright, *God's Soldiers: Adventure, Politics, Intrigue and Power – A History of the Jesuits* (New York, 2004), pp. 148, 153–4; V. Barbour, *Henry Bennet Earl of Arlington Secretary of State to Charles II* (Oxford, 1914), p. 44.

18 R. Ollard, *Clarendon and his Friends* (New York, 1988), pp. 202–3; B. H. G. Wormwald, *Clarendon, History, Politics, Religion* (Cambridge, 1964), p. 210.

19 Smith, *The Cavaliers in Exile*, pp. 166–7.

20 T. C. Barnard, 'Conclusion. Settling and unsettling Ireland: The Cromwellian and Williamite Revolutions' in J. Ohlmeyer (ed.), *Ireland From Independence to Occupation 1641–1660* (Cambridge, 1995), p. 247; G. Davies, *The Restoration of Charles II 1658–1660* (Oxford, 1955), pp. 340–1.

21 Jenny Uglow, *A Gambling Man: Charles II and the Restoration 1660–1670* (London, 2009), p. 150; Anthony Adolph, *The King's Henchman: Henry Jermyn Stuart Spymaster and Architect of the British Empire* (London, 2012), pp. 227–8; J. D. Davies, 'International relations, war and the armed forces' in L. Glassey (ed.), *The Reigns of Charles II and James VII & II* (Basingstoke, 1997), p. 212.

22 G. Rommelse, *The Second Anglo-Dutch War (1665–1667): Raison d'État, Mecantilism and Maritime Strife* (Hilversum, 2006), p. 64; R. A. Stradling, 'Spanish Conspiracy in England, 1661–1663' in *EHR*, vol. 87, no. 343 (Apr. 1972), p. 270.

23 Anthony Hamilton, *Memoirs of the Comte de Gramont*, ed. D. Hughes (London, 1965), p. 125.

24 E. Gregg, *Anne, Queen of Great Britain* (London, 1980), p. 65.

25 A. Bryant, *King Charles II* (London, 1931), pp. 92, 103–4.

26 Chapman, *Great Villiers*, p. 107; Linda Levy Peck, *Court Patronage and Corruption in Early Stuart England* (Boston MA, 1990), pp. 49–50; N. Cuddy, 'Reinventing a monarchy: the changing structure and political function of the Stuart court, 1603–88' in E. Cruickshanks (ed.), *The Stuart Courts* (Stroud, 2000), pp. 59, 61, 71.

27 G. Aylmer, 'Patronage at the court of Charles II', p. 191.

28 Brian Weiser, *Charles II and the Politics of Access* (Woodbridge, 2003), pp. 26–7.

29 Alan Marshall, *The Age of Faction Court Politics, 1660–1702* (Manchester, 1999), pp. 21, 25; W. E. Buckeley (ed.), *Memoirs of Thomas, Earl of Ailesbury* (2 vols, London, 1890), i, pp. 22–3.

30 Levy Peck, *Court Patronage and Corruption*, pp. 16–17, 27, 273.

31 Smith, *The Cavaliers in Exile*, pp. 119, 122, 131; D. Wilson, *All the King's Women; Love, Sex and Politics in the Life of Charles II* (London, 2003), p. 70.

32 R. B. Shoemaker, 'The taming of the duel: masculinity, honour and ritual violence in London, 1660–1800', *Historical Journal*, 45 (2002), pp. 528, 531.

33 James Kelly, *That Damn's Thing Called Honour: Duelling in Ireland 1570–1800* (Cork, 1995), pp. 30, 88, 89; Marku Peltonen, *The Duel in Early Modern England: Civility, Politeness and Honour* (Cambridge, 2003), pp. 2, 60; V. G. Kiernan, *The Duel in European History: Honour and the Reign of Aristocracy* (Oxford, 1988), p. 113; Smith, *The Cavaliers in Exile*, pp. 123–4; *HMC* 5th Rep., p. 147; Taaffe to Charles II, 'neer Antwerp' 20 Aug. 1658, *Clarendon MS 58*, fos. 181–3.

34 Levy Peck, *Court Patronage and Corruption*, pp. 38, 52, 56; Marshall, *Age of Faction*, p. 38.

35 Lionel K. J. Glassey, 'Politics, finance and government', in Glassey (ed.), *The Reigns of Charles II and James VII & II*, p. 52; N. H. Keeble, *The Restoration England in the 1660s* (Oxford, 2002), pp. 61–2.

36 Magalotti, *Relazione d'Inghilterra*, pp. 32–4.

37 Miller, *James II*, p. 43; Clarendon, *Continuation*, iii, p. 691.

38 Clarke, *Life*, i, 397, 412; Uglow, *A Gambling Man*, p. 138; C. H. Hartmann, *The King's Friend; a Life of Charles Berkeley, Viscount Fitzhardinge* (London, 1951), p. 114.

39 G. Aylmer, 'Patronage at the court of Charles II', p. 194..

40 Granville Penn, *Memorials of Sir William Penn* (2 vols, London, 1833), ii, 273, 321.

41 '...orders touching severall offices...', *HMC* 8th Report (London, 1881), pp. 278–279; E. Walker, *A Circumstantial Account of the Preparations for the Coronation of His Majesty King Charles the Second* (London, 1820), p. 14.

42 Callow, *The Making of King James II*, p. 149; Smith, *The Cavaliers in Exile*, pp. 180–1, 192;

Tyrconnel, p. 114; G. Steinman, 'Memorials preserved at Bruges of King Charles the Second's residence in that city' in *Archaeologia or Miscellaneous Tracts relating to Antiquity*, vol. xxxv (London, 1853), pp. 341–342.

43 Andrew Marvell, 'Second advice to a painter' in *Poems on Affairs of State; Augustan Satirical Verse, 1660–1714*, ed. G. deF. Lord (3 vols, New Haven, CT, 1963), i, p. 38; V. Vale, 'Clarendon, Coventry, and the sale of naval offices, 1660–8', *Cambridge Historical Journal*, vol. xii, no. 2 (1956), pp. 107–9, 122–3.

44 Henry Cobbett, *Parliamentary History of England* (6 vols, London, 1810), vi, p. 209; J. Macpherson (ed.), *Original Papers; Containing The Secret History of Great Britain* (2 vols, London, 1775), i, p. 56; C. Dennehy, 'The cabal ministry and Irish Catholic Politics, 1667–73', in Dennehy (ed.), *Restoration Ireland*, p. 146; J. N. Pearson, *The Whole Works of Robert Leighton DD Archbishop of Glasgow* (2 vols, London, 1827), i, p. 16.

45 Smith, *Cavaliers in Exile*, p. 197.

46 'Ormond', p. 43.

47 Keeble, *England in the 1660s*, pp. 82, 96, 100; H. W. Chapman, *Great Villiers*, p. 139; T. Stackhouse (ed.), *Bishop Burnet's History of His Own Times* (London 1906) p. 34; G. Smith, *The Cavaliers in Exile 1650–1660* (Basingstoke, 2003), p. 201; Uglow, *A Gambling Man*, pp. 207–8.

48 'Ormond', p. 37.

49 'Irish Narrative', p. 25

50 Smith, *The Cavaliers in Exile*, p. 174; Carte, *Ormond*, ii, pp. 273–4; Keeble, *England in the 1660s*, pp. 36, 96–9; Uglow, *A Gambling Man*, pp. 203–4, 208.

51 Uglow, *A Gambling Man*, p. 139; Murray (ed), *The Diary of Samuel Pepys* (London, 1891), p. 590.

52 Lord Braybrooke (ed.), *Diary and Correspondence of Samuel Pepys* (5 vols, London, 1849), v, p. 132; Anon., *A New and General Biographical Dictionary* (11 vols, London 1761), ii, pp. 126–7; Reynolds, 'The Stuart court and courtiers in exile' p. 169.

53 Magalotti, *Relazione d'Inghilterra*, pp. 48–9.

54 Marvell, 'Third advice to a painter' in *Poems on Affairs of State; Augustan Satirical Verse, 1660–1714*, ed. G. deF. Lord (3 vols, Yale, 1963), p. 78; Wilson, *Court Satires of the Restoration*, p. 11.

55 J. Miller, *The Stuarts* (Hambledon, 2004), pp. 183–4.

56 A. Barclay, 'The rise of Edward Colman' in *Historical Journal*, vol. 42, no 1 (Mar. 1999), pp. 123–6; *Memorials of Sir William Penn*, ii, pp. 273, 321.

57 Keeble, *England in the 1660s*, pp. 96–7.

58 Marvell, 'Third advice to a painter', p. 78; Wilson, *Court Satires of the Restoration*, p. 11.

59 *Memoirs of the Comte de Gramont*, pp. 120–3.

60 'Irish Narrative', p. 27; Callow, *The Making of King James II*, p. 91; Magalotti, *Relazione d'Inghilterra*, p. 78.

61 *Dick Talbot*, i, p. 129.

62 *Memoirs of the Comte de Gramont*, p. 126; W. Fraser, *History of the Carnegies* (2 vols, Edinburgh, 1857), i, p. 145; *Dick Talbot*, i, pp. 110–11.

63 Richard Talbot to Fitzhardinge 30 Sept. and 20 Nov. 1662, Sackville Correspondence *CKS-U269C303*, Centre for Kentish Studies, Maidstone, Kent

64 F. Dabhoiwala, 'The construction of honour, reputation and status in late seventeenth- and

early eighteenth-century England', *Transactions of the Royal Historical Society*, vol. vi (1996), pp. 203–6.

65 Anon., *Memoirs of the Court of France and City of Paris* (London, 1702), p. 25.

66 W. F. Butler, *Confiscation in Irish History* (Dublin, 1913), p. 185.

67 L. Stone, *The Family, Sex and Marriage in England 1500–1800* (Harmondsworth, 1977), pp. 206–7.

68 Clarendon, *Continuation*, iii, p. 690; Berwick, *Memoirs*, vol. i. p. 94.

69 Wilson, *Court Satires of the Restoration*, pp. 25, 26, 30; Marshall, *Age of Faction*, pp. 61–2.

70 *Memoirs of the Comte de Gramont*, pp. 84, 158: 'Irish Narrative', p. 7.

71 S. Shifrin, '"Subdued by a famous Roman dame": picturing foreigness, notoriety, and prerogative in the portraits of Hortense Mancini, Duchess Mazarin', J Marciari Alexander and C. MacLeod (eds), *Politics, Transgression and Representation at the Court of Charles II* (New Haven, CT, 2007), pp. 149, 151–3, 157, 166–7; J. Marciari Alexander and C. MacLeod (eds), *Painted Ladies; Women at the Court of Charles II* (London, 2001), pp. 21, 111–12.

72 Chapman, *Great Villiers*, pp. 125–6.

73 *HMC 7th Report* (London, 1879), p. 484.

74 *Dick Talbot*, i, p. 140; *Memoirs of the Comte de Gramont*, p. 193.

75 G. Aylmer, 'Patronage at the court of Charles II', p. 195.

76 *Dick Talbot*, i, pp. 144–5, 152–3; 'Irish Narrative', p. 8; Carte, *Ormonde*, ii, p. 545.

77 Creighton, 'The Remonstrance of Dec. 1661', p. 22

78 Hutton, *Charles II*, p. 237; See for instance, Richard Talbot to Williamson, 2 Nov. 1668 *Calendar of State Papers Domestic; Charles II, 1668–9* (1894), pp. 45–86 [www.british-history.ac.uk/report, accessed 5 Jan. 2012].

79 Sir Arnold Braems to Edward Montagu, Earl of Sandwich, Lisbon Roads, 16/26 Jan. 1662, Bodl. Carte MS 73, fo. 531.

80 E. Corp, 'Catherine of Braganza and cultural politics', C. Campbell Orr (ed.), *Queenship in Britain, 1660–1837: Royal Patronage, Court Culture and Dynastic Politics*, pp. 53, 55; Alexander and Macleod, *Politics, Transgression, and Representation* (Manchester, 2002), p. 9.

81 *Dick Talbot*, i, p. 131; Uglow, *A Gambling Man*, p. 164: M. Hay, *The Jesuits and the Popish Plot* (London, 1934), p. 86.

82 Hartmann, *The King's Friend*, pp. 76–7; 'Irish Narrative', pp. 27, 29; Hutton, *Charles II*, pp. 160, 187; *The Friar Disciplind*, p. 74.

83 Talbot to Fitzhardinge, 30 Sept. and 20 Nov. 1662, Sackville Correspondence CKS-U269 C303, Centre for Kentish Studies, Maidstone, Kent.

84 T. Clavin, 'Talbot, Peter (1618/20–1680), Roman Catholic Archbishop of Dublin' in *ODNB* [www.oxforddnb.com/view/printable/26937, accessed 16/06/2005].

85 Hartmann, *The King's Friend*, p. 84; Peter Talbot to Fitzhardinge, Dublin, 27 June 1663 CKS-U269/4/5/1/8 *Sackville Correspondence*, Centre for Kentish Studies; S. Wynne 'The Mistresses of Charles II and Restoration court politics' in E. Cruickshanks (ed.), *The Stuart Courts* (Stroud, 2000), pp. 176–8.

86 Hutton, *Charles II*, pp. 147–8; J. O'Hart, *The Irish and Anglo-Irish Landed Gentry*, ed. E. Mac Lysaght (Shannon, 1969), p. 427; G. Davies, *The Restoration of Charles II 1658–1660* (Oxford, 1955), p. 254.

87 K. S. Bottigheimer, 'The restoration land settlement in Ireland: a structural view' in *IHS*, vol. 18, no. 69 (Mar. 1972), pp. 2, 6, 8, 10; S. J. Connolly, *Religion, Law and Power: The Making of Protestant Ireland 1660* (Oxford, 1992), pp. 12, 16.

88 P. Lenihan, *Consolidating Conquest: Ireland 1603–1727* (London, 2008), pp. 98–102; H. Simms, 'Violence in County Armagh, 1641' in Brian Mac Cuarta (ed.), *Ulster 1641 Aspects of the Rising* (Belfast, 1997); Nicholls, 'The other massacre: English killings of Irish, 1641–2'; *Thomason Tracts E180* (15), p. 1.

89 Cited in J. C. Beckett, *The Cavalier Duke: A Life of James Butler, 1st Duke of Ormond* (Belfast, 1990), p. 80; Hutton, *Charles II*, pp. 147–8; 'Ormond', p. 41; Kevin J. McKenny, *The Laggan Army in Ireland 1640–1685* (Dublin, 2005), pp. 133–4.

90 J. J. Jusserand (ed.), *A French Ambassador at the Court of Charles the Second* (London, 1892), p. 227; Magalotti, *Relazione d'Inghilterra*, p. 28.

91 Bottigheimer, 'The Restoration land settlement in Ireland', p. 2.

92 Edward Earl of Clarendon, *The History of the Rebellion and Civil Wars in Ireland* (London, 1720), pp. 12, 134, 155, 248, 262, 264, 278–279, 284; T. Ellison Gibson (ed.), *A Cavalier's Note Book: Being Notes, Ancedotes & Observations of William Blundell* (London, 1880), pp. 230–1.

93 'Ormond', p. 34; Gilbert, *Jacobite Narr.*, p 7.

94 Carte, *Ormonde*, ii, p. 298; T. C. Barnard, 'Aristocratic values and the careers of the dukes of Ormond' in T. C. Barnard and J. Fenlon (eds), *The Dukes of Ormonde, 1610–1745* (Woodbridge, 2000), p. 164.

95 J. Cunningham, *Conquest and Land in Ireland: The Transplantation to Connaught, 1649–1680* (Woodbridge, 2011), pp. 120, 122.

96 S. H. Bindon (ed.), *The Historical Works of the Rev. Nicholas French* (Dublin, 1846), i, pp. 100–1.

97 Joyce Lee Malcolm, 'Charles II and the reconstruction of royal power' in *Historical Journal*, vol. 35, no. 2 (Jun. 1992), pp. 308–9; Gilbert, *Jacobite Narr.*, p 25; McGuire, 'Richard Talbot earl of Tyrconnell (1630–91) and the Catholic counter-revolution', p. 76; T. Harris, *Restoration: Charles II and His Kingdoms 1660–1685* (Harmondsworth, 2005), pp. 60, 70–1, 78–9, 97–8.

98 Hutton, *Charles II*, p. 177; Creighton, 'Remonstrance', pp. 24–5.

99 Peter Walsh quoted in Creighton, 'Remonstrance', p. 100.

100 Creighton, 'Remonstrance', p. 36; Rev. J. C. MacErlean (ed.), *Duanaire Dháibhidh Ó Bhruadair* (3 vols, London, 1913), ii, pp. 2–5.

101 *The Thirty-Second Annual Report of the Deputy Keeper of the Public Records: appendix one* (London, 1871), p. 123.

102 J. G. Simms, 'The Restoration, 1660–85' in *New History of Ireland*, pp. 429–30; *The Thirty-Second Annual Report*, p. 125.

103 R. Briggs, *Early Modern France 1560–1715* (Oxford, 1998), p. 156.

104 Creighton, 'Remonstrance', pp. 35–6, 40; E. Ó Ciardha, 'The unkinde deserter and the bright Duke' in T. C. Barnard and J. Fenlon (eds), *The Dukes of Ormonde, 1610–1745* (Woodbridge, 2000), p. 164.

105 'Ormond', p. 41.

106 Ormond to Michael Boyle, Bishop of Cork, 2 June 1663, in *The Third Report of the Deputy*

Keeper of the Public Records in Ireland (Dublin, 1871), p. 153; Carte *Ormonde*, ii, p. 261; 'Ormond', p. 36; J. Oldmixon, *Memoirs of Ireland from the Restoration to the Present Time* (London, 1726), p. 5.

THREE: ARLINGTON'S FRIEND

1   'Ormond', p. 36; J. Oldmixon, *Memoirs of Ireland from the Restoration to the Present Time* (London, 1726), p. 5.
2   Sir Alan Broderick to Ormond, 9 Sept. 1663 (Bodl., Carte MS 44, fol 624); M. F. Bond (ed.), *The Diaries and Papers of Sir Edward Dering 1644 to 1688* (London, 1976), p. 11; Henry Coventry to Ormond, Whitehall, 1663 (Bodl., Carte MS 47, fos. 411; Bagwell, *Stuarts*, iii, p. 42; Unk., to W. Donellan (Bodl., Carte MS 214 fos. 489–90); K. S. Bottigheimer, 'The Restoration land settlement in Ireland'; BL Add. MS 46947A, fo. 20.
3   Ollard, *Clarendon and his Friends*, pp. 279–82.
4   Sir Alan Broderick to Ormond, 9 Sept. 1663 (Bodl., Carte MS 44, fo. 624 v); Talbot to unk., 20 Dec. 1662 (Centre for Kentish Studies, Maidstone, Kent, Sackville Correspondence, CKS-U269/4/5/1/8).
5   M. J. Lennon, 'Winston Churchill, Dublin, 1662–1668' in *Dublin Historical Record*, vol. 43, no. 2 (Autumn, 1990), p. 101; *Thirty-second Annual Report*, p. 152.
6   Talbot to Bennet, 8 Nov. 1662 (SP 63/310 p. 262); Talbot to Bennet, 13 Dec. 1662 (SP 63/311 p. 14); Talbot to Bennet, 13 Dec. 1662 (SP 63/311, p. 14); Talbot to Bennet, 7 Nov. 1662, Talbot to Bennet, 8 Nov. 1662, Talbot to Bennet, 15 Apr. 1663 in R. P. Mahaffy (ed.), *Calendar of the State Papers Relating to Ireland 1663–1665* (London, 1907), pp. 62, 612–13.
7   Talbot to Bennet, 28 Apr. 1663 (SP 63/313 p. 119).
8   'Petition and Appeal of Sir Robert Newgent', *HMC 8th Report* (London, 1881), p. 144.
9   *Mercurius Hibernicus or Ireland's Intelligencer*, no. 2, 27 Jan. 1663 p. 10.
10 Sir Alan Broderick to Ormond, 9 Sept. 1663 (Bodl., Carte MS 44, fo. 625).
11 Ormond to Clarendon Dublin, 8 Jan 1663, *The Third Report of the Deputy Keeper of the Public Records in Ireland* (Dublin, 1871), p. 153; G. Hill (ed.), *The Montgomery Manuscripts* (Belfast, 1869), pp. 233–4; Talbot to unk., Dublin 16 Oct. (Sackville Correspondence, CKS-U269/4/5/1/8); *Mercurius Hibernicus*, no. 2, p. 14.
12 Talbot to Bennet, 4 Feb. 1663, Mount Alexander to unk., 7 Feb. 1663, *CSPI 1663–1665*, pp. 17–20.
13 H. F. Hore, 'Richard Talbot, Earl and Duke of Tyrconnell' in *Ulster Journal of Archaeology*, vol. 5 (Belfast, 1857), p. 279; L. J. Arnold, *The Restoration Land Settlement in County Dublin 1660–1688* (Dublin, 1993), p. 139.
14 Talbot to Fitzhardinge, Dublin 7 Jan. 1663 (Sackville Correspondence U269 C303 (58)).
15 'Irish Narrative', p. 22.
16 'Lord Lieutenant's Report' 25 Feb 1676, F. H. Blackburne Daniell (ed.), *Calendar of State Papers Domestic* (London, 1907), p. 578.
17 *Mercurius Publicus* 5 Mar. 1662, p. 148; Bottigheimer, 'The Restoration land settlement', p. 19; Lennon, 'Winston Churchill', p. 106.
18 J. Murray (ed), *The Diary of Samuel Pepys* (London, 1891), p. 176.

19 Bottigheimer, 'The Restoration land settlement', pp. 12–15; J. C. Beckett, *The Cavalier Duke* (Belfast, 1990), pp. 84–85.

20 T. Harris, *Restoration: Charles II and his Kingdoms 1660–1685* (London, 2005), p. 96; D. Hanrahan, *Colonel Blood: The Man Who Stole the Crown Jewels* (Stroud, 2003), pp. 37–40; 'Ormond', p. 36; R. Greaves, *Enemies under his Feet: Radicals and Non-Conformists in Britain, 1664–1677* (Stanford, Calif., 1990), pp. 103–5, 110, 111.

21 J. Ohlmeyer, *Civil War and Restoration in the Three Stuart Kingdoms: The Career of Randal MacDonnell Marquis of Antrim, 1609–1683* (Cambridge, 1993), pp. 263–70; Oldmixon, *Memoirs of Ireland*, p. 5.

22 Beckett, *The Cavalier Duke*, p. 88.

23 Carte, *Ormond*, ii, pp. 296–7.

24 *Dick Talbot*, i, p 153.

25 Fr Thomas Talbot to Ormond, 27 Aug. 1663 (Bodl., Carte MS 33, fos. 74–5); Bennet to Ormond, Bath 9 Sept. 1663 (Bodl., Carte MS. 46, fos. 82–3); Ormond to Bennet, Dublin 14 Oct. 1663 (Bodl., Carte MS 143, fos. 192–5); Richard Talbot to Ormond, Whitehall, 7 Nov. 1663 (Bodl., Carte MS 214, fos. 566–9); Earl of Carlingford to Ormond, 10 Nov. 1663 (Bodl., Carte MS 214, fos. 574–5).

26 Bagwell, *Ireland under the Stuarts*, iii, p. 42; Arlington to Ormond, Whitehall, 27 Oct. 1663, T. Brown (ed.), *Miscellanea Aulica: or a Collection of State-Treatises* (London, 1702), p. 312; V. Barbour, *Henry Bennet Earl of Arlington* (Oxford, 1914), pp. 55–7.

27 Carte, *Ormond*, ii, pp. 274–6; Toby Barnard, 'Butler, James, first duke of Ormond (1610–1688)', *ODNB* [www.oxforddnb.com/view/article/4191, accessed 19 Aug 2013].

28 Bennet to Ormond, Hampton Court 6 Aug. 1662 (Bodl., Carte MS 221, fos. 5–6).

29 Talbot to Bennet 8 Nov. 1662 (SP 63/310, p. 262); Talbot to Bennet, 13 Dec. 1662 (SP 63/311, p. 20); Patrick Brien to Bennet, 27 Dec. 1662, *CSPI 1660–1662*, pp. 666–7.

30 Talbot to Joseph Williamson, 18 June 1663, *CSPI 1663–1665*, pp. 133–4; Lord Aungier to Bennet, 3 Dec. 1662, *CSPI 1660–1662*, pp. 641–2.

31 Talbot to Bennet, 13 Mar. 1664, *CSPI 1663–1665*, p. 375.

32 Ormond to Bennett, 21 Oct. 1662 (Bodl., Carte MS 143, fos. 26–7).

33 Talbot to Bennet 13 Dec. 1662 (SP 63/311, p. 20); Talbot to Bennet, 20 Dec. 1662, *CSPI 1660–1662*, pp. 663–4.

34 Martha Nelson to Orrery, 26 Feb 1666, in R. P. Mahaffy (ed.), *CSPI 1666–1669* (London, 1908), p. 46.

35 Lord Aungier to Bennet, 3 Dec. 1662, *CSPI 1663–1665*, p. 642.

36 Hutton, *Charles II*, pp. 209–10, 237.

37 Carte, *Ormond*, ii, pp. 300–4; Hill, *Montgomery Manuscripts*, p. 232; J. G. Simms, 'The Restoration, 1660–85', in *New History of Ireland*, p. 425.

38 'Memorandum criticising the Restoration settlement in Ireland' *c.*1667, *CSPI 1666–1669*, p. 549.

39 *Thirty-second Annual Report*, pp. 87–8, 92.

40 Arnold, *The Restoration Land Settlement*, pp. 76–7.

41 Oldmixon, *Memoirs of Ireland* p. 5; Carte, *Ormond*, ii, p. 296.

42 Patrick Moore to Ormond, 2 July, 13 Aug. and 28 Oct. 1664, HMC, *Calendar of the*

Manuscripts of the Marquess of Ormonde (London, 1904), pp. 177, 179, 182; E. More O'Ferrall (ed.), 'The dispossessed landowners of Ireland, 1664' in *The Irish Genealogist*, pp. 277, 278, 288; Hamilton to Ormond, London 23 May 1663 (Bodl., Carte MS 214, fo. 493); *Mercurius Hibernicus*, no. 4, p. 30, no. 8 p. 63, no. 12, p. 91; *Dick Talbot*, i, p. 236.

43 Charles II to Lord Lieutenant, 12 May 1671, F. H. B. Daniell (ed.), *CSPD Charles II 1671* (London, 1895), p. 234.

44 Arnold, *Restoration Land Settlement*, p. 76; W. J. Smith (ed.), *Herbert Correspondence* (Cardiff and Dublin, 1963), p. 181; Gilbert, *Jacobite Narr.*, p. 156.

45 'Petition and Appeal of Sir Robert Newgent', pp. 143–4.

46 Ormond to Clarendon, 16 Nov. 1663 (Bodl., Carte MS 143, fos. 214–16).

47 He conveyed 8,192 of the acres he was decreed to kinsmen like Dunboyne and Ikerrin and to others he favoured like Wogan of Rathcoffey Co. Kildare whose father had been killed at the Battle of Rathmines; Carte, *Ormond*, ii, p. 437.

48 Ormond to Charles II, Dublin, 16 Aug. 1662 (Bodl., Carte MS 143, fos. 1–2); Butler, *Confiscation in Irish History*, pp. 178, 185.

49 Massareene to Ormond, 29 Oct. 1662 (Bodl., Carte MS 214, fo. 383).

50 Richard Talbot to Ossory, Whitehall 13 Oct. 1663 (Bodl., Carte MS 214, fo. 562) and P. F. Moran (ed.), *Spicilegium Ossoriense* (3 vols, Dublin 1874–8), ii, p. 190; Ormond to Colonel Richard Talbot, 16 Nov. 1663 (Bodl. Carte MS 49, fos. 242–3).

51 Richard Talbot to Ormond, 1 Dec. 1663 (Bod. Carte MS 214, fos. 590–2); Sir George Hamilton to Ormond, 12 Dec. 1663 (Bodl. Carte MS 33, fos. 249–50; Talbot to Ormond, Whitehall, 7 Nov. 1663 (Bodl., Carte MS 49, fos. 242–3).

52 Patrick Moore to Ormond 2 July 1664, *Manuscripts of the Marquess of Ormonde*, p. 177; T. C. Barnard, *Irish Protestant Ascents and Descents 1641–1770* (Dublin, 2004), p. 105; T. C. Barnard and J. Clark, *Lord Burlington: Architecture, Art and Life* (London, 1995), p. 192.

53 Orrery to Conway, Charleville, 11 Aug. 1666 in *CSPI*, p. 180.

54 K. M. Lynch, *Roger Boyle First Earl of Orrery* (Knoxville, TN, 1965), p. 161; Creighton 'Grace and favour', p142; (Bodl., Carte MS 220, fos. 424, 396, 426; 48, 290); T. Morrice (ed.), *A Collection of the State Letters of the Right Honourable Roger Boyle The First Earl of Orrery* (London, 1742), p. 53.

55 A. Creighton, 'The remonstrance of Dec. 1661 and Catholic politics in Restoration Ireland', *IHS* vol. xxxiv, no. 133 (May 2004), p. 20; *HMC Tenth Report Ormonde Manuscripts* (London, 1885), p. 3; Morrice, *State Letters*, p. 347.

56 Richard Talbot to Ormond, Whitehall, 3 Apr. 1664 (Bodl., Carte MS 215, fos 24–5).

57 Orrery to Bennet, 16 Jan. 1666, *CSPI 1666–1669*, p. 7.

58 *The Friar Disciplind*, pp. 75–6; *Continuation of the Life of Edward Earl of Clarendon* (3 vols, Dublin, 1729), iii, p. 688; Sir George Hamilton to Ormond, 12 Dec. 1663 (Bodl., Carte MS 33, fos. 249–50).

59 Patrick Moore to Ormond, 13 Aug. 1664 and 28 Oct. 1664, *Manuscripts of the Marquess of Ormonde*, pp. 179, 182.

60 P. Ua Duinnín, *Dánta Sheafraidh Uí Dhonnchadha* (Dublin, 1912), p. 27.

61 Charles, Viscount Muskerry to Ormond, undated, and Ormond to Donogh, Lord

Clancarty, undated (Bodl., Carte MS 128, fos 388–9); A. Creighton, 'The cabal ministry and Irish Catholic Politics, 1667–73' in Dennehy (ed.), *Restoration Ireland*, p. 142.

62 Bindon, *Historical Works of Nicholas French*, pp. 15, 152–5, 168, 171, 194; T. Clavin, 'Talbot, Peter (1618/1620–1680), Roman Catholic Archbishop of Dublin' in *ODNB* [www.oxforddnb. com/view/printable/26937 accessed 16 Jun. 2005].

63 'Irish Narrative', p. 19: 'Ormond', pp. 36–7.

64 *Life of Edward Earl of Clarendon*, iii, p. 687; Ormond to Ossory, Whitehall, 24 Dec. 1664 (Bodl., Carte MS 48, fo. 179).

65 *Dick Talbot*, i, pp. 176–180; R. Holmes, *Marlborough: England's Fragile Genius* (London, 2008), p. 178.

66 'Irish Narrative', p. 20.

67 *Life of Edward Earl of Clarendon*, p. 693; Bennet to Ormond, 21 Feb. 1665 (Bodl., Carte MS 221 fos. 94–5, Carte MS 48, fo. 189); Sir J. Perceval to R. Southwell, Dublin. Jan. 28, 1665, HMC *Egmont MS* (London, 1909), ii, p. 12.

68 G. Rommelse, *The Second Anglo-Dutch War* (Hilversum, 2006), pp. 79–82, 113, 126; Keeble, *England in the 1660s*, p. 102.

69 Edmund Waller, 'Instructions to a painter' (1665) in G. de F. Lord (ed.), *Poems on Affairs of State: Augustan Satirical Verse, 1660–1714* (3 vols, New Haven, CT, 1963), i, p. 27.

70 R. Latham and W. Matthews (eds), *The Diary of Samuel Pepys: Companion* (Cambridge, 1983), p. 407; Henry Savile to Lady Dorothy Savile, London, 4 June 1665, in W. Durrant Cooper (ed.), *Savile Correspondence* (London, 1858), p. 7.

71 Andrew Marvell, 'Second advice to a painter', p. 44; Granville Penn, *Memorials of Sir William Penn* (2 vols, London, 1833), ii, pp. 316, 338, 339; Callow, *The Making of King James II*, p. 220.

72 Penn *Memorials*, ii, p. 321; P. Seaward, *The Cavalier Parliament and the Reconstruction of the Old Régime, 1661–1667* (Cambridge, 2002), p. 234.

73 *Dick Talbot*, pp. 196, 221, 223.

74 Jusserand, *A French Ambassador at the Court of Charles the Second*, pp. 153, 155, 156.

75 *Dick Talbot*, pp. 144–55; Hamilton, *Memoirs of the Comte de Gramont*, pp. 171–2, 192–4, 200.

76 Carte *Ormonde*, ii, p. 316.

77 A. Grey, *Debates of the House of Commons from the year 1667 to the year 1694* (10 vols, London, 1763), ii, p. 124; McGuire, 'Richard Talbot earl of Tyrconnell (1630–91) and the Catholic counter-revolution', p. 75.

78 'An Abridgement of the Act for Settling of Estates, &c. in Ireland' in Anon., *An Exact Abridgement of all the Publick Printed Irish Statutes* (Dublin, 1724), p. 25; Dunlop, *Ireland under the Commonwealth*, i, pp. 196–197.

79 He may have gotten the Castlesallagh estate back since the Forfeiture Trustees in 1702–03 return him as having 1, 530 acres in Co. Wicklow. However, other contemporaneous official reports state he 'had not any considerable estate' and the Jacobite outlawry lists give his home address as Carton: J. G. Simms, *The Williamite Confiscation in Ireland 1691–1703* (London, 1956), p. 181; *HMC Appendix to 8th Report* (London, 1881), p. 499.

80 Charles Calvert to Cecilius [Cecil] Lord Baltimore, 26 Apr. 1672, and Charles Calvert to

Cecilius [Cecil] Lord Baltimore, 2 June 1673 in J. W. M. Lee (ed.), *The Calvert Papers* (Baltimore, 1889), pp. 254, 256, 268, 274, 276, 277, 282–3.

81 Simms, 'Irish Jacobites', pp. 61–2.

82 *Dick Talbot*, i, pp. 323, 332.

83 Fitzgerald, 'Carton', pp. 7, 11–13.

84 T. Barnard, *Making the Grand Figure: Lives and Possessions in Ireland 1641–1770* (New Haven, CT, 2004), pp. 68–70.

85 P. Elmer, *The Miraculous Conformist: Valentine Greatrakes, the Body Politic, and the Politics of Healing in Restoration Britain* (Oxford, 2013), p. 205.

86 Arthur Colclough to Ormond, 16 July 1665 (Bodl., Carte MS 34, fo. 327); Creighton, 'The cabal ministry and Irish Catholic politics', p. 143; Ollard, *Clarendon and his Friends*, pp. 276, 291; Hutton, *Charles II*, pp. 250–1; C. Roberts, 'The impeachment of the earl of Clarendon', *Cambridge Historical Journal*, xiii (1957), pp. 4, 10–11; Keeble, *England in the 1660s*, p. 101.

87 John Wilson, *A Treatise on Religion and Government* (1670), pp. 471, 549; Clavin, 'Peter Talbot', *ODNB*.

88 Smith, *The Double Crown*, p. 225; G. Smith, *The Cavaliers in Exile 1650–1660* (Basingstoke, 2003), p. 195; Ollard, *Clarendon and his Friends*, p. 293; Hutton, *Charles II*, p. 259; Cuddy, 'Reinventing a monarchy', pp. 75–5.

89 J. Miller, *The Stuarts* (Hambledon, 2004), pp. 161–3: Hutton, *Charles II*, pp. 263–4.

90 Beckett, *The Cavalier Duke*, p. 96.

91 'Ormond', p. 45; Knowles, *Relazione d'Inghilterra, p.* 52.

92 J. McGuire, 'Why was Ormond dismissed in 1669?' in *IHS*, vol. xviii, no. 71 (1973), pp. 295–8; Lynch, *Roger Boyle*, p. 134.

93 Ranelagh to Stepney, 13 Apr. 1672 (Bodl., Carte MS 69, fo. 156).

94 'Ormond', p. 39.

95 Creighton, 'The cabal ministry and Irish Catholic politics', p. 142; Ormond to Sir William Coventry, 30 June 1666 (Bodl., Carte MS 51, fo. 462).

96 'Ormond', pp. 39, 43–4.

97 Ranelagh to Stepney, 13 Apr. 1672 (Bodl., Carte MS 69, fo. 156).

98 [undated] 1674, *CSPD Charles II, 1673–1675*, p. 162; Wilson, *Court Satires of the Restoration*, pp. 279–80; Charles II to the Vice-Treasurer of Ireland, 3 May 1669, *CSPD Charles II, 1668–1669*, p. 308; Hutton, *Charles II*, pp. 281, 316–317; D. Hughes, *Memoirs of Gramont*, p. 192.

99 F. Harris, *Transformations of Love: The Friendship of John Evelyn and Margaret Godolphin* (Oxford, 2003), pp. 106–7, 127; Rev. C. V. Collier, *An Account of the Boynton Family and the Family Seat of Burton Agnes* (Middlesbrough, 1914), pp. 22–3; A. Somerset, *Ladies in Waiting* (Edison, NJ, 1984), pp. 134, 154.

100 Keeble, *England in the 1660s*, p. 174.

101 Wilson, *Court Satires of the Restoration*, p. 4; Hamilton, *Memoirs of the Comte de Gramont*, pp. 165, 167; N. Smith (ed.), *The Poems of Andrew Marvell* (Harlow, 2007), p. 392.

102 Wauchope, 'Richard Talbot', *ODNB*.

103 H. Love, *The Works of John Wilmot, Earl of Rochester* (Oxford, 1998), p. 432.

104 Creighton, 'The Cabal ministry and Irish Catholic politics', p. 142; T. Clavin, 'Talbot, Peter (1618/20–1680), Roman Catholic Archbishop of Dublin' in *ODNB* [www. oxforddnb. com/view/printable/26937, accessed 16/06/2005].

105 P. F. Moran, *Memoir of the Ven Oliver Plunkett* (Dublin, 1895), p. 31.

106 McGuire, 'Richard Talbot earl of Tyrconnell (1630–91) and the Catholic Counter-Revolution', pp. 78–9.

107 Anon., *The Secret History of Europe* (London, 1712), part iii, p. 165.

108 Creighton, 'The cabal ministry and Irish Catholic politics', p. 151.

109 Ibid., pp. 145, 147, 151; Carte *Ormonde,* ii, pp. 415–19.

110 Moran, *Oliver Plunkett*, pp. 137–8, 244–5, 265, 269; A. Forrestal, *Catholic Synods in Ireland, 1600–1690* (Dublin, 1998), pp. 100–1; Creighton, 'The cabal ministry and Irish Catholic politics', pp. 147–8.

111 Moran, *Oliver Plunkett*, pp. 254–6, 261–2; Oliver Plunkett to Padre Oliva, 22 Oct. 1672, *Manuscripts of the Marquess of Ormonde*, p. 361.

112 Michael Boyle, Archbishop of Dublin and Lord Chancellor, to Arlington, 2 Nov. 1672 in F. H. Blackburne Daniell (ed.), *CSPD Charles II, 1672–1673* (London, 1901), p. 117; Notes by Joseph Williamson, in Dec. 1671 (SP 29/294, fo. 240).

113 Creighton, 'The Cabal Ministry and Irish Catholic Politics', p. 149.

114 Lynch, *Roger Boyle*, p. 163; Creighton, 'The Cabal Ministry and Irish Catholic Politics', p. 142.

115 Harris, 'Restoration Ireland – themes and problems', pp. 10–11

116 Creighton, 'The Cabal Ministry and Irish Catholic Politics', p. 151.

117 Ormonde to Ossory Dublin 23 Apr. 1679, *Manuscripts of the Marquess of Ormonde*, p. 287; 'Order in Council, on the petition of Colonel Richard Talbot, on behalf of his Majesty's most distressed subjects of Ireland, who were outed of their estates by the late usurped governments…', 18 Jan. 1671, F. H. Blackburne Daniell (ed.), *CSPD Charles II 1671* (London, 1895), p. 30; Hutton *Charles II*, p. 275.

118 Petition of the Earl of Westmeath and of many others of his Majesty's Roman Catholic subjects of Ireland to the King Dublin, 28 Nov. 1670 (Bodl., Carte MS 118, fo. 45v).

119 Hutton, *Charles II*, p. 274; Creighton, 'The Cabal Ministry and Irish Catholic Politics', pp. 153–4.

120 Creighton, 'The Cabal Ministry and Irish Catholic Politics', p. 155; 'Ormond', pp. 48–9.

121 Report of Sir Heneage Finch, 1 Feb 1671 in T. Carte, *An History of the Life of James Duke of Ormonde* (2 vols, London 1736), ii, pp. 72, 75, 79.

122 Creighton, 'The Cabal Ministry and Irish Catholic Politics', pp. 153, 156.

123 Robert Leigh to Williamson 8 July 1671, *CSPD Charles II 1671*, p. 375: Sir N. Armorer to Williamson, 2 Nov. 1672, *CSPD Charles II 1672–1673*, p. 118; Creighton, 'The Cabal Ministry and Irish Catholic Politics', pp. 158–9.

124 *Dick Talbot*, i, p. 241.

125 Nicholas Armorer to Williamson, 27 Aug. 1668 (SP 29/245, fo. 103); H. Hyde, *The State Letters of Henry Earl of Clarendon* (2 vols, Oxford, 1763), pp. 7, 21, 34, 48, 63, 67; E. McLysaght, *Irish Life in the Seventeenth Century* (4th edn, Dublin, 1979), pp. 263–4; H. C. Foxcroft (ed.), *The Life and Letters of Sir George Savile* (2 vols, London, 1898), i, p. 150.

126 Foxcroft, *Life and Letters of Sir George Savile*, i, p. 99.

127 A. Clarke, *Prelude to Restoration: The End of the Commonwealth 1659–1660* (Cambridge, 1999), p. 30; Sir Henry Ingoldesby to Lord O'Brien [Mar. .] 1673, F. H. Blackburne Daniell (ed.), *CSPD Charles II 1673* (London, 1902), p. 108; Clavin, 'Peter Talbot'.

128 Hutton, *Charles II*, pp. 282, 285; Miller, *James II*, p. 63.

129 'Irish Narrative', p. 33.

130 E. Carp, 'France, Rome and the exiled Stuarts, 1689–1713', in ibid. (ed.), *A Court in Exile The Stuarts in France 1689–1718* (Cambridge, 2004), p. 18.

131 J. Childs, *Warfare in the Seventeenth Century* (London, 2001), pp. 165–7; J. A. Lynn, *The Wars of Louis XIV 1667–1714* (London, 1999), pp. 113–17; C. J. Ekberg, 'From Dutch to European war: Louis XIV and Louvois are tested' in *French Historical Studies*, vol. 8 (1973), pp. 394–8.

132 G. Carleton, *Military Memoirs* (London, 1727), pp. 2–3.

133 Rev. E. Berwick (ed.), *The Rawdon Papers* (London, 1819), p. 253.

134 Henry Savile to Arlington, 6 June 1672 (SP 29/310, fo. 259).

135 Sir C. Lyttelton to Williamson, 27 May 1672, *CSPD Charles II 1672*, p. 74 and (SP 29/309, fo. 202).

136 Carleton, *Military Memoirs*, p. 1.

137 C. Carlton, *This Seat of Mars: War and the British Isles 1485–1746* (New Haven, CT, 2001), p. 212.

138 Berwick, *Rawdon Papers*, p. 253; Sir C. Lyttleton to Williamson, 29 May 1672 (SP 29/310, fo. 40); Lord O'Brien to Williamson, 30 May 1672 (SP 29/310, fo. 64); H. A. Hansen, 'The opening phase of the third Dutch War described by the Danish envoy in London, Mar.– June 1672' in *Journal of Modern History*, vol. 21, no. 2 (Jun. 1949), p. 105.

139 Col. T. Middleton to Williamson 29 May 1672 (SP 29/310 f. 47a); Silas Taylor to Williamson, 30 May 1672 (SP 29/310 fo. 62).

140 G. Brandt (ed.), *La Vie de Michel de Ruiter* (Amsterdam, 1698), p. 492; Callow, *The Making of King James II*, p. 226; Robert Custis to the Commissioners for the Sick and Wounded, 8 June 1672 (SP 29/311, f. 26 a); Unk. to unk., London, 1 June 1672 in E. Berwick (ed.), *The Rawdon Papers: consisting of letters on various subjects, literary, political, and ecclesiastical, to and from Dr John Bramhall, primate of Ireland* (London, 1819), p. 253.

141 Hansen, 'The Third Dutch War', pp. 107–8; Carleton, *Military Memoirs*, p. 4.

FOUR: ORMOND'S ENEMY

1 J. P. Montano, *Courting the Moderates: Ideology, Propaganda, and the Emergence of Party, 1660–1678* (Newark/London, 2002), pp. 254–5.

2 M. A. Mullett, *Catholics in Britain and Ireland 1558–1829* (London, 1998), pp. 30, 98.

3 Basil Duke Henning, *The House of Commons, 1660–1690* (3 vols, London, 1983), i, pp. 241, 298, 632, 729.

4 Sir N. Armorer to Williamson, 30 Oct. 1673 (SP 29/337, fo. 224).

5 'General Index: D, E', *CSPD Charles II*, 1671 (1895), pp. 627–35 [www. british-history. ac. uk/report. aspx?compid=55073& strquery=Talbot, accessed 5 Jan. 2012].

6   Garroway and Sir Thomas Higgons: 'Debates in 1673: Mar. (17th–22nd)', *Grey's Debates of the House of Commons: volume 2* (1769), pp. 116–54 [www.british-history.ac. uk/report. asp ?compid=40962&strquery=richard%20talbot, accessed 20 June 2006, pp. 2/28 to 4/28, 7/28 to 9/28].

7   Francis Godolphin to Essex, 18 Mar. 1673, Osmund Airy (ed.), *Essex Papers 1672–1679* (London, 1890), i, p. 61.

8   'Irish Narrative', p. 33.

9   C. H. Hartmann, *Clifford of the Cabal: A Life of Thomas, First Lord Clifford of Chudleigh, Lord High Treasurer of England 1630–1673* (London, 1937), pp. 259–61, 264.

10 Smith, *The Double Crown*, pp. 229–30.

11 Henry Ball to Joseph Williamson, 26 June 1673, W. D. Christie (ed.), *Letters Addressed from London to Sir Joseph Williamson* (2 vols, London, 1874), i, p. 68.

12 Aungier to Essex, 15 Mar. 1673, Airy (ed.), *Essex Papers*, p. 60.

13 D. Wilson, *All the King's Women: Love, Sex and Politics in the Life of Charles II* (London, 2004), pp. 212–13.

14 Harris, *Transformations of Love*, p. 127; Hutton, *Charles II*, p. 270; Uglow, *A Gambling Man*, pp. 462–3: Miller, *James II*, p. 70.

15 'Irish Narrative', pp. 28–30; W. P. Burke, *The Irish Priests in the Penal Times (1660–1760)* (Waterford, 1914), p. 105.

16 Miller, *James II*, pp. 71–3.

17 S. C. A Pincus, 'Republicanism, absolutism and universal monarchy' in G. M. MacLean (ed.), *Culture and Society in the Stuart Restoration: Literature, Drama and History* (Cambridge, 1995), p. 260.

18 E. Gregg, 'New light on the authorship of the life of James II' in *EHR*, vol. 108, no. 429 (1993), pp. 960–1.

19 A. Strickland, *Lives of the Queens of England* (London, 1846), ix, pp. 14–25; 'Irish Narrative', pp. 31–2; Louis XIV to Croissy, Versailles 18 July 1673, Louis XIV to Croissy, Versailles 25 July 1673 in Marquise Campana di Cavelli, *Les Derniers Stuarts à Saint-Germain en Laye* (2 vols, Paris, 1871), i, pp. 3–5.

20 'Irish Narrative', pp. 31–2.

21 M. Haile, *Queen Mary of Modena: Her Life and Letters* (London, 1905), pp. 29–30: Abbé Rizzini to Count Graziani, 11 Oct. 1673 in Campana di Cavelli, *Les Derniers Stuarts*, i, pp. 92–3.

22 Henry Ball to Williamson 6 June 1673, Henry Ball to Williamson 26 June 1673, John Richards to Joseph Williamson, 26 Sept. 1673, Thomas Ross to Joseph Williamson, 3 Oct. 1673 in W. D. Christie (ed.), *Letters Addressed from London to Sir Joseph Williamson* (2 vols, London, 1874), i, pp. 24, 26, 30, 68; Peter Talbot to Padre Oliva General of the Jesuits, 29 Dec. 1673 in *HMC 10th Report*, p. 363: M. B. Curran, 'The correspondence of an English diplomatic agent in Paris, 1669–1677' in *Transactions of the Royal Historical Society*, vol. 15 (1901), p. 149.

23 W. A. Speck, *James II: Profiles in Power* (London, 2002), p. 25.

24 Smith, *The Double Crown*, pp. 250–1; H. C. Foxcroft (ed.), *The Life and Letters of Sir George Savile* (2 vols, London, 1898), i, pp. 62–3; Miller, *James II*, p. 76.

25   G. Tapsell, *The Personal Rule of Charles II, 1681–85* (Woodbridge, 2007), pp. 23, 33.

26   Countess of Burlington to Duchess of Ormond, 16 Nov. 1674, *HMC Manuscripts of the Marquess of Ormonde*, p. 356; Sir W. Throckmorton to E. Coleman, Paris 20 Dec. 1674, *HMC, Thirteenth Report Fitzherbert MS* (London, 1893), pp. 57–8.

27   K. Feiling (ed.), 'Two unprinted letters of Henrietta Stuart, Duchess of Orleans', *EHR*, vol 43, no. 171 (Jul. 1928), p. 397; Essex to Sir Henry Capel, Dublin Castle 10 Feb. 1675, ? *Letters written by his Excellency Arthur Capel Earl of Essex* (London, 1770), p. 72.

28   C. E. Pike (ed.), *Selections from the Correspondence of Arthur Capel Earl of Essex 1675–1677* (London, 1913), p. 3.

29   Pike, *Essex Correspondence*, pp. 121, 127, 139; Lord Lieutenant Essex to Arlington, Dublin Castle, 8 Nov. 1673, *CSPD: Charles II, 1673–5* (1904), pp. 1–40 [www.british-history.ac.uk, accessed 5 Jan. 2012].

30   Talbot to Essex, London, 26 May 1676 (BL Stowe MS 200–17, fo. 256–8).

31   D. Dickson, *New Foundations: Ireland 1660–1800* (Dublin, 1987), p. 15

32   Hutton, *Charles II*, pp. 339–340; 'Irish Narrative', p. 7: Colonel Fitzpatrick to unk., 22 May 1677, *6th Report on Historical Manuscripts*, part 1 (London, 1877), p. 776; Anon., *A Collection of State Tracts published during the reign of William III* (3 vols, London, 1707), pp. 624–5.

33   Hay, *The Jesuits and the Popish Plot*, pp. 26–8.

34   Mullett, *Catholics in Britain and Ireland*, pp. 75–6, 140–1; G. H Tavard, *The Seventeenth-Century Tradition: A Study in Recusant Thought* (Leiden, 1978), p. 237, 239; T. Cartwright and J. Hunter (eds), *The diary of Dr. Thomas Cartwright, bishop of Chester* (London, 1843), p. 23.

35   Viscount Granard to Viscount Conway, [Aug.?] 1677, *CSPD: Charles II, 1677–1678*, p. 335; A. Grey, *Debates of the House of Commons from the year 1667 to the year 1694* (10 vols, London, 1763), viii, p. 253; *Dick Talbot*, i, pp. 265, 285–6; Burke, *Irish Priests*, pp. 105–6.

36   Hay, *Popish Plot*, pp. 152, 156, 162–3.

37   Harris, *Restoration*, pp. 175–7; B. Weiser, *Charles II and the Politics of Access* (Woodbridge, 2003), pp. 80–1.

38   M. Kishlansky, *A Monarchy Transformed Britain 1603–1714* (London, 1996), p. 253; Harris, *Restoration*, p. 137; P. Hinds, 'The Horrid Popish Plot': Roger L'Estrange and the Circulation of Political Discourse in late Seventeenth-Century London* (Oxford, 2010), pp. 32–3.

39   J. Kenyon, *The Popish Plot* (Harmondsworth, 1972), p. 74.

40   N. Tindall, *Rapin de Thoyras' History of England*, ii, p. 695.

41   Harris, *Restoration*, pp. 146–7.

42   G. Tapsell, *The Personal Rule of Charles II, 1681–85* (Woodbridge, 2007), pp. 15–16; L. Glassey, *The Reigns of Charles II and James VII & II* (Basingstoke, 1997), p. 61; J. Gibney, *Ireland and the Popish Plot* (Basingstoke, 2009), p. 7.

43   J. Miller, *Popery and Politics in England 1660–1688* (Cambridge, 1973), p. 170.

44   Tapsell, *The Personal Rule of Charles II*, pp. 24–5.

45   James Macpherson, *Original Papers Containing the Secret History of Great Britain…* (2 vols, Dublin, 1775), i, p. 140.

46   Notes by Joseph Williamson, 28 Sept. 1678 (SP 29/406, fo. 125).

47   Harris, *Restoration*, p. 151.

48 Anon., *An Account of the Publick Affairs in Ireland since the discover of the Late Plot* (London 1679), pp. 3, 8, 19.

49 HMC Marquess of Ormond New Series, vol. 4 (London, 1906), pp. 221, 222, 232, 234.

50 Anon., *The Secret History of Europe* (London, 1712), pp. 164–5: 'Edmond Everard's Information', 21 Dec. 1678, in *HMC: FitzHerbert Manuscripts*, pp. 141–5.

51 E. Everard, *The Depositions and Examinations of Mr. Edmund Everard* (London, 1679), pp. 3–6.

52 R. Walsh, *A True Narrative and Manifest, set forth by Sir Robert Walsh* (London, 1679) pp. 3, 4, 10, 24, 26, 28; A. Marshall, 'Sir Robert Walsh and the fragmented world of the double agent' in D. Szechi (ed.), *The Dangerous Trade. Spies, Spymasters and the Making of Europe* (Dundee, 2010), pp. 66–92.

53 J. O'Hart, *The Irish and Anglo Irish Landed Gentry when Cromwell came to Ireland*, ed. E. McLysaght (2nd edn, New York, 1969), pp. 502–3; J. A. Lynn, *Giant of the Grand Siècle: The French Army, 1610–1715* (Cambridge, 1, 1997), p. 300; Jean-Philippe Cénat, *Le Roi stratège, Louis XIV et la direction de la guerre 1661–1715* (Rennes, 2010), pp. 64, 100.

54 Alan Marshall, 'Everard, Edmund (*fl.* 1673–1691)', *ODNB* [www.oxforddnb. com/view/article/67394, accessed 14 Nov 2013].

55 Peter Walsh to Ormond, London 25 Mar. 1679 (Bodl., Carte MS 216, fos. 5–6).

56 Harris, *Restoration*, pp. 172–3; F. Hargrave (ed.), *A Complete Collection of State Trials* (2 vols, Dublin, 1795), ii, p. 724; A. Grey (ed.), *Debates of the House of Commons* (10 vols, London, 1763), viii, p. 253.

57 Ormond to Ossory, Dublin, 1 Mar. 1679, *HMC Calendar of the Manuscripts of the Marquess of Ormonde* (London, 1911), p. 284; Gibney, *Popish Plot*, pp. 33, 125.

58 *CSPD: Charles II, 1679–80* (London, 1915), pp. 63–92 [www.british-history.ac. uk/report, accessed 5 Jan. 2012]; 'Articles against the Duke of Ormond ...', 4 Dec. 1680, *CSPD: Charles II, 1680–1681*, p. 98.

59 'Recognizances of Lord Dungan and others to the Duke of Ormond, Lord Lieutenant, for the safe custody of Colonel Richard Talbot, now a prisoner in Dublin Castle, but permitted by his Grace to visit his sick wife, upon obligation to return upon command', Dublin 1679 (Bodl., Carte MS 38, fo. 687).

60 Tapsell, *The Personal Rule of Charles II*, p. 188.

61 *New History of Ireland*, p. 432; *An Account of the Publick Affairs in Ireland*, pp. 3, 9; Gibney, *Popish Plot*, p. 154.

62 Gibney, *Popish Plot*, pp. 24–5, 40–2, 152.

63 *Dick Talbot*, i, p. 272; Ormond to Henry Coventry, Dublin 8 Nov. 1679 (Bodl., Carte MS 146, fos. 227–9). Richard Talbot to Ormond, Dublin Castle, 20 Mar. 1679 (Bodl., Carte MS 38, fo. 691; Sir Robert Southwell to Ormond, 21 June 1679, *HMC Manuscripts of Marquess of Ormond*, vi (London, 1911), pp. 533–4; Gibney, *Popish Plot*, p. 68; 'Warrant for Sir Thomas Newcomen Baronet of Sutton, Co. Dublin to be a privy councillor of Ireland', 1676 (BL Stowe MS 210, fo. 127).

64 *Dick Talbot*, i, pp. 272–3.

65 Sept. 1 1679?, Windsor, 'Pass for Mistress Mary Boynton with Catherine and Charlotte Talbot, her nieces, and Katherine Luttrell, her kinswoman, 4 women servants and 7 men

servants with a coach and 7 horses, wearing apparel and equipage', *Entry Book* 51, p. 287, *CSPD: Charles II, 1679–80* (London, 1915), pp. 232–55 [www.british-history.ac.uk/report, accessed 5 Jan. 2012]; Harris, *Charles II*, p. 189

66 Ormond to Henry Coventry, 8 Nov. 1678 (Bodl. Carte MS 146, fo. 228); Harris, *Charles II*, p. 190.

67 Uglow, *A Gambling Man*, p. 516; 'Duc de Tirconnell', pp. 4–5.

68 David Fitzgerald, *A Narrative of the Irish Popish Plot, for the betraying that Kingdom into the hands of the French, Massacring all English Protestants there, and utter subversion of the Government and Protestant Religion....* (London 1680), pp. 4–7 [eebo. chadwyck. com/ search, accessed 16 Nov. 2010]; J. Gibney, 'An Irish informer in Restoration England: David Fitzgerald and the 'Irish Plot' in the exclusion crisis, 1679–81' in *Éire-Ireland*, vol. 42, nos. 3 & 4 (Fall/Winter, 2007), p. 255; Thomas Samson, *A Narrative of the Late Popish Plot in Ireland* (London, 1680), pp. 11–12; Carte, *Ormonde*, ii, p. 496.

69 J. Gibney, 'Edward Murphy, 'Oliver Plunkett and the Popish plot', *History Ireland*, vol. 12, no. 4 (Winter, 2004), p. 22; Gibney, 'An Irish informer…', p. 272.

70 Gibney, 'Edmund Murphy, Oliver Plunkett, and the Popish plot', p. 23; Gibney, *Popish Plot*, p. 153; S. J. Connolly, *Religion, Law, and Power: The Making of Protestant Ireland 1660–1760* (Oxford, 1992), p. 23.

71 Kenyon, *The Popish Plot*, pp. 225, 233–4.

72 Connolly, *Religion, Law and Power*, p. 23.

73 Gibney, *Popish Plot*, pp. 149, 151.

74 Moran, *Memoir of the Ven Oliver Plunkett*, p. 268; Moran, *Priests in the Penal Times*, pp. 107–9.

75 S. Schama, *A History of Britain: The British Wars 1603–1776* (London, 2001), p. 207; Smith, *The Double Crown* (Oxford, 1998), pp. 253–9, 262–3; M. Knights, *Politics and Opinion in Crisis, 1678–81* (Cambridge, 1994), p. 42; M. Mullett, *James II and English politics 1678–1688* (London, 1994), pp. 26, 31.

76 Kenyon, *The Popish Plot*, p. 281.

77 Hutton, *Charles II*, p. 421; G. Tapsell, *Personal Rule of Charles II*, pp. 27–9.

78 'Duc de Tirconnell', p. 5.

79 C. T. Atkinson, 'Charles II's regiments in France, 1672–1678', *Journal of Army Historical Research*, no. 23 (1945), pp. 54–5, 133, 162, 166.

80 Piers Wauchope, 'Talbot, Frances, duchess of Tyrconnell (1648–1731)', *ODNB* [www. oxforddnb. com/view/article/14756, accessed 19 Aug 2013].

81 Marciari Alexander and MacLeod, *Painted Ladies*, p. 182.

82 John Churchill to Sarah Churchill, 15 Jan. 1680 (BL Add MS 61327, fo. 97v).

83 R. Holmes, *Marlborough: England's Fragile Genius* (London, 2008), p. 92; Bryan Bevan, *Marlborough the Man: A Biography of John Churchill first Duke of Marlborough* (London, 1975).

84 Marciari Alexander and MacLeod, *Painted Ladies*, p. 243; *Dick Talbot*, pp. 280–1; O'Kelly, *Macariae Excidium*, pp. 69, 129–30.

85 'Irish Narrative', pp. 11–12.

86 *HMC 7th Report* (London, 1879), pp. 334–8.

87 Richard Talbot to Ormond, Paris 17 Feb 1683, *Calendar of the Manuscripts of the Marquess of Ormonde*, vi, p. 533.

88 Charles Paulet 6th Marquess of Winchester to Sir Leoline Jenkins Secretary of State, Bolton 20 Oct. 1683 (SP 29/433 fo. 295); J. Scodel, *The English Poetic Epitaph: Commemoration and Conflict from Jonson to Wordsworth* (Ithaca, NY, 1991), pp. 244–5.

89 *CSPD: Charles II, 1683: July–Sept.* (1934), pp. 94–129 [www.british-history.ac. uk/report, accessed 5 Jan. 2012].

90 R. Refaussé and C. Lennon (eds), *The Registers of Christ Church Cathedral Dublin* (Dublin, 1998), p. 95; *Dick Talbot*, i, pp. 286–7.

91 Hutton, *Charles II*, pp. 436, 437; Simms, *Jacobite Ireland*, pp. 11, 19; John Gibney, 'Forbes, Sir Arthur 1st earl of Granard', in *DIB* [dib.cambridge.org/viewReadPage.do?articleId=a3320].

92 Beckett, *The Cavalier Duke*, p. 133.

93 Earl of Sutherland to the Lords Justices, 12 May 1685, *CSPD: James II*, p. 149; James to Archbishop of Armagh and the Earl of Granard 7 May 1685, *CSPD: James II*, p. 147.

94 J. G. Simms, *Jacobite Ireland, 1685–91* (Dublin, 2000), p. 20; T. C. Barnard, 'Introduction: the dukes of Ormond' in T. Barnard and J. Fenlon (eds), *The Dukes of Ormond 1610–1745* (Suffolk, 2000), p. 8; *Tyrconnel*, p. 143.

95 'Lord Mountjoy's history' (Dublin Corporation Library, Gilbert Collection MS 109, p. 45).

96 Ibid., p. 67.

97 Kenyon, *Robert Spencer, Earl of Sunderland, 1641–1702*, p. 120; D. Ogg, *England in the Reigns of James II and William III* (Oxford, 1955), p. 163.

98 'Lord Mountjoy's history', p. 67

99 Richard Talbot to James II, Dublin 29 Aug. 1685 (BL Add MS 32095, fos. 224–224v).

100 G. A. Ellis (ed.), *The Ellis Correspondence* (2 vols, London, 1829), i, p. 57; Simms, *Jacobite Ireland*, pp. 23–5.

101 J. Elrington-Ball, *The Judges in Ireland, 1221–1921* (2 vols, London, 1929), ii, p. 295.

102 D. W. Hayton, 'The Williamite revolution in Ireland, 1689–91' in J. I. Israel, *The Anglo-Dutch Moment: Essays on the Glorious Revolution* (Cambridge, 1991), p. 191.

103 *Dick Talbot*, i, pp. 301–2.

104 Unk. to John Ellis, London 12 Jan. 1686; unk. to unk., London 16 Jan. 1686; unk. to John Ellis, London, 9 Mar. 1686; unk. to John Ellis, London, 15 Mar. 1686; unk. to John Ellis, London 10 Apr. 1686, *Ellis Correspondence*, i, pp. 11, 18, 63, 66, 68, 97; 'Lord Mountjoy's history', p. 67.

105 *Dick Talbot*, i, pp. 308–9.

106 Unk. to John Ellis, London, 15 Mar. 1686, *Ellis Correspondence*, i, p. 68

107 Stuart Handley, 'Petre, Sir Edward, third baronet (1630–1699)', *ODNB* [www.oxforddnb. com/view/article/22046, accessed 15 Nov 2013]; O. Lutaud, *Des revolutions d'Angleterre a la revolution française: le tyrannicide & killing no murder* (Leiden, 1973), p. 173.

108 Mary of Modena to Tyrconnell, Saint Germain, 5 Apr. 1690 in Haile, *Mary of Modena*, pp. 262–4.

109 Miller, *James II*, p. 211.

110 Ibid.

111 James II to Clarendon, May 1686, McNeill, 'Rawlinson manuscripts', *Anal. Hib.* 1 (Mar., 1930) p. 35; Kenyon, *Robert Spencer, Earl of Sunderland 1641–1702*, pp. 131–2, 140; J. Childs, *The Army, James II, and the Glorious Revolution* (Manchester, 1980), p. 60; 'Mountjoy's history', p. 61.

112 Simms, *Jacobite Ireland*, pp. 20–1.

113 *Life* pp. 59–61.

114 Childs, *The Army, James II, and the Glorious Revolution*, pp. 56, 60.

115 *Life*, p. 60.

116 Childs, *The Army, James II, and the Glorious Revolution*, pp. 63, 65.

117 Tyrconnell to ?Sunderland, 16 May 1688 in McNeill, 'Rawlinson manuscripts', pp. 38–9.

118 Anon., *A Vindication of the Present Government of Ireland under his excellency Richard, earl of Tirconnel* (London, 1688), pp. 10–11.

119 Clarendon to James II, 14 Aug. 1686 (BL, Western Manuscripts, Add MS 15894, fo. 119).

120 Clarendon to Sunderland, Dublin Castle, 2: June 1686, *CSPD: James II, 1686–7* (1964), pp. 149–93. J. Childs, *The Army, James II, and the Glorious Revolution*, p. 64; Earl of Longford to Ormond, Dublin 6 Sept. 1686, and 22 Nov. 1686, *HMC 8th Report*, pp. 433, 444, 473, 477.

121 *Dick Talbot*, i, pp. 326–30.

122 King, *State of the Protestants*, pp. 59–60.

123 Lynch, *Roger Boyle*, p. 241.

124 Childs, *The Army, James II, and the Glorious Revolution*, pp. 61, 62, 74.

125 Simms, *Jacobite Ireland*, p. 25; Turner, *James II*, p. 384.

126 King, *State of the Protestants*, p. 60.

127 L. G. Schwoerer, 'Propaganda in the revolution of 1688–89' in *American Historical Review*, vol. 82, no. 4 (1977), pp. 853, 867.

128 J. MacErlean (ed.), *Duanaire Dháibhidh Ó Bhruadair* (3 vols, London, 1917), pp. 128–9.

129 J. Childs, *The Williamite Wars in Ireland, 1688–91* (London, 2007), pp. 38, 40, 52.

130 Childs, *The Army, James II, and the Glorious Revolution*, pp. 101–2.

131 Clarendon to James II, 14 Aug. 1686 (BL, Hyde Papers and Correspondence, Add MS 15894, fo. 118).

132 H. Hyde, Earl of Clarendon, *The Correspondence of Henry Hyde, Earl of Clarendon, and of his Brother Laurence Hyde, Earl of Rochester*, ed. S. W. Singer (2 vols, London, 1828), I, pp. 432, 451, 464.

133 Kenyon, *Sunderland*, p. 331.

134 Henry Hyde Earl of Clarendon, *The State Letters of Henry Earl of Clarendon Lord Lieutenant of Ireland during the reign of King James the Second: and his Lordship's diary for the years 1687, 1688, 1689, and 1690* (2 vols, Oxford, 1763), i, p. 305.

135 Bagwell, *Ireland under the Stuarts*, iii, p. 177.

136 Ibid.; 'A list of the names of such persons as are to be sheriffs in the severall counties of Ireland for the ensuing year', 6 Oct. 1686, McNeill, 'Rawlinson Manuscripts', pp. 37–8.

137 Bagwell, *Ireland under the Stuarts*, iii, p. 171.

138 J. McGuire, 'A lawyer in politics, the career of Sir Richard Nagle *c*.1636–1699' in J. Devlin and H. B. Clarke (eds), *European Encounters, Essays in Memory of Albert Lovett* (Dublin, 2003), pp. 121–3.

139 T. Bruce, Earl of Ailesbury, *Memoirs*, ed. W. E. Buckley (2 vols, Cambridge, 1890), i, p. 126;

Miller, *Popery and Politics*, p. 224; Kenyon, *Sunderland*, pp. 141–2; S. Pincus, 'Gallicanism, Innocent XI, and Catholic opposition', in A. I. MacInnes and A. H. Williamson (eds), *Shaping the Stuart World, 1603 - 1714: The Atlantic Connection* (Leiden, 2006), pp. 86, 105–6.

140 Victor Stater, 'Herbert, William, styled first marquess of Powis and Jacobite first duke of Powis (*c.*1626–1696)', *ODNB* [www.oxforddnb.com/view/article/13060, accessed 14 Nov 2013]; Andrew J. Hopper, 'Belasyse, John, first Baron Belasyse of Worlaby (*bap.* 1615, *d.* 1689)', *ODNB* [www.oxforddnb.com/view/article/1977, accessed 14 Nov 2013].

141 W. Bray (ed.), *The Diary of John Evelyn* (2 vols, London, 1937), ii, pp. 118–19; Turner, *James II*, p. 391.

142 Thomas Sheridan 'Narrative', *HMC Stuart MSS*, vi, pp. 8–9.

143 Sir James MacKintosh, *Review of the Causes of the Revolution of 1688* (Philadelphia, 1846), p. 318; G. Southcombe and G. Tapsell, *Restoration Politics, Religion and Culture* (Basingstoke, 2010), p. 118; *Foreign Quarterly Review*, iii (London, 1829), p. 102.

144 James II to Clarendon, 6 Oct. 1686, C. McNeill (ed.), 'Rawlinson Manuscripts', p. 37.

145 J. Miller, 'Thomas Sheridan and his "Narrative"', in *IHS*, vol. 20, no. 78 (1976), p. 117; Glassey, *The Reigns of Charles II and James VII & II*, p. 84.

146 Cardinal d'Adda to Cardinal Cibo, London, 15 Nov. 1686 in Padraig Eric Mac Finn (ed.), 'Scríbhinní i gCartlainn an Vatican: Tuarascbhail', *Anal. Hib.* no. 16 (Mar. 1946) pp. 55–6.

147 Simms, *Jacobite Ireland*, p. 31; Gilbert, *Jacobite Narr.* p. 196.

148 Kenyon, *Sunderland*, p. 143.

149 Sir H. Verney to unk., London 6 Oct., 19 Oct. and 27 Oct. 1686, *HMC 7th Report*, p. 500.

150 Cardinal d'Adda to Cardinal Cibo, London, 15 Nov. 1686 in 'Scríbhinní i gCartlainn an Vatican', p. 55.

151 John Egan to unk., Lille 7 Feb. 1688, 'Tyrconnell's Papers'.

152 Sir J. Dalrymple, *Memoirs of Great Britain and Ireland* (Dublin, 1773), p. 182; 'JH' to John Ellis, 23 Feb. 1686, *Ellis Correspondence*, i, p. 48

153 Thomas Sheridan, 'Narrative', *HMC Stuart MSS*, vi, p. 7; Simms, *Jacobite Ireland*, p. 38.

154 Miller, 'Thomas Sheridan and his "Narrative"', p. 126.

155 Thomas Sheridan, 'A discourse on the rise and power of parliaments', in S. Bannister (ed.), in *Some Revelations in Irish History* (London, 1870) p. 92;

156 Vincent Geoghegan, 'Sheridan, Thomas', in *DIB* [dib.cambridge.org/viewReadPage.do?articleId=a8045].

157 J. Oldmixon, *Memoirs of Ireland* (London, 1716), pp. 19–21, 67.

158 Anon to J Ellis 30 Nov. 1686 and Anon. to J. Ellis, 14 Dec. 1686 in Ellis *Correspondence*, i, pp. 56, 196, 206.

159 Miller, *James II*, p. 149; Kenyon, *Sunderland*, p. 331.

160 Hunter, *Diary of Dr. Thomas Cartwright*, p. 23.

161 Anon. to J. Ellis, 11 Jan 1687 and Anon. to J. Ellis 12 Feb 1687 in *Ellis Correspondence*, i, pp. 225–6, 237.

162 A. Carpenter (ed.), *Verse in English from Tudor and Stuart Ireland* (Cork, 2003), pp. 504–5, 521, 530.

163 Ó Buachalla, 'Lillibulero agus Eile', *Comhar Teoranta*, vol. 46, no. 4 (1987), p. 29; no. 6 (1987), pp. 25–6, no. 7 (1987), pp. 18–20.

164 Kenyon, *Sunderland*, p. 150; P. Sonnino, 'The origins of Louis XIV's wars' in J. Black (ed.), *The Origins of War in Early Modern Europe* (Edinburgh, 1987), pp. 112–31.

165 E. Mallet (ed.), *Négociations du comte d'Avaux en Hollande depuis 1679 jusqu'en 1688* (4 vols, Paris, 1754), iv, p. 31.

FIVE: LORD DEPUTY

1 Mac Erlean, *Duanaire Uí Bhruadair*, pp. 104–5.

2 *Tyrconnel*, p. 150; J. Miller, 'The earl of Tyrconnel and James II's Irish policy, 1685–1688' in *Historical Journal*, vol. 20, no. 4 (Dec. 1977), p. 806.

3 T. Harris, *Revolution: The Great Crisis of the British Monarchy, 1685–1720* (London, 2007), p. 135.

4 J. Miller, 'Thomas Sheridan and his narrative', p. 120.

5 Simms, *Jacobite Ireland*, pp. 28, 33, 35, 36.

6 Anon, *An Exact list of the lords spiritual and temporal who sat in the pretended parliament at Dublin…* (London, 1689), p. 12.

7 H. Maynard, 'The Irish legal profession and the Catholic revival 1660–89' in J. Kelly, J. McCafferty and C. I McGrath (eds), *People, Politics and Power: Essays on Irish History in honour of James I. McGuire* (Dublin, 2009), pp. 40–1; Hayton, 'Williamite revolution in Ireland', p. 196; Southcombe and Tapsell, *Restoration Politics, Religion and Culture*, p. 119.

8 J. C. Beckett, 'The Irish viceroyalty in the Restoration period', *Transactions of the Royal Historical Society*, vol. 20 (London, 1970), pp. 66, 69.

9 *Dick Talbot*, ii, pp. 373, 382.

10 Simms, *Jacobite Ireland*, p. 28.

11 Éamonn Ó Ciardha, 'Tyrrell, Patrick', in *DIB* [dib.cambridge. org/viewReadPage. do?articleId=a8701]

12 Murray, *Journal of John Stevens*, pp. 54–5; Hugh Fenning, 'Dominic Maguire, O. P. Archbishop of Armagh: 1684–1707' in *Seanchas Ardmhacha: Journal of the Armagh Diocesan Historical Society*, vol. 18, no. 1 (1999/2000), p. 45; Oldmixon, *Memoirs of Ireland*, i, pp. 70–1.

13 Kenyon, *Sunderland*, p. 162; Glassey, *The Reigns of Charles II and James VII & II*, p. 84; Oldmixon, *Memoirs of Ireland*, i, pp. 76–7.

14 *Ailesbury Memoirs*, i, p. 149.

15 Bagwell, *Ireland under the Stuarts*, iii, p. 172.

16 Ibid., iii, p. 174.

17 J. Miller, 'The Earl of Tyrconnel and James II's Irish policy, 1685–1688' in *Historical Journal*, vol. 20, no. 4 (Dec. 1977), p. 810; James McGuire, 'Talbot, Richard duke of Tyrconnell', in *DIB* [dib.cambridge.org/view]; J. Carwell, *The Descent on England: A Study of the English Revolution of 1688 and its European background* (London, 1969), p. 101.

18 Kenyon, *Sunderland*, p. 208.

19 Smith, *The Double Crown*, pp. 278, 280; J. R. Jones, *The Revolution of 1688 in England* (London, 1972), pp. 81–2, 99; P. Seaward, *The Restoration* (London, 1991), pp. 131–2.

20 Bonrepaux to Seignelay, London 4 Sept. 1687 in Sir James Mackintosh, *History of the Revolution in England in 1688* (Philadelphia, 1835), p. 468.

21 S. Pincus, *1688: The First Modern Revolution* (New Haven, CT, 2011), pp. 142, 475.

22 Southcombe and Tapsell, *Restoration Politics, Religion and Culture*, p. 80.

23 Bagwell, *Ireland under the Stuarts*, iii, p. 172.

24 Harris, *Revolution*, p. 136.

25 Tyrconnell to James II, Dublin 28 Mar. 1688 (BL, Hyde Papers and Correspondence, Add MS 32095, fo. 259); Simms, *Jacobite Ireland*, p. 41; Miller, 'Tyrconnel and James II's Irish Policy', p. 810.

26 'Robert Spencer, 2nd Earl of Sunderland: Letter to a friend: 1689' (BL, Osborne Correspondence, Add MS 28053, fo. 386).

27 Piers Wauchope, 'Ellis, Sir William, in *ODNB* [www.oxforddnb.com/view/article/8717, accessed 7 Sept 2013].

28 Miller, 'Thomas Sheridan and his narrative', p. 120; McNeill, 'Rawlinson Manuscripts, pp. 43–5, 48–51.

29 G. M. Crump, *Poems on Affairs of State: Augustan Satirical Verse, 1660–1714* (4 vols, New Haven, CT, 1963–8), iv, p. 262.

30 James Johnston to unk., 6/16 Feb. 1688 (University of Nottingham archive, Pw A 2141) [www.nottingham.ac.uk/mss/elearning/conflict/theme1/documents.aspx].

31 *Vindication*, p. 12.

32 King, *State of the Protestants*, p. 329.

33 Lord Deputy and Council, Proclamation (Dublin, 22 Mar. 1689).

34 Unless otherwise specified: *Dick Talbot*, ii, pp 643–5; Gilbert, *Jacobite Narr.*, p. 148.

35 Aoife Duignan, 'Cusack, Nicholas', in *DIB* (dib. cambridge. org/viewReadPage. do?articleId=a2348)

36 Gilbert, *Jacobite Narr.*, p. 102

37 Ibid., p. 241; Mulloy, *Franco-Irish Correspondence*, iii, p. 198; *HMC 8th Report*, pp. 444, 453.

38 D'Alton, *Irish Army List*, p. 61.

39 *HMC, 10th report*, appendix 5 (1885), p. 154.

40 G. Steinman, *Althorp Memoirs* (Oxford, 1869), pp. 67–8.

41 E. Kimber, *The Peerage of Ireland: A Genealogical and Historical Account* (2 vols, London, 1768), i, p. 14.

42 Hazel Maynard, 'Nugent, Thomas 1st Baron Nugent of Riverston', in *DIB* [dib.cambridge. org/viewReadPage. do?articleId=a6262].

43 H. Maynard 'The Irish legal profession and the Catholic revival 1660–89' in Kelly, McCafferty and McGrath (eds), *People, Politics and Power*, pp. 38–9; J. McGuire, 'A lawyer in politics', p. 124.

44 Earl of Limerick to Tyrconnell, 10 June 1690, 'Tyrconnell Papers'.

45 P. Kelly 'Ireland and the Glorious Revolution: From Kingdom to Colony' in R. Beddard (ed.), *The Revolutions of 1688* (Oxford, 1991), p. 168.

46 J. Mackintiosh, *The Miscellaneous Works of Sir James Mackintosh* (3 vols, London, 1854), ii, p. 134.

47 Thomas Sheridan, 'Narrative', *HMC Stuart MSS*, vi, pp. 8–10.

48 J. Childs, *The Army, James II, and the Glorious Revolution* (Manchester, 1980), pp. 66, 69, 77; 'Estat des troupes du Roy d'Angleterre Irlande, 1689' in Gilbert, *Jacobite Narr.*, pp. 201–233.

49 Lynn, *Giant of the Grand Siecle*, pp. 205, 311.

50 Walter Dungan to Tyrconnell, Curragh Camp, 5 Apr. 1688, 'Tyrconnell Papers'.

51 Childs, *The Army, James II, and the Glorious Revolution*, pp. 66, 69–71.

52 Breandán Ó Buachalla, 'Lillibulero agus Eile' in *Comhar Teoranta*, vol. 46, no. 4 (1987), p. 27.

53 Mac Erlea, *Duanaire Uí Bhruadair*, pp. 105–9; Anon., *An Account of the Late, Horrid and Bloody Massacre in Ireland* (London, 1689), pp. 1–2.

54 Bevan, *Marlborough the Man*, p. 83; J. R. Jones, *The Revolution of 1688 in England* (London, 1972), p. 85; E. Gregg, *Anne, Queen of Great Britain* (London, 1980), p. 45; Seaward, *Restoration*, p. 135; M. Mullett, *James II and English Politics 1678–1688* (London, 1994), p. 81.

55 P. Sonnino, 'The origins of Louis XIV's wars' in Jeremy Black (ed.), *The Origins of War in Early Modern Europe* (Edinburgh, 1987), pp. 112–31.

56 G. M. Crump *Poems on Affairs of State: Augustan Satirical Verse, 1660–1714* (4 vols, New Haven, CT, 1963–8), iv, p. 262. Frances came over in June 1688 to assist at the birth and apartments were assigned her in Whitehall: 'But Orange nam'd, the royal elf, / The sweet, sweet babe besh- himself. Frances "lick'd him clean"'.

57 H. Verney to unk., 29 Aug. 1688 HMC 7th Report, p. 500; Simms, *Jacobite Ireland*, p. 46; C. E. Levillain, *Vaincre Louis XIV: Angleterre-Hollande-France Historie d'une relation triangulaire 1665–1689* (Seyssel, 2010), p. 360; D. Ogg, *England in the Reigns of James II and William III* (Oxford, 1955), pp. 211–14; Miller, *James II*, pp. 194–5.

58 Miller, *James II*, p. 202.

59 Unk. to Duke of Queensberry, London 25 Dec. 1688 (BL Add MS 28053, fo. 380).

60 King, *State of the Protestants*, p. 120.

61 Tyrconnell to James II, Dublin 17 Mar. 1688 (BL Add MS 28053S, fos 253–4); Henri & Barbara van der Zee, *1688: Revolution in the Family* (New York, 1988), p. 104.

62 Tyrconnell to Sunderland, 9 and 29 May 1688, Mc Neill, 'Rawlinson Manuscripts', pp. 39, 41.

63 P. G. Melvin, 'The Irish army and the revolution of 1688' in *Irish Sword*, ix (1969), pp. 294–5; J. Childs, The *Williamite Wars in Ireland 1688–1691* (London, 2007), p. 33; Simms, *Jacobite Ireland*, p. 48.

64 H. Murtagh, 'The Irish Jacobite army, 1689–91' in *Irish Sword*, no. 70 (1990), pp. 33, 45; Tyrconnell to James II, Dublin 29 Jan. 1689, BL, Add MS 28053, p. 387.

65 Tyrconnell to James II, Dublin 3 Oct. 1688 (BL, Add MS 28053S, fos 34–6); J. McGuire, 'A lawyer in politics', p. 56.

66 Walter Dawson to Darce Barrett, 16 Mar. 1689 (PRONI, Barrett–Lennard Papers, T2529/6, no. 108). My thanks to Alan Smyth of Trinity College Dublin for this reference.

67 Anon, *A True and Impartial Account of the Most Material Passages in Ireland* (London, 1689), pp. 4–5; C. Leslie, *An Answer to a Book intituled The State of the Protestants of Ireland* (London, 1692), pp. 79, 83–97. J. Bolton to unk., Derry 13 Oct. 1706 (Letters and Papers of the Talbot Family Barons de Malahide', NLI Microfilm no 9741, p. 100).

68 Anon, *The Judgement and Indictment of John Price esq* (London, 1689), p. 4.

69 J. Mackenzie, *A Narrative of the Siege of Londonderry: Or the late memorable transactions of that city* (London, 1690), p. 11: R. Doherty, *The Williamite War in Ireland 1688–1691* (Dublin, 1998), p. 40; Anon., *A True and Impartial Account*, p. 9.

70 Gilbert, *Jacobite Narr.*, p. 36.

71 'Duc de Tyrconnel', p. 477.

72 *Dick Talbot*, pp. 403–4, 440; A. Chalmers, *The General Biographical Dictionary* (London, 1816), xxix, p. 211; Luttrell, *A Brief Relation of State Affairs*, i, p. 495.

73 Simms, *Jacobite Ireland*, p. 51; Childs, *Williamite Wars*, p. 34.

74 *Dick Talbot*, pp. 406–7.

75 Though Clarendon records that a letter posted from Dublin on 12 Jan. 1689 reached him on the night of the 16th: T. Stackhouse (ed.), *Abridgement of Bishop Burnet's History of His Own Times* (London, 1724), p. 432; King, *State of the Protestants*, p. 112: E. Mac Lysaght, *Irish Life in the Seventeenth Century* (4th edn, Dublin, 1979), p. 259; Clarendon, *State Letters*, ii, p. 300.

76 Simms, *Jacobite Ireland*, p. 52; Childs, *Williamite Wars*, p. 34.

77 'Information of John Phillips', 9 Aug. 1689', Statement of James Hamilton', 15 June 1689, 'Statement of Robert Rochfort', June 1689 in *HMC 12th Report part vi The Manuscripts of the House of Lords 1689–90* (London, 1889), pp. 137–40, 190–1; Simms, *Jacobite Ireland*, pp. 51–2; *Dick Talbot*, ii, p. 400.

78 William Ellis to Colonel Henry Dillon, Dublin, 30 Dec. 1688; Tyrconnell to Colonel Henry Dillon, Dublin 6 Jan. 1689 ('Dillon Papers', NLI microfilm no. 9741, np)

79 T. Harris, 'Restoration Ireland: themes and problems' in Dennehy (ed.), *Restoration Ireland*, p. 11.

80 Roger Kenyon to William Stanley, Earl of Derby, 18 Dec. 1688, 'The manuscripts of Lord Kenyon', *HMC 14th Report, Appendix Part IV* (London, 1894), p. 211; *Dick Talbot*, ii, p. 402; King, *State of the Protestants*, pp. 342, 345.

81 Simms, *Jacobite Ireland*, p. 53: Tyrconnell to James II, Dublin 29 Jan. 1689 (BL Add MS 28053, fo. 387); N. Luttrell, *A Brief Relation of State Affairs* (6 vols, Oxford, 1857), i, p. 488; A. Hamilton (ed.), *Actions of the Enniskillen Men* (Belfast, 1813), p. xiv; Statement of Archbishop of Dublin', 15 June 1689, *HMC 12th Report*, p. 141; Unk. to Duke of Queensberry, London 25 Dec. 1688 (BL Add MS 28053, fo. 381); Denis Scott to Sir Edward Scott, Dublin 15 Dec. 1688; HMC, *Dartmouth Manuscripts* (London, 1887) p. 234.

82 Anon, *A Faithful History of the Northern Affairs of Ireland from the late K. James accession to the crown, to the siege of Londonderry* (London, 1690) pp. 10–11.

83 Tyrconnell to James II, Dublin 29 Jan. 1689 (BL Add MS 28053, fos 386, 388).

84 Anon, *The Judgement and Indictment of John Price esq* (London, 1689), p. 28.

85 C. Hatton to Viscount Hatton, 20 Apr. and 23 Apr. 1689 in E. Maunde Thompson (ed.), *Correspondence of the Family of Hatton* (2 vols, London 1878), ii, pp. 131–3: J. Dunn, *Read My Heart: A Love Story in England's Age of Revolution* (New York, 2008), pp. 344–5; Chalmers, *Biographical Dictionary*, p. 211.

86 Childs, *Williamite Wars*, pp. 31–2; Stackhouse, *Bishop Burnet's Own Times*, p. 431.

87 Simms, *Jacobite Ireland*, pp. 51–2; *HMC 12th Report*, p. 140.

88 Foxcroft, *Life and Letters of Sir George Savile*, ii, pp. 203–4.

89 Clarendon, *State Letters*, ii, pp. 270, 286–7, 289.

90 Luttrell, *A Brief Relation of State Affairs*, i, p. 495.

91 Mountjoy to Ormonde 10 Jan. 1689, *HMC Calendar of the Manuscripts of the Marquess of Ormonde*, p. 14.

92 Longford to Ormond, Dublin, 12 Jan. 1689 in P. Melvin and Lord Longford (eds), 'Letters of Lord Longford and others on Irish affairs 1689–1702', *Anal. Hib.*, no. 32 (1985), p. 47.

93 Anon., *A True and Impartial Account*, p. 9; Childs, *Williamite Wars*, p. 35; Gilbert, *Jacobite Narr.*, p. 43.

94 F. G. James, *Lords of the Ascendancy; The Irish House of Lords and its Members, 1600–1800* (Dublin, 1995), p. 48; William Stewart Viscount Mountjoy to Lord Middleton, 6 Mar. 1688 (BL Add MS 41805, fo. 16); R. Gillespie 'The Irish Protestants and James II, 1688–90' in *IHS*, vol. 28, no. 110 (Nov. 1992), pp. 127, 130; Clarendon, *State Letters*, p 300.

95 J. Boyce, *A Vindication of the Reverend Mr. Alexander Osborn, in reference to the affairs of the north of Ireland* (London, 1690) pp. 12, 15, 17; C. Leslie, An *Answer to a Book Intituled The State of the Protestants in Ireland* (London, 1692), pp. 82–3

96 Simms, *Jacobite Ireland*, pp. 50, 52, 56.

97 Dominic Sheldon to Tyrconnell, Derry, 3 May 1688, 'Tyrconnell Papers'.

98 Childs, *Williamite Wars*, pp. 25, 41; Murray Pittock, *Jacobitism*, p. 20.; H. Murtagh, 'The war in Ireland 1689–91' in W. A. Maguire, *Kings in Conflict The Revolutionary War in Ireland and its Aftermath 1689–1750* (Belfast, 1990), p. 62; Simms, *Jacobite Ireland*, pp. 58–61.

99 Tyrconnell to James II, Dublin 29 Jan. 1689 (BL Add. MS 28053, fos. 387–8); Piers Wauchope, 'Talbot, Richard, first Earl of Tyrconnell and Jacobite Duke of Tyrconnell (1630–1691)', *ODNB*.

100 D'Avaux to Louis XIV, Charlemont, 23 Apr. 1689 in J. Hogan (ed.), *Négociations de M. Le Comte D'Avaux en Irlande 1689–90* (Dublin, 1934), pp. 87–8: Tyrconnell to James II, Dublin 29 Jan. 1689, BL Add. MS 28053, fo. 387).

101 Dublin, 25 Feb. 1689, *By the Lord Deputy General…A Declaration*; Childs, *Williamite Wars*, p. 48; Anon., *The Popish Champion* (London, 1689) and 'Tyrconnel's proceedings in Ireland' Dublin, 17 Jan. 1690 in (NLI microfilm no. 9741, p. 22).

102 'Minute and entry book of the Committee for Ireland' (Privy Council Office: Miscellaneous Books and Correspondence Registers, SP, PC 6/2, fos 2–3, 9–10); W. Bray (ed.), *Diary and Correspondence of John Evelyn* (4 vols, London, 1854), iii, p. 29; Anon., *The Popish Champion* p. 21.

103 Childs, *Williamite Wars*, p. 34.

104 King, *State of the Protestants*, p. 319; Doherty, Williamite War, p. 41.

105 D'Avaux to Louis XIV, Dublin 4 Apr. 1689 in Hogan, *Négociations*, p. 53.

106 Childs, *Williamite Wars*, pp. 56–57, 61–62, 67.

107 Doherty, *Williamite War*, pp. 48–49 Childs Williamite Wars pp. 70–4.

108 'Depart du Roy d'Angleterre de France pour l'Irlande' (BNF Fr 12160, fo. 130)

109 Anon., *Ireland's Lamentation* (London, 1689), pp. 26–8; J. Macpherson, *Original papers containing the Secret History of Great Britain* (2 vols, London, 1776), p. 177; M. B. 'Entry of King James into Dublin', *Dublin Literary Gazette* (Dublin, 1830), xi, 13 Mar. 1830, p. 174.

110 Hogan, *Négociations*, p. 2.

111 D'Avaux to Louis XIV, D'Avaux to Louvois, Kinsale 13/23 Mar. 1689, D'Avaux to Louis XIV, Cork, 16 and 27 Mar., D'Avaux to Louvois, Cork, 19 Mar. 1689, D'Avaux to Louis XIV, D'Avaux to Louvois, Dublin 26 Mar./4 Apr. 1689, D'Avaux to Louis XIV Dublin, 4/14 Apr. 1689, Hogan *Négociations* pp. 23, 25, 27, 30, 36, 37, 42, 49–52; Simms, *Jacobite Ireland*, pp. 63–4.

112 D. Szechi, 'The Jacobite revolution settlement, 1689–1696' in *EHR*, no. 428 (1993), pp. 615–16.

113 E. Carp, 'France, Rome and the exiled Stuarts, 1689–1713' in E. Carp (ed.), *A Court in Exile The Stuarts in France 1689–1718* (Cambridge, 2004), pp. 21, 24; Miller *James II*, pp. 224–5; D. Szechi 'A blueprint for tyranny? Sir Edward Hales and the Catholic Jacobite response to the revolution of 1688' in *EHR*, vol. 116, no. 466 (2001), p. 346.

114 Gilbert, *Jacobite Narr.*, p. 110; P. M. Kerrigan, 'Ireland in naval strategy 1641–1691' in P. Lenihan (ed), *Conquest and Resistance: War in Seventeenth Century Ireland* (Leiden, 2001), p. 170; D'Avaux to Louis XIV 17/12 May 1689, Hogan, *Négociations*, p. 180 ; Edward Corp, 'Drummond, John, styled first earl of Melfort and Jacobite first duke of Melfort (1649–1714)', *ODNB* [www.oxforddnb. com/view/article/8077, accessed 19 June 2013].

115 Vincent Morley, 'The continuity of disaffection in Eighteenth-Century Ireland' in *Eighteenth-Century Ireland / Iris an dá chultúr* 22 (2007), pp. 193–4.

116 Gilbert, *Jacobite Narr.*, p. 83

117 Bishop O'Molony to Bishop Tyrrell, Mar. 1690, King, *State of the Protestants*, pp. 356–7.

118 P. Kelly, '"A light to the blind": the voice of the dispossessed elite in the generation after Limerick' in *IHS*, no. 96 (1985), pp. 433–4.

119 G. N. Plunkett and E. I. Hogan (eds), *The Jacobite War in Ireland 1688–1691* (Dublin, 1894), pp. 14–15.

120 Philip Sidney, 'Astrophell his song of Phillida and Coridon' in J. Payne Collier (ed.), *Seven English Poetical Miscellanies* (London, 1867) p. 63; B. W. Breed, *Pastoral Inscriptions: Reading and Writing Virgil's Eclogues* (London, 2006), p. 32; A. M. Patterson, *Pastoral and Ideology: Virgil to Valéry* (Berkeley, CA, 2008), p. 11.

121 Lord Clare to Louvois 22 Aug. 1690 in S. Mulloy (ed.), *Franco-Irish Correspondence Dec. 1688–Feb. 1692* (3 vols, Dublin, 1983–4), iii, p. 138.

122 E. Ó Ciardha, *Ireland and The Jacobite Cause, 1685–1766: A Fatal Attachment* (Dublin, 2001), p. 86.

123 'Poema', 4. 196–200

124 Ó Ciardha, *Ireland and The Jacobite Cause*, p. 64.

125 Hayton, 'Williamite revolution in Ireland', p. 197; Simms, *Jacobite Ireland*, pp. 81–2.

126 Simms, *Jacobite Ireland*, pp. 80, 82, 88; M. G. H. Pittock, *Jacobitism* (New York, 1998), p. 20.

127 Hayton, 'Williamite revolution in Ireland', p. 198; M. G. H. Pittock, *Poetry and Jacobite Politics in Eighteenth-Century Britain and Ireland* (Cambridge, 1994), pp. 188, 201; Ellis, *Original Letters*, iv, p. 188.

128 Pittock, *Jacobitism*, p. 20; B. Ó Buachalla, 'Briseadh na Bóinne', in *Éigse* vols 23–5 (1989), pp. 83–105; É. Ó Ciardha, *Ireland and the Jacobite cause, 1685–1766: A Fatal Attachment* (Dublin, 2002), pp. 57–8; 'Caithréim Cing Séamais' (BL Add MSS 29614, fo. 11, line 14).

129 Carp, 'France, Rome and the exiled Stuarts', pp. 12–14; T. Ó hAnnracháin, 'The strategic involvement of continental powers in Ireland 1596–1691' in Lenihan (ed.), *Conquest and Resistance*, pp. 46–7; P. Kelly 'Ireland and the Glorious Revolution: from kingdom to colony' in R. Beddard (ed.), *The Revolutions of 1688* (Oxford, 1991), p. 172.

130 Childs, *Williamite Wars*, p. 53; Madame de Sévigné, 28 Feb. 1689 in M. Haile, *Mary of Modena*, p. 244; Murtagh, 'The Irish Jacobite army', pp. 73–4; R. Pillorget, 'Louis XIV and

Ireland in B. Whelan (ed.), *The Last of the Great Wars: Essays on the Wars of the Three Kings in Ireland 1688–91* (Limerick, 1995), p. 10.

131 R. Biggs, *Early Modern France 1560–1715* (Oxford, 1997), p. 143; A. W. H. Pearsall, 'The war at sea' in Maguire, *Kings in Conflict*, pp. 102–5; T. Ó hAnnracháin, 'Strategic involvement of continental powers in Ireland 1596–1691', p. 47.

132 R. Doherty, *The Williamite War in Ireland 1688–1691* (Dublin, 1998), p. 38.

133 Murtagh, 'The Irish Jacobite army', p. 74.

134 Louis XIV to D'Avaux, Versailles, 4 Jan. 1690, and Louvois to D'Avaux Versailles, 4 Jan. 1690 in Hogan, *Négociations*, pp. 648–9, 654–5; D. Szechi, *The Jacobites: Britain and Europe 1688–1788* (Manchester, 1994), pp. 55, 87.

135 D'Avaux to Louis XIV, D'Avaux to Louvois, Dublin 26 Mar. /4 Apr. 1689, D'Avaux to Louis XIV Dublin, 4 Apr. 1689, *Négociations*, pp. 49–52, 54; Simms, *Jacobite Ireland*, p. 63.

136 Tyrconnell to James II, Dublin 29 Jan. 1689 (Correspondence, chiefly between Thomas Osborne, Earl of Danby, 1st Duke of Leeds, and officers of state and other official persons …' (BL Add. MS 28053, fo. 388).

137 Lord Clare to Louvois, 22 Aug. 1690, in Mulloy, *Franco-Irish Correspondence*, iii, p. 138.

138 Tyrconnell to Mary of Modena, 7 Mar. 1690, 24 June 1690, Tyrconnell to Barrillon 23 Apr. 1690, 'Letter-book of Richard Talbot', ed. Lilian Tate. in *Anal. Hib.*, no. 4 (1932), pp. 111–13, 123–4, 131.

139 B. Lenman, *The Jacobite Risings in Britain 1689–1746* (London, 1980), p. 31; *Life*, ii, p. 352; Pittock, *Jacobitism*, pp. 20–2; Childs, Williamite Wars, p. 125.

140 G. Story, *A True and Impartial History of the most material occurrences in the kingdom of Ireland during the last two years* (London, 1691), p. 5; D'Avaux to Louis XIX, Dublin, 16 Apr. 1689, Hogan, *Négociations* p. 61.

141 D'Avaux to Louvois, Dublin 14 Apr. 1689, D'Avaux to Louis XIV, Dublin 23 Apr. 1689, D'Avaux to Louis XIV, Charlemont, 27 Apr. 1689; Hogan, *Négociations* pp. 75, 85, 88, 104–5, 112.

142 Childs, *Williamite Wars*, p. 135; B. G. Scott et al., *The Great Guns Like Thunder: The Cannon from the City of Derry* (Derry, 2008), pp. 66–7, 85–93; P. W. Kerrigan, *Castles and Fortifications in Ireland 1485–1945* (Cork, 1995), pp. 74–5; J. S. Wheeler, 'The logistics of conquest' in Lenihan (ed.), *Conquest and Resistance*, p. 202.

143 Lynn *Wars of Louis XIV*, p. 235; M. Virol 'Le siège de Namur en 1692: l'héroisme et la technique' in *XVII Siècle*, no. 228 (2005), p. 476.

144 Carlo Gébler, *The Siege of Derry* (London, 2005), pp. 178–9, 182–3, 189–190, 212–15; James Macpherson, *Original Papers Containing the Secret History of Great Britain...* (2 vols, Dublin, 1775), i, p. 203; Gilbert, *Jacobite Narr.*, pp. 66, 68, 70, 79, 111.

145 Childs, *Williamite Wars*, pp. 85–6, 120–1, 133.

146 Ibid., p. 135.

147 'Poema', 4. 306–11, 490–3, 652–4.

148 J. G. Simms, 'Sligo in the Jacobite War, 1689–91,' in *Irish Sword*, vii, no. 27 (1965), pp. 133–4; J. G. Simms, 'Schomberg at Dundalk, 1689' in D. W. Hayton and G. O'Brien (eds), *War and Politics in Ireland 1649–1730* (London, 1986), p. 95; Childs, *Williamite Wars*, pp. 150, 154.

149 P. Lenihan, *1690 Battle of the Boyne* (Stroud, 2003), p. 63; Childs, *Williamite Wars*,

pp. 144–7, 148–9; M. Glozier, *Marshal Schomberg 1615–1690* (Sussex, 2005), pp. 138–44.

150 D'Avaux to Louis XIV, Charlemont 27 Apr. 1689, D'Avaux to Louis XIV, Dublin 12 May 1689, D'Avaux to Louis XIV, Dublin 27 May 1689, D'Avaux to Louvois, 29 May 1689, Hogan, *Négociations*, pp. 104, 182, 188.

151 Unk. to Tyrconnell, 2 May 1689, 'Tyrconnell Papers'.

152 D'Avaux to Louis XIV, Dublin 26 June, Hogan, *Négociations*, p. 219; Pusignan to Louvois, Dublin, 11 Apr. NS 1689, Fumeron to Louvois, Limerick 28 Jan. 1691, Mulloy, *Franco-Irish Correspondence*, ii, p 207, iii, p. 9; Tyrconnell to Queen Mary of Modena, 27 Nov. 1689 in 'Letter-Book of Richard Talbot', p. 105.

153 Hutton, *Charles II*, p. 414; H. Mantel, 'Royal Bodies' in *London Review of Books*, vol. 35, no. 4, 21 Feb. 2013, p. 7.

154 Mac Erlean, *Duanaire Uí Bhruadair*, pp. 122–3.

155 Tyrconnell to Mary of Modena, Dublin, 30 Apr., 26 June 1690 in 'Letter-Book of Richard Talbot', pp. 121, 130.

156 Melfort to Innes, Rome 30 Sept. 1690 in H. Ellis (ed), *Original Letters Illustrative of English History* (4 vols, London, 1827), iv, p. 187; *Dick Talbot*, pp. 458–65.

157 D'Avaux to Louis XIV, Hogan, *Négociations*, Dublin 27 May, 26 June, 10 July 1689, pp. 180–3, 218, 247–9, 251–2.

158 Mackenzie, *Narrative of the Siege of Londonderry*, p. 46; G. Walker, *A True Account of the Siege of Londonderry* (London, 1689), p. 42: Colles's diary, 13 Aug. 1689, *HMC Ormonde MSS*, viii, p. 369. My thanks to Alan Smyth Trinity College Dublin for the latter reference. M. Rosen to James II, 30 June 1689 and M. Fumeron to Louvois, 13 Aug. 1689, in L. Tate (ed.), 'Franco-Irish correspondence in the Archives Nationales, Paris: Dépôt de la Guerre', *Anal. Hib.*, no. 21 (1959), letters no. 232 and 242; Mackenzie, *Narrative of the Siege of Londonderry*, p. 46.

159 D'Avaux to Louis XIV, Hogan, *Négociations*, Dublin 14 Aug. 1688, p. 375–6.

160 D'Avaux to Louis XIV, Dublin 18 Aug. 1688; Hogan, *Négociations* pp. 390–1, 394, 395.

161 Rosen to Louvois, Dundalk 13 Oct., 1688; Hogan, *Négociations*, p. 83.

162 T. Crofton Croker (ed.), 'Macariae Excidium', *Narratives Illustrative of the Contests in Ireland in 1641 and 1690* (London, 1849) pp. 55, 69, 98, 129–130; *Dick Talbot*, p. 463.

163 E. Carp, 'France, Rome and the exiled Stuarts', p. 23.

164 Fumeron to Louvois, Dublin 2 Sept., Drogheda, 20 Sept. (N.S.) 1689, Girardin to Louvois, Dublin, 4 Sept. (N.S.) 1689, in Mulloy *Franco-Irish Correspondence*, iii, pp. 57, 66, 70; Edward Corp, 'Drummond, John, styled first earl of Melfort and Jacobite first duke of Melfort (1649–1714)', *ODNB* [www. oxforddnb. com/view/article/8077, accessed 9 July 2012]; D'Avaux to Louis XIV, Dublin 30 Aug., 4 Sept. 1688, D'Avaux to Colbert de Croissy, Dublin 30 Aug. (N.S.) 1689 in Hogan, *Négociations*, pp. 431, 430, 433, 445.

165 D'Avaux to Louis XIV, Dublin 6 Dec. (N. S.) 1689 in Hogan, *Négociations*, p. 617; Fumeron to Louvois, Limerick, 10 Feb. (N.S.) 1690 in Mulloy *Franco-Irish Correspondence*, i, p. 259.

166 J. F. A. Kazner, *Leben Friedrichs von Schonburg* (2 vols, Mannheim, 1789), i, p. 301.

167 G. Story, *A True and Impartial History of the Most Material Occurrences* (London, 1691), pp. 30, 35–6, 39, 46.

168 Childs, *Williamite Wars*, pp. 149–150; Simms, *Jacobite Ireland*, pp. 125–6; D'Avaux to Louis XIV, Drogheda 7 Sept., D'Avaux to Colbert de Croissy, 30 Aug. in Hogan, *Négociations*, pp. 443, 461; Fumeron to Louvois, Drogheda 20 Sept. 1689 in Mulloy, *Franco-Irish Correspondence*, iii, p. 69.

169 Macpherson, *Original Papers*, i, p. 224.

170 P. Lenihan, 'Unhappy campers: Dundalk (1689) and after' in T. Pollard and I. Banks (eds), *Scorched Earth: Studies in the Archaeology of Conflict* (Leiden, 2008), pp. 198–200; D'Avaux to Louis XIV, Drogheda, 20 Sept. 1688, Knockbridge 2 Oct. 1688, D'Avaux to Louvois, Knockbridge, 30 Sept. 1688, in Hogan, *Négociations*, pp. 464–5, 478–9.

171 O'Kelly cited in Harris, *Revolution*, p. 141.

SIX: LORD LIEUTENANT

1   Soulié et al. (eds), *Journal du Marquis de Dangeau* (Paris, 1854), iii, p. 36.

2   Simms, *Jacobite Ireland*, pp. 119, 133; Childs, *Williamite Wars*, pp. 200–3; Tyrconnell to Mary of Modena, Dublin 22 Apr. 1690, L. Tate (ed.), 'Letter Book of Richard Talbot' in *Anal. Hib.*, 4 (1932), p. 119.

3   Gilbert, *Jacobite Narr.*, p. 90; D'Avaux to Louis XIV, Dublin 11 Feb. 1690, Hogan, *Négociations*, pp. 644–5.

4   Tyrconnell to Mary of Modena, 27 Nov. 1689, 20 Feb. 1690, Tyrconnell to Barrillon, 23 Apr. 1690, 'Letter Book of Richard Talbot', pp. 103–6, 110, 112, 124.

5   J. C. O'Callaghan, *History of the Irish Brigades in the Service of France* (Glasgow, 1870), pp. 8–9, 27–8.

6   Tyrconnell to D'Avaux, 23 Apr. 1690, 'Letter Book of Richard Talbot' p. 125; G. S. Steinman, *Althorp Memoirs* (1869), pp 67–8; Commissaire Bouridal to Louvois, Brest 7 May 1690, Mulloy *Franco-Irish Correspondence*, i, p. 296.

7   Galway's mother Helen Mac Carthy was the daughter of Donagh Mac Carthy, 1st earl of Clancarthy; J. Lodge, *The Peerage of Ireland* (7 vols, London 1789), i, pp. 138–40; Gilbert, *Jacobite Narr.*, p. 147; T. Wall (ed.), T. Burke, *Hibernia Dominicana* (Cologne, 1762 repub. London, 1970), p. 144.

8   D'Avaux to Louvois, Ardee 21 Sept. 1689, *Négociations*, pp. 517–21.

9   M. F. Sandars, *Lauzun: Courtier and Adventurer The Life of a Friend of Louis XIV* (2 vols, London, 1908), i, pp. 7, 16, 37, 169–70, ii, pp. 465, 472, 495, 497, 498, 502, 538, 551, 563; V. Sackville West, *Daughter of France, the life of Anne Marie Louise D'Orléans duchesse de Montpensier* (London, 1959), pp. 239–41, 254, 338–9.

10 Tyrconnell to Mary of Modena, Ardee, 20 Oct. 1689, Tyrconnell to Mary of Modena Dublin 27 Nov. 1689, 'Letter Book of Richard Talbot', pp. 101, 104; T. Stackhouse (ed), *An Abridgement of Bishop Burnet's History of his own Times* (London, 1906), pp. 309–10.

11 Lauzun to Louvois Dublin 7 June 1690, Mulloy, *Franco-Irish Correspondence*, i, pp. 411–2.

12 Lord Dover to Tyrconnell, Bantry, 2 May 1690, 'Tyrconnell Papers'.

13 Lauzun to Louvois, Dublin 20 May, 7 and 26 June 1690, Mulloy *Franco-Irish Correspondence*, i, pp. 392, 412, 432; Tyrconnell to Queen Mary, Dublin 2 Apr. 1690, Tate, 'Letter-Book of Richard Talbot' p. 117; Miller, *James II*, pp. 229–30.

14 Miller, *Glorious Revolution*, pp. 43–4; Simms, 'Schomberg at Dundalk, 1689', pp. 91–104.

15 Lauzun to Louvois, Rochescastle, 30 July 1690, Mulloy, *Franco-Irish Correspondence*, i, p. 438.

16 R. Caulfield (ed.), *Journal of the Rev. Rowland Davies* (London, 1858), p. 121; Lauzun to Louvois, Ardee, 4 July 1690, Girardin to Louvois, Limerick, 19 July 1690, Mulloy *Franco-Irish Correspondence* i, pp. 443, 447.

17 Tyrconnell to Queen Mary, 26 June 1690 in 'Letter Book of Richard Talbot', p. 133.

18 *Life*, ii, pp. 392–3.

19 Tyrconnell to Mary of Modena 7 Mar. 1690, 24 June 1690, Tyrconnell to Barrillon 23 Apr. 1690, 'Letter Book of Richard Talbot', pp. 111–13, 123–4, 131; A. W. H. Pearsall, 'The War at Sea' in Maguire, *Kings in Conflict*, pp. 102–5.

20 Tyrconnell to Barillon, Dublin, 23 Apr. 1690, Tyrconnell to D'Avaux, Dublin, 23 Apr. 1690, Tyrconnell to Queen Mary, 20 May 1690, Tyrconnell to Queen Mary, 26 June 1690 in 'Letter Book of Richard Talbot', pp. 124, 127, 129–130.

21 Louvois to Lauzun, Versailles, 10 June 1690, Mulloy, *Franco-Irish Correspondence*, i, pp. 46–7.

22 Story, *Impartial History*, pp. 74–4; John Shirley, *The True and Impartial History and Wars of the Kingdom of Ireland...* (1692), p. 69.

23 Story, *Impartial History*, p. 88.

24 Jean Payen de la Fouleresse to Christian V, Duleek, 2/13 July 1690, ed. L. Barbé in *Notes and Queries* 5th series, vol. viii, 14 July 1877, p. 22.

25 Gilbert, *Jacobite Narr.*, p. 100.

26 Ibid.

27 Ibid., p. 99; Story, *Impartial History*, p. 79.

28 J. Fitzjames, *Mémoires du Maréshal de Berwick* (2 vols, Paris, 1780), pp. 70, 104.

29 Story, *Impartial History*, p. 80.

30 David Chandler, *The Art of Warfare in the Age of Marlborough* (Staplehurst, 1990), p. 77.

31 Michael McNally, *Battle of the Boyne 1690: The Irish Campaign for the English Crown* (Colchester, 2005), pp. 72–3.

32 Diarmuid and Harman Murtagh, 'The Irish Jacobite army, 1689–91' in *Irish Sword*, no. 70 (1990), p. 39; J. G. Simms, 'Lord Sarsfield of Kilmallock' in D. W. Hayton and G. O'Brien (eds), *War and Politics in Ireland 1649–1730* (London, 1986), p. 132.

33 Anon., *Missive van Syne Koninghl. Majesteyt van Groot Brittannien Geschreven in het Leger by Daleck den 12 July 1690* (The Hague, 1690), p. 2; *Life, ii, p.* 398; H. Murtagh, *The Battle of the Boyne 1690* (Drogheda, 2006), p. 45.

34 Lenihan, P. and Sheridan, G. 'A *Swiss Soldier in Ireland* 1689–1690' in *Irish Studies Review* (2005), vol. 13, no. 4, pp. 479–97.

35 George Clarke Secretary at war cited in Murtagh, *Battle of the Boyne*, p. 45.

36 *Journal of Rev. Rowland Davies*, pp. 123–4.

37 Gilbert, *Jacobite Narr.*, p. 101.

38 Lenihan, *1690 Battle of the Boyne*, pp. 177, 178; P. Berresford Ellis, *The Boyne Water, the Battle of the Boyne*, 1690 (Belfast, 1976), pp. 85–90; Story, *Impartial History*, p. 80; 'Autobiography of Dr. George Clarke' in HMC *Leyborne–Popham MS* (London, 1899), p. 271.

39 Gilbert, *Jacobite Narr.*, pp. 101–2.

40 'Poema', 6. 122–5.

41 'Duc de Tirconnell', p. 18.

42 Kjeld Hald Galster, *Danish Troops in the Williamite Army in Ireland, 1689–91* (Dublin, 2012), pp. 125–6.

43 M. Richard (ed.), *Mémoires D'Issac Dumont de Bostaquet* (Paris, 1968), pp. 236–8; Berresford-Ellis, *Boyne Water*, p. 109.

44 Lenihan, *1690 Battle of the Boyne*, pp. 214–16; Murtagh, *Battle of the Boyne*, pp. 64–5.

45 Story, *Impartial History*, p. 88; Robert Southwell to the Earl of Nottingham, Finglas, 6 July 1690, *HMC Finch MS* (2 vols, London, 1889), ii, p. 345.

46 Story, *Impartial History*, p. 86; Famechon to Louvois, Limerick 9 Aug. 1690, Mulloy, *Franco-Irish Correspondence*, iii, pp. 131–2.

47 De La Hoguette to Louvois, Limerick, 10 Aug. 1690, Mulloy, *Franco-Irish Correspondence*, ii, p 81.

48 Lenihan, *1690 Battle of Boyne*, p. 176.

49 M. O'Conor, *Military Memoirs of the Irish Nation* (Dublin, 1845), p. 109.

50 Lauzun to Seignelay, Limerick, 26 July 1690 in L. Von Ranke, *History of England* (Oxford, 1875), p. 120; Boisseleau to his wife, Cork, 16 July 1690, Zurlauben to Louvois, Limerick, 20 July 1690, Bouridal to Louvois, Brest, 28 July 1690, Mulloy *Franco-Irish Correspondence*, i, pp. 322–3, 446, 451.

51 Zurlauben to Luvois, 12 Sept. 1690, Mulloy *Franco-Irish Correspondence*, ii, p. 111.

52 C. Leslie, *An Answer to A Book Intituled The State of the Protestants in Ireland* (London, 1692), Appendix p. 71

53 Laisné to Louvois, 18 July 1690, Mulloy, *Franco-Irish Correspondence*, iii, pp. 125–6.

54 *Dick Talbot*, pp. 500–1; Lenihan, *Battle of the Boyne*, pp. 246–7; S. Mulloy, 'French eye-witnesses of the Boyne' in *Irish Sword*, no. 59 (1982), p. 109.

55 Corp, *Stuart Court in Exile*, p. 27.

56 Gilbert, *Jacobite Narr.*, p. 105; *Life*, ii, pp. 406–9.

57 *Mémoires du Maréchal de Berwick*, i, p. 104.

58 Murray, *Journal of John Stevens*, pp. 133–8

59 Bouridal to Louvois, Brest, 25 Aug. and 2 Sept. 1690, Mulloy, *Franco-Irish Correspondence*, ii, pp. 15–16, 18–19.

60 'Memoire concernant les affaires d'Irlande' nd, Mulloy, *Franco-Irish Correspondence*, iii, pp. 146–7.

61 Murray, *Journal of John Stevens*, p. 144.

62 Lord Clare to Louvois, 22 Aug. 1690, Mulloy, *Franco-Irish Correspondence*, iii, pp. 137–8.

63 Samuel Mullenaux, 'Diary of the siege of Limerick' in *The Old Limerick Journal 1690 Siege Edition*, no. 28 (1990), p. 193; J. G. Simms, 'Williamite peace tactics' in Hayton and O'Brien (eds), *War and Politics in Ireland*, p. 187.

64 Simms, 'Williamite Peace Tactics', pp. 183–4; HMC, *Finch MSS*, ii, p. 337.

65 Gilbert, *Jacobite Narr.*, p. 105; Simms, 'Williamite Peace Tactics', p. 187.

66 *HMC 12th Report, Le Fleming MSS* (London, 1890), pp. 281, 300.

67 Robert Southwell to Nottingham, 9 July 1690, HMC, *Finch MSS*, ii, p 373.

68 Sir George Clarke to Earl of Nottingham, 28 July 1690, HMC, *Finch MSS*, ii, p. 387; Lauzun to Louvois, Limerick, 10 Aug. 1690, Lauzun to Louvois, Galway, 26 Aug. 1690, Lauzun to Louvois, Galway, 3 Sept. 1690, Mulloy, *Franco-Irish Correspondence*, ii, pp. 83, 97, 104.

69 O'Connell's identity is unclear: the outlawry lists include several possible candidates, 'Maurice Connell' of Ashtown, Co. Dublin, 'Morrish Connell', Ballycarbery Co. Kerry, 'Maurice Connell', Killeveragh, Co. Kerry and 'Morgan Connell', Parteen, Co. Clare in Simms, 'Irish Jacobites', pp. 31, 74, 92, 122; D'Alton, *Irish Army List*, p. 877; Anon., *The Report of the Trustees of the Forfeited Estates in Ireland* (Dublin, 1704) pp. 149, 320; Lauzun to Louvois 26 Aug. 1690, Commissaire Fumeron to Louvois 25 Feb. 1691, Mulloy *Franco-Irish Correspondence* i, p. 237 and ii, p. 96; Sheridan, 'Narrative', p. 57; *Dick Talbot*, ii, p. 512.

70 O'Kelly, *Macariae Excidium*, pp. 46–8, 98; Marquis d'Albeville to James II, 27 Oct. 1690, Limerick, HMC, *Finch MSS*, ii, pp. 472, 474.

71 Murray, *Journal of John Stevens*, pp. 144–5.

72 Anon., *An Account of the Transactions of the Late King James in Ireland* (London, 1690), p. 61.

73 Mulloy, *Franco-Irish Correspondence*, ii, p. 445

74 G. Symcox, *The Crisis of French Sea Power 1688–1697* (The Hague, 1974), p. 101.

75 Baron Riverston to Colonel Henry Dillon, Galway 16 Aug. 1690 ('Dillon Papers', NLI microfilm no. 5312, np).

76 Thomas Sheridan 'Narrative', *HMC Stuart MSS*, vi, pp. 8–9; *Mémoires du Maréchal de Berwick*, i, p. 80; Childs, *Williamite Wars*, pp. 244–7; Lauzun to Louvois, 3 Sept. 1690, Mulloy, *Franco-Irish Correspondence*, ii, pp. 103, 105.

77 Gilbert, *Jacobite Narr.*, pp. 114, 146.

78 Constantijn Huygens den zoon, *Journaal* (Utrecht, 1876), p. 319; L. Irwin, 'Sarsfield: the man and myth' in B. Whelan (ed.), *The Last of the Great Wars* (Limerick), pp. 114–15; Rev. E. Berwick (ed.), *The Rawdon Papers* (London, 1819), p. 332.

79 Anon., *The New Method of Fortification as practiced by Monsieur de Vauban...* (London, 1691), p. 18.

80 Marquis de Feuquières, *Mémoires* (4 vols, Amsterdam, 1741), iv, pp. 193, 197; J. Turner, *Pallas Armata: Military Essayes of the Ancient Grecian, Roman and Modern Art of War ...* (London, 1683), p. 330; C. Duffy, *Fire & Stone. The Science of Fortress Warfare 1660–1860* (London, 1975), pp. 57–9; P. Lenihan, 'Ballaí Luimnigh: the sieges of Limerick' in L. Irwin et al. (eds), *Limerick History and Society* (Dublin, 2009), pp. 140–7.

81 Gilbert, *Jacobite Narr.*, pp. 115–16; Chandler, *Warfare in the Age of Marlborough*, pp. 266–7; *Mémoires du Maréchal de Berwick*, ii, pp. 168, 172, 186–7.

82 Childs, *Williamite Wars*, p. 255; Southwell to Nottingham, 28 Aug. 1690, *HMC Finch MS*, p. 429; K. Danaher and J. G. Simms (eds), *The Danish Force in Ireland 1690–1691* (Dublin, 1962), p. 72; A. Jullien (ed.), 'Journal de Jean -Francois de Morsier' in *Soldats Suisses au service étranger* (8 volumes Geneva 1908–19), vii (Geneva, 1915), p. 100.

83 Murray, *Journal of John Stevens*, pp. 176, 180; *Journal of Rev. Rowland Davies*, p. 141; R. Parker, *Memoirs of the Most Remarkable Military Transactions* (London, 1757), p. 27: R. Kane, *Campaigns of King William and Queen Anne....* (Dublin, 1748), p. 13: 'Journal de Jean-Francois de Morsier', pp. 87–105.

84 Story, *Impartial History*, p. 130; Gilbert, *Jacobite Narr.*, pp. 260–7; Boisseleau to Louvois, 20 Sept. 1690 (N. S.) in Kemmy and Walsh (eds), *The Old Limerick Journal 1690 Siege Edition*, no. 28 (1990), p. 106; S. Pufendorf, *Rebus Gestis Friderici Wilhelmi Magni* (Berlin, 1695), p. 258; Murray, *Journal of John Stevens*, pp. 177–8; *Mémoires d'Issac Dumont de Bostaquet*, p. 249.

85 Story, *Impartial History*, p. 130; W. Harris, *The History of the Life and Reign of William-Henry, Prince of Nassau and Orange* (Dublin, 1749), p. 288; R. Parker, *Memoirs of the Most Remarkable Military Transactions* (London, 1757), p. 27; Pufendorf, *Rebus Gestis*, p. 258; The figures relating to Danish troops are extracted from Würtemberg's war journal in *The Danish Force in Ireland*, pp. 73–4; A. Claudianus, *Mavor Irlandicus sive Historia de bello Hibernico* (Copenhagen, 1718), p. 55: Jean Payen de la Fouleresse to Christian V, D. Campbell to Sir Arthur Rawdon, in Kemmy and Walsh, *Old Limerick Journal 1690 Siege Edition*, pp. 120, 126, 183; G. Story *A Continuation of the Impartial History* (London, 1693), p. 39.

86 Lauzun to Louvois, Galway, 3 Sept. (N. S), Quin, 7 Sept. NS 1690, Mulloy, *Franco-Irish Correspondence*, iii, pp. 105, 107–8.

87 J. de la Brune, *Histoire de la Revolution d'Irlande* (Amsterdam, 1691), p. 164; Gilbert, *Jacobite Narr.*, p. 266; Story, *Impartial History*, p. 132; Robert Southwell to Nottingham, 28 Aug. 1690, *HMC Finch MS*, p. 434.

88 Gilbert, *Jacobite Narr.*, p. 266; *Histoire de la Revolution d'Irlande*, p. 164.

89 Cited in J. Gibney, '"Sarsfield is the word": the heroic afterlife of an Irish Jacobite', *New Hibernia Review*, vol. 15, no. 1 (Spring 2011), p. 72; Liam Irwin, 'Sarsfield: The man and the myth' in B. Whelan (ed.), *The Last of the Great Wars: Essays on the War of the Three Kings in Ireland 1688–91* (Limerick, 1995), pp. 108–26; M. McNally, *The Battle of Aughrim 1691* (Stroud, 2008), pp. 51–2.

90 Tyrconnell to Louvois, Galway, 10 Sept. 1690, NS, Mulloy, *Franco-Irish Correspondence*, ii, p. 110.

91 Simms, *Jacobite Ireland*, p. 173; Gilbert, *Jacobite Narr.*, p. 118.

92 Tyrconnell to Henry Dillon, Galway 12 Sept. 1690 ('Dillon Papers', NLI microfilm no. 5312, np).

93 D'Alton, *King James's Irish Army List*, p. 71.

94 Lauzun to Louvois, 26 Aug. 1690 (N. S.), Mulloy *Franco-Irish Correspondence*, i, p. 97; Lauzun to Louvois, Galway 13 Sept. 1690, Mulloy, *Franco-Irish Correspondence*, ii, p. 113

95 La Hoguette to Louvois, 9 Oct. 1690 (N. S.), Lauzun to Louvois, 9 Oct. 1690 (N. S.), 'Estat abregé des troupes francaises…', nd, Mulloy, *Franco-Irish Correspondence*, ii, pp. 31–3, 117–21.

96 Childs, *Williamite Wars*, pp. 277–8.

97 *Mémoires du Maréchal de Berwick*, i, pp. 88–90; Gilbert, *Jacobite Narr.*, p. 112.

98 O'Kelly, *Macariæ Excidium*, p. 54; *Dick Talbot*, ii, p. 527.

99 'Mémoire de Mylord Tirconel', Nov. 1690, Mulloy, *Franco-Irish Correspondence*, iii, p. 185.

100 'Instructions pour le sieur Fumeron', Versailles, 8 Nov. 1690 (N. S.), Mulloy, *Franco-Irish Correspondence*, i, p. 85.

101 T. Ó hAnnracháin, 'The strategic involvement of continental powers in Ireland, 1596–1691' in P. Lenihan (ed.), *Conquest and Resistance: War in Seventeenth Century Ireland* (Leiden, 2001), p. 47.

102 Bouridal to Louvois, Brest, 11 Dec. 1690 (N. S.), Bouridal to Louvois, 22 Dec. 1690 (N. S.),

Fumeron to Louvois Vannes, 22 Dec. 1690 (N. S.), Fumeron to Louvois, Brest, 8 Jan. 1691 (N. S.), Mulloy, *Franco-Irish Correspondence*, ii, pp. 64–6, 144.

103 MacErlean, *Duanaire Uí Bhruadair*, p. 140.

104 Tyrconnell to Louvois, 5 Jan. 1691, Mulloy *Franco-Irish Correspondence* ii, pp. 142–3; Macariae Excidium, pp. 74–5.

105 Abbé de Gravel to Louvois, Galway, 15/25 Dec. 1690, Mulloy, *Franco-Irish Correspondence*, iii, pp. 164–5.

106 Simms, *Jacobite Ireland*, p. 191; Santons Boullain to Louvois, 12 Jan. 1691, Mulloy, *Franco-Irish Correspondence*, ii, p. 203; O'Kelly, *Macariae Excidium*, pp. 70–1; Childs, *Williamite Wars*, p. 292.

107 Santons Boullain to Louvois, Portumna, 12 Jan. 1691 (N. S.), Sarsfield to Mountcashel, Limerick, 24 Feb. 1691 (N. S.), Mulloy, *Franco-Irish Correspondence*, ii, pp. 203, 230; Wauchope, *Patrick Sarsfield and the Williamite War*, pp. 174–5; J. Todhunter, *Life of Patrick Sarsfield Earl of Lucan* (London, 1895), pp. 122–5.

108 *Mémoires du Maréchal de Berwick*, i, p. 90.

109 Cited in P. Wauchope, *Patrick Sarsfield and the Williamite War* (Dublin, 1992), p. 192.

110 N. Genet Rouffiac, 'The wild geese in France, 1688–1715: a French perspective' in *Irish Sword*, no. 103 (2008), p. 33; R. Pillorget, 'Louis XIV and Ireland' in *The Last of the Great Wars*, p. 4.

111 Lenihan, *1690 Battle of the Boyne*, pp. 65–6; Gravel to Louvois, Mulloy, *Franco-Irish Correspondence*, iii, pp. 164, 166; M. McNally, *The Battle of Aughrim 1691* (Stroud, 2004), pp. 52–3.

112 James McGuire, 'Talbot, Richard duke of Tyrconnell', in *DIB* [dib.cambridge.org/view]; O'Kelly, *Macariæ Excidium*, p. 77.

113 O'Donnell to D'Avaux, Limerick, 4 Nov. 1690, Hogan, *Négociations*, pp. 736, 740; . J. G. Simms 'Sligo in the Jacobite war, 1689–91' in *Irish Sword*, vii, no. 27 (1965), pp. 133–4.

114 Gilbert, *Jacobite Narr.*, p. 5; P. Kelly, '"A light to the blind": the voice of the dispossessed élite in the generation after the defeat at Limerick' in *IHS*, no. 96 (Nov. 1985), p. 434.

115 Abbé de Gravel to Louvois, Galway, 25 Dec. 1690 (N. S.), Mulloy, *Franco-Irish Correspondence*, iii, p. 166; O'Kelly, *Macariae Excidium*, p. 99.

116 O'Kelly, *Macariæ Excidium* p. 75.

117 Ibid., pp. 76, 77, 81.

118 Ibid., p. 76.

119 J. A. Murphy, *Justin McCarthy Lord Mountcashel* (Cork, 1959), p. 39; Fumeron to Louvois, 28 Jan. and 16 July 1691 (N. S.), Mulloy, *Franco-Irish Correspondence*, ii, pp. 207, 363.

120 Fumeron to Louvois, Limerick, 25 Feb. 1691, Mulloy, *Franco-Irish Correspondence*, ii, pp. 236–7; Story, *Continuation*, p. 61.

121 Rev J. Trench to Bishop William King, 9 May 1691 ('Lyons Collection of the correspondence of William King', *TCD MSS 1995–2008*, fo. 126 v).

122 S. Mulloy, 'The French navy and the Jacobite war in Ireland, 1688–91' in *Irish Sword*, no. 70 (1990), p. 29; P. Lenihan, 'Strategic geography, 1641–1691' in Leniham (ed.), *Conquest and Resistance*, p. 142.

123 Tyrconnell to Louvois, camp near Athlone, 4 July 1691 (N. S.), Fumeron to Louvois,

Limerick, 10 June, 9 July 1691 (N. S.), Mulloy, *Franco-Irish Correspondence*, ii, pp. 334, 357–8, 360–1; p. 452; *Life*, ii, pp. 452, 456.

124 Fumeron to Louvois, Limerick, 25 Feb. 1691 (N. S.), Mulloy, *Franco-Irish Correspondence*, ii, pp. 237, 239; Simms, *Jacobite Ireland*, pp. 210–11.

125 'Poema', 6. 989–1000.

126 Murray, *Journal of John Stevens*, p. 208; Wauchope, *Patrick Sarsfield*, p. 212. Story, *Continuation*, p. 115; R. Doherty, *The Williamite War in Ireland* (Dublin, 1998), p. 166; H. Murtagh, 'The siege of Athlone, 1691' in *Journal of the Old Athlone Society*, vol. i, no. 3 (1972–3), p. 175; Childs, *Williamite Wars* p. 135; E. Hogan and G. Plunkett (eds), *The Jacobite War in Ireland 1688–1691* (Dublin, 1894), p. 84.

127 Gilbert, *Jacobite Narr.*, p. 131.

128 Anon., *An Exact Journal of the Victorious Progress of their Majestie's Forces…* (London, 1691), p. 20: R. Parker, *Memoirs of the Most Remarkable Military Transactions* (London, 1757), p. 34.

129 *Life* ii, p. 456; Fumeron, 19 July 1691 (N. S.), Mulloy, *Franco-Irish correspondence*, ii, p. 376; Murray, *Journal of John Stevens*, p. 19.

130 Gilbert, *Jacobite Narr.*, p. 143; *Life*, ii, p. 457; Parker, *Memoirs*, p. 34; Story, *Impartial History*, pp. 34, 128; H. Mackay, *Memoirs of the War carried on in Scotland and Ireland* (Edinburgh, 1833), p. 162.

131 Simms, *Jacobite Ireland*, p. 228; O'Kelly, *Macariae Excidium*, p. 546; M. McNally, *The battle of Aughrim 1691* (Stroud, 2008), pp. 172–3.

132 Tyrconnell to Louvois, Limerick 24 July 1691 (N. S.), Mulloy, *Franco-Irish Correspondence*, i, p. 380; Gilbert, *Jacobite Narr.*, p. 281.

133 Hogan and Plunkett, *The Jacobite War in Ireland*, p. 87; Gilbert, *Jacobite Narr.*, p. 145; Childs, *Williamite Wars*, p. 318.

134 Tyrconnell to Louvois, Limerick, 24 Aug. 1691 (N. S.), Mulloy, *Franco-Irish Correspondence*, ii, p. 380.

135 Simms, *Jacobite Ireland*, pp. 230–1; Doherty, *Williamite War*, pp. 184–5.

136 Simms, *Jacobite Ireland*, pp. 214–15; Simms, 'Williamite peace tactics', p. 194.

137 Tyrconnell to Louis XIV Limerick, 15 Aug. 1691 (N. S.), Fumeron to de Barbezieux, 16 Aug. 1691 (N.S.), Fumeron to de Barbezieux, 17 Aug. 1691 (N.S.), Tessé and d'Usson to de Barbezieux, 17 Aug. 1691 (N. S.), in Mulloy, *Franco-Irish Correspondence*, ii, pp. 396–7, 401–2, 414–15.

138 W. Harris, *History of the Life and Reign of William Henry* (3 vols, Dublin, 1789), iii, p. 177; Thomas Nugent, Earl of Westmeath to Walter Harris, 22 Aug. 1749 in J. Ferrar, *The History of Limerick, Ecclesiastical, Civil and Military* (Limerick, 1787), p. 354.

139 B. Ó Buachalla, 'Seacaibíteachas Thaidhg Uí Neachtain' in *Studia Hibernica*, no. 26 (1992), p. 44; *Life*, ii, pp. 460–1.

140 Tessé and d'Usson to de Barbezieux, 17 Aug. 1691 (N.S.), Mulloy, *Franco-Irish Correspondence*, ii pp. 414–15.

141 O'Kelly, *Macariae Excidium*, p. 97; Simms, *Jacobite Ireland*, p. 242; Childs, Williamite Wars, p. 366.

142 *Dick Talbot*, pp. 560–1.

143 'Poema' 6. 1497–1502.

SEVEN: POST MORTEM

1 Gilbert, *Jacobite Narr.*, p. 175.

2 J. McGuire 'James II and Ireland 1685–90' in W. A. Maguire (ed.), *Kings in Conflict. The Revolutionary War in Ireland and its Aftermath 1689–1750* (Belfast, 1990), p. 57.

3 Simms, *Jacobite Ireland*, p. 242.

4 H. Murtagh, 'The war in Ireland 1689–91' in Maguire (ed), *Kings in Conflict*, p. 89.

5 *The Danish Force in Ireland*, pp. 126–8, 310; William III to Ginckel, 27 Sept. 1691, N. Japiske (ed.), *Correspondentie van Willem III* (The Hague, 1927), iii, p. 27; HMC *Leyborne-Poham MS* (London, 1899), p. 279; Story, *Continuation*, pp. 224, 538.

6 Simms, *Jacobite Ireland*, pp. 242–3; Tate, 'Franco-Irish correspondence', pp. 226–8; J. G. Simms, 'Williamite peace tactics 1690–1' in *IHS*, vol. 8 no. 32 (1953) p. 320; Fumeron to Barbezieux, Limerick, 18 Sept. (N. S.) 1691, Mulloy, *Franco-Irish Correspondence*, ii, pp. 489, 491–2.

7 Story, *Continuation*, pp. 207, 216; Mulloy, *Franco-Irish Correspondence*, ii, p. 540; Doherty, *Williamite War*, pp. 190–2.

8 Childs, *Williamite Wars*, pp. 378–9; O'Kelly, *Macariae Excidium*, p. 102; Gilbert, *Jacobite Narr.*, pp. 161–3; Sarsfield to Mountcashel, Limerick, 24 Feb. 1691, Commissaire Bouridal to de Berbezieux, Brest, 17 Oct. (N. S.) 1691, Fumeron to de Berbezieux, Limerick, 26 Sept. (N. S.) 1691, Mulloy, *Franco-Irish Correspondence*, ii, pp. 232–3, 433, 502.

9 Story, *Continuation*, p. 225; Mulloy, *Franco-Irish Correspondence*, ii, pp. 401–2, p. 541.

10 Ginckel to Lords Justices, 23 Sept. 1691, *HMC, Fourth Report* (London, 1874), p. 323.

11 *Mémoires du Maréchal de Berwick*, i, pp. 102–3: Simms, *Jacobite Ireland*, p. 257; HMC, Leyborne-Popham MS, pp. 280–1; Simms, 'Williamite Peace Tactics, p. 322.

12 C. Rousset, *Histoire de Louvois* (Paris, 1891), iv, pp. 542–3.

13 Parker, *Memoirs*, p. 38. Childs, *The British Army of William III 1689–1702*, pp. 215–8.

14 Gilbert, *Jacobite Narr.*, p. 178.

15 Simms, 'The treaty of Limerick' in *War and Politics in Ireland*, p. 205; Idem, *The Williamite Confiscation in Ireland 1690–1703* (London, 1956), p. 161.

16 Anon., *A Diary of the Siege and Surrender of Lymerick with the Articles at Large, both Civil and Military* (London, 1692), p. 19; Anon., *An Account from Ireland of the Death of the Late Earl of Tyrconnell* (London, 1691) p. 1.

17 Claudianus, *Mavor Hibernicus*, p. 134.

18 Charles O'Kelly. *The Jacobite War in Ireland 1688–1691*, eds Plunkett and Hogan (Dublin, 1894), p. 107.

19 Simms, *The Williamite Confiscation*, p. 56.

20 J. Macpherson (ed.), *Original Papers Containing the Secret History of Great Britain from the Restoration to the Accession of the House of Hannover* (2 vols, London), i, p. 202; Gilbert, *Jacobite Narr.*, p. 148.

21 W. A. Maguire, 'The land settlement' in Maguire (ed.), *Kings in Conflict*, p. 143; Warrant to Lord Lieutenant Sydney, 22 Mar. 1693, *CSPD, William & Mary 1693*, p. 77; W. Troost, 'Letters from Van Homrigh to Ginkel, 1692–1799' in *Anal. Hib.*, no 33 (1986), pp. 62–3, 67.

22 J. F. Michaud and J. J. Poujelet (eds), *Mémoires du Maréchal de Villars* (Paris, 1839), p. 44.

23 Gilbert, *Jacobite Narr.*, p. 178.

24 J. Debrett, *The Peerage of the United Kingdom of Great Britain & Ireland* (2 vols, London, 1814), i, p. 442.

25 Simms, *Williamite Confiscation*, p. 182.

26 Duchess of Tyrconnell to Duchess of Marlborough, 3 Oct. 1698; Idem, 6 Nov. 1698 (BL Add. MSS 61453 fos 85, 90).

27 G. S. Steinman, *Althorp Memoirs* (1869), pp. 68–9; D. W. Hayton (ed.), *The Parliamentary Diary of Sir Richard Cocks 1698–1702* (Oxford, 1996), p. 230.

28 *Althorp Memoirs*, pp. 67–8; Lady Rachel. V. Russell to Dr Fitzwilliam, 15 Jan. 1686 in T. Selwood (ed.), *The Letters of Lady Rachel Russell* (2 vols, London, 1819), i, p. 81.

29 Melville Henry Massue Ruvigny, *The Jacobite Peerage, Baronetage, Knightage, and Grants of Honour*, Extracted … (Edinburgh, 1904), p. 177; Deirdre Bryan, 'Talbot, Frances Jennings duchess of Tyrconnell', in *DIB.* (dib. cambridge. org/viewReadPage. do?articleId=a8447)

30 *Dublin Weekly Journal* 13 Mar. 1730–1; Hore, 'Richard Talbot Earl and Duke of Tyrconnell', p. 285; D. Ryan, *Blasphemers and Blackguard: The Irish Hellfire Clubs* (Dublin, 2012), pp. 22–4.

31 F. Elrington Ball, *The Judges in Ireland, 1221–1921* (2 vols, London, 1926), i, p. 365; *Dick Talbot*, ii, p. 643.

32 James II to the Archbishop of Armagh, 7 May 1685, *CSPD James II, p.* 149; O'Callaghan, *Irish Brigades*, p. 262; G. E. Cokayne, *The Complete Peerage of England, Scotland, Ireland, Great Britain and the United Kingdom, Extant, Extinct, or Dormant* (13 vols, London, 1910), 12, p. 123.

33 Marc Serge Rivière, 'The earl of Tyrconnell's impact on Franco-Prussian relations (1750–2)' in *Eighteenth-Century Ireland*, vol. 15 (2000), pp. 120–1.

34 Anon., *Memoirs of the Court of France and City of Paris* (London, 1702), p. 25.

35 J. Childs, *The Army, James II, and the Glorious Revolution* (Manchester, 1980), p. 42.

36 *HMC 8th Report* (London, 1881), p. 391: Childs, *Williamite Wars* (London, 2007), pp. 45–6.

37 R. Hayes, 'Biographical dictionary of Irishmen in France: Part XX' in *Studies: An Irish Quarterly Review*, vol. 36, no. 142 (Jun., 1947), p. 221; O'Callaghan, *Irish Brigades*, p. 39.

38 *Memoirs of the Court of France and City of Paris*, p. 26

39 Haile, *Mary of Modena*, pp. 292, 313.

40 Quincy, *Histoire Militaire*, iii, p. 680.

CONCLUSION: A STUDY IN FAILURE

1 Anon., *A Vindication of the Present Government of Ireland* (London, 1688), p. 4.

2 Jenny Wormald, *Mary Queen of Scots: A Study in Failure* (London & New York, 1991); John Callow, *The Making of James II: The Formative Years of a Fallen King* (Stroud, 2000); S. R. Gardiner, *Oliver Cromwell* (London, 1899), p. 316; J. S. Morrill, *Oliver Cromwell and the English Revolution* (Cambridge, 1990), p. 283.

3 B. Ó Buachalla, 'Irish Jacobite poetry', *Irish Review*, no. 12 (Spring–Summer 1992), p. 48: Ó Ciardha, *Fatal Attachment*, pp. 347–67.

4 Albertus Warren, *A Panegyrick to his Excellency…* (Dublin, 1686).

5   Eamon Darcy, *The Irish Rebellion of 1641 and the Wars of the Three Kingdoms* (Woodbridge, 2013), p. 165.

6   Gilbert, *Jacobite Narr.* p. 22.

7   'Irish Narrative', p. 20; John Lynch, *De Praesulibus Hiberniae* (2 vols, Dublin, 1944), i, p. 323.

8   Earl of Sutherland to the Lords Justices, 12 May 1685 and James II to the Archbishop of Armagh and the Earl of Granard, 7 May 1685, *CSPD James II*, pp. 147, 149.

9   *Mémoires du Maréchal de Berwick*, i, p. 94.

10 Demetrius McEncroe, *Calamus Hibernicus* (Paris, 1728), p. 21.

11 Letter from Sir Richard Nagle to Viscount Merrion, Limerick, 14 Aug. 1691, Gilbert, *Jacobite Narr.*, p. 282.

12 McGuire, 'Richard Talbot earl of Tyrconnell (1630–91) and the Catholic counter-revolution', p. 75; 'Cui Tros et Rutulus simul indiscreta fuere Nomina', 'Poema', 6.1495.

13 Sir Walter Scott, *A Collection of Scarce and Valuable Tracts, on the Most Interesting and Entertaining Subjects* (London, 1814), p. 97.

14 *Life*, pp. 392–3.

15 Murray, *Journal of John Stevens*, p. 144; Lord Clare to Louvois, 22 Aug. (N. S.) 1690, in Mulloy (ed.), *Franco-Irish Correspondence*, iii, p. 137; Simms, 'Williamite peace tactics 1690–91', p. 187.

16 O'Kelly, *Macariae Excidium*, pp. 100–1.

Bibliography

MANUSCRIPT SOURCES

1641 Depositions (TCD MS 810, 813, 816, 818) (1641.tcd.ie).

A. L., *A True Relation of the Late Expedition...*, 1642 (NLI LO P 39 (4)).

Anon., Le Duc de Tirconnell, c.1700 (NLI MS 118).

A. Anselme, 'L'homme Fidele où Discours Panegerique en faveur De Monsieur Le Comte de Tirconnel Viceroi d'Irlande', in Recueil de copies de pièces françaises et latines, en prose et en vers, sur les affaires d'Angleterre, d'Irlande et de France, sous Jacques II, Jacques III et Louis XIV, etc.' (BNF, MS Français 12160, fos 169–194).

Sir N. Armorer to Williamson, 30 Oct. 1673 (SP 29/337, fo. 224).

J. Bolton to unk, Derry 13 October 1706 ('Letters and Papers of the Talbot Family Barons de Malahide', NLI, microfilm, No. 9741).

Sir Arnold Braems to Edward Montagu, Earl of Sandwich, Lisbon Roads, 16/26 Jan. 1662 (*Carte MS* 73, fo. 531).

Walter Dawson to Darce Barrett, 16 Mar., 1689 ('Barrett–Lennard papers', PRONI T2529/6, no. 108).

William Ellis to Colonel Henry Dillon, Dublin 30 December 1688 ('Dillon Papers', NLI microfilm, no. 9741).

George Fitzgerald, The Earl of Kildare's Letter Book (PRONI MS D.3078/3.1/5).

James Johnston to unk, 6/16 Feb. 1688 (University of Nottingham archive, Pw A 2141) [www.nottingham.ac.uk/mss/elearning/conflict/theme1/documents.aspx].

'The Lyons Collection of the correspondence of William King' (TCD, MS 1995–2008).

Baron Nugent of Riverston, 'Poema de Hibernia', c.1695 (Dublin City Public Library, Gilbert MS 141).

'Minute and entry book of the Committee for Ireland' (Privy Council Office: Miscellaneous Books and Correspondence Registers, SP, PC 6/2, fos 2–3, 9–10).

Recognizances of Lord Dungan and others to the Duke of Ormond, Lord Lieutenant, for the safe custody of Colonel Richard Talbot, now a prisoner in Dublin Castle, but permitted by his Grace to visit his sick wife, upon obligation to return upon command, Dublin 1679 (Bodl. Carte MS 38, fo. 687).

Ormond to Henry Coventry, Dublin 8 November 1679 (Bodl. Carte MS 146, fos 227–9).

Richard Talbot to Ormond, Dublin Castle, 20 March 1679 (Bodl. Carte MS 38, fo. 691).

Warrant for Sir Thomas Newcomen Baronet of Sutton, Co. Dublin to be a privy councillor of Ireland, 1676 (BL Stowe MS 210, fo. 127).

John Churchill to Sarah Churchill, 15 January 1680 (BL Add MS 61327, fo.97 v).

Henry Hyde Earl of Clarendon to James II, 14 August 1686, ('Western Manuscripts', BL Add. MS 15894, fo. 119).

Charles Paulet 6th Marquess of Winchester to Sir Leoline Jenkins Secretary of State, Bolton 20 Oct. 1683 (SP 29/433, fo. 295).

Robert Spencer, 2nd Earl of Sunderland, Letter to a friend, 1689 ('Osborne Correspondence', BL Add MS 28053, fo. 386).

William Stewart, 'Lord Mountjoy's History' ('Gilbert Collection', Dublin Corporation Library, MS 109).

William Stewart Viscount Mountjoy to Lord Middleton, 6 March 1688 (BL Add. MS 41805, fo. 16).

Richard Talbot to Fitzhardinge, 30 September and 20 November 1662 ('Sackville Correspondence', Centre for Kentish Studies, Maidstone, CKS-U269C30).

Richard Talbot to Essex, London, 26 May 1676, (BL Stowe MS 200–17, fos 256–8).

Tyrconnell to James II, Dublin 17 March 1688 (BL Add MS 28053S, fos 253–4).

Tyrconnell to James II, Dublin 28 March 1688 ('Hyde Papers and Correspondence', BL, Add MS 32095, fo. 259).

Tyrconnell to James II, Dublin 3 October 1688 (BL Add MS 28053S, fos, 34–6).

Tyrconnell to James II, Dublin 29 January 1689 (BL Add MS 28053, fo. 387).

Tyrconnell to Colonel Henry Dillon, Dublin 6 January 1689 ('Dillon Papers', NLI microfilm no. 9741).

Tyrconnel's proceedings in Ireland' Dublin, 17 January 1690 (NLI microfilm no. 9741).

Rev J. Trench to Bishop William King', 9 May 1691 ('Lyons Collection of the correspondence of William King', TCD MSS 1995–2008, fo.126 v).

Unk to Duke of Queensberry', London 25 December 1688 (BL Add. MS 28053, fo. 380).

Peter Walsh to Ormond, London 25 March 1679 (Bodl. Carte MS 216, fos. 5–6).

Notes by Joseph Williamson, 28 September 1678 (SP 29/406, fo. 125).

PRINTED SOURCES

Airy, Osmund (ed.), *Essex Papers 1672–1679*. London, 1890.

Anon, *A Great Fight at Sea… Also a bloudy Fight in Ireland.* London, 6 November 1651.

Anon, *An Account of the Publick Affairs in Ireland since the discover of the Late Plot.* London 1679.

Anon, *A Vindication of the Present Government of Ireland under his excellency Richard, earl of Tirconnel.* London, 1688.

Anon, *An Account of the Late, Horrid and Bloody Massacre in Ireland.* London, 1689.

Anon, *An Exact list of the lords spiritual and temporal who sat in the pretended parliament at Dublin…* London, 1689.

Anon, *A True and Impartial Account of the Most Material Passages in Ireland.* London, 1689.

Anon, *The Judgement and Indictment of John Price esq.* London, 1689.

Anon, *The Popish Champion.* London, 1689.

Anon, *A faithful history of the northern affairs of Ireland from the late K. James accession to the crown, to the siege of Londonderry.* London, 1690.

Anon, *Missive van Syne Koninghl. Majesteyt van Groot Brittannien Geschreven in het Leger by Daleck den 12 July 1690*. The Hague, 1690.

Anon, *An Exact journal of the victorious progress of their Majestie's forces...* London, 1691.

Anon, *The New Method of Fortification as practiced by Monsieur de Vauban...* London, 1691.

Anon, *Memoirs of the Court of France and City of Paris*. London, 1702.

Anon, *The Report of the Trustees of the forfeited estates in Ireland*. Dublin, 1704.

Anon, *A Collection of State Tracts published during the reign of William III*. 3 vols, London, 1707.

Anon, *The Secret History of Europe*. London, 1712.

Anon, *A New and General Biographical Dictionary*. 11 vols, London 1761.

Barbé, Louis (ed.), 'The Battle of the Boyne', in *Notes and Queries*, Fifth Series, viii, 185 July 1877.

Berwick, Edward (ed.), *The Rawdon Papers*. London, 1819.

Bindon, S. H. (ed.), *The Historical Works of the Rev. Nicholas French*. Dublin, 1846.

Boyce, Joseph, *A Vindication of the Reverend Mr. Alexander Osborn, in reference to the affairs of the north of Ireland*. London, 1690.

Buckeley, W. E. (ed.), *Memoirs of Thomas, Earl of Ailesbury*. 2 vols, London, 1890.

De Burgh, Ulick, *Letter Book of the Earl of Clanricard 1643–47*, ed. John Lowe. Dublin, 1983.

Bray, William (ed.), *Diary and Correspondence of John Evelyn*. 4 vols, London, 1854.

Bruce, Thomas, Earl of Ailesbury, *Memoirs*, ed. W. E. Buckley. 2 vols, Cambridge, 1890.

De la Brune, Jean, *Histoire de la Revolution d'Irlande*. Amsterdam, 1691.

Calendar of the Patent and Close Rolls of Chancery in Ireland: of the Reign of Charles the First. First to Eight Year, Inclusive, ed. James Morrin. Dublin, 1863.

Campana, Emilia, Marquise di Cavelli, *Les Derniers Stuarts à Saint-Germain en Laye*. 2 vols, Paris, 1871.

Capel, Arthur, Earl of Essex, *Letters written by his Excellency Arthur Capel Earl of Essex*. London, 1770.

Carpenter, Andrew (ed.), *Verse in English from Tudor and Stuart Ireland*. Cork, 2003.

Carte, Thomas (ed.), *A Collection of Original Letters and Papers concerning the Affairs of England from among the Duke of Ormond's Papers*. 2 vols, London, 1739.

Cartwright, Thomas, *The Diary of Dr. Thomas Cartwright, Bishop of Chester*, ed. Joseph Hunter. London, 1843.

Caulfield, Richard (ed.), *Journal of the Rev. Rowland Davies*. London, 1858.

Christie, W. D. (ed.), *Letters Addressed from London to Sir Joseph Williamson*. 2 vols, London, 1874.

Claudianus, Andreas, *Mavor Irlandicus sive Historia de bello Hibernico*. Copenhagen, 1718.

Coate, Mary (ed.), *The Letter-Book of John Viscount Mordaunt 1658–1660*. London, 1945.

Crofton Croker, Thomas (ed.), *Narratives Illustrative of the Contests in Ireland in 1641 and 1690*. London, 1849.

CSPD Charles II, 1668–9, ed. M. A. Everett Greene. London, 1894 [www.british-history.ac.uk/source].

CSPD Charles II, 1671, ed. F. H. Blackburne Daniell. London, 1895 [www.british-history.ac.uk/source].

CSPD Charles II, 1673–5, ed. F. H. Blackburne Daniell. London, 1904 [www.british-history.ac.uk/source].

CSPD Charles II, 1679–80, ed. F. H. Blackburne Daniell. London, 1915 [www.british-history. ac.uk/source].

CSPD Charles II, 1680–1681, ed. F. H. Blackburne Daniell. London, 1921 [www.british-history. ac.uk/source].

CSPD Charles II, 1683: July–September, eds F. H. Blackburne Daniell and Francis Bickley. London, 1934 [www.british-history.ac.uk/source].

CSPD James II, 1686–7, ed. E. K. Timings. London, 1964 [www.british-history.ac.uk/ source].

CSPI James I, 1606–08, eds C.W. Russell and J. P. Prendergast. London, 1874.

CSPI James I, 1611–1614, eds C.W. Russell and J.P. Prendergast. London, 1877.

Deputy keeper of the public records, *Thirty-second annual report: appendix one* London, 1871.

Deputy Keeper of the Public Records in Ireland, *The Third Report of the Deputy Keeper of the Public Records in Ireland* Dublin, 1871.

Ellis, G. A. (ed.), *The Ellis Correspondence*. 2 vols, London, 1829.

Ellis, Henry (ed.), *Original Letters Illustrative of English History*. 4 vols, London, 1827.

Ellison Gibson, Thomas (ed.), *A Cavalier's Note Book; Being Notes, Ancedotes & Observations of William Blundell*. London, 1880.

Everard, Edmund, *The Depositions and Examinations of Mr. Edmund Everard*. London, 1679.

Feiling, Keith (ed.), 'Two unprinted letters of Henrietta Stuart, Duchess of Orleans' in *EHR*, vol 43, no. 171, Jul. 1928.

Ferrar, John, *The History of Limerick, Ecclesiastical, Civil and Military*. Limerick, 1787.

Firth, C. H. (ed.), 'Thomas Scot's account of his actions as intelligencer during the Commonwealth' in *EHR*, vol. xii, no. 45, Jan. 1897.

Fitzgerald, David, *A Narrative of the Irish Popish Plot, for the betraying that Kingdom into the hands of the French, Massacring all English Protestants there, and utter subversion of the Government and Protestant Religion...* London 1680.

Fitzjames, James, *Mémoires du Maréshal de Berwick*. 2 vols, Paris, 1780.

Foxcroft, H. C. (ed.), *The Life and Letters of Sir George Savile*. 2 vols, London, 1898.

Gibney, John (ed.), 'Some remarks on those who were friends and enemyes to the Duke of Ormond and to the Acts of Settlement of Ireland', *Anal. Hib.*, no. 42, 2011.

Gilbert, J.T. (ed.), *A contemporary history of affairs in Ireland, from 1641 to 1652...* 3 vols, Dublin, 1879.

——— (ed.), *A Jacobite Narrative of the War in Ireland, 1688–91*. Dublin, 1892: reprint, with introduction by idem, Shannon, 1971.

Grey, Anchitell (ed.), *Debates of the House of Commons from 1667 to 1694*. 10 vols, 1769.

Griffin, Richard, Lord Braybrooke (ed.), *Diary and Correspondence of Samuel Pepys*. 5 vols, London, 1849.

Hamilton, Anthony, *Memoirs of the Comte de Gramont*, ed. D. Hughes London, 1965.

Hargrave, Francis (ed.), *A Complete Collection of State Trials*. 2 vols, Dublin, 1795.

Harris, Walter, *The History of the Life and Reign of William-Henry, Prince of Nassau and Orange*. Dublin, 1749.

HMC *Sixth Report of the Royal Commission on Historical Manuscripts*. London, 1877.

HMC *Twelfth Report: Appendix Part VI The Manuscripts of the House of Lords 1689–90*. London, 1889.

HMC *Twelfth Report: Appendix Part VII The Manuscripts of S. H. Le Fleming and Others.* London, 1890.

HMC *Report on the Manuscripts of Sir William Fitzherbert, Bart., and Others.* London, 1893.

HMC *Fourteenth Report: Appendix Part IV.* London, 1894.

HMC *Report on the Manuscripts of F. W. Leyborne-Popham.* London, 1899.

HMC *Calendar of the Manuscripts of the Marquess of Ormonde at Kilkenny Castle, New Series.* 8 vols, London, 1902–20.

HMC *Reports on the Manuscripts of George Allen Finch, of Burley-on-the-Hill, Rutland.* 4 vols, London, 1913–65.

Hogan, Edmind (ed.), *History of the Warr of Ireland from 1641 to 1653 by a British Officer.* Dublin, 1873.

Hogan, James (ed.), *Négociations de M. Le Comte D'Avaux en Irlande 1689–90.* Dublin, 1934.

Hore, H. F. (ed.), 'The Rental Book of Gerald, ninth Earl of Kildare, AD 1518', in *Kilkenny Arch. Soc. Jn.*, v, Dublin, 1867.

Huygens, Constantijn, *Journaal van Constantijn Huygens, den Zoon, van 21 Oct. 1688 tot 2 Sept. 1696.* Utrecht, 1876.

Hyde, Edward, Earl of Clarendon, *The History of the Rebellion and Civil Wars in Ireland.* London, 1720.

——— *The Continuation of the Life of Edward Earl of Clarendon.* 3 vols, Dublin, 1759.

Hyde, Henry, *The State Letters of Henry Earl of Clarendon Lord Lieutenant of Ireland during the reign of King James the Second: and his Lordship's diary for the years 1687, 1688, 1689, and 1690.* 2 vols, Oxford, 1763.

Jennings, Brendan (ed.), *Wild Geese in Spanish Flanders 1582–1700: Documents relating to Irish regiments from the Archives Genéral du Royaume and other sources.* Dublin, 1964.

Jullien, A. (ed.), 'Journal de Jean-François de Morsier' in *Soldats Suisses au service étranger* 8 volumes. Geneva, 1908–1919.

Jusserand, J. J. (ed.), *A French Ambassador at the Court of Charles the Second.* London, 1892.

Kane, Richard, *Campaigns of King William and Queen Anne...* Dublin, 1748.

Kazner, J. F. A., *Leben Friedrichs von Schonburg.* 2 vols, Mannheim, 1789.

Kemmy, Jim and Larry Walsh (eds), *The Old Limerick Journal*, 1690 Siege edition, no 28, 1990.

Leslie, Charles, An *Answer to a Book Intituled The State of the Protestants in Ireland.* London, 1692.

Lodge, John, *The Peerage of Ireland.* 7 vols, London 1789.

Ludlow, Edmund, *Memoirs.* 3 vols, London, 1721.

Luttrell, Nicholas, *A Brief Relation of State Affairs from September 1678 to April 1714.* 6 vols, Oxford, 1857.

Lynch, John, *Cambrensis Eversus*, ed. Matthew Kelly. 3 vols, Dublin 1848–52.

——— *De Praesulibus Hiberniae*, ed. J. F. O'Doherty. 2 vols, Dublin, 1944.

Lynch, Patrick (ed.), *The Earl of Castlehaven's Memoirs.* Dublin, 1815.

Lytton Sells, Arthur (ed.), *The memoirs of James II: His Campaigns as Duke of York.* London, 1962.

Mac Fhinn, P. E. (ed.), 'Scríbhinní i gCartlainn an Vatican: Tuarascbhail' in *Anal. Hib.*, no. 16, Mar. 1946.

MacErlean, J. C. (ed.), *Duanaire Dháibhidh Uí Bhruadair.* 3 vols, London, 1913.

Mackay, Hugh, *Memoirs of the War Carried on in Scotland and Ireland.* Edinburgh, 1833.

Mackenzie, John, *A Narrative of the Siege of Londonderry: Or the late memorable transactions of that city.* London, 1690.

Mackintosh, James, *Review of the Causes of the Revolution of 1688*. Philadelphia, 1846.

—— *The Miscellaneous Works of Sir James Mackintosh*. 3 vols, London, 1854.

Macpherson, James (ed.), *Original Papers: Containing The Secret History of Great Britain*. 2 vols, London, 1775.

Magalotti, Lorenzo, *Lorenzo Magalotti at the court of Charles II: his Relazione d'Inghilterra of 1668*, ed. W. E. Knowles Middleton. Ontario, 1980.

Marvell, Andrew, 'Second advice to a painter' in *Poems on Affairs of State; Augustan Satirical Verse, 1660–1714*, ed. G. F. Lord. 3 vols, New Haven, 1963.

Maunde Thompson, Edward (ed.), *Correspondence of the Family of Hatton*. 2 vols, London 1878.

McNeill, Charles (ed.), *The Tanner Letters*. Dublin, 1943.

Meehan, C. P., *The Rise and Fall of the Irish Franciscan Monasteries: and memoirs of the Irish hierarchy in the seventeenth century...* 5th edn, Dublin, 1877.

Melvin, Patrick and Lord Longford (eds), 'Letters of Lord Longford and Others on Irish Affairs 1689–1702', in *Anal. Hib.*, no. 32, 1985.

De Mesmes, Claude, Comté d'Avaux, *Négociations du comte d'Avaux en Hollande depuis 1679 jusqu'en 1688*. 4 vols, Paris, 1754.

Mhág Craith, Cuthbert, 'Toirdhealbhach Ó Conchubhair' in Franciscan Fathers (eds), *Father Luke Wadding Commemorative Volume*. Dublin, 1957

Moran, P. F. (ed.), *Spicilegium Ossoriense: Being a Collection of Original Letters and Papers Illustrative of the history of the Irish Church*. 3 vols, Dublin 1874–8.

——, (ed.), *Memoir of the Ven. Oliver Plunket, archbishop of Armagh and primate of all Ireland...* Dublin, 1895.

Mulloy, Sheila (ed.), *Franco-Irish Correspondence December 1688–February 1692*. 3 vols, Dublin, 1983–4.

Murray, John (ed.), *The Diary of Samuel Pepys*. London, 1891.

Murray, R. H. (ed.), *The Journal of John Stevens containing a brief account of the war in Ireland, 1689–1691*. Oxford, 1912.

'NN', *The Polititians Cathechisme*. Antwerp, 1658.

O'Conor, Matthew, *Military Memoirs of the Irish Nation*. Dublin, 1845.

Ó Donnchadha, Tadgh (ed.), 'Cín Lae Ó Mealláin', in *Anal. Hib.*, no. 3. Dublin, 1931.

O'Kelly, Charles, *Macariae Excidium or The Destruction of Cyprus*, ed. J. C. O'Callaghan. Dublin, 1850.

—— *The Jacobite War in Ireland 1688–1691*, ed. Edmund Hogan and George Plunkett Dublin, 1894.

O'Mahony, Conor, *An Argument Defending the Right of the Kingdom of Ireland 1645*, ed. John Minihane Aubane. Cork, 2010.

Oldmixon, John, *Memoirs of Ireland*. London, 1716.

Parker, Robert, *Memoirs of the Most Remarkable Military Transactions*. London, 1757.

Partington, Thomas, *Worse and worse newes from Ireland...* London, 1641.

Pas, Antoine de, Marquis de Feuquières, *Mémoires de M. le Feuquières, contenans ses maximes sur la guerre, et l'application des exemples aux maximes...* 4 vols, Amsterdam, 1741.

Payne Collier, John (ed.), *Seven English Poetical Miscellanies*. London, 1867.

Pearson, J. N. (ed.), *The Whole Works of Robert Leighton, D.D.: Archbishop of Glasgow*. 2 vols, London, 1827.

Penn, Granville (ed.), *Memorials of Sir William Penn.* 2 vols, London, 1833.

Pike, C. E. (ed.), *Selections from the Correspondence of Arthur Capel, Earl of Essex, 1675–1677.* London, 1913.

Plunkett, G. N. and E. I. Hogan (eds), *The Jacobite War in Ireland 1688–1691.* Dublin, 1894.

De Pufendorf, Samuelis, *Rebus Gestis Friderici Wilhelmi Magni.* Berlin, 1695.

Ramsay, Andrew, the Chevalier, *The Memoirs of the Viscount de Turenne.* London, 1765.

Refaussé, Raymond and Colin Lennon (eds), *The Registers of Christ Church Cathedral Dublin.* Dublin, 1998.

Richard, Michel (ed.), *Mémoires D'Issac Dumont de Bostaquet.* Paris, 1968.

Samson, Thomas, *A Narrative of the Late Popish Plot in Ireland.* London, 1680.

Savile, Henry, 'Advice to a painter to draw the duke by' in G. F. Lord (ed.), *Poems on Affairs of State: Augustan Satirical Verse, 1660–1714.* 3 vols, New Haven, CT, 1963.

Sévin, Charles, marquis de Quincy, *Histoire militaire du regne de Louis le Grand, roy de France.* 7 vols, Paris, 1726.

Sheridan, Thomas, 'A discourse on the rise and power of parliaments', in Saxe Bannister ed., *Some Revelations in Irish history: or, Old Elements of Creed and Class Conciliation* London, 1870.

———— 'An historical account of some remarkable matters concerning King James the Second's succession…' in HMC, *Stuart Manuscripts, vi.* London, 1916.

Shirley, John, *The true and impartial history and wars of the Kingdom of Ireland…* London, 1692.

Simington, R. C., *Civil Survey: County of Meath, v.* Dublin, 1940.

———— and John MacLellan eds. 'Oireachtas List of Outlaws, 1641–1647' in *Anal. Hib.,* no. 23, 1966.

Singer, S. W. (ed.), *The Correspondence of Henry Hyde, Earl of Clarendon, and of his brother, Laurence Hyde Earl of Rochester.* 2 vols, London, 1828.

Stackhouse, Thomas (ed.), *Abridgement of Bishop Burnet's History of his own times.* London, 1724.

———— (ed.), *Bishop Burnet's History of His Own Times.* London 1906.

Story, George, *A True and Impartial History of the most material occurrences in the kingdom of Ireland during the last two years.* London, 1691.

———— *A Continuation of the Impartial History.* London, 1693.

De Rapin, Paul, *The History of England,* ed. Nicholas Tindal. London, 1732.

Talbot, Richard, Earl of Tyrconnel, *By the Lord Deputy General… A Declaration.* Dublin, 1688.

———— 'Letter-book of Richard Talbot' ed. Lilian Tate, in *Anal. Hib.,* no. 4, 1932.

Tate, Lilian (ed.), 'Franco-Irish Correspondence in the Archives Nationales, Paris: Dépôt de la Guerre', *Anal. Hib.,* no. 21, 1959.

Thurloe, John, *A collection of the State Papers of John Thurloe, Secretary of State 1652–8,* ed. Thomas Birch. 7 vols, London, 1742.

Turner, James, *Pallas Armata: Military Essays of the Ancient Grecian, Roman and Modern Art of War.* London, 1683.

Walker, Edward, *A Circumstantial Account of the Preparations for the Coronation of His Majesty King Charles the Second.* London, 1820.

Walker, George, *A True Account of the Siege of Londonderry.* London, 1689.

Wall, Thomas (ed.), Thomas Burke, *Hibernia Dominicana*. Cologne, 1762: republished London, 1970.

Walsh, Robert, *A True Narrative and Manifest, set forth by Sir Robert Walsh*. London, 1679.

Warner, G. F. (ed.), *The Nicholas Papers, Correspondence of Sir Edward Nicholas*. 4 vols, London, 1897.

Williams, Lynn (ed.), *Letters from the Pyrenees: Don Luis Méndez de Haro's Correspondence to Philip IV of Spain, July to September 1659*. Exeter, 2000.

Wilson, Robert, *The Friar Disciplined or Animadversions on Friar Peter Walsh*. Ghent, 1674.

SECONDARY WORKS

Adolph, Anthony, T*he King's Henchman: Henry Jermyn Stuart Spymaster and Architect of the British Empire*. London, 2012.

Aiazza, Giuseppe, *The Embassy in Ireland of Monsignor G. B. Rinuccini, archbishop of Fermo in the years 1645–49*, trans. Annie Hutton. Dublin, 1873.

Aubrey, Philip, *Mr Secretary Thurloe: Cromwell's Secretary of State, 1652–1660*. Athlone, 1990.

Atkinson, C. T., 'Charles II's Regiments in France, 1672–1678', in *Journal of Army Historical Research*, no. 23, 1945.

Barclay, Andrew, 'The Rise of Edward Colman' in *Historical Journal*, vol. 42, no. 1, Mar. 1999.

Barnard, T. C., 'Conclusion. Settling and Unsettling Ireland' and 'The Cromwellian and Williamite Revolutions' in Jane Ohlmeyer ed., *Ireland From Independence to Occupation 1641–1660* Cambridge, 1995.

——— 'Introduction: The Dukes of Ormond' in idem and Jane Fenlon (eds), *The Dukes of Ormond 1610–1745*. Suffolk, 2000.

Beckett, J. C., *The Cavalier Duke: a life of James Butler, 1st Duke of Ormond*. Belfast, 1990.

Berresford Ellis, Peter, *The Boyne Water, the Battle of the Boyne, 1690*. Belfast, 1976.

Bevan, Bryan, *Marlborough the Man: A Biography of John Churchill first Duke of Marlborough*. London, 1975.

Bottigheimer, K. S., *English Money and Irish Land*. Oxford, 1971.

——— 'The Restoration land settlement in Ireland; A Structural View' in *IHS*, vol. xviii, no. 69, Mar. 1972.

Breed, Brian, *Pastoral Inscriptions: Reading and Writing Virgil's Eclogues*. London, 2006.

Briggs, Robin, *Early Modern France 1560–1715*. 2nd edn, Oxford, 1998.

Burke, James, 'The new model army and the problems of siege warfare, 1648–51' in *IHS*, no. 105, May 1990.

——— 'Siege warfare in seventeenth-century Ireland' in Pádraig Lenihan (ed.), *Conquest and Resistance war in Seventeenth-Century Ireland*. Leiden, 2001.

Burke, W. P., *The Irish Priests in the Penal Times 1660–1760*. Waterford, 1914.

Butler, W. F., *Confiscation in Irish History*. Dublin, 1913.

Brudenell-Bruce, C. S. C., Earl of Cardigan, *The Life and Loyalties of Thomas Bruce: A Biography of Thomas, Earl of Earl of Ailesbury and Elgin, Gentleman of the Bedchamber to King Charles II and to King James II, 1656–1741*. London, 1951.

Bryant, Arthur, *King Charles II*. London, 1931.

Callow, John, *The Making of King James II; The Formative Years of a Fallen King.* Stroud, 2000.

Canny, Nicholas, *The Upstart Earl: A Study of the Social and Mental World of Richard Boyle first Earl of Cork 1566–1643.* Cambridge, 1982.

——— 'Religion, politics and the Irish rising of 1641' in Judith Devlin and Ronan Fanning (eds), *Religion and Rebellion: Historical Studies, XX.* Dublin, 1997.

——— *Making Ireland British.* Oxford, 2001.

Carrington, P. J. et al. (eds), *Models and Methods in Social Network Analysis.* Cambridge, 2005.

Carte, Thomas, *History of the Life and Times of James the first Duke of Ormonde.* 3 vols, London, 1735.

Casway, J. T., *Owen Roe O'Neill and the Struggle for Catholic Ireland.* Philadelphia, 1984.

Cénat, Jean-Philippe, *Le Roi stratège: Louis XIV et la direction de la guerre 1661–1715.* Rennes, 2010.

Chalmers, Alexander, *The General Biographical Dictionary.* London, 1816.

Chapman, H. W., *Great Villiers: A Study of George Villiers Second Duke of Buckingham 1628–1687.* London, 1949.

Chandler, David, *The Art of Warfare in the Age of Marlborough.* London, 1997.

Childs, John, *The Army, James II, and the Glorious Revolution.* Manchester, 1980.

———, The *Williamite Wars in Ireland: 1688–1691.* London, 2007.

Aidan Clarke, 'Ireland and the General Crisis' in *Past and Present*, no. 48, Aug. 1970.

———, *The Old English in Ireland, 1625–42.* 2nd edn, Dublin, 2000.

Clavin, Terry. 'Talbot, Peter 1618/1620–1680, Roman Catholic Archbishop of Dublin' in *ODNB* [www.oxforddnb.com/view/printable/26937].

Claydon, Tony. *William the Third and the Godly Revolution.* Cambridge, 2004.

Cobbett, Henry, *Parliamentary History of England.* 6 vols, London, 1810.

Connolly, S. J., *Religion, Law and Power: The Making of Protestant Ireland 1660.* Oxford, 1992.

Corish, P. J.. 'The Cromwellian regime, 1650–60' in T. W. Moody, F. X. Martin and F. J. Byrne (eds), *A New History of Ireland III: Early Modern Ireland 1534–1691.* Oxford, 1976.

Corp, Edward, 'Catherine of Braganza and cultural politics', in Clarissa Campbell Orr (ed.), *Queenship in Britain, 1660–1837: Royal Patronage, Court Culture and Dynastic Politics.* Manchester, 2002.

——— 'Drummond, John, styled first earl of Melfort and Jacobite first duke of Melfort 1649–1714', *ODNB* [www.oxforddnb.com/view/article/8077 19 June 2013].

——— 'France, Rome and the exiled Stuarts, 1689–1713' in Corp (ed.), *A Court in Exile The Stuarts in France 1689–1718.* Cambridge, 2004.

Cuddy, Neil, 'Reinventing a monarchy: the changing structure and political function of the Stuart court, 1603–88', in Eveline Cruickshanks (ed.), *The Stuart Courts.* Stroud, 2000.

Cunningham, John, *Conquest and Land in Ireland: The Transplantation to Connaught, 1649–1680.* London, 2011.

Curry, John, *An Historical and Critical Review of the Civil Wars in Ireland.* Dublin, 1775.

Cregan, D. F., 'An Irish cavalier: Daniel O'Neill', *Studia Hibernica*, no. 3, 1963.

———. 'The Confederate Catholics of Ireland: the personnel of the Confederation, 1642–9', in *IHS*, vol. xxix, no. 116, Nov. 1995.

Creighton, Anne, 'The Remonstrance of December 1661 and Catholic Politics in Restoration Ireland' in *IHS*, vol. xxxiv, no. 133, May 2004.

Cronin, J. J., 'The Irish Royalist elite of Charles II in exile, *c.*1649–1660'. PhD thesis, European University Institute, Florence, 2007.

——'The political activities of an exiled royal court and the role played by its Irish Courtiers' in Philip Mansel and Torsten Riotte (eds), *Monarchy and Exile: The Politics of Legitimacy from Marie de Médicis to Wilhelm II*. London, 2011.

Crump, G. M., *Poems on Affairs of State: Augustan Satirical Verse, 1660–1714*. 4 vols, New Haven, CT, 1963–8.

Curran, M. B., 'The correspondence of an English diplomatic agent in Paris, 1669–1677' in *Transactions of the Royal Historical Society*, vol. 15, 1901.

Dabhoiwala, Faramerz, 'The construction of honour, reputation and status in late seventeenth- and early eighteenth-century England' in *Transactions of the Royal Historical Society*, vol. vi, 1996.

Dale Kerr, Ronald, '"Why should you be so furious?" The violence of the Pequot war' in *Journal of American History*, vol. 85, no. 3, Dec. 1998.

Dalrymple, John, *Memoirs of Great Britain and Ireland*. Dublin, 1773.

Danaher, Kevin and J. G. Simms (eds), *The Danish Force in Ireland 1690–1691*. Dublin, 1962.

Davies, Godfrey, *The Restoration of Charles II 1658–1660*. Oxford, 1955.

Davies, J. D., 'International relations, war and the armed forces' in Lionel Glassey (ed.), *The Reigns of Charles II and James VII & II*. London, 1997.

Dennehy, Coleman (ed.), *Restoration Ireland: Always Settling and Never Settled*. Dublin, 2008.

Dickson, David, *New Foundations: Ireland 1660–1800*. Dublin, 1987.

Doherty, Richard, *The Williamite War in Ireland 1688–1691*. Dublin, 1998.

Donagan, Barbara, 'Codes and conduct in the English Civil War' in *Past & Present*, no. 118, Feb. 1988.

Duffy, E. P., 'The siege and surrender of Galway 1651–1652' in *Journal of the Galway Archaeological and Historical Society*, vol. xxxix, 1983–4.

Duffy, Christopher, *Fire & Stone: The Science of Fortress Warfare*. London, 1975.

Duignan, Aoife, 'Cusack, Nicholas', in *DIB* [www.dib.cambridge.org/view]

Duke Henning, Basil, *The House of Commons, 1660–1690*. 3 vols, London, 1983.

Dunlop, Robert, *Ireland under the Commonwealth: Being a Selection of Documents Relating to the Government of Ireland*. 2 vols, Manchester, 1913.

Dunn, James, *Read My Heart: A Love Story in England's Age of Revolution* New York, 2008.

Eden Quainton, C., 'Colonel Lockhart and the peace of the Pyrenees', in *Pacific Historical Review*, vol. iv, no. 3, Sept. 1935.

Elrington-Ball, Francis, *The Judges in Ireland, 1221–1921*. 2 vols, London, 1926.

Fenning, Hugh, 'Dominic Maguire, O. P. Archbishop of Armagh: 1684–1707' in *Seanchas Ardmhacha: Journal of the Armagh Diocesan Historical Society*, vol. 18, no. 1, 1999–2000.

Fitzgerald, Walter, 'The County Wicklow barony of Upper Talbotstown, and whence its name' in *Kildare Arch. Soc. Jn.*, vol. v, 1906–8

—— 'Miscellanea' in *Kildare Arch. Soc. Jn.*, vol. vi, 1909–11.

Fox, C. J., *A History of the Early Part of the Reign of James the Second*. London, 1808.

Fraser, William, *History of the Carnegies*. 2 vols, Edinburgh, 1857.

Gébler, Carlo, *The Siege of Derry*. London, 2005.

Genet Rouffiac, Nathalie. 'The wild geese in France, 1688–1715: A French perspective' in *Irish Sword*, no. 103, 2008.

Geoghegan, Vincent, 'Sheridan, Thomas', in *DIB* [www.dib.cambridge.org/viewRead-Page.do?articleId=a8045].

Gibney, John, '"Sarsfield is the word": the heroic afterlife of an Irish Jacobite' in *New Hibernia Review*, vol. 15, no 1, Spring 2011.

—— 'Edward Murphy, Oliver Plunkett and the Popish Plot' in *History Ireland*, vol. 12, no. 4, Winter 2004.

—— 'An Irish informer in Restoration England: David Fitzgerald and the 'Irish plot' in the exclusion crisis, 1679–81' in *Éire-Ireland*, vol. 42, nos 3 & 4, Fall–Winter 2007.

—— *Ireland and the Popish Plot*. Basingstoke, 2009.

Gillespie, Raymond, 'The Irish Protestants and James II, 1688–90' in *IHS*, vol. 28, no. 110, Nov. 1992.

—— *Seventeenth Century Ireland*. Dublin, 2006.

Glassey, Lionel, *The Reigns of Charles II and James VII & II*. London, 1997.

Glozier, Matthew, *Marshal Schomberg, 1615–1690: 'The Ablest Soldier of His Age'*. Sussex, 2005.

Greenspan, Nicole, *Selling Cromwell's Wars: Media, Empire and Godly Warfare, 1650–1658*. London, 2012.

Gregg, Edward, *Anne: Queen of Great Britain*. London, 1980.

—— 'New light on the authorship of the life of James II' in *EHR*, vol. 108, no. 429, 1993.

Guizot, François, *History of Richard Cromwell and the Restoration of Charles II*. 2 vols, London, 1856.

Haile, Martin, *Queen Mary of Modena Her Life and Letters*. London, 1905.

Hald Galster, Kjed. *Danish Troops in the Williamite Army in Ireland, 1689–91*. Dublin, 2012.

Handley, Stuart, 'Petre, Sir Edward, third baronet', *ODNB* [www.oxforddnb.com/view/article/22046 accessed 15 Nov. 2013].

Harris, Tim, *Restoration: Charles II and His Kingdoms 1660–1685*. London, 2005.

—— *Revolution: The Great Crisis of the British Monarchy, 1685–1720*. London, 2007.

—— 'Restoration Ireland – themes and problems' in Coleman Dennehy (ed.), *Restoration Ireland: Always Settling and Never Settled*. Aldershot, 2008.

Hartmann, C. H., *Clifford of the Cabal A Life of Thomas, First Lord Clifford of Chudleigh, Lord High Treasurer of England 1630–1673*. London, 1937.

—— *The King's Friend: A Life of Charles Berkeley, Viscount Fitzhardinge*. London, 1951.

Hay, Malcolm, *The Jesuits and the Popish Plot*. London, 1934.

Hayes-McCoy, G. A., *Irish Battles*. 2nd edn, Dublin, 1980.

Hayton, D. W., 'The Williamite Revolution in Ireland, 1689–91' in J. I. Israel (ed.), *The Anglo-Dutch Moment: Essays on the Glorious Revolution*. Cambridge, 1991.

Hill, George, *An Historical Account of the MacDonnells of Antrim: Including Notices of Some Other Septs, Irish and Scottish*. Belfast, 1873.

Hinds, Peter, *'The Horrid Popish Plot': Roger L'Estrange and the Circulation of Political Discourse in late Seventeenth-Century London*. Oxford, 2010.

Hogan, Edmund, *Ibernia Ignatiana*. Dublin, 1880.

Holmes, Richard, *Marlborough: England's Fragile Genius*. London, 2008.

Hopper, Andrew, 'Belasyse, John, first Baron Belasyse of Worlaby *bap.* 1615, *d.* 1689', *ODNB* [www.oxforddnb.com/view/article/1977].

Hutton, Ronald, *Charles the Second: King of England, Scotland and Ireland*. Oxford, 1989.

Irwin, Liam, 'Sarsfield: the man and myth' in Bernadette Whelan (ed.), *The Last of the Great Wars: Essays on the Wars of the Three Kings in Ireland 1688–91*. Limerick, 1995.

James, F. G., *Lords of the Ascendancy: The Irish House of Lords and its Members, 1600–1800*. Dublin, 1995.

Jones, J. R., *The Revolution of 1688 in England*. London, 1972.

Keeble, N. H., *The Restoration: England in the 1660s*. Oxford, 2002.

Kelly, Patrick, 'A light to the blind: the voice of the dispossessed élite after the defeat at Limerick' in *IHS*, vol. xxiv, no. 96, 1985.

——— 'Ireland and the Glorious Revolution: from kingdom to colony' in Robert Beddard (ed.), *The Revolutions of 1688*. Oxford, 1991.

Kelly, James, *That Damned Thing Called Honour: Duelling in Ireland 1570–1800*. Cork, 1995.

Kenyon, J. P., *Robert Spencer, Earl of Sunderland 1641–1702*. London, 1958.

———. *The Popish Plot*. London, 1972.

Kerrigan, P. M., *Castles and Fortifications in Ireland 1485–1945*. Cork, 1995.

——— 'Ireland in naval strategy 1641–1691' in Pádraig Lenihan (ed.), *Conquest and Resistance: War in Seventeenth Century Ireland*. Leiden, 2001.

Kiernan, V. G., *The Duel in European History; Honour and the Reign of Aristocracy*. Oxford, 1988.

Kimber, Edward, *The Peerage of Ireland: A Genealogical and Historical Account*. 2 vols, London, 1768.

Kishlansky, Mark, *A Monarchy Transformed: Britain, 1603–1714*. London, 1996.

Knights, Mark, *Politics and Opinion in Crisis, 1678–81*. Cambridge, 1994.

Krugler, J. D., *English and Catholic: The Lords Baltimore in the Seventeenth Century*. Baltimore, MD, 2004.

Lee Malcolm, Joyce, 'Charles II and the reconstruction of royal power' in *Historical Journal*, vol. 35, no. 2, Jun. 1992.

Lenihan, Pádraig, 'Unhappy campers: Dundalk 1689 and after' in Tony Pollard and Iain Banks (eds), *Scorched Earth: Studies in the Archaeology of Conflict*. Leiden, 2008.

——— 'War and population' in *Journal of the Economic and Social History Society of Ireland*, Spring, 1998.

——— *Confederate Catholics At War, 1641–49*. Cork, 2001.

——— *1690 Battle of the Boyne*. Stroud, 2003.

——— 'Strategic geography, 1641–1691' in Lenihan (ed.), *Conquest and Resistance: Warfare in Seventeenth Century Ireland*. Leiden, 2001.

——— 'The Leinster army and the battle of Dungan's Hill' in Harman Murtagh (ed.), *Irishmen in War: Essays from the Irish Sword*, i. Dublin, 2006, pp 90–104.

——— *Consolidating Conquest: Ireland 1603–1727*. London, 2008.

——— and Geraldine Sheridan, 'A Swiss soldier in Ireland 1689–1690' in *Irish Studies Review*, vol. 13, no. 4, 2005.

Lenman, Bruce, *The Jacobite Risings in Britain 1689–1746*. London, 1980.

Levillain, C. E., *Vaincre Louis XIV: Angleterre-Hollande-France Histoire d'une relation triangulaire 1665–1689*. Seyssel, 2010.

Levy Peck, Linda, *Court Patronage and Corruption in Early Stuart England*. London, 1990.

Little, Patrick, 'The marquess of Ormond and the English parliament, 1645–1647' in T. C. Barnard and Jane Fenlon (eds), *The Dukes of Ormonde, 1610–1745*. Woodbridge, 2000.

Loftis, John and Paul Hardacre, *Colonel Joseph Bampfield's Apology: 'Written by Himself and Printed at His Desire' 1685*. London, 1993.

Lutaud, Oliver, *Des Révolutions d'Angleterre à la Révolution Française: Le Tyrannicide & Killing no Murder*. Leiden, 1973.

Lydon, J. F., *The Making of Ireland From Ancient Times to the Present*. London, 1998.

Lynn, J. A., *Giant of the Grand Siècle: The French Army, 1610–1715*. Cambridge, 1997.

Macaulay, T. B., *The History of England from the Accession of James II*, 2 vols, London, 1849.

MacCuarta, Brian, 'Religious violence against settlers in South Ulster, 1641–2' in David Edwards, Pádraig Lenihan and Clodagh Tait (eds), *Age of Atrocity: Violence and Political Conflict in Early Modern Ireland*. Dublin, 2007.

MacLysaght, Edward, *Irish life in the Seventeenth Century*. 4th edn, Dublin, 1979.

Mackintosh, James, *History of the Revolution in England in 1688*. Philadelphia, 1835.

Mantel, Hilary, 'Royal bodies' in *London Review of Books*, vol. 35, no. 4, 21 Feb. 2013.

Marciari Alexander, Julia and Catharine MacLeod (eds), *Painted Ladies: Women at the Court of Charles II*. London, 2001.

Marshall, Alan, *The Age of Faction Court Politics, 1660–1702*. Manchester, 1999.

—— 'Everard, Edmund *fl.* 1673–1691', *ODNB* [www.oxforddnb.com/view/article/67394].

—— '"Woeful knight": Sir Robert Walsh and the fragmented world of the double agent' in Daniel Szechi (ed.), *The Dangerous Trade: Spies, Spymasters and the Making of Europe*. Dundee, 2010.

Maynard, Hazel, 'The Irish legal profession and the Catholic revival 1660–89' in James Kelly, John McCafferty and Charles Ivar McGrath (eds), *People, Politics and Power: Essays on Irish History in Honour of James I. McGuire*. Dublin, 2009.

—— 'Nugent, Thomas 1st Baron Nugent of Riverston', in *DIB* [www.dib.cambridge.org]

McElligott, Jason, *Cromwell our Chief of Enemies*. Dundalk, 1994.

McGuire, James, 'Why was Ormond dismissed in 1669?' in *IHS*, vol. xviii, no. 71, 1973.

—— 'Richard Talbot earl of Tyrconnell 1630–91 and the Catholic counter-revolution' in Ciaran Brady (ed.), *Worsted in the Game: Losers in Irish History*. Belfast, 1989.

—— 'A lawyer in politics, the career of Sir Richard Nagle *c.*1636–1699' in Judith Devlin and H. B. Clarke (eds), *European Encounters: Essays in Memory of Albert Lovett*. Dublin, 2003.

—— 'Talbot, Richard duke of Tyrconnell' in *DIB* [dib.cambridge.org/viewReadPage.do?articleId=a8460}.

McKenny, K. J., *The Laggan Army in Ireland 1640–1685*. Dublin, 2005.

McNally, Michael, *Battle of the Boyne 1690: The Irish Campaign for the English Crown*. Oxford, 2005.

—— *The Battle of Aughrim 1691*. Stroud, 2008.

McNeill, Charles, 'Rawlinson Manuscripts', *Anal. Hib.*, 1 Mar. 1930.

Melvin, P. G., 'The Irish army and the revolution of 1688' in *Irish Sword*, no. ix, 1969.

Miller, John. *Popery and Politics in England 1660–1688*. Cambridge, 1973.

—— 'Thomas Sheridan 1646–1712 and his "Narrative"' in *IHS*, vol. xx, no. 78, Sept. 1976.

———— 'The earl of Tyrconnel and James II's Irish policy, 1685–1688' in *Historical Journal*, vol. 20, no. 4, Dec. 1977.

———— *James II: A Study in Kingship*. London, 1978.

Montano, J. P., *Courting the Moderates: Ideology, Propaganda, and the Emergence of Party, 1660–1678*. London, 2002.

Morley, Vincent, 'The continuity of disaffection in eighteenth-century Ireland' in *Eighteenth-Century Ireland / Iris an dá chultúr*, vol. 22, 2007.

Morrill, John, 'The Drogheda massacre in Cromwellian context' in David Edwards, Pádraig Lenihan and Clodagh Tait (eds), *Age of Atrocity: Violence and Political Context in Early Modern Ireland*. Dublin, 2007.

Mullenaux, Samuel, 'Diary of the siege of Limerick' in *The Old Limerick Journal*, 1690 Siege edition, no. 28, 1990.

Mullett, M. A., *James II and English Politics 1678–1688*. London, 1994.

———— *Catholics in Britain and Ireland 1558–1829*. London, 1998.

Mulloy, Sheila, 'French eye-witnesses of the Boyne', in *Irish Sword*, no. 59, 1982.

———— 'The French navy and the Jacobite war in Ireland, 1688–91' in *Irish Sword*, no. 70, 1990.

Murphy, Dennis, *Cromwell in Ireland: A History of Cromwell's Irish Campaign*. Dublin, 1883.

Murphy, J. A., *Justin McCarthy, Lord Mountcashel*. Cork, 1959.

Murtagh, Harman, 'The siege of Athlone, 1691' in *Journal of the Old Athlone Society*, vol. i, no. 3, 1972–3.

———— 'The Irish Jacobite army, 1689–91' in *Irish Sword*, no. 70, 1990.

———— 'The war in Ireland 1689–91' in W. A. Maguire (ed.), *Kings in Conflict: The Revolutionary War in Ireland and its Aftermath 1689–1750*. Belfast, 1990.

———— *The Battle of the Boyne 1690: A Guide to the Battlefield*. Drogheda, 2006.

Nicholls, Kenneth, 'The other massacre: English killings of Irish, 1641–2' in David Edwards, Pádraig Lenihan and Clodagh Tait (eds), *Age of Atrocity: Violence and Political Conflict in Early Modern Ireland*. Dublin, 2007.

Ó hAnnracháin, Tadhg, 'The strategic involvement of continental powers in Ireland 1596–1691' in Pádraig Lenihan (ed.), *Conquest and Resistance: Warfare in seventeenth century Ireland*. Leiden, 2001.

———— *Catholic Reformation in Ireland: The Mission of Rinuccini 1645–1649*. Oxford, 2002.

Ó Buachalla, Breandán, 'Lillibulero agus Eile' in *Comhar Teoranta*, vol. 46, nos 4, 6–7, 1987.

———— 'Briseadh na Bóinne', *Éigse: A Journal of Irish Studies*, vols 23–5, 1989.

———— 'Seacaibíteachas Thaidhg Uí Neachtain', *Studia Hibernica*, no. 26, 1992.

Ó Ciardha, Éamonn, 'The unkinde deserter and the bright Duke' in T. C. Barnard and Jane Fenlon (eds), *The Dukes of Ormonde, 1610–1745*. Woodbridge, 2000.

———— *Ireland and The Jacobite Cause, 1685–1766: A Fatal Attachment*. Dublin, 2001.

———— 'Tyrrell, Patrick d. 1692', in *DIB* [www.dib.cambridge.org/view].

Ó Fiach, Tomás, 'Edmund O'Reilly, Archbishop of Armagh, 1657–1669', Franciscan Fathers (eds), *Father Luke Wadding Commemorative Volume*. Dublin, 1957

Ó Siochrú, Micheál, *Confederate Ireland 1642–1649: A Constitutional and Political Analysis*. Dublin, 1999.

———— *God's Executioner: Oliver Cromwell and the Conquest of Ireland*. London, 2008.

O'Callaghan, J. C., *History of the Irish Brigades in the Service of France*. Glasgow, 1870.

O'Hart, John, *The Irish and Anglo Irish Landed Gentry when Cromwell came to Ireland*, ed. Edward MacLysaght. 2nd edn, New York, 1969.

Ogg, David, *England in the Reigns of James II and William III*. Oxford, 1955.

Ohlmeyer, Jane, *Civil War and Restoration in Three Stuart Kingdoms*. Cambridge, 1993.

—— *Making Ireland English: The Irish Aristocracy in the Seventeenth Century*. New Haven CT, 2012.

Ollard, Richard, *Clarendon and his Friends*. New York, 1988.

Pearsall, A. W. H., 'The war at sea' in W. A. Maguire (ed.), *Kings in Conflict: The Revolutionary War in Ireland and its Aftermath 1689–1750*. Belfast, 1990.

Patterson, A. M., *Pastoral and Ideology: Virgil to Valéry*. Berkeley, CA, 2008.

Peltonen, Markku, *The Duel in Early Modern England: Civility, Politeness and Honour*. Cambridge, 2003.

Perceval-Maxwell, Michael, *The Outbreak of the Irish Rebellion of 1641*. Dublin, 1994.

Pérez Tostado, Igor, *Irish Influence at the Court of Spain in the Seventeenth Century*. Dublin, 2008.

Pillorget, René, 'Louis XIV and Ireland' in Bernadette Whelan (ed.), *The Last of the Great Wars: Essays on the Wars of the Three Kings in Ireland 1688–91*. Limerick, 1995.

Pincus, Steven, 'Republicanism, absolutism and universal monarchy' in G. M. MacLean, *Culture and Society in the Stuart Restoration: Literature, Drama and History*. Cambridge, 1995.

——, 'Gallicanism, Innocent XI, and Catholic opposition', in A. I. MacInnes and A. H. Williamson (eds), *Shaping the Stuart World, 1603–1714: The Atlantic Connection*. Leiden, 2006.

—— *1688: The First Modern Revolution*. New Haven, CT, 2011.

Puttock, Murray, *Poetry and Jacobite Politics in Eighteenth-Century Britain and Ireland*. Cambridge, 1994.

—— *Jacobitism*. Basingstoke, 1998.

Prendergast, J. P., *The Cromwellian Settlement of Ireland*. New York, 1868.

Ranke, Leopold von, *History of England: Principally in the Seventeenth Century*. Oxford, 1875.

Recio Morales, Óscar, *Ireland and the Spanish Empire 1600–1825*. Dublin, 2010.

Reynolds, N. A. C., 'The Stuart court and courtiers in exile 1644–54'. PhD thesis, University of Cambridge, 1996.

Rommelse, Gijs, *The Second Anglo-Dutch War 1665–1667: Raison d'État, Mercantilism and Maritime Strife*. Hilversum, 2006.

Routledge, F. J., *England and the Treaty of the Pyrenees*. Liverpool, 1953.

Ruiz Rodriguez, Ignacio, *Don Juan José de Austria en la Monarquiá Hispánica; Entre la Política, el poder y la intriga*. Madrid, 2007.

Russell, Conrad, *The Fall of the British Monarchies*. Oxford, 1991.

Sackville-West, Vita, *Daughter of France: The Life of Anne Marie Louise D'Orléans 1627–1693*. London, 1959.

Sandars, M. F., *Lauzun: Courtier and Adventurer The Life of a Friend of Louis XIV*. 2 vols, London, 1908.

Schama, Simon, *A History of Britain: The British Wars 1603–1776*. London, 2001.

Schwoerer, L. G., 'Propaganda in the revolution of 1688–89' in *American Historical Review*, vol. 82, no. 4, 1977.

Scodel, Joshua, *The English Poetic Epitaph: Commemoration and Conflict from Jonson to Wordsworth.* Ithaca, NY, 1991.

Scott, B. G. et al., *The Great Guns Like Thunder: The Cannon from the City Of Derry.* Derry, 2008.

Scott, D. L., 'Counsel and cabal in the king's party, 1642–1646' in Jason McElligott and D. L. Smith (eds), *Royalists and Royalism during the English Civil Wars.* Cambridge, 2007.

Scott, Eva, *The Travels of the King: Charles II: In Germany and Flanders 1654–1660.* London, 1907.

Scott Wheeler, James, *Cromwell in Ireland.* Dublin, 1999.

———— 'The logistics of conquest' in Pádraig Lenihan (ed.), *Conquest and Resistance War in Seventeenth-Century Ireland.* Leiden, 2001.

Seaward, Paul, *The Restoration, 1660–88.* London, 1991.

Sergeant, P. W., *Little Jennings and Fighting Dick Talbot.* 2 vols, London, 1913.

Shifrin, Susan, '"Subdued by a famous Roman dame": picturing foreigness, notoriety, and prerogative in the portraits of Hortense Mancini, Duchess Mazarin', in Julia Marciari Alexander and Catharine MacLeod (eds), *Politics, Transgression and Representation at the Court of Charles II.* New Haven, CT, 2007.

Shoemaker, R. B., 'The taming of the duel: masculinity, honour and ritual violence in London, 1660–1800' in *Historical Journal*, vol. 45, 2002.

Simms, Hilary, 'Violence in County Armagh, 1641' in Brian MacCuarta (ed.), *Ulster 1641: Aspects of the Rising.* Belfast, 1997.

Simms, J. G., 'A Jacobite colonel, Lord Sarsfield of Kilmallock', in *Irish Sword*, vol. ii, no. 7, 1955.

————, *The Williamite Confiscation in Ireland 1690–1703.* London, 1956.

————, 'Sligo in the Jacobite War, 1689–91' in *Irish Sword* vol. vii, no. 27, 1965.

————, *Jacobite Ireland.* London, 1969.

————, 'Review: The Great Tyrconnell' in *IHS*, vol. xviii, no. 72, Sept. 1973.

————, 'The Restoration, 1660–85' in *New History of Ireland.*

————, 'Schomberg at Dundalk, 1689' in D. W. Hayton and Gerard O'Brien (eds), *War and Politics in Ireland, 1649–1730.* London, 1986.

————, 'Williamite peace tactics' in D. W. Hayton and Gerard O'Brien (eds), *War and Politics in Ireland, 1649–1730.* London, 1986.

————, *Jacobite Ireland, 1685–91.* Dublin, 2000.

————, 'Cromwell at Drogheda, 1649' in Harman Murtagh (ed.), *Irishmen at War: Essays from the Irish Sword.* Dublin, 2006.

Smith, D. L., *A History of the Modern British Isles 1603–1707: The Double Crown.* Oxford, 1998.

Smith, Geoffrey, *The Cavaliers in Exile 1650–1660.* Basingstoke, 2003.

———— *Royalist Agents, Conspirators and Spies: Their Role in the British Civil Wars, 1640–1660.* London, 2011.

Smyth, William, *Map-making, Landscapes and Memory A Geography of Colonial and Early Modern Ireland c.1530–1750.* Cork, 2006.

Sonnino, Paul, 'The origins of Louis XIV's wars' in Jeremy Black (ed.), *The Origins of War in Early Modern Europe.* Edinburgh, 1987.

Southcombe, George and Grant Tapsell. *Restoration Politics, Religion and Culture.* Basingstoke, 2010.

Speck, W. A., *James II: Profiles in Power*. London, 2002.

Stater, Victor, 'Herbert, William, styled first marquess of Powis and Jacobite first duke of Powis c.1626–1696', *ODNB* [www.oxforddnb.com/view/article/13060 accessed 14 Nov. 2013].

Steinman, George, 'Memorials preserved at Bruges of King Charles the Second's residence in that city' in *Archaeologia or Miscellaneous Tracts relating to Antiquity*, vol. xxxv. London, 1853.

———— *Althorp Memoirs: or, Biographical notices of Lady Denham…* Oxford, 1869.

Stevenson, David, 'Cromwell, Scotland and Ireland' in John Morrill (ed.), *Oliver Cromwell and the English Revolution*. London, 1990.

Stone, Lawrence, *The Family, Sex and Marriage in England 1500–1800*. New York, 1977.

Stradling, R. A., *The Spanish Monarchy and Irish Mercenaries The Wild Geese in Spain 1618–68*. Dublin, 1994.

Strickland, Agnes, *Lives of the Queens of England*. London, 1846.

Symcox, Geoffrey, *The Crisis of French Sea Power 1688–1697*. The Hague, 1974.

Szechi, Daniel. 'The Jacobite revolution settlement, 1689–1696' in *EHR*, no. 428, 1993.

———— *The Jacobites: Britain and Europe 1688–1788*. Manchester, 1994.

———— 'A blueprint for tyranny? Sir Edward Hales and the Catholic Jacobite response to the revolution of 1688' in *EHR*, vol. 116, no. 466, 2001.

Tapsell, Grant, *The Personal Rule of Charles II, 1681–85*. Woodbridge, 2007.

Tavard, G. H., *The Seventeenth-Century Tradition: A Study in Recusant Thought*. Leiden, 1978.

Todhunter, John, *Life of Patrick Sarsfield, Earl of Lucan*. London, 1895.

Treadwell, Victor, *Buckingham and Ireland 1616–1628* Dublin, 1998.

Treasure, G. R., *Mazarin: The Crisis of Absolutism in France*. London, 1995.

Turner, F. C., *James II*. London, 1948.

Uglow, Jenny, *A Gambling Man Charles II and the Restoration 1660–1670*. London, 2009.

Vale, Vivian, 'Clarendon, Coventry, and the sale of naval offices, 1660–8', *Cambridge Historical Journal*, vol. xii, no. 2, 1956.

Venning, Timothy, *Cromwellian Foreign Policy*. London, 1995.

Virol, Michèle. 'Le Siège de Namur en 1692: l'héroisme et la technique', in *XVII Siècle*, no. 228, 2005.

Wauchope, Piers, 'Ellis, Sir William', *ODNB* [www.oxforddnb.com/view/article/8717].

———— 'Talbot, Richard, first earl of Tyrconnell and Jacobite duke of Tyrconnell 1630–1691', *ODNB* [www.oxforddnb.com/view/article/26940].

Weiser, Brian, *Charles II and the Politics of Access*. Woodbridge, 2003.

Wheeler, J. S., *The Irish and British Wars 1637–1654*. London, 2002.

White, M. A., *Henrietta Maria and the English Civil War*. Farnham, 2008.

Wiener, C. Z., 'The beleaguered isle. "A study of Elizabethan and Jacobean Anti-Catholicism"' in *Past and Present*, no. 51, May 1971.

Williams, M. R. F., 'Between king, faith and reason: Father Peter Talbot SJ and Catholic royalist thought in exile' in *EHR*, vol. cxxvii, no. 528, 2012.

Wilson, Derek, *All the King's Women: Love, Sex and Politics in the Life of Charles II*. London, 2003.

Wilson, J. H., *Court Satires of the Restoration*. Columbus, OH, 1976.

Wynne, Sonya, 'The mistresses of Charles II and Restoration court politics' in Eveline Cruickshanks (ed.), *The Stuart Courts*. Stroud, 2000.

Zee, Van der, Henry and Barbara, *1688: Revolution in the Family*. New York, 1988.

Index